Confronting Academic Mobbing in Higher Education:

Personal Accounts and Administrative Action

Caroline M. Crawford
University of Houston – Clear Lake, USA

A volume in the Advances in Higher Education and Professional Development (AHEPD) Book Series

IGI Global
DISSEMINATOR OF KNOWLEDGE

Published in the United States of America by
   IGI Global
   Information Science Reference (an imprint of IGI Global)
   701 E. Chocolate Avenue
   Hershey PA, USA 17033
   Tel: 717-533-8845
   Fax: 717-533-8661
   E-mail: cust@igi-global.com
   Web site: http://www.igi-global.com

Copyright © 2020 by IGI Global. All rights reserved. No part of this publication may be reproduced, stored or distributed in any form or by any means, electronic or mechanical, including photocopying, without written permission from the publisher.
Product or company names used in this set are for identification purposes only. Inclusion of the names of the products or companies does not indicate a claim of ownership by IGI Global of the trademark or registered trademark.

                Library of Congress Cataloging-in-Publication Data

Names: Crawford, Caroline M., 1968- editor.
Title: Confronting academic mobbing in higher education : personal accounts
   and administrative action / Caroline M. Crawford, editor.
Description: Hershey, PA : Information Science Reference, [2019] | Summary:
   "This book provides qualitative analysis of academic mobbing stories and
   experiences. It also examines the academic mobbing phenomenon, support
   for higher education professionals who are currently dealing with the
   academic mobbing phenomenon, and role of both higher education academic
   leadership and the human resources departments in the academic mobbing
   phenomenon"-- Provided by publisher.
Identifiers: LCCN 2019002540 | ISBN 9781522594857 (hardcover) | ISBN
   9781522594871 (ebook) | ISBN 9781522594864 (softcover)
Subjects: LCSH: College teachers. | Victims of bullying. | Mobs. |
   Universities and colleges. | Intellectual freedom.
Classification: LCC LB1778 .C65 2019 | DDC 378.1/25--dc23
LC record available at https://lccn.loc.gov/2019002540

This book is published in the IGI Global book series Advances in Higher Education and Professional Development (AHEPD) (ISSN: 2327-6983; eISSN: 2327-6991)

British Cataloguing in Publication Data
A Cataloguing in Publication record for this book is available from the British Library.

All work contributed to this book is new, previously-unpublished material.
The views expressed in this book are those of the authors, but not necessarily of the publisher.

For electronic access to this publication, please contact: eresources@igi-global.com.

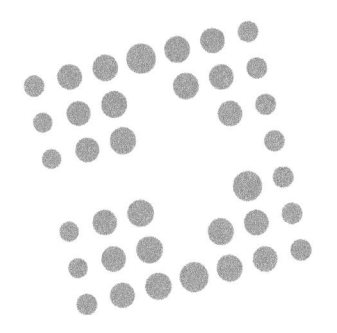

Advances in Higher Education and Professional Development (AHEPD) Book Series

ISSN:2327-6983
EISSN:2327-6991

Editor-in-Chief: Jared Keengwe, University of North Dakota, USA

MISSION

As world economies continue to shift and change in response to global financial situations, job markets have begun to demand a more highly-skilled workforce. In many industries a college degree is the minimum requirement and further educational development is expected to advance. With these current trends in mind, the **Advances in Higher Education & Professional Development (AHEPD) Book Series** provides an outlet for researchers and academics to publish their research in these areas and to distribute these works to practitioners and other researchers.

AHEPD encompasses all research dealing with higher education pedagogy, development, and curriculum design, as well as all areas of professional development, regardless of focus.

COVERAGE

- Adult Education
- Assessment in Higher Education
- Career Training
- Coaching and Mentoring
- Continuing Professional Development
- Governance in Higher Education
- Higher Education Policy
- Pedagogy of Teaching Higher Education
- Vocational Education

IGI Global is currently accepting manuscripts for publication within this series. To submit a proposal for a volume in this series, please contact our Acquisition Editors at Acquisitions@igi-global.com or visit: http://www.igi-global.com/publish/.

The Advances in Higher Education and Professional Development (AHEPD) Book Series (ISSN 2327-6983) is published by IGI Global, 701 E. Chocolate Avenue, Hershey, PA 17033-1240, USA, www.igi-global.com. This series is composed of titles available for purchase individually; each title is edited to be contextually exclusive from any other title within the series. For pricing and ordering information please visit http://www.igi-global.com/book-series/advances-higher-education-professional-development/73681. Postmaster: Send all address changes to above address. ©© 2020 IGI Global. All rights, including translation in other languages reserved by the publisher. No part of this series may be reproduced or used in any form or by any means – graphics, electronic, or mechanical, including photocopying, recording, taping, or information and retrieval systems – without written permission from the publisher, except for non commercial, educational use, including classroom teaching purposes. The views expressed in this series are those of the authors, but not necessarily of IGI Global.

Titles in this Series

For a list of additional titles in this series, please visit:
https://www.igi-global.com/book-series/advances-higher-education-professional-development/73681

The Formation of Intellectual Capital and Its Ability to Transform Higher Education Institutions and the Knowledge Society
Edgar Oliver Cardoso Espinosa (Instituto Politécnico Nacional, Mexico)
Information Science Reference • ©2019 • 312pp • H/C (ISBN: 9781522584612) • US $195.00

Engaging Teacher Candidates and Language Learners With Authentic Practice
Chesla Ann Lenkaitis (Binghamton University, USA) and Shannon M. Hilliker (Binghamton University, USA)
Information Science Reference • ©2019 • 368pp • H/C (ISBN: 9781522585435) • US $195.00

Case Study Methodology in Higher Education
Annette Baron (William Paterson University, USA) and Kelly McNeal (William Paterson University, USA)
Information Science Reference • ©2019 • 393pp • H/C (ISBN: 9781522594291) • US $195.00

Workforce Education at Oil and Gas Companies in the Permian Basin Emerging Research and Opportunities
Julie Neal (Dearing Sales, USA) and Brittany Lee Neal (Axip Energy Services, USA)
Business Science Reference • ©2019 • 131pp • H/C (ISBN: 9781522584643) • US $160.00

Handbook of Research on Educator Preparation and Professional Learning
Drew Polly (University of North Carolina at Charlotte, USA) Christie Martin (University of South Carolina at Columbia, USA) and Kenan Dikilitaş (Bahçeşehir University, Turkey)
Information Science Reference • ©2019 • 459pp • H/C (ISBN: 9781522585831) • US $245.00

Preparing the Higher Education Space for Gen Z
Heidi Lee Schnackenberg (State University of New York at Plattsburgh, USA) and Christine Johnson (University of Western Kentucky, USA)
Information Science Reference • ©2019 • 253pp • H/C (ISBN: 9781522577638) • US $175.00

For an entire list of titles in this series, please visit:
https://www.igi-global.com/book-series/advances-higher-education-professional-development/73681

IGI Global
DISSEMINATOR OF KNOWLEDGE

701 East Chocolate Avenue, Hershey, PA 17033, USA
Tel: 717-533-8845 x100 • Fax: 717-533-8661
E-Mail: cust@igi-global.com • www.igi-global.com

Editorial Advisory Board

Billi Bromer, *Brenau University, USA*
Terri E. Bubb, *San Jacinto College, USA*
Annette Digby, *Independent Researcher, USA*
Terry L. Dupler, *Adams State University, USA*
Sandra L. Hardy, *Hardy Education Resources, USA*
Elaine Hendrix, *University of Houston – Clear Lake, USA*
Thomas A. Lucey, *Illinois State University, USA*
Bonnie Mackey, *University of Houston – Clear Lake, USA*
Noran L. Moffett, *Fayetteville State University, USA*
John E. Simons, *Azusa Pacific University, USA*
Melissa A. Simons, *Independent Researcher, USA*
Jennifer Young Wallace, *Jackson State University, USA*
Sharon A. White, *University of Houston – Clear Lake, USA*

Table of Contents

Foreword *by Sandra L. Hardy* xv

Foreword *by Noran L. Moffett* xvii

Foreword *by Melissa A. Simons* xix

Preface xxi

Acknowledgment xxxii

Section 1
What Is Mobbing? An Introduction and Overview

Chapter 1
Overcoming the Onslaught: A Tale of Woe from One Adjunct Professor 1
    Janelle Christine Simmons, Walden University, USA

Chapter 2
Bullied by the Best: Why the Bully Paradigm Is a Bad Fit for Understanding
the Mob 29
    Janice Harper, Independent Researcher, USA

Chapter 3
The Role of Passive Evil in Perpetuating Downward Academic Mobbing 44
    Theodore W. McDonald, Boise State University, USA
    Sandina Begic, Boise State University, USA
    R. Eric Landrum, Boise State University, USA

Section 2
Organizational Culture and Leadership Accountability

Chapter 4
Narcissistic and Sociopathic Leadership and the World of Higher Education:
A Place for Mentoring, Not Mobbing 69
    David B. Ross, Nova Southeastern University, USA
    Melissa T. Sasso, Nova Southeastern University, USA
    Cortney E. Matteson, Orange County School District, USA
    Rande W. Matteson, Nova Southeastern University, USA

Chapter 5
Mobbability: Understanding How a Vulnerable Academia Can Be
Healthier 104
    Naomi Jeffery Petersen, Central Washington University, USA
    Rebecca L. Pearson, Central Washington University, USA

Chapter 6
Neoliberal Technocracy and Opposition Exams for Hiring Tenured Full-Time
Professors in a Mexican Public University 132
    Silvia Karla Fernández Marín, National School of Anthropology and
        History, Mexico
    Florencia Peña-Saint-Martin, National School of Anthropology and
        History, Mexico

Chapter 7
A Remedy for Improving the Culture in Higher Education: Toxic Leadership
to Servant Leadership 159
    David B. Ross, Nova Southeastern University, USA
    Rande W. Matteson, Nova Southeastern University, USA
    Melissa T. Sasso, Nova Southeastern University, USA
    Gina L. Peyton, Nova Southeastern University, USA

Section 3
Accounts from the Ivory Tower Arena

Chapter 8
My Campus Administration, Faculty Association, Senate, and Me: A Case
Study in Academic Mobbing 187
    Peter Wylie, University of British Columbia – Okanagan, Canada

Chapter 9
Sins of a Syndicate: Arresting Malicious Mob Assaults Against
Academics..211
    Denise M. McDonald, University of Houston – Clear Lake, USA

Chapter 10
In the Midst of the Maelstrom: Struggling Through the Revulsions of
Academic Mobbing While Maintaining One's Ethical Compass 241
    Caroline M. Crawford, University of Houston – Clear Lake, USA

Compilation of References 267

About the Contributors 293

Index 299

Detailed Table of Contents

Foreword *by Sandra L. Hardy* xv

Foreword *by Noran L. Moffett* xvii

Foreword *by Melissa A. Simons* xix

Preface xxi

Acknowledgment xxxii

Section 1
What Is Mobbing? An Introduction and Overview

An overview of the phenomenon of academic mobbing and bullying efforts within higher education institutions is vital towards understanding the nuances of the manifestation.

Chapter 1
Overcoming the Onslaught: A Tale of Woe from One Adjunct Professor 1
   Janelle Christine Simmons, Walden University, USA

This chapter seeks to explore and examine the phenomenon known as mobbing and more specifically academic mobbing. First, a brief introduction to bullying at the workplace as well as mobbing ensues. Second, the definitions of mobbing and academic mobbing as well as clear descriptions are delineated. Third, various topics surrounding academic mobbing are introduced such; the phases of mobbing, a description of the bully, a description of the "mobbers," a description of the bystanders and a description of the target. Other topics are introduced as well such as statistics that surround the phenomenon of mobbing at the workplace as well as workplace engagement results of academic mobbing. Then the methodology is introduced. This research study is qualitative in nature. An autoethnography is utilized and the data is seen through a constructivist/interpretivist lens. The author than introduces her experience via narrative form, which is followed by a discussion and conclusion, limitations of the study, recommendations for future research, and a statement of conflict.

Chapter 2
Bullied by the Best: Why the Bully Paradigm Is a Bad Fit for Understanding
the Mob 29
    Janice Harper, Independent Researcher, USA

As the prevalence of academic mobbing gains increasing notice, the concept is almost always framed in terms of bullying perpetrated by a group of "bullies." While mobbing is seemingly bullying writ large, upon closer examination bullying and mobbing are very different forms of aggression. In this chapter, the author discusses how the prevailing bully paradigm has conflated bullying with mobbing, and why doing so is problematic. By focusing on the behavior of animals, she shows how signs of submission and/or domination can end or escalate the aggression, attract others to join in, and cause leaders to ignore or encourage the abuse. She then turns to the ways in which workplace aggression has been cast in moral terms of bullies and powerless victims, while failing to account for the complexity and nuance of workplace aggression, as well as the role of the victim. Finally, she discusses the organizational context of the university, suggesting that there are specific features of the academy that make it ripe for mobbing.

Chapter 3
The Role of Passive Evil in Perpetuating Downward Academic Mobbing 44
    Theodore W. McDonald, Boise State University, USA
    Sandina Begic, Boise State University, USA
    R. Eric Landrum, Boise State University, USA

Downward academic mobbing occurs when unethical administrators initiate a pattern of bullying, intimidation, and the commission of personal and career damage on undeserving faculty members (most often principled, tenured professors who question their decisions or call attention to unethical behavior such as policy violations and lack of academic due process). Once these unethical administrators succeed in framing a faculty victim as a target (often through innuendo, factual distortions, or outright lies), the victim's colleagues—many of whom have known and benefited from the victim for years—either fail to support the victim (a problem known as passive evil) or begin actively participating in the persecution themselves (often in pursuit of personal gain). The purpose of this chapter is to focus on the first instance (i.e., passive evil), and to discuss how passive evildoers' failure to stand up for victims of downward academic mobbing effectively encourages future acts of persecution—including against the passive evildoers themselves.

Section 2
Organizational Culture and Leadership Accountability

The organizational culture is analyzed, including individual, administrative and operationalized structural contributing factors.

Chapter 4
Narcissistic and Sociopathic Leadership and the World of Higher Education:
A Place for Mentoring, Not Mobbing 69
    David B. Ross, Nova Southeastern University, USA
    Melissa T. Sasso, Nova Southeastern University, USA
    Cortney E. Matteson, Orange County School District, USA
    Rande W. Matteson, Nova Southeastern University, USA

This chapter was designed to explore mobbing and bullying within higher education. This chapter per the researchers revealed the theoretical framework, the schema of people making versus bullying and mobbing, as well as differentiating between bullying and mobbing. Moreover, an array of examples of types of dark leadership and toxicity was provided. Furthermore, the researchers felt it was imperative to include the organizational culture applied to bullying and mobbing, in addition to the emphasis of counterproductive behavior. Also, the physiological and psychological impact on individuals under that leadership was provided as well as bullying and mobbing case studies. Preventative measures of bullying and mobbing within all levels was discussed and included a solution such as the TSTL survey created by Dr. David B. Ross. Lastly, a conclusion was provided.

Chapter 5
Mobbability: Understanding How a Vulnerable Academia Can Be
Healthier 104
    Naomi Jeffery Petersen, Central Washington University, USA
    Rebecca L. Pearson, Central Washington University, USA

This chapter discusses mobbing as a predictable institutional disorder with significant community effect. Academic departments are particularly vulnerable as contexts where conflicting motivations and tacit power differentials may allow undetectable and infectious incivility, and while there are research tools to measure experience, there are few effective practical campus-based strategies to monitor these issues. The authors explore mobbing through the lenses of epidemiology, public health, and organizational psychology. As part of this exploration the terms "mobbable" and "mobbability" are proposed, connoting the degree of incivility tolerated in the workplace climate, people's and institution's vulnerabilities, and the potential for improved capacity surrounding mobbing prevention. Outlining a story of academic mobbing, the chapter highlights contributing factors at both personal and organizational levels. The authors close with practical suggestions for recognizing symptoms and opportunities.

Chapter 6
Neoliberal Technocracy and Opposition Exams for Hiring Tenured Full-Time
Professors in a Mexican Public University 132
    Silvia Karla Fernández Marín, National School of Anthropology and
        History, Mexico
    Florencia Peña-Saint-Martin, National School of Anthropology and
        History, Mexico

In this chapter, the introduction of technocratic neoliberal policies in Mexico, starting in the mid-1980s, and their repercussions in higher education are analyzed. Special focus is set on its negative consequences for hiring tenured full-time professors at public universities. A case study from a public university is used to demonstrate how suppressing candidates and arbitrarily favoring others through sham dealing are almost part of the formal procedures now. This case was used because access to all the documentation was granted, and it was possible to interview in depth a female candidate who was suppressed twice. Unfortunately, experiencing suppression, workplace bullying, and mobbing for some candidates is almost the norm now. Also, when suppressed, they are left in a powerless position with almost no resources to confront injustice.

Chapter 7
A Remedy for Improving the Culture in Higher Education: Toxic Leadership
to Servant Leadership 159
    David B. Ross, Nova Southeastern University, USA
    Rande W. Matteson, Nova Southeastern University, USA
    Melissa T. Sasso, Nova Southeastern University, USA
    Gina L. Peyton, Nova Southeastern University, USA

The purpose of this chapter is to examine how servant-centered leadership should align with the values of higher education institutions than other forms of leadership. Servant leadership follows a value system, ethical philosophy, rather than a standard set of leadership practices. This chapter explores adult education and leadership-power philosophies, the historical perspective of leadership and management, followed by literature of servant leadership and toxic leadership. In addition, crises of higher education were discussed as well as the need to remedy a toxic culture toward servant-centered environment and that institutions of higher education must be the proactive educators. The researchers concluded that in order for an academic institution to thrive, the utilization and implementation of servant-centered leadership is paramount. It is also equally critical to teach students the philosophy of servant leadership so they in turn can give back to their communities.

Section 3
Accounts from the Ivory Tower Arena

Personal storytelling as a means through which to describe, explain and interpret academic mobbing as competently insidious.

Chapter 8
My Campus Administration, Faculty Association, Senate, and Me: A Case Study in Academic Mobbing 187
    Peter Wylie, University of British Columbia – Okanagan, Canada

This chapter recounts recent experiences of the author with the University of British Columbia (UBC), its Faculty Association (FA), this association's relationship with the author's campus administration at UBC Okanagan campus (UBCO), and the relationship of the campus administration with the senate of the campus. The chapter is a case study of academic mobbing. The author's targeting, exclusion, and ostracism is fully documented in the chapter and fully explained by the concepts of academic bullying, harassment, and mobbing. It is a case study of where an elected union representative of faculty members and an elected senator was targeted, excluded, and ostracized by the powers that be in the union and university administration, working in collusion and complicity.

Chapter 9
Sins of a Syndicate: Arresting Malicious Mob Assaults Against Academics 211
    Denise M. McDonald, University of Houston – Clear Lake, USA

This chapter presents a fictitious and satirical story, which explores how individuals and groups of privilege in a university structure exert their power (through intimidation and other oppressive actions) on targeted individuals who are perceived as challenging or disruptive to the power group's existing control. The story is presented as an allegory of the 1920-1940's mafia.

Chapter 10
In the Midst of the Maelstrom: Struggling Through the Revulsions of Academic Mobbing While Maintaining One's Ethical Compass 241
    Caroline M. Crawford, University of Houston – Clear Lake, USA

Academic mobbing's impact upon the target and the target's professional world can throw one's world off kilter to the point that the target has difficulty maintaining a semblance of psychological and cognitive balance. This story is one target's approach towards maintaining a semblance of balance within the midst of the horrors of academic mobbing and bullying attacks. This target's ethical compass and balance are maintained through the support and guidance of outstanding colleagues, yet in more personal moments the target's sense of psychological equilibrium and emotional stability are drawn from the lifetime accumulation of quotations, lyrics, and poems that articulate one's ethical compass and steadfast psychological center.

Compilation of References 267

About the Contributors 293

Index 299

Foreword

PIVOTING PENDULUMS OF POLARIZATION

Confronting Academic Mobbing in Higher Education: Personal Accounts and Administrative Action is a mindful masterpiece, and a must read! This revolutionary book is brought to a cutting-edge of artful fruition by the brilliantly skilled orchestration of editor, author, and scholar, Dr. Caroline Crawford in cooperation with the noteworthy contributions of chapter contributors. The chapters paint the pictures of pivoting pendulums of good and malice in the tunnels and chambers of ivory towers may result in the targeting of productive members who stand-up for ethical reasons against the status quo. The authors reveal many sources of power that when mismanaged may yield potentially coercive tenets of deconstructionism and associated polarizations may be collectively encountered behind the scenes of what is primarily perceived as academic equality and opportunity (Ostby, Urdal, & Dupuy, 2019).

Confronting Academic Mobbing in Higher Education: Personal Accounts and Administrative Action ushers to the forefront a long overdue and brilliantly executed discourse of higher education and sometimes hidden happenings and harsh realities found as divisiveness and misuse of power. The many forms of academic mobbing are highlighted in the chapters by the author's personal and professional accounts as well as by their knowledge of the professional literature. Of these accounts are including the fabrication of stories and other varied forms of bullying that take place not only in the institutions of higher education but also may permeate complexity outside the halls and walls of academia to the private lives of targeted individuals, the general public, and indeed society at large (Jacobson, Levin, & Kapur, 2019).

The dynamic works contained in this must-read academic masterpiece will lead to further awareness, action, and therefore research and justice for targets of academic mobbing and bullying for decades to come.

Sandra L. Hardy
Hardy Education Resources, USA

REFERENCES

Jacobson, M. J., Levin, J. A., & Kapur, M. (2019). Education as a complex system: Conceptual and methodological implications. *Educational Researcher*, *48*(2), 112–119. doi:10.3102/0013189X19826958

Ostby, G., Urdal, H., & Dupuy, K. (2019). Does education lead to pacification? A systematic review of statistical studies on education and political violence. *Review of Educational Research*, *89*(1), 46–92. doi:10.3102/0034654318800236

Foreword

EXPLORING STRANGE NEW WORLDS

Ideally, the academy should be a place of intellectually discovery where the universe is the only limitation. Dr. Crawford has presented a collection of experiences on the subject of mobbing that allows us to look deeper into the academy for the cancerous nature of the academic mobbing enterprise. It is the belief that each chapter can be viewed as part of the metaphorical experiences of Star Trek, namely the "…voyages of the starship *Enterprise*" (Smithsonian National Air and Space Museum, 2016, 0:15-0:18).

The character of Mr. Spock would remind Captain Kirk that human beings are imminently *illogical*. For any of us who have seen the concept of mobbing at work, keeping with the Star Trek analogy, the intellectual description of the voyages can be found in the chapters of this text, *Confronting Academic Mobbing in Higher Education: Personal Accounts and Administrative Action*.

The challenge of this book is to acknowledge that these accounts are like the voyages of Star Trek's *Enterprise* but, unless the academic community from Boards of Governors through Faculty Promotion and Tenure Committees and even the Faculty Search Committees choose to suggest that these voyages are real and do occur for many of our academic colleagues, then we stand the chance of having two of the most memorable Star Trek phrases to have been captured through the series to endure on our halls of academy; specifically Spock quotations that "Logic is the beginning of wisdom, not the end" (Clarke, 2015, 0:40-0:44) and, "Highly illogical" (DarthNub, 2007, 0:18-0:20).

To the outsider, it might seem improbably or highly illogical for academic mobbing to be a reality. The chapters presented herein allow us to consider the contributors as members of the academic Star Trek voyage, seeking to contribute to the body of knowledge in the universe, but finding that adventures may await that make the episodes of immediate danger portrayed in the episodes of Star Trek seem like a nursery rhyme.

As the reader constructively reads these episodes in the lives of the contributors, consider your role as a member of the university setting or other organizations wherein a breeding ground for academic mobbing can become a culture of acceptance. Perhaps, the Opening Monologue for the Original classic Star Trek Series can be considered.

At its best and its worst, the operational existence of our work in the academy can be characterized through the words spoken by Captain James T. Kirk, wherein the full quotation as pulled from the voiceover introduction to each episode being:

Space: the final frontier. These are the voyages of the starship Enterprise. Its five-year mission: to explore strange new worlds, to seek out new life and new civilizations, to boldly go where no man has gone before. (Smithsonian National Air and Space Museum, 2016, 0:05-0:30)

In fact, Geraghty, Palumbo, and Sullivan (2014) suggests that fans can engage with Star Trek in complex ways; therefore, it is suggested that the higher education institutions are a gift to the world and should be eradicated of tangible instances of academic mobbing.

At our best, we should be seeking to take these stories and working to eradicate their existence from the academic *Enterprise* (Gregory, 2000).

Noran L. Moffett
Fayetteville State University, USA

REFERENCES

Clarke, P. (2015, February 27). *Spock and Valeris*. Retrieved from https://www.youtube.com/watch?v=F4Op4vc3GBs

DarthNub. (2007, January 30). *Leonard Nimoy's Highly Illogical*. Retrieved from https://www.youtube.com/watch?v=Ru9e2rTHeuk

Geraghty, L., Palumbo, D. E., & Sullivan, C. W. III. (2014). *The Influence of Star Trek on Television, Film and Culture*. McFarland.

Gregory, C. (2000). *Introduction: "to boldly go…" — approaching the texts of Star Trek*. Star Trek. doi:10.1057/9780230598409_1

Smithsonian National Air and Space Museum. (2016, October 13). *Star Trek Original Series – Opening Credits* [video file]. Retrieved from https://www.youtube.com/watch?v=4pptCGR9N4g

Foreword

YOU'RE JUST NOT GOOD ENOUGH

As a learner who has enjoyed attending six different higher education institutions at the undergraduate and graduate levels of academic engagement, I have viewed bullying and academic mobbing from a close up and very personal viewpoint. I've heard and experienced the depth of cruelty and bullying behaviors that might shock those who have been less assertively engaged in the learning process, including statements such as:

"Your only novices."

"Didn't you read the Chapter? Then you should have passed the test."

"I know the syllabus does not match the required textbook. Just look at my slides, that's all you need."

"[announcing publicly the student's name] is failing the course, they are not smart enough for this field."

"Sorry, can't help you, the faculty in question is tenured."

"This is going to be hard. Deal with it."

    The internal pandemonium that occurs in the mind of a vulnerable student, trying to propagate her or his own cognitive understandings around new subject matter, is negatively impacted through the trauma and dissonance achieved by the higher education personnel who consider the students as disposable. All the while, the student is progressively dealing with new information and perversely negative comments that ultimately combust into trauma, distressing the student and damaging not only the student's higher education experience but also negatively impacting the cognitive ability of the student. The damage experienced is distracting from the learner's coursework and knowledge attainment while, the next moment, the student's self-efficacy and hope are incinerated. The student's internal messaging system defines one's own knowledge base and student efforts as *less than,* clearly articulating the sense that the student *does not belong* and somehow deserves the traumatically unprofessional and cruel treatment displayed by higher education faculty, administrative leadership and staff. This treatment of the student decreases the potential towards positive outcomes, establishing and reinforcing the student's slowly internalized message – "You're just not good enough."

The faculty and administrative leadership's subtle and unsubtle comments spread abusive bullying behaviors, negatively influencing the student population and the organization's collegial community. One might suggest some academic communities accept such practices by those faculty and administrative leadership who, perhaps privately, seek power and control over not only their professional equals but even the student body over whom they have ultimate callous control. These internal-to-the-organization bullying behaviors can develop to form an academic mobbing culture that directly impacts the students, with bullying and mobbing behaviors impacting the student through the faculty, the administrative leadership, the staff and even other students who have had these behaviors modeled as acceptable.

The organizational sickness, defined as bullying and academic mobbing, develops into an inherent organizational reality that slowly overtakes faculty, administration, staff and students. The modeled negative and traumatic behaviors result in an organizational sickness inside the higher education structure that is also upon full display within the profession as well as within the surrounding community. The reputation of the academic institution is forever tarnished.

The book chapters clearly outline the negative academic mobbing outcomes that have been achieved. The immoral compass eventually skews and overtakes positive diversity and inclusionary efforts, creativity, fiscal accountability, and ultimately shuns returning or academically strong students who are unwilling to attempt to survive within this type of organizational culture. Long-term, the development of a fear-based, bullying organizational culture will repress teaching, research and service strengths through the loss of stronger faculty and administrators, leaving the organization with lower quality faculty who achieved influence through bullying and academic mobbing, with the mantra clearly focused upon – "It's all about me".

Melissa A. Simons
Independent Researcher, USA

Preface

Higher education has always been its own world, set apart from the real-world expectations found within other environments that also includes societal imperatives. Therefore, one may recognize academia as its own cultural milieu and with standards of expectation that may not always align with the societal expectations and cultural laws of appropriate practice. Within this type of world, one can find the autonomy to think and work freely and differently, towards attaining astounding positive, constructive and progressive additions to the larger knowledge base. Yet there is always a yin to the yang within any balanced approach. Specifically, with the good comes the bad, always offering complimentary opposites that are actually interconnected towards a balanced life experience. This is equally true within the hallways of academia, as the interrelation between strengths and weaknesses, different collegial talents, interrelated engagement of ideas, offers an interconnected synergy amongst individual selves and personalities within the academic community. In most instances, the academics meld into mutually respectful and complimentary colleagues. However, what happens when mutual respect and collegial support shifts to the darker side of humanity's being, such as bullying and mobbing of colleagues?

Workplace bullying is a growing organizational concern throughout society, yet bullying within academia takes on a totally different understanding due to the style of bullying that has come to be referred to as academic mobbing. Of interest, is that bullying in the workplace has developed into a significant area of study; however, within the bounds of scholarly practice and focus, academic forms of bullying have only recently begun to receive attention. This does not suggest that academic bullying and academic mobbing is a new phenomenon, as there have always been jealousy and greed throughout the hallways of the ivory tower, with power and control being desired outcomes. Instead, the prerequisites of the academy ensured the silencing of persons who were willing to speak out against these behaviors. The suppression of the distasteful underbelly of academia was a self-serving approach towards maintaining the societal impression of eminence and value throughout higher education. Yet with the shifting cultural and societal norms, the growing recognition of academia's disquieting ethos has fractured, disintegrating the ivory tower and allowing a glimpse into the world of academia that can be gloriously scholarly and creatively innovative, while also offering the potential towards displaying lesser qualities of human nature that includes the normative ethics of the seven deadly sins of lust, gluttony, greed, sloth, wrath, envy, and pride (Capps, 2000; DeYoung, 2009; Schimmel, 1997).

Yet called from the depths of the seven deadly sins is an alternative view. The virtues that are highlighted amongst the wreckage of the seven deadly sins are beautifully laid out by Capps (2000) while representing an overview of virtues as found within Chaucer's *Canterbury Tales* (2010):

Deadly Sins	Virtues
Gluttony	Abstinence, temperance, sobriety
Anger	Patience
Greed	Mercy
Envy	Love of God, neighbor, and enemy
Pride	Humility
Lust	Chastity, continence
Acedia and sloth	Fortitude. (Capps, 2000, p. 74)

Viewing the seven deadly sins against the more virtuous humanist understandings reflects an intriguing dichotomy that also offers a metaphoric understanding around the creative and scholarly efforts that are consistently occurring within the ivory tower, focused upon the triad of effort designated as teaching, research and service.

THE CHALLENGES

There is a growing interest in bullying within higher education, specifically labeled as *academic mobbing*, reflecting the bullies who focus upon a specific target faculty member. Notice the faculty member is referred to as a *target* and not a *victim* because, as described by Ken Westhues:

Preface

Leymann [a researcher] studies the non-violent, polite, sophisticated kind of mobbing that happens in ostensibly rational workplaces. Universities are archetype. If professors despise a colleague to the point of feeling desperate need to put the colleague down, pummeling the target is a foolish move. The mobbers lose and the target gains credibility.

The more clever and effective strategy is to wear the target down emotionally by shunning, gossip, ridicule, bureaucratic hassles, and withholding of deserved rewards. The German word Todschweigen, death by silence, describes this initial, informal stage of workplace mobbing. This is often enough to achieve the goal. . . .

If the target refuses to leave or acquiesce, the mobbing may escalate to a formal outburst of aggression. Mobbers seize upon a critical incident, some real or imagined misbehavior that they claim is proof of the target's unworthiness to continue in the normal give and take of academic life. A degradation ritual is arranged, often in a dean's office, sometimes in a campus tribunal. The object is to destroy the good name that is any professor's main resource, to expose the target as not worth listening to. Public censure by the university administration leaves the target stigmatized for life. Formal dismissal with attendant publicity is social elimination in its most conclusive form. (Westhues, n.d.a, para. 4-7)

This has become a growing phenomenon throughout higher education.

As further described by Westhues (n.d.b), he identifies as strategy number five, "*In the face of demands that a professor be punished, entertain not just the null hypothesis but the mobbing hypothesis*" (para. 29):

Often, an issue is already couched in exclusionary, stigmatizing, forensic language by the time one learns of it. Waterloo philosopher Jan Narveson has nicely phrased a request commonly brought to university administrators: "Git my enemies!" Chair or dean receives a delegation that says essentially, "Professor Z is a racist [sexist, plagiarist, thief, bully, abuser, harasser, nutbar, terrorist, or some other discrediting label]. This has to stop. Do something."

Faced with this proffered hypothesis of Professor Z's guilt of some offense, an unskilled administrator simply accepts it out of personal respect for its authors or personal aversion to Z . . .

A somewhat more skilled administrator acknowledges the proffered hypothesis but weighs it against the contrary or null hypothesis, that Z has not in fact behaved in a way that warrants administrative interference with Z's work . . .

A highly skilled administrator entertains the first two hypotheses but also a third one, that this is no mere misunderstanding, that Z's accusers are caught up in a panic or hysteria that prevents them from thinking and seeing straight, that their zealous demand for Z's punishment fits the bill of what researchers call workplace mobbing.

The advantage of knowing this third hypothesis is that it broadens the range of possible interpretations to place on the usually confusing data of disputes. (Westhues, n.d.b, para. 30-33)

Of importance is highlighting that the faculty being mobbed are capable instructors and researchers, with a strong moral compass who contribute greatly to the university in multiple ways. Some of the characteristics of those who tend to be targets are designated by Khoo (2010) as:

Women faculty members who are outspoken about ethical and unjust matters are usually the targets being mobbed. Their competence and professional success are perceived as threats by the bullies. (para. 5)

As well, Khoo (2010) notes that:

Those with integrity to withstand the efforts of the bully to create a group of "yes men or women" risk being victimized. It is often the person who is potentially an organization's best asset who becomes the target of bullying. (para. 9)

These are references that may be viewed as lacking in recent impact. However, instead of the suggestion that this is no longer a viable topic that is worthy of addressed focus, what has currently been offered is merely a framework through which to understand the basics associated with the topic. More recent articles have been highlighted in The Chronicle of Higher Education (2009, 2018) and The Guardian (Farley & Sprigg, 2014), while innumerable publications are recognized merely within the current 2018 year (McDonald, Stockton & Landrum, 2018; Miley, 2018; Pheko, 2018a, 2018b; Prevost & Hunt, 2018); Samier & Miley, 2018; Wylie, 2018) with the extensiveness of the list beyond recognition. Farley and Sprigg (2014) suggest that "…the percentage of people who have experienced bullying within academic settings is higher than the national average. UK Higher education studies have found the percentage of people experiencing it ranges between 18% to 42%" (para. 11). As well, authors such as Yaman (2010) have highlighted the impact of mobbing upon the higher education institution, negatively reflecting upon organizational culture and climate within the institution. This suggests a lack of faculty engagement and lessens the institution's reputation.

Preface
SEARCHING FOR A SOLUTION

The shifting realities of higher education over the past few decades have disquieted the metaphoric ivory tower that traditionally perceived itself to be comfortably cared for by the larger populace as being a *greater good*. Yet with the slowly lessened support for public instructions by the state governments along with the shift in cultural norms towards workforce competency and parity, the shifts have become swift and impactful. This may be partially based within the Internet's growth that supported online and blended learning environments but also based within the economic and customer-centric shift towards privatized for-profit higher education institutions. One may suggest that it is too early to know the outcome of the earthquakes impacting the world of higher education and slowly shifting the life of academics from comfortably secure towards struggling and scraping for yearly merit raises and student retention. This type of environment enhances the fight, flight, face or freeze base reactive responses within humans. Recognizing this, Maslow's hierarchy of needs (Maslow, 1943, 1954, 1961, 1962a, 1962b, 1963, 1964, 1969a, 1969b, 1970, 1971, 1979, 1982, 1987, 1993a, 1993b, 1993c, 1996, 1999a, 1999b, 1999c) becomes a pyramid upon which academia stumbles and people's natural motivations and fear-based responses may begin to be more openly displayed. As Koltko-Rivera (2006) emphasizes, the later work of Maslow recognized the hierarchy did not end by reaching self-actualization but actually the level of self-transcendence must be embraced.

Maslow's hierarchy of needs is impactful, when considering the quality of people's motivational needs within an academic environment. The understanding around bullying and academic mobbing may be well represented by Koltko-Rivera's (2006) representation of Maslow's hierarchy of needs (1943, 1954, 1969a, 1979, 1982) as representing six motivational levels (Table 1).

The interesting aspects of Maslow's hierarchy of needs is the recognition that people move between motivational levels, dependent upon one's quality of purpose

Table 1.

A Rectified Version of Maslow's Hierarchy of Needs	
Motivational Level	Description of person at this level
Self-transcendence	Seeks to further a cause beyond the self and to experience a communion beyond the boundaries of the self through peak experience.
Self-actualization	Seeks fulfillment of personal potential.
Esteem needs	Seeks esteem through recognition or achievement.
Belongingness and love needs.	Seeks affiliation with a group.
Safety needs	Seeks security through order and law.
Physiological (survival) needs	Seeks to obtain the basic necessities of life.
(Koltko-Rivera, 2006, p. 303)	

and personality, environment in which one finds oneself, and one's response to environmental factors that might directly focus upon fight, flight, face or freeze. The actors within bulling and academic mobbing experiences, whether actively engaged or bystanders, may find oneself moving between different levels of motivation. The bullies, the mobbers, the targets, the bystanders, and the valued few who attempt to protect and support the targets are on display throughout chapters of this book. The work of impressive book chapter authors may support recognition and differentiation between these hierarchy of needs and action or response to stimuli.

ORGANIZATION OF THE BOOK

The book is organized into 10 chapters. A brief description of each of the chapters follows:

Chapter 1 by Simmons is titled "Overcoming the Onslaught: A Tale of Woe from One Adjunct Professor." This chapter offers an introduction and overview to the phenomenon of bullying as a workplace experience, then delves into a differentiated understanding around the academic mobbing experience. The different topics that support and impact academic mobbing are also discussed, including labels of bully, mobber, target, as well as bystanders. Along with this welcome overview framework, the author shares a personal account of academic mobbing.

Chapter 2 by Harper, titled "Bullied by the Best: Why the Bully Paradigm Is a Bad Fit for Understanding the Mob," furthers the discussion around bullying versus academic mobbing. The conceptual discussion emphasizes the differentiated approaches to the aggressive actions of bullies versus the mobbing enterprise. Her understanding around workplace aggression and the impactful comprehensions around the idiosyncratic distinctions and convoluted intricacies of the workplace are established within contextual understandings of the workplace.

Chapter 3 by McDonald, Begic, and Landrum, titled "The Role of Passive Evil in Perpetuating Downward Academic Mobbing," focuses upon the administrative leadership as the bullies and enact academic mobbing within organizational structures. The concept of passive evil and passive evildoers is presented, as the silent majority who ignore the bullying and mobbing behaviors by failing to support or protect the target of the bullying and mobbing behaviors.

Chapter 4 by Ross, Sasso, Matteson, and Matteson is titled "Narcissistic and Sociopathic Leadership and the World of Higher Education: A Place for Mentoring, Not Mobbing." This chapter's intriguing discussions around dark leadership and organizational toxicity as a culture are brought forward, while also focusing upon the physiological and psychological short-term impact and long-term impact on the target. Potential preemptive and precautionary measures are discussed.

Preface

Chapter 5 by Petersen and Pearson, titled "Mobbability: Understanding How a Vulnerable Academia Can Be Healthier," focuses upon academic mobbing as an organizational disorder that results in an institutional community impact. This intriguing discussion grows out of an understanding of an organization's vulnerabilities and potential towards improved capacity, at both personal and organizational levels of engagement and impact, with practical opportunistic suggestions towards recognizing and addressing burgeoning signs, symptoms and indicative warnings associated with bullying and academic mobbing concerns.

Chapter 6 by Fernández Marín and Peña-Saint-Martin is titled "Neoliberal Technocracy and Opposition Exams for Hiring Tenured Full-Time Professors in a Mexican Public University." This discussion is important and timely, as the inherent institutional toxicity can reach into the faculty hiring process, towards suppressing superior candidate applications while at the same time favoring other candidate applications that may be less desirable, deliberately designed for different motives and towards achieving different aims and desired outcomes.

Chapter 7 by Ross, Matteson, Sasso, and Peyton, titled "A Remedy for Improving the Culture in Higher Education: Toxic Leadership to Servant Leadership," focuses upon the values, mission, and vision of the organizational institution while also highlighting differentiated forms of leadership. Articulated are leadership and power philosophies from a historical perspective as well as toxic leadership based within the literature, resulting in the suggestion that servant-centered leadership is a necessary and critical approach within an academic institution.

Chapter 8 by Wylie is titled "My Campus Administration, Faculty Association, Senate, and Me: A Case Study in Academic Mobbing." This is a case study, in fact a self-study, of one academic's experiences around academic mobbing. The gut wrenching experiences represented throughout this chapter emphasizes the toxicity of an organization that supports collusion and complicity while targeting an academic representing an impressive standing within the larger scholarly community. The story of a superior academic colleague's experience should be a distressing inducement to all within higher education.

Chapter 9 by McDonald is titled "Sins of a Syndicate: Arresting Malicious Mob Assaults Against Academics." This enjoyably satirical and fictitious metaphorical frame through which storytelling articulates the ravages of academic mobbing upon academicians is significant and troublingly insightful. The recognition of the story as based within the author's experiential observations undergirds the impact of bullying and academic mobbing upon not only the targets, but upon every person within the organizational structure.

Chapter 10 by Crawford is titled "In the Midst of the Maelstrom: Struggling Through the Revulsions of Academic Mobbing While Maintaining One's Ethical Compass." This chapter focuses upon ways that one target attempts to maintain their implicit ethical compass and integrity throughout bullying and academic mobbing assaults. Inherent within this story is the depth of emotional angst and trauma that a target undergoes, while attempting to and striving towards maintaining a level of balance and composed serenity that reflects a personal integrity and a strong moral and ethical compass.

Caroline M. Crawford
University of Houston – Clear Lake, USA

REFERENCES

Capps, D. (2000). *Deadly sins and saving virtues*. Eugene, OR: Wipf and Stock Publishers.

Chaucer, G. (2010). The Canterbury Tales. *World Public Library*. Retrieved from http://117.211.153.211:8001/jspui/bitstream/123456789/940/1/canterbury.pdf

DeYoung, R. K. (2009). *Glittering vices: A new look at the seven deadly sins and their remedies*. Grand Rapids, MI: Brazos Press.

Farley, S., & Sprigg, C. (2014, November 3). Culture of cruelty: Why bullying thrives in higher education. *The Guardian*. Retrieved from https://www.theguardian.com/higher-education-network/blog/2014/nov/03/why-bullying-thrives-higher-education

Khoo, S. B. (2010). Academic mobbing: Hidden health hazard at workplace. *Malaysian Family Physician, 5*(2), 61-67. Retrieved from https://www.ncbi.nlm.nih.gov/pmc/articles/PMC4170397/

Koltko-Rivera, M. E. (2006). Rediscovering the later version of Maslow's hierarchy of needs: Self-transcendence and opportunities for theory, research, and unification. *Review of General Psychology, 10*(4), 302–317. doi:10.1037/1089-2680.10.4.302

Maslow, A. H. (1943). A theory of human motivation. *Psychological Review, 50*(4), 370–396. doi:10.1037/h0054346

Maslow, A. H. (1954). *Motivation and Personality*. New York: Harper.

Maslow, A. H. (1961). Are our publications and conventions suitable for the personal sciences? *The American Psychologist, 16*(6), 318–319. doi:10.1037/h0039674

Preface

Maslow, A. H. (1962a). Lessons from the peak experiences. *Journal of Humanistic Psychology*, *2*(1), 9–18. doi:10.1177/002216786200200102

Maslow, A. H. (1962b). Notes on being-psychology. *Journal of Humanistic Psychology*, *2*(2), 47–71. doi:10.1177/002216786200200205

Maslow, A. H. (1963). Further notes on the psychology of being. *Journal of Humanistic Psychology*, *3*(1), 120–135. doi:10.1177/002216786300300112

Maslow, A. H. (1964). Further notes on the psychology of being. *Journal of Humanistic Psychology*, *4*(1), 45–58. doi:10.1177/002216786400400105

Maslow, A. H. (1969a). The farther reaches of human nature. *Journal of Transpersonal Psychology*, *1*(1), 1–9.

Maslow, A. H. (1969b). Toward a humanistic biology. *The American Psychologist*, *24*(8), 724–735. doi:10.1037/h0027859

Maslow, A. H. (1971). *The Farther Reaches of Human Nature*. New York: Viking.

Maslow, A. H. (1979). *The Journals of A. H. Maslow* (R. J. Lowry, Ed.; Vols. 1–2). Monterey, CA: Brooks/Cole.

Maslow, A. H. (1982). The Journals of Abraham Maslow (R. J. Lowry, Ed., & J. Freedman, Abridger). Brattleboro, VT: Lewis.

Maslow, A. H. (1987). Motivation and Personality (3rd ed.; R. Frager, J. Fadiman, C. McReynolds, & R. Cox, Eds.). Boston, MA: Addison Wesley.

Maslow, A. H. (1993a). A theory of metamotivation: The biological rooting of the value-life. In A. H. Maslow (Ed.), *The Farther Reaches of Human Nature* (pp. 289–328). New York: Penguin/Arkana.

Maslow, A. H. (1993b). Theory Z. In A. H. Maslow (Ed.), *The Farther Reaches of Human Nature* (pp. 270–286). New York: Penguin/Arkana.

Maslow, A. H. (1993c). Various meanings of transcendence. In A. H. Maslow (Ed.), *The Farther Reaches of Human Nature* (pp. 259–269). New York: Penguin/Arkana.

Maslow, A. H. (1996). Critique of self-actualization theory. In E. Hoffman (Ed.), *Future visions: The Unpublished Papers of Abraham Maslow* (pp. 26–32). Thousand Oaks, CA: Sage.

Maslow, A. H. (1999a). Cognition of being in the peak-experiences. In A. H. Maslow (Ed.), *Toward a Psychology of Being* (3rd ed.; pp. 81–111). New York: Wiley.

Maslow, A. H. (1999b). Peak-experiences as acute identity experiences. In A. H. Maslow (Ed.), *Toward a Psychology of Being* (3rd ed.; pp. 113–125). New York: Wiley.

Maslow, A. H. (1999c). Some dangers of being cognition. In A. H. Maslow (Ed.), *Toward a Psychology of Being* (3rd ed.; pp. 127–138). New York: Wiley.

Maslow, A. H. (1964). Religions, Values, and Peak Experiences. New York: Penguin.

McDonald, T. W., Stockton, J. D., & Landrum, R. E. (2018). Civility and academic freedom: Who defines the former (and how) may imperil rights to the latter. *The College Quarterly*, *21*(1), n1.

Milley, P. (2018). *Strategies of discursive closure maladministrators use to 'manage' their misdeeds*. In International Perspectives on Maladministration in Education: Theories, Research, and Critiques. New York: Routledge.

Pheko, M. M. (2018a). Autoethnography and cognitive adaptation: Two powerful buffers against the negative consequences of workplace bullying and academic mobbing. *International Journal of Qualitative Studies on Health and Well-being*, *13*(1), 1459134. doi:10.1080/17482631.2018.1459134 PMID:29667923

Pheko, M. M. (2018b). Rumors and gossip as tools of social undermining and social dominance in workplace bullying and mobbing practices: A closer look at perceived perpetrator motives. *Journal of Human Behavior in the Social Environment*, 1–17.

Prevost, C., & Hunt, E. (2018). Bullying and Mobbing in Academe: A Literature Review. *European Scientific Journal, 14*(8).

Samier, E. A., & Milley, P. (2018). Introduction: The Landscape of Maladministration in Education. In *International Perspectives on Maladministration in Education* (pp. 11–26). New York: Routledge. doi:10.4324/9781315150222-1

Schimmel, S. (1997). The seven deadly sins: Jewish, Christian, and classical reflections on human psychology. *Oup Usa*. Retrieved from The PhilPapers Foundation: https://philpapers.org/rec/SCHTSD

The Chronicle of Higher Education. (2009, June 11). *'Mobbing' Can Damage More Than Careers, Professors are Told at Conference*. Retrieved from https://www.chronicle.com/article/Mobbing-Can-Damage-More-Than/47736

The Chronicle of Higher Education. (2018). *The Awakening: Women and Power in the Academy*. Retrieved from https://www.chronicle.com/interactives/the-awakening?cid=wcontentgrid_hp_2

Westhues, K. (Ed.). (2006). *The Remedy and Prevention of Mobbing in Higher Education: Two Case Studies.* Lewiston, NY: The Edwin Mellen Press.

Westhues, K. (n.d.a). The unkindly art of mobbing. *Academic Matters: The Journal of Higher Education*, 18-19. Retrieved from http://kwesthues.com/unkindlyart.htm

Westhues, K. (n.d.b). *The Waterloo Strategy for Prevention of Mobbing in Higher Education.* Retrieved from http://www.kwesthues.com/waterloostrategy.htm

Wylie, P. (2018). My Campus Administration, Faculty Association and Me: Academic Mobbing and Sweetheart Unionism. *Workplace: A Journal for Academic Labor*, (31).

Yaman, E. (2010, Winter). Perception of faculty members exposed to mobbing about the organizational culture and climate. *Educational Sciences: Theory and Practice*, *10*(1), 567–578. Retrieved from https://files.eric.ed.gov/fulltext/EJ882735.pdf

Acknowledgment

The editor would like to acknowledge the help of all the people involved in this project and, more specifically, to the authors and reviewers that took part in the review process. Without their support, this book would not have become a reality.

First, the editor would like to thank each one of the authors for their contributions. My sincere gratitude goes to the chapter's authors who contributed their time and expertise to this book.

Second, the editor wishes to acknowledge the valuable contributions of the reviewers regarding the improvement of quality, coherence, and content presentation of chapters. The timely engagement and superiority of evaluative review offered collegial support towards the author's vision as well as the consequential distinction of the completed book.

Caroline M. Crawford
University of Houston – Clear Lake, USA

Section 1
What Is Mobbing? An Introduction and Overview

An overview of the phenomenon of academic mobbing and bullying efforts within higher education institutions is vital towards understanding the nuances of the manifestation.

Chapter 1
Overcoming the Onslaught:
A Tale of Woe from One Adjunct Professor

Janelle Christine Simmons
Walden University, USA

ABSTRACT

This chapter seeks to explore and examine the phenomenon known as mobbing and more specifically academic mobbing. First, a brief introduction to bullying at the workplace as well as mobbing ensues. Second, the definitions of mobbing and academic mobbing as well as clear descriptions are delineated. Third, various topics surrounding academic mobbing are introduced such; the phases of mobbing, a description of the bully, a description of the "mobbers," a description of the bystanders and a description of the target. Other topics are introduced as well such as statistics that surround the phenomenon of mobbing at the workplace as well as workplace engagement results of academic mobbing. Then the methodology is introduced. This research study is qualitative in nature. An autoethnography is utilized and the data is seen through a constructivist/interpretivist lens. The author than introduces her experience via narrative form, which is followed by a discussion and conclusion, limitations of the study, recommendations for future research, and a statement of conflict.

DOI: 10.4018/978-1-5225-9485-7.ch001

INTRODUCTION

For centuries, workers have endured treatment that belittles their pride and robs the artistry from their craft. Stud Terkel (Murphy, 2016, p. 1).

The workplace is a seemingly important facet of one's life (Osborne & Hammond, 2017; Pheko, 2018; Tigrel & Kokalan, 2009). Sigmund Freud once noted that working is an action that continues to be the strongest link to reality (Pheko, 2018). The social environment of a workplace is extremely important to establishing normalcy. "The emotional state of an employee also relates to motivation" (Osborne & Hammond, 2017, p. 52); and employee engagement is critical to any organization (Osborne & Hammond, 2017).

A positive social work environment where an employee is healthy and happy is necessary due to the fact that people spend a large amount of their time at the workplace (Tigrel & Koklan, 2009). This may be because "many scholars concur that organizational life, jobs and work are fundamental to the human condition, to human beings' sense of identity [...], and are central to establishing personally meaningful self-definitions [...]" (Pheko, 2018, p. 1). It also important to point out that employee engagement is necessary for organizational productivity (Osborne & Hammond, 2017). An employee's emotional state relates to motivation (Osborne & Hammond, 2017) - their "basic needs of satisfaction have been found to directly relate to the dedication of employees" (Osborne & Hammond, 2017, p. 52). It has become apparent that a byproduct of sound leadership is literally healthy employee engagement (Osborne & Hammond, 2017). Employees must be allowed to have psychological autonomy and be encouraged to be extrinsically motivated (Murphy, 2016; Osborne & Hammond, 2017). While workplace conflict is normal in small doses; it can also have detrimental effects to employees (Murphy, 2016). Nonetheless, normal conflict in the workplace is not equivalent by any means to the "art" of mobbing.

MOBBING

The term mobbing was first used in the 19th century by biologists to define/describe birds' behaviors of protecting themselves and their needs by flying around their enemies (Tigrel & Kokalan, 2009). It is based on the premise of a mob, which is a lawless and disorderly crowd (Staub, 2015; Tigrel & Kokalan, 2009). The term evolved through a handful of scientists and researchers (Tigrel & Kokalan, 2009), which included Konrad Lorenz (Staub, 2015) until it was applied to complex behaviors that occur at actual workplaces (Murphy, 2016; Tigrel & Kokalan, 2009). "Mobbing is considered a severe social stressor, a traumatic life event, an epidemic that causes work dissatisfaction, a psychological distress, & a physical problem" (Taspinar, Taspinar, Guclu, Nalbart, Calik, Uslu & Inal, 2013, p. 405). Moreover, "mobbing [is] a rising issue in the occupational health area [which] has recently [..] paid attention more and more in the academic and business settings" (Gul, 2009, p. 515). Mobbing leads to acts, behaviors, gestures and words or even writings that strip the target of their dignity, physical well-being and their "psychological integrity" (Gul, 2009, 515).

Khoo (2010) states: "mobbing is a 'form of organizational pathology in which co-workers essentially "ganged up," and engaged in ongoing rituals of humiliation, exclusion, unjustified accusations, emotional abuse and general harassment in their malicious attempt to force a targeted worker out of the workplace" (p. 61). It is a form of discrimination and the experience of mobbing can be devastating (Pheko, 2018). Mobbing occurs at workplaces when various individuals at a particular workplace "try to protect their positions from a successful person that can be dangerous for them and start to make decisions based on the natural instinct" (Tigrel & Kokalan, 2009, p. 1474); which is deliberate, harmful and repetitive (Keim & McDermott, 2007).

Mobbing is equivalent to a disease (Tigrel & Kokalan, 2009), which is deliberate and harmful (Kein & McDermott, 2007; Yaman, 2010); and is a "repeated, malicious, and irrational behavior that is directed towards a person or a group of people - it creates a risk of health and safety" (p. 400). Ironically, it usually occurs more within non-profit organizations than at any other type of organization (Tigrel & Kokalan, 2009). "The term itself, *mobbing,* describes its four essential characteristics: it is a collective, violent and [a] deliberate process in which the individual psychologies of the aggressors and their victim provide no keys to understanding the phenomenon." (Seguin, 2016, p. 1) Bullying and mobbing activities that occur on college and university campuses are classified differently (Gorlewski, Gorlewski & PorFilio, 2014; Khoo, 2010; Martin & Beese, 2018; Seguin, 2016). However, when mobbing takes place at a place of higher learning, the term utilized is "academic mobbing" (Harper, 2013; Khoo, 2010; Seguin, 2016; Tigrel & Kokalan, 2009).

ACADEMIC MOBBING

Over the years, a serious situation has arisen in the form of bullying at the workplace (Harper, 2013; Housker & Saiz, 2006; Khoo, 2010; Seguin, 2016; Tigrel & Kokalan, 2009). Bullying activities tend to include actions such as follows; limiting a person's self-expression, targeting a person's social relations, attacking or seeking to destroy a person's reputation, attacking a person's professional life and attacking a person's mental and physical health (Khoo, 2010). However, the act of bullying is not equivalent to mobbing (Khoo, 2010). This type of abuse tends to wear the target down (Khoo, 2010).

Specific to institutions of higher learning, a term made its way into the literature as early as the 1990s (Gul, 2009; Staub, 2015), which was coined by Heinz Leymann (Taspinar, Taspinar, Guclu, Nalbart, Calik, Uslu & Inal, 2013; Staub, 2015). Outside of reframing the concept and coining the term, Leymann and Gustafsson created the 5 stages of mobbing, which will be discussed later in this chapter (Gorlewski, Gorlewski & Porfilio, 2014; Staub, 2015; Seguin, 2016). As a result of this research, Leymann also found that 10-20% of research participants in his study, under various forms of mobbing contracted serious illnesses or eventually committed suicide (Housker & Saiz, 2006). When academic mobbing occurs in the academic workplace it is indicative of the fact that the academic workplace is no longer balanced (Petrina, Matheson & Ross, 2015). Moreover, overall academic workplaces have a higher risk for mobbing as do certain other types of workplaces (Taspinar, et al., 2013). In actuality, academic mobbing has increased to such an extent that it has become normal, especially as a form of gentrification (Murphy, 2016). However, the initial and continuous attack usually takes place between six to eighteen months (Gorlewski, Gorlewski, Porfilio, 2014; Khoo, 2010; Staub, 2015; Seguin, 2016).

What is more disturbing, is that academic mobbing is often encouraged by various universities (Seguin, 2016). Thus, the target is targeted on purpose with the university's consent. When they begin to present certain types of symptomatology due to the torment, the employee is often blamed for the torment (Seguin, 2016) - just as a battered wife would be blamed for the emotional and physical abuse that she had suffered at the hands of her husband. Instead of being a victim in a personal relationship, the person is a target of their workplace bullies (Gorlewski, Gorlewski & Porfilio, 2014; Khoo, 2010; Martin & Beese, 2018; Petrina, Matheson & Ross, 2015; Pheko, 2018; Seguin, 2016). This is particularly the case with females, since "their competencies and professional success are perceived as threats by the bullies" (Khoo, 2010, p. 61). This occurs because there is a lack of traditional academic positions available overall and an increased level of competition for certain positions amongst female colleagues (Martin & Beese, 2018). Although there are various reasons for academic mobbing, one thing is for sure - that academic mobbing never produces a positive outcome for anyone (Gorlewski, Gorlewski & Porfilio, 2014).

The Reason for Workplace Mobbing/Academic Mobbing

Academia tends to include some of the brightest minds of each generation's time. In fact, "academic settings have organizational and work characteristics that increase the possibility of interpersonal hostile behaviors" (Taspinar, et al., 2013, p. 401), and that naturally give birth to further trends of bullying and more specifically mobbing (Pheko, 2018). In such places of higher learning, "the most prominent results is a lack of continuity. Organizational problems, time pressure, lack of leadership task definition, etc. are defined to be potential risk factors" (Gul, 2009, p. 515). Since institutions of higher learning also have higher job security, demanding personal and corporate objectives, and subjective performance ratings and criteria, they are more prone to mobbing over all (Taspinar, et al., 2013). In addition, there is a lack of positions that each person is vying for and thus a "competition" occurs (Petrina, Matheson & Ross, 2015). The target is usually "targeted" by a supervisor or a senior colleague who chooses the target because they appear to be vulnerable (Pheko, 2018).

Petrina, Matheson & Ross (2015) states the following; "The balance of the academic workplace workforce has been reduced and casualized or segmented "at whim" insecure, unsalaried part-time labor pool, the 8-hour workday and 40-hour academic work week collapsed to 60 - 80 hours [...]" (p. 58). Thus, with limited resources and limited positions or limited secure positions (Petrina, Matheson & Ross, 2015), often colleagues feel threatened by another colleague for various reasons such as; being highly intelligent, highly skilled, et al. (Khoo, 2010). When prompted by a bully who has decided to target the individual, they (i.e., the mob) often mob an individual to cover up their own deficiencies and weaknesses (Khoo, 2010).

The Inception of Workplace Mobbing and Its Phases

Workplace mobbing usually includes the act of utilizing insulting comments, whispering whenever the person comes around and criticism that is not concrete in nature (Staub, 2015). It should be noted once colleagues feel threatened, a series of occurrences or happenstance occurs (Khoo, 2010). They tend to begin by spreading rumors about the target (Khoo, 2010). Once the campaign of rumors has begun, then bullying activities begin. These activities continue anywhere from six months (Housker & Saiz, 2006) to 18 months, or several months and years (Seguin, 2016; Staub, 2015). The goal is for the complete systematic elimination of the target (Khoo, 2010).

Phases of Mobbing

There are five phases of mobbing (Gorlewski, Gorlewski, Porfilio, 2014; Khoo, 2010, Staub, 2015; Seguin, 2016). They are as follows; Phase 1 - Critical incident (Conflict Phase); Phase 2 - Mobbing & Stigmatizing; Phase 3 - Personnel Management; Phase 4 - Incorrect Diagnosis, and Phases 5 - Expulsion (Gorlewski, Gorlewski, Porfilio, 2014; Harper, 2013; Khoo, 2010; Seguin, 2016; Staub, 2015). First, a critical incident occurs and lingers with no results - eventually leading to mobbing (Gorlewski, Gorlewski, Porfilio, 2014; Khoo, 2010; Seguin, 2016). Second, the target is mobbed and stigmatized with the intent of punishing the target to get them psychologically in order to break their resolve down (Gorlewski, Gorlewski, Porfilio, 2014; Khoo, 2010; Seguin, 2016). Targets face "intense, collective humiliation [which often leaves them] scarred for life (Westhues, 2006) and/or an ostracization (Seguin, 2016). Third, in Stage 3, personnel and/or administration finally step in but by this point the target usually has been ostracized, and blamed for the abuse they have endured (Seguin, 2016). This leads to a serious infringement on the target's civil liberties/rights (Gorlewski, Gorlewski, Porfilio, 2014; Khoo, 2010). Fourth, the target is usually told that s/he is paranoid or being a whistleblower (Gorlewski, Gorlewski, Porfilio, 2014; Khoo, 2016; Seguin, 2016) and suffers the social stigma of someone else's actions (Seguin, 2016). The abuse and bullying behavior is minimized and the target may have trouble in their career and in seeking vocational rehabilitation (Gorlewski, Gorlewski, Porfilio, 2014; Housker & Saiz, 2006; Khoo, 2016; Seguin, 2016). Fifth, the target is pressured to leave and is expelled through force, or pushed to resign, retire, etc. (Gorlewski, Gorlewski, Porfilio, 2014; Khoo, 2016; Seguin, 2016).

Descriptions of the Bully

"There is considerable consensus that workplace bullies are selfish, inadequate, insecure and totally insensitive. They can be evasive, manipulative, dishonest and convincing" (Khoo, 2010, p. 63). However, the main bully who orchestrates the mob within an academic institution is often clever since they are utilizing an effective strategy in order to dispel of the target by wearing them down (Westhues, 2006). They often utilize covert tactics to accomplish their goal (Housker & Saiz, 2006).

Description of the Mob

Often other co-workers fail to warn their colleagues of what is to come. In fact, they tend to fail to support the target at all, but rather engage with further negative activities in support of the bully (Khoo, 2010). They are often scared to be the next victim (Khoo, 2010). Thus, they engage in shunning, gossiping, whispering and ridiculing of the target (Staub, 2015; Westhues, 2006). Housker & Saiz (2006) describes the mobbers with the following adjectives: angry, critical, inadequate, jealous, manipulative, poorly developed people, and unpredictable. Often the mob serves as a reinforcer of their own actions and continues to encourage colleagues to torment the chosen target(s) (Gorlewski, Gorlewski & Porfilio, 2014). The goal of the primary bully and the mob is to complete a "systematic eliminative process" of the target(s) (Khoo, 2010, p. 64) by using coert tactics (Housker & Saiz, 2006).

Description of the Bystanders

Bystanders are not the initiating mob leader, nor are they part of the mob (Khoo, 2010; Tigrel & Kokalan, 2009). Rather, they are persons of no interest who also never take a stance either way in regard to the target, the bully or even the mob. Unlike the bully or the mob, the bystander is not utilizing covert tactics (Housker & Saiz, 2006). They are seemingly cowards who may be more interested in protecting their position than intervening on behalf of another person/colleague.

Description of the Target

The most common trait of targets of academic mobbing is that they are high achieving and usually superior or an expert in their field (Khoo, 2010; Tigrel & Kokalan, 2009). They usually are trying to blow the whistle on a practice or wrongdoing (Khoo, 2010; Tigrel & Kokalan, 2009) "by a powerful person in the workplace" (Khoo, 2010, p. 63). However, they tend to be the best asset of the institution (Khoo, 2010), and are successful within the organization (Tigrel & Kokalan, 2009). They may be successful due to the very descriptors used for them such as; promoters of human rights, high achievers, being a whistleblower, being female (Martin & Beese, 2018; Tigrel & Kokalan, 2009) or even cooperative, creative, devoted, empathetic, experienced, fair, just, loyal, and organized (Tigrel & Kokalan, 2009; Housker & Saiz, 2006), they may also be married women and/or are the religious minority at the institution (Tigrel & Kokalan, 2009). In addition, they are usually loyal to their organization. More specific, as creatives, the target(s) tend to promote new ideas and this becomes a challenge and a threat to the establishment (Housker & Saiz, 2006).

In fact, "many mobbing targets love their work; they derive purpose and pleasure from it" (Khoo, 2010, p. 63). And this makes sense since "the basic needs of satisfaction have been found to directly relate to dedication of employees" (Osborne & Hammond, 2017, p. 52). This is the irony of academic mobbing, the individuals who are the strongest assets and who are best equipped to instruct tend to be the ones who are targeted and forced to leave. Especially since the target(s) usually stay in a toxic workplace or ignores the problem in order to bring transformation, because they really do enjoy their work (Housker & Saiz, 2006). However, once, attacked, the target is caught off guard (Harper, 2013), which was the purpose of the attack (Gorlewski, Gorlewski & Porfilio, 2014; Gul, 2009; Harper, 2013; Housker & Saiz, 2006; Khoo, 2010; Martin & Beese, 2018; Osborne & Hammond, 2017; Pheko, 2018; Staub, 2015; Tigrel & Kokalan, 2099).

The problem lies in the fact that the target is usually overwhelmed, confused and does not understand why they were targeted (Khoo, 2010). They often have few resources to fight such an onslaught (Harper, 2013). They begin to have a lower level of self-confidence, feel a loss of their dignity, have higher levels of non-work stress, their productivity lessens and they may experience other health-related issues (Pheko, 2018). Usually, when they try to resolve the issue, they find that they are given an incorrect diagnosis (Staub, 2015). Sometimes, they are forced to take voluntary or involuntary leave(s) from work (Staub, 2015). They also have no "frame of reference, no language to describe what is happening. When their attempts to change the situation fail and they feel all avenues have been exhausted, they are pushed as far as committing suicide or even murder" (Khoo, 2010, p. 64). The marriages and other relationships of targets are also affected, they often have many doctors' appointments, go to therapy, take medication, face financial difficulties, etc. (Houseker & Saiz, 2006). To understand this phenomenon further, statistics regarding the prevalence of issues relating to academic mobbing will be delineated in the next section.

The Statistics on Workplace Engagement and Academic Mobbing

According to the U.S. Department of Labor in 2015; "employee engagement [is] a challenge, with a negative percentage of 35% or higher for organizations" (Osborne & Hammond, 2017, p. 54). In other words, 35% of employees across various organizations are not engaged at work or pleased at work at all (Osborne & Hammond, 2017). Linkedin found 2014 that of 18,000 employees only 15% (2,700) are satisfied at work (Murphy, 2016) and only 13% are actually engaged at work (Murphy, 2016; Osborne & Hammond, 2017). Murphy (2016) noted that 26% of employees are completely disengaged (Osborne & Hammond, 2017).

According to Housker & Saiz (2006), "due to the lack of reporting, the number of mobbing victims is uncertain" (p. 4). However, when it comes to academic mobbing, the statistics that are available are even more telling (Tigrel & Kokalan, 2009). In the United States, it has been estimated that approximately four (4) million people are exposed to academic mobbing on a yearly basis (Housker & Saiz, 2006). Moreover, ¼ of faculty and staff are in danger of or at risk for suffering from academic mobbing (Housker & Saiz, 2006). In New Zealand, 65.3% of employees had been mobbed (Taspinar, et al., 2013; Tigrel & Kokalan, 2009). In Finland, 30% of men were mobbed and 55% of women were mobbed while at work (Tigrel & Kokalan, 2009). In Norway, 5.2% of academics reported suffering through mobbing (Gorlewski, Gorlewski & Porfilio, 2014). It was found that 12-25% of academic personnel had been subjected to mobbing through very specific tactics such as; gossip, lowering performance grades/reviews, verbal harassment and by being attacked based on race and/or sex (Tigrel & Kokalan, 2009).

In a study completed by Taspinar, et al. (2013), after surveying/interviewing 100 academicians between September 2012 to October 2012, it was found that 13.6% of the respondents reported that they had dealt with academic mobbing. In addition, eight percent (8%) reported suffering from other psychosomatic problems (Taspinar, et al., 2013). This was comparable with 13% of the academic population had being a target of academic mobbing and reported psychological complaints (Gorlewski, Gorlewski & Porfilio, 2014). In addition, Taspinar, et al. (2013) found that 6% of the sample who had suffered from academic mobbing also reported musculoskeletal problems. Thus, overall Taspinar, et al. (2013) noted that there was a moderate association between academic mobbing and issues of the musculoskeletal nature.

Outside of those statistics, 43.9% of those who had endured academic mobbing literally became ill (Tigrel & Kokalan, 2009). 30.8% changed their position, but remained at the same institution of higher learning (Tigrel & Kokalan, 2009). 22.5% literally left the institution (Tigrel & Kokalan, 2009). 14.8% were unceremoniously dismissed (Tigrel & Kokalan, 2009). In Sweden, 12% of instructors committed suicide (Tigrel & Koklan, 2009). 25% of academic personnel chose early retirement (Tigrel & Kokalan, 2009). Overall, 10% committed suicide and/or committed murder (Tigrel & Kokalan, 2009).

RESULTS OF ACADEMIC MOBBING

The targets of academic mobbing are often the ones who anticipate the "workday with dread and a sense of impending doom" (Pheko, 2018, p. 7). They are often on heightened alert and they are vigilant in order to fight off the next attack (Pheko,

2018), which is an emotional attack (Tigrel & Kokalan, 2009). Moreover, the target of the "intense, collective humiliation is ordinarily scarred for life" (Westhues, 2006, p. 19). They may experience stress, burnout, depression, etc. (Kein & McDermott, 2007; Khoo, 2010; Pheko, 2018; Taspinar, et al., 2013) or major depression (Housker & Sazi, 2006). They also suffer from PTSD, panic attacks, heart attacks, et al. (Housker & Saiz, 2006).

Once ostracized, they may suffer from various symptomologies. According to Housker & Saiz (2006) targets often suffer from the following: becoming less productive, questioning their abilities, becoming less creative, their life becomes tumultuous, feeling embarrassed, uncharacteristic fearfulness, frustration, persistent crying, become untrusting, having high blood pressure, gastrointestinal issues, etc. Targets tend to suffer from feelings of loneliness and experience of heightened levels of stress (Kein & McDermott, 2007), which increases cortisol levels (Taspinar, et al., 2013). According to Taspinar, et al. (2013), "mental stress plays an important role in the increase in the prevalence of musculoskeletal discomfort in physically light but psychologically stressful jobs" (Taspinar, et al., 2013, p. 401). In addition, the continued stress may also bring stress to the target's family, further injuries, etc. (Khoo, 2010).

Targets are denied tenure (Pheko, 2018), eventually resign, are fired or even commit suicide (Kein & McDermott, 2007; Pheko, 2018), especially since they did not have access to many resources in order to fight the onslaught of the mob (Harper, 2013). Other results may be that they remove themselves from responsibilities, take permanent sick leave or continue to take sick days, and may even retire early (Pheko, 2018). Moreover, "non-tenure track faculty are hit particularly hard, indicating "contingency or the precariousness of their position" as relentless stressors" (Murphy, 2016, p. 58). Sometimes, targets actually move through the psychological states of Elizabeth Kubler-Ross' stages of grief (Harper, 2013). When targets seek help, they then are able to grieve their losses, assess their financial challenges, change their life perspectives and seek job possibilities (Housker & Saiz, 2006).

Another result of academic mobbing is a dismantling of the actual work place (Yaman, 2010). Yaman (2010) states the following: a "collapse in organizational values, negative climate disputes and conflicts between individuals. Distrust media, general reduction of respect, and restriction of the creativity of the employers because of their willingness to restrict creativity" (p. 569) is what winds up occurring in said organizations. To explore this topic further, the methodology portion of this research is introduced for this chapter.

THE METHODOLOGY

The methodology utilized for this study is qualitative in nature (Creswell, 2013; Creswell, 2014; Pheko, 2018). Qualitative research seeks to explore a phenomenon or happenstance with in-depth and rich description, by collecting data on an individual(s) via interviews, surveys, questionnaires, etc. (Creswell, 2013; Creswell, 2014). However, it does occur in natural settings where humans interact on a regular basis (Creswell, 2013; Creswell, 2014). It should be noted that "McIlveen (2018) explains that while qualitative data and methods have regained a legitimate place in psychological theory, research and practice, the story as data and as method is not yet comprehensively articulated with field" (Pheko, 2018). Moreover, "[...] Johnson (2014) observes theory and research literature and outcomes on bullying and mobbing make sense" (Pheko, 2018, p. 6). This study is formed and founded in constructivism-interpretivism, which seeks to explore "lived experiences" (Pheko, 2018, p. 3). According to Gray (2014), constructivism is when "truth and meaning [...] are created by the subjects' interactions with the world" (p. 20). Interpretivism is "culturally derived and historically situated interpretation of the social life world" (Gray, 2014, p. 23).

The Purpose of This Study

The purpose of this qualitative research study is to explore the phenomenon of academic mobbing. The author has chosen to utilize an autoethnography (Creswell, 2013; Creswell, 2014; Pheko, 2014) because ethnographies and autoethnographies allow for a holistic exploration of a phenomenon by allowing the author/researcher to tell their story within an academic framework to address a problem (Creswell, 2013; Creswell, 2014). They are also often utilized to explore social problems within the field of the arts, education and psychology (Creswell, 2013; Creswell, 2014) to examine or study culture (Gray, 2014).

According to Pheko (2018), "In similar work, Akella (2016) suggests that when using ethnography in cases of workplace bullying, it is advantageous to focus on one single case study or on one victim's pain, humiliation and stress, as this will allow the reader to effectively deconstruct workplace bullying and classify it as a horrific and degrading process" (p. 2). This chapter will introduce the reader to the phenomenon that appears to be ever-growing when it comes to academic mobbing. It will also allow her to document her experience and contribute to the growing body of research. With that being said, she will now introduce her role as the researcher.

Role of the Researcher

The author has worked in higher education as an adjunct professor of psychology for approximately ~10+ at a handful of colleges and universities in New York and New Jersey and at an international high school in China. Additionally, she taught research methods for one year at a music institution in New York and half a year at a university in New Jersey. Moreover, she taught conversational English at a top-tier university in Seoul, South Korea to science and engineering students for a semester and at other locales.

Concurrently, she served in AmeriCorps during the beginning of her teaching career in the United States in a high-crime, high-poverty town/city in New Jersey for a year. Thereafter, she worked as a Social Work Supervisor until almost the close of the institution. She supervised five men and was supervised by a licensed social worker and a reverend who was the Executive Director. The institution was part of a consortium that focused on housing homeless people who had mental illnesses. Thereafter, she was hired as a Coordinator of High School Services and ran a credit recovery program at a high school in New Jersey. As part of her duties, she engaged in grant writing, meeting with donors including large corporations such as Johnson and Johnson, attending trainings, learning budgeting, etc. Previous to leaving the country to study abroad in 2002, she worked at a District Attorney's Office in a borough of New York in the research department as well as various law firms.

As a survivor of academic mobbing as well as mobbing at the workplace in general, she has a unique positionality to the topic. She also knows that in some ways she may be biased in evaluating such situations do to these experiences. Nonetheless, it should be pointed out that this information was introduced to address the issue of reliability in this chapter. According to Pheko (2018) stated the following: "reliability in this content means that the narrator's credibility is juxtaposed with available "factual evidence" is essential" [...] (p. 10).

Data Collection Procedure

Data collection was based on the author's recollection, reviewing emails, photos, etc. It should be repeated that before this chapter was due, the author's email account was hacked and twenty years of emails were deleted - even emails from people who had died. In addition, the author has access to class review scores, etc. She also re-accessed her ratings from https://www.ratemyprofessors.com/. The narrative of the next section is written in the first person.

EVIDENCE OF MOBBING/ACADEMIC MOBBING

Previous to experiencing academic mobbing, I experienced mobbing at a non-profit organization where I worked concurrently. It was a small organization in a semi-city like area. The Executive Director ran a tight ship. He expected loyalty, which included remaining at only that organization. In other words, he was not happy that I had a part-time adjunct position and that I volunteered in church. My co-worker also was competing with me to be E.D. although I had told him and our supervisor that I had no interest.

The year was 2012. I was flourishing at the university and at the non-profit. At that point, I had already completed two of the two and a half years on the contract of which the last six months or so were completed under harrowing circumstances. Nonetheless, the program had been improved and was approximately 400% more effective than it had been previously.

Rumors began and were untrue. Evidently, I was a whore, a lesbian, a homewrecker, a liar and I had HIV. Through this organization, I had two offices (i.e. at the base and at the high school). Behind my back, the superintendent and my supervisor locked me out of my office at the school with no cause. I went to obtain paperwork and could not enter since someone else needed the office. My things were given to me in a box. The security guards were laughing at me. Everybody was laughing at me except for the bystanders. I called the E.D. immediately and told him off on the phone in the midst of the mobbers. When I returned he attempted an apology and feigned ignorance, but the truth is he always knew everything that happened in that city.

At some point, a student allegedly became ill. Please note: There were always multiple, licensed adults in the classrooms. At that time, I was supervising at least five to six teachers - one was younger than me and the rest were older. The majority had families and tended to be honest people. And they were all in the room at the time and reported to me what had occurred.

However, one teacher began crying and telling me that he had been hospitalized for schizophrenia and then was re-trained to obtain a position in teaching and that I would need to do the same. He also told me in incoherent bits of information about various things. Another female teacher told me that she was raped by the police at the age of 17 and that she hated the police. Another teacher told me that he played dumb to stay afloat. At this point, I had no idea what was going on but to have people of integrity - mostly Christians begin to have meltdowns was beyond my capacity for comprehension.

That same week, as was noted, a student allegedly became ill. The hospital was near and the E.D. was friends with much of the staff. I returned to the classroom to find that EMT personnel were bringing her to the hospital. I recorded their contact information. When I came out of the classroom, I saw the Vice Principal. He looked mortified. He would not come near me as if he had heard something very bad. Please note: This vice-principal died only a number of months before this publication. He was hit by a car.

When I returned to my primary office, I informed the E.D. and his assistant of what happened. However, I had a strange feeling. They were almost mocking me. The next morning, I called the student's grandmother to check on the student. The grandmother did not even know what I was talking about. Finally, she responded; "Oh, yeah she is fine. Uhh...no, you don't have to visit the hospital."

At some point, the Executive Director kept telling me that I should go to the doctor. (Please note: I am rarely ever sick.) The only time I became deathly ill was related to this particular job. The male counterpart that I previously noted and one of his coaches hid my phone in the ceiling which turned out to have lime and other unmentionables that can make people deathly ill due to the fact that it was an old untreated house - that had been converted to an office space. I contracted a respiratory infection. When I was finally able to see my doctor, I could barely breathe. He literally was concerned for my life and prescribed steroids - otherwise, I would have to be hospitalized long-term. I began the treatment and gained an unmentionable amount of weight. He then suddenly retired.

Whenever I was driving to work - at an interval of a handful of months, someone would hit my vehicle (e.g., someone from Haifa, Israel). Each time, I had to take time from work to go through the process of having my car towed or driving the vehicle to the mechanic, getting a rental, paying a $500 deductible, etc. For someone clearing all debt, the bills were beginning to add up quickly. One day, after I had a flat returning to the office from a training and the vehicle literally spun out of control on the ice (i.e., it was winter), I barely made it back to the parking area in time. I called the E.D. outside to explain what took so long. He looked at the car and said the following; "How come nothing ever happens to you?" It was a perplexing question. In fact, by this point, I must have had at least six to seven accidents, two flat tires, a cracked windshield from an ice storm in October, etc. And all I knew to say was - "It was because of God!" Do remember, I had only worked at this place for two years. Count - two years.

Right before the end of my contract, my father almost died. In addition, the man I knew as a friend and had come to adore did die at ~40. I was devastated. I also began driving to NY to visit my father in the hospital on top of all of the other duties mentioned above. When I went to church, I was being mocked even though they knew that my father had almost died and that my friend had died. The only person who showed any concern was the pianist (a music producer). It was one of the most untoward attacks I had ever encountered during the course of my life.

I finally completed the contract. Simultaneously, I was still being harassed at church. I was serving as a Bible Study Leader and Choir Member/Worship Leader. The head female pastor wanted me to assist her - to which I declined the offer. She became angry. One day, during rehearsal, all of the leadership including the pianist were gone. The bullying began from the tenor section. When all was said and done, my Bible study members stopped attending, but sent cards, and other messages telling me that I was wonderful, but that they could not attend anymore. I assumed that they had been bullied too, but then I saw that each person was promoted or suddenly had a group of new friends - or positioned on stage.

In November of 2012, I left the church with the female pastor's blessing. I always suspected that she had recorded that conversation. Then she said; "You will thank God when you get raped!" I could not believe what I was hearing. Through tears, I left. It would not be until years later that I thought to myself - "Why don't you thank God when your two daughters are raped?" It was only a thought but...

My contract was completed and I had left the church. I was independent but I needed capital. All of the game-playing people had done made me lose a lot of money over the course of a number of years. In fact, I believe that the loss of not working full-time from 2012 and ending teaching at the university in 2015 led to a loss of approximately ½ a million dollars. I wasn't able to purchase my condo in Montclair (which now costs twice as much), have not been able to marry or have children, etc.

So, I decided to teach psychology in China. After my father was well, I received an amended contract. I flew to Shanghai and was transported to my residence, and was deemed by the government of China as an expert in the field of psychology. Most of the high school students did not want to do any work, so they dropped the class. I was left with two students who had come from wealthy families.

The first month or two was fine. Since I was the only psychology instructor, I had to create a whole new curriculum. It was a daunting process. I was offered the option to move to a new apartment complex which was off-campus, and I accepted. The other female instructors remained in the old building. The male instructors and I moved to the new complex.

First, things were moved around in my apartment (e.g., my textbook disappeared). However, I later found out that the office assistant had a key to each apartment unit, which I had not known initially. Second, my shower head literally flew out of the ceiling (something similar had happened at the non-profit - the ceiling caved in but for some reason I was stuck in traffic and missed the opportunity for my head to be crushed in by pounds of cement, lime, dust, glass and whatever else had been up there.), and I jumped out of the way. My colleague (B)'s shower door shattered and a chunk of her leg had been cut out. The New York office was contacted, but they never did anything. Third, my computers were continuously hacked. I went to the American Embassy a number of times to complain (Please note: They never took a report), but informed me that often Chinese students hack their teacher's computer, because they want to go on vacation early.

This was appalling to me and the fact that American citizens were being terrorized and that their embassy did nothing was appalling. (Please note: This occurred at the same time that Edward Snowden was bringing the system to its knees). Fourth, the worst thing to occur left me shaking in tears. I heard a recording. The recording was the voice of my dead friend. I finally thought it was coming from the floor upstairs. I ran upstairs to check, but there was no one there. There was mail strewn across the doorstep. I knocked and rang the bell and tried to open the door. I wrote the contact person in NY, who flew to Shanghai and informed me that is the way China is and China's ways are China's. At this point, I knew I would leave early. I completed ALL duties and left on a Delta flight two weeks early. Something like me hearing his voice only happened one other time on an American Airlines flight some years later. This time, I told the stewardesses off. It never happened again!

Notation

It should also be noted that right before leaving for China, I had been talking to a man who briefly spoke to my mother. I was not officially dating him but I brought him food because he claimed to be sick. After some time - I was assaulted. I went to the hospital, reported the crime, brought evidence, and went through all medical follow-ups. For someone who hates going to the hospital, this was not a fun time for me. Also, I was not sure how to tell my family so I did not tell them until after I had returned. What occurred thereafter also brought much division amongst my most trusted and closest family members. As for friends, I believe I lost almost every single one as they blamed me for my own rape. To this day, I am not always sure who to trust.

The Return

After returning from China, I decided to visit my neighbors and inquire about the comments they had made about Russians and spies before I left. A few blocks away from my apartment (i.e., which was still being paid for), I was in a major car accident - albeit not one scratch could be found on my body. The police unbuckled my seat belt and carried me to the stretcher. I was placed in a room with a purple seat - somewhat like a chaise after being semi-examined by approximately five people including someone who was referred to as a scribe. In another room, my pressure was taken and then I was reported as being too fidgety.

They kept pressuring me to be admitted for observation, which I finally agreed to at that time but denied me a phone call. My mother and aunt came and took my items. I slept, saw a psychiatrist (i.e., a tall Persian man) who felt my glands. He asked me why I had been so fidgety and I told him that I do not like being held in small rooms against my will and that I had been assaulted only a handful of months before. My father and I spoke on the phone and he begged me to "stay for two." I had no idea what he was talking about and told him I was signing myself out and that the people were insane. Outside of one pill (e.g., anti-anxiety), I took no medications. It should also be noted that my hospital bracelet had the names of two individuals that were not me (i.e., a previous co-worker and a previous student - both Hispanic or related to Spanish-speaking people).

I was picked up and returned home (i.e., my original home - not Jersey). I was devastated. I also found out I had been diagnosed without any clear assessment or documentation. I rested, took a semester off and then returned to teaching and studying. I leased a car. I decided that I needed to return to teaching and my supervisor had sent a new contract. Although my aunt begged me not to return (i.e., something I did not understand), I did. I received a pay increase, and then I moved through the semester with relative ease. I was teaching a class and then two within the Psychology Department. Sometimes, I subbed for other instructors or picked up an additional class. This carried me through 2014.

It turns out that other colleagues had found out that I was being given more opportunities to teach and there may have been a bit of jealousy. I started to hear rumors. Instructors began whispering around me in the hallway, by my classroom whenever I passed. However, since I did much of my work in the adjunct office; I ignored much of it. In my opinion, it had not become too bad yet and it did not involve multiple car accidents, a respiratory infection or possible poisoning (i.e., this will be referred to in an upcoming book), etc.

During 2015, outside of the whispers and instructors who I did not know gathering to talk about me in front of me in the hallway (Please note: I had no way of identifying them as either they were not in my department which means they were Occupational Therapy or they were randomly rude people); I had noticed that Jewish and Christian adjunct professors were disappearing since 2014 (i.e, in particular a history professor who also taught at Brooklyn College and another professor who taught psychology). Their names were always replaced by the name of a Muslim. This probably corresponded with the intent of the president who was himself a Muslim whose CV had been proven to be falsified and still received a $250,000 raise.

Attacks were being made on good, solid, hard-working instructors who loved their students and spent unpaid hours with them. They were actually educating them correctly. They were not evangelizing by any means and I can attest to that as before they closed the adjunct office. They taught them and re-taught them and tutored them in the subject that they were enrolled in...period.

By Fall of 2015, I had also been hired on the main campus to teach research methods. I had not told my supervisor that I was teaching research methods as well as the classes did not conflict. The GE department was well-organized. There were trainings, chances to meet colleagues and do team-building. An office was also offered to me, but then the mobbing truly began.

Some of the students began to act strangely. They kept mentioning that they were suddenly getting tuition discounts for my classes. They began comparing me to other instructors. Eventually, I heard that other instructors were upset that I would throw a party and bake for my students, which only occurred at the end of the class during grade check. In addition, my students in one particular class (i.e., approximately 30+) within the Psychology Department would rapid-fire question me for lack of a better term. Going to class to teach became exhausting.

The Dissertation

By October, I requested two weeks off in order to collect dissertation data in South Korea. Each supervisor from each respective campus would only give me one week. I was confident that I could not complete everything within a week since everything had been unclear. Thus, I requested a sub. Right after, I arranged to leave and was replaced; I received an email that my research methods class had been chosen for a visit from middle school/high school students due to the superiority and quality of my class. In other words, I was doing better than I had thought and I had been toyed with so (i.e., as I believe) that someone else could re-position her/himself based on the work I had done. Instead of just telling me this and saying this is why you only have a week, the various supervisors were vague - perhaps purposely vague.

I suspect that since my supervisor from the Psychology Department heard about this and was not pleased. Then my student review scores dropped significantly. My scores had always been quite high and that was the first semester that they lowered significantly. However, at that point, I knew - I would not be returning to this institution to teach within the Psychology Department.

I left the third week of November and was in Seoul. For a handful of days, I met with old friends, visited my previous university, et al. Then, I went to my research site. I had completed approximately half of the interviews, and became ill. I was whispering to my roommate. I finally fell back to sleep. I awoke early and then I awoke again to a phone call. It was my mother and my brother informing me that my father had passed away. I also found out that Verizon had lied about the call plan and I had been charged $800 worth of roaming charges. In addition, when I went to inform the "case" of the case study, she was flippant, careless, and mean. I had known her since I was a young teenager and I was hurt by her actions. To this day, I have not forgiven her. The other *samonim* (pastor's wife) replied in Korean something to the effect of - "Oh. He's dead. Oh, I am so sorry." And then she slammed the door in my face. I had known her and that pastor since I was in my early twenties. I have not yet returned to South Korea due to the ills that occurred during that trip.

Upon returning to the United States, I began assisting with funeral preparations and I can remember my father's words; "Janelle, just stay one week." Perhaps, he knew what would occur somehow. After everything was over, I was empty. I entered 2016 extremely drained, however I was hired to teach at a college.

The area was mainly a Muslim neighborhood. They had often asked me to return to the mosque and to pray for them, which I did for many in the street or in their shops. From this point on, I came to realize that I needed to rebuild my career. I thought back to the words of the teacher who was crying that I supervised. However, I knew that I would not give up.

An Analysis

According to various researchers, academic mobbing has several phases (Gorlewski, Gorlewski, Porfilio, 2014; Harper, 2013; Khoo, 2010; Seguin, 2016; Staub, 2015). Based on the narrative, two tables (Table 1, Table 2) are available for review, that highlights key events, occurrences and descriptive words/themes. The first table presented (Table 1) focuses upon the non-profit-based key events, occurrences and descriptive words and theories.

The second table offered (Table 2) focuses upon the university-based key events, occurrences and descriptive words and themes.

How to Prevent and/or Address Academic Mobbing

There are a number of steps that individuals and institutions can take to "[...] prevent[...] academic mobbing is to ensure that workplaces are psychologically safe and healthy places" (Khoo, 2010, p. 64). Respect and dignity should be the hallmark of the institution (Khoo, 2010). If academic mobbing can be properly addressed at Phase 1 (Gorlewski, Gorlewski, Porfilio, 2014; Harper, 2013; Khoo, 2010; Seguin, 2016; Staub, 2015); then academics and college and university staff would not

Table 1.

Non-Profit key events, occurrences and descriptive words/themes.	
Phases	Non-Profit Organization
Phase 1: Critical Incident	Actually filed a complaint against my colleague.
Phase 2: Mobbing and Stigmatizing	Closure of my office at the school without notification. Rumors, Slander, etc.
Phase 3: Personnel Management	Mediation with the person I filed a complaint against and the E.D.
	E.D. turned on me and began o=mocking me with my counterpart
	("Let me show you!").
Phase 4: Incorrect Diagnosis	No diagnosis while at the nonprofit.
Phase 5: Expulsion	Completion of the four-year contract, but the contract was not renewed.
	While I was given a glowing written recommendation letter, I surmise that whenever anyone called, they were told the opposite of what was written.
	I returned to the office to see the E.D. but they claimed he was not there. Please note: He was always the first person in the office.
	All communication cut.

need to needlessly go through various forms of abuse while trying to accomplish educating our next generations.

However, if academic mobbing has already occurred or is occurring - then it is necessary to take steps to address the bully, the mobbers, the bystanders and the institution. One of the first steps will be documenting each act of mobbing. For those who decide to fight back and/or report academic mobbing, **you** must know that it takes a lot of courage and that **you** are a person who has shown a great deal of resolve (ICES, 2014).

To fight these injustices, first, record the names of the perpetrator. Second, record dates and times of all incidents (Pheko, 2018). Third, record/document why you thought the person(s) were bullying you (Pheko, 2018). Fourth, document if there were any witnesses or bystanders present at the time of said incident (Pheko, 2018). Fifth, document any action that was taken by you or someone else (Pheko, 2018). Sixth, especially for those who may have been in the author's situation, and could not identify the perpetrators, begin to take pictures with your cell phone. Be ready to address the bully, the mobbers and even the bystanders through university management and via a union if your institution has one. Then, the institution will need to respond.

Table 2.

University key events, occurrences and descriptive words/themes.	
Phases	University Organization
Phase 1: Critical Incident	Vague and Unknown. Possibly a vicious rumor. But there had been no initial conflict.
Phase 2: Mobbing and Stigmatizing	University: Rumors, slander and whisperings. Refusal of enough vacation time to complete data collection and transcribing. Did not tell me that my class had been chosen for a special event/program.
Phase 3: Personnel Management	I did not confront my supervisor after she appeared in my classroom to "check on me." Sent all documentation to the Union Office - they did not take the matter seriously.
Phase 4: Incorrect Diagnosis	No diagnosis given amongst licensed psychologists (i.e., dozens of them), however, many of my colleagues were suddenly given disabled diagnoses in order to refute their complaints and documentation. Paranoid diagnosis via car accident (which was unknown and undocumented) and after my assault (African Psychiatrist asked me if I wanted to be a schizophrenic. I replied no and contested the diagnosis in written form)
Phase 5: Expulsion	Hired a sub. Formally retired after being denied the possibility to do so or to withdraw money from my retirement funds circa 2016/2017.

The Institution's Response

As far as from an institutional perspective, each institution needs to be clear that a healthy work environment is linked to sound leadership (Murphy, 2016). Organizational culture is formed by having employees who share beliefs, values, norms, et al. (Yaman, 2010). However, when academic mobbing has occurred, the organization needs to re-institute sound leadership.

Sound Leadership

"Leaders that are authentic influence the engagement of employees" (Osborne & Hammond, 2017, p. 53). Also, leaders and employees who are intrinsically motivated tend to be psychologically autonomous (Osborne & Hammond, 2017), and have a lot to offer their place of employment. "Engaged employees deliver improved organizational and individual performance" (Osborne & Hammond, 2017, p. 59), and employee engagement (Osborne & Hammond, 2017). It has been found that "organizations must provide a psychologically safe workplace to improve employer engagement" (Osborne & Hammond, 2017, p. 54).

For institutions such as those described at the onset of this chapter - where academic mobbing occurs on a regular basis, transformational leaders are needed (Osborne & Hammond, 2017). Fonseca (2014) emphasized that workplaces where academic mobbing has run rampant need to introduce alternative leaders since "central administration" has failed to employ sound monitoring methods (Fonseca, 2014). With sound leadership, people will be able to "create an environment that positions people to do their best work and also become better human beings" (Murphy, 2016, p. 2).

Also, it is clear that there "is a need for standardization, and studies to define and evaluate mobbing behavior in order to make a comparison between different cultures and occupations" (Gul, 2009, p. 515). Murphy (2016) noted that if one cannot address the academic culture, then they need to address the climate. In other words, they will need to create a healthy workplace environment - not just to avoid lawsuits.

Creating a Healthy Workplace Environment

There are a number of things that been introduced to a workplace in order to create healthy workplace (Murphy, 2016; Osborne & Hammond, 2017). Osborne & Hammond (2017) notes it is pertinent for the employer to create a safe work environment. Part of creating a safe workplace environment is to infuse it with joy and a measure of optimism (Murphy, 2016). Some managers note that employees need to provide necessary training and that workplace trainings should impart an employee a feeling of confidence in their skills and their ability to accomplish personal and company goals (Murphy, 2016; Osborne & Hammond, 2017). Employers need to attract extraordinary people who contribute the workplace and can keep them (Murphy, 2016; Osborne & Hammond, 2017) with incentives that can be initiated to attract and keep employees such as follows; recognition for doing a good/company goal, employee/work stability and insurance, snacks, extended breaks, gift cards, raffle drives, et al. (Osborne & Hammond, 2017). In addition, more research needs to be done on the topic.

Research on Reducing Academic Mobbing

There have been a number of questionnaires that have been created in order to measure the levels of academic/mobbing within workplaces/institutions of higher learning such as the Negative Acts Questionnaire (Civilidag & Sargin, 2013). For organizations and institutions of higher learning that are serious about improving the health of their institutions, it would behoove them to administer said questionnaire to measure the health of their organization. If the reported scores point to a problem, than it is imperative for leadership to re-evaluate their leadership as well as bring in transformational leaders to address such issues (Osborne & Hammond, 2017).

DISCUSSION AND CONCLUSION

This chapter was written in order to address the phenomenon of academic mobbing. The author established a literature review and utilized a qualitative research method in order to explore the topic. By utilizing an autoethnography, the author hoped to introduce her lived experience to discuss the phenomenon of academic mobbing. She also analyzed (briefly) and applied her experience to the five phases of academic mobbing (Gorlewski, Gorlewski, Porfilio, 2014; Harper, 2013; Khoo, 2010; Seguin, 2016; Staub, 2015). While this may not be the most extensive chapter, it is one that will be a contribution to the field due to the need for a conglomeration of voices who have suffered, survived and went on to conquer to communicate their experiences. The author will now address the limitations of the study.

LIMITATIONS OF THE STUDY

Since this study is an autoethnography, the lived experience of the author cannot be generalized. However, the experience is not atypical when it comes to the topic of academic mobbing. Nonetheless, in order for the results to be generalizable, a large scale quantitative and/or mixed methods study would need to be conducted in order to address this topic more thoroughly. Then and only then would it be possible to determine how to address the issue of academic mobbing en masse.

In regard to reliability, how can the reader determine the reliability of this chapter? According to Creswell (2013; 2014) qualitative reliability relies on the consistency of the reporting. Pheko (2018) stated the following: "reliability in this content means that the narrator's credibility is juxtaposed with available "factual evidence" is essential" [...] (p. 10). Therefore, the author introduced herself in order to allow the reader to know enough information about her background to understand that she had the necessary experience and cultural adaptation to succeed in such a position.

Qualitative validity refers to the accuracy or the checking of the findings (Creswell, 2013; Creswell, 2014). Specific to this chapter, the author had to review emails and photos, recall incidents, etc. It should be noted, that less than one month before completing this publication, the author's first email account was hacked. Twenty years of emails were deleted. Thus, she had to check a secondary account. However, for those emails and documentation that cannot be solidified, copies had already been sent to the author's Union at the time.

Since the author presented her own "lived experiences," member checking was not necessary (Creswell, 2013; Creswell, 2014). . Regardless, there was rich, thick and deep descriptions (Creswell, 2013; Creswell, 2014) that were proffered. Triangulation in the research presented was based on certain principles by finding different points of data collection (Creswell, 2013; Creswell, 2014; Denzin, 1978; Patton, 1999) such as; examining the literature as well as reading cases such as presented in the case of Pheko (Pheko, 2018),by examining the perception of the author (myself) (Denzin, 1978; Patton, 1999), et al.

RECOMMENDATIONS FOR FUTURE RESEARCH

Future research needs to focus on exploring the topic and consequences of academic mobbing. Both colleges and universities should be examined and surveyed. A large-scale meta-analysis as well as a longitudinal study should be established to examine said phenomena. In addition, those who are being mobbed and have documentation, may wish to consider further legal action.

Statement of Conflict

The author reports that there is no potential conflict of interest.

REFERENCES

Çivilidağ, A., & Sargin, N. (2013). Academics' Mobbing and Job Satisfaction Levels. *Online Journal of Counseling & Education, 2*(2).

Creswell, J. W. (2013). *Qualitative inquiry and research design: Choosing among five approaches* (3rd ed.). Thousand Oaks, CA: Sage Publications.

Creswell, J. W. (2014). *Research design: Qualitative, quantitative, and mixed methods approaches*. Thousand Oaks, CA: Sage Publications.

Denzin, N. K. (1978). *Sociological methods*. New York, NY: McGraw-Hill.

Fonseca, A. P. (2014). Pathogenic versus healthy biofilms: A metaphor for academic mobbing. *Workplace, 24*, 52–55.

Gorlewski, J., Gorlewski, D., & Porfilio, B. J. (2014). Beyond bullies and victims: Using case story, analysis and Freirean insight to address academic mobbing. *Workplace, 24*, 9–18.

Gray, D. E. (2014). *Doing research in the real world*. Washington, DC: Sage Publications.

Gul, H. (2009). An important psychosocial risk in occupational health: Mobbing. *TAF Preventative Medicine Bulletin, 8*(6), 515-520. Retrieved from https://www.ejmanager.com/mnstemps/1/khb_008_06-515.pdf?t=1561405895

Harper, J. (2013, March 28). *Surviving workplace mobbing: Identify the stages*. Retrieved on January 19, 2019 from https://www.psychologytoday.com/us/blog/beyond-bullying/201303/surviving-workplace-mobbing-identify-the-stages

Health & Safety Executive. (n.d.). *Healthy workplace, healthy workforce, better business delivery*. Retrieved on January 21, 2019 from http://www.hse.gov.uk/pubns/misc743.pdf

Housker, J. E., & Saiz, S. G. (2006). *Warning: Mobbing is legal, work with caution*. Retrieved on January 21, 2019 from https://www.counseling.org/resources/library/vistas/vistas06_online-only/Housker.pdf

Impressum. (2018). *Anti-mobbing: Help for scientists*. Retrieved on January 21, 2019, from http://www.antimobbing.eu/introduction/index.html

Johnson, P. (2014). Bullying in academia up close and personal: My story. *Workplace: A Journal for Academic Labor, 24*, 33–41.

Kein, J., & McDermott, J. C. (2007). *Consulting with academics: Mobbing, stress and workplaces of Violence.* Paper presented at the meeting of the American Psychological Association, San Francisco, CA.

Khoo, S. B. (2010). Academic mobbing hidden health hazard at workplace. *Malaysian Family Physician, 5*(2), 61–67. PMID:25606190

Martin, J.L. & Beese, J.A. (2018). Disappearing feminists: Remaining critical voices from academe. *Forum on Public Policy Online, 1*(22). Abstract retrieved from Walden University Library Databases.

McIlveen, P. (2008). Autoethnography as a method for reflexive research and practice in vocational psychology. *Australian Journal of Career Development, 17*(2), 13–20. doi:10.1177/103841620801700204

Murphy, S. (2016). *The optimistic workplace: Creating an environment that employees everyone.* New York, NY: American Management Association.

Osborne, S., & Hammond, M. S. (2017). Effective employee engagement in the workplace. *International of Journal of Applied Management in Technology, 16*(1), 50–67. doi:10.5590/IJAMT.2017.16.104

Patton, M. Q. (1999). Enhancing the quality and credibility of qualitative analysis. *HSR: Health Services Research, 34*(5), 1189–1208. PMID:10591279

Petrina, A., Matheson, S., & Ross, E. W. (2015). Threat convergence: The new academic work, bullying, mobbing & freedom. *Workplace, 24*, 58–69.

Pheko, M. M. (2018). Autoethnography and cognitive adaptation: Two powerful buffers against the negative consequences of workplace bullying and academic mobbing. *International Journal of Qualitative Studies on Health and Well-being, 13*(1), 1–12. doi:10.1080/17482631.2018.1459134 PMID:29667923

Seguin, E. (2016). Academic mobbing or how to become campus tormentors. *University Affairs.* Retrieved on January 17, 2019 from https://www.universityaffairs.ca/opinion/in-my-opinion/academic-mobbing-become-campus-tormentors/

Staub, S. (2015). Mobbing in academia: Case analysis. *International Journal of School and Cognitive Psychology, 2*(2), 121. doi:10.4172/2469-9837.1000121

Taspinar, B., Taspinar, F., Guclu, S., Nalbart, A., Calik, B. B., Uslu, A., & Innal, S. (2013). Investigation of the association between mobbing and musculoskeletal discomfort in academicians. *The Japanese Psychological Research, 55*(4), 400–408. doi:10.1111/jpr.120130

Tigrel, E.U. & Kokalan, O. (2009). Academic mobbing in Turkey. *International Journal of Social Behavioral, Educational, Economic, Business and Industrial Engineering, 3*(7), 1473-1481.

Westhues, K. (2006). The unkindly art of mobbing. *The Journal of Higher Education*, 18–19.

Yaman, E. (2010). Perception of Faculty members exposed to mobbing about the organizational culture and climate. *Educational Sciences: Theory and Practice, 10*(10), 567-578.

ADDITIONAL READING

Brown, J. E., & Duffy, M. (2018). Best Practices in Coaching for Targets of Workplace Bullying and Mobbing. In M. Duffy & D. C. Yamada (Eds.), *Workplace Bullying and Mobbing in the United States* (pp. 315–334).

Duffy, M., & Brown, J. E. (2018). Best Practices in Psychotherapy for Targets of Workplace Bullying and Mobbing. In M. Duffy & D. C. Yamada (Eds.), *Workplace Bullying and Mobbing in the United States* [2 volumes]. (pp. 291–314).

Leymann, H., & Gustafsson, A. (1996). Mobbing at work and the development of post-traumatic stress disorders. *European Journal of Work and Organizational Psychology, 5*(2), 251–275. doi:10.1080/13594329608414858

Malik, N. A., & Björkqvist, K. (2018). Workplace Bullying and Occupational Stress Among University Teachers: Mediating and Moderating Factors. *Europe's Journal of Psychology, 15*(2), 240–259. doi:10.5964/ejop.v15i2.1611

Qureshi, M. I., Iftikhar, M., Janjua, S. Y., Zaman, K., Raja, U. M., & Javed, Y. (2015). Empirical investigation of mobbing, stress and employees' behavior at work place: Quantitatively refining a qualitative model. *Quality & Quantity, 49*(1), 93–113. doi:10.100711135-013-9976-4

Steffgen, G., Sischka, P., Schmidt, A. F., Kohl, D., & Happ, C. (2016). The Luxembourg Workplace Mobbing Scale. *European Journal of Psychological Assessment*, *35*(2), 164–171. doi:10.1027/1015-5759/a000381

Yamada, D. C. (2018). The American Legal Landscape: Potential Redress and Liability for Workplace Bullying and Mobbing. In M. Duffy & D. C. Yamada (Eds.), *Workplace Bullying and Mobbing in the United States* (pp. 413–434).

KEY TERMS AND DEFINITIONS

Academic: Something that is related to education or a higher level of scholarship pertinent to a specific field.

Academic Mobbing: The act of ganging up on a colleague within an institution of higher learning by targeting the individual in order to force them to leave the workplace.

Adjunct: An instructor at a college or university that usually holds a Master-level degree and teaches 1-2 courses per semester in their specialization.

Bullying: a form of intimidation that involves various forms of harassment and sometimes physical abuse/assault.

Mobbing: The act of a group of people targeting one specific person for some shared purpose (i.e., dislike, envy, etc.).

Professor: A person who teaches and lectures students at a place of higher learning in the field of their specialization. Said individual may also serve on committees, engage in research, attend faculty meetings/trainings, et al.

Tenured Professor: An instructor at a place of higher learner whose position is protected and can work at the same institution until the time of their retirement.

Chapter 2
Bullied by the Best:
Why the Bully Paradigm Is a Bad Fit for Understanding the Mob

Janice Harper
Independent Researcher, USA

ABSTRACT

As the prevalence of academic mobbing gains increasing notice, the concept is almost always framed in terms of bullying perpetrated by a group of "bullies." While mobbing is seemingly bullying writ large, upon closer examination bullying and mobbing are very different forms of aggression. In this chapter, the author discusses how the prevailing bully paradigm has conflated bullying with mobbing, and why doing so is problematic. By focusing on the behavior of animals, she shows how signs of submission and/or domination can end or escalate the aggression, attract others to join in, and cause leaders to ignore or encourage the abuse. She then turns to the ways in which workplace aggression has been cast in moral terms of bullies and powerless victims, while failing to account for the complexity and nuance of workplace aggression, as well as the role of the victim. Finally, she discusses the organizational context of the university, suggesting that there are specific features of the academy that make it ripe for mobbing.

DOI: 10.4018/978-1-5225-9485-7.ch002

INTRODUCTION

As the prevalence of academic mobbing gains increasing notice, the concept is almost always framed in terms of bullying perpetrated by a group of "bullies." While mobbing is seemingly bullying writ large, upon closer examination bullying and mobbing are very different forms of aggression. Bullying is typically a series of aggressive actions perpetrated by one or a few aggressive individuals against a weaker person. Bullying may be excused by leadership, even condoned in some cases, but the aggression remains limited to those individuals who find pleasure or profit in abusing someone. They may want the target gone, or they may prefer having them around to enjoy the power they experience by bullying them. The abuse itself is the objective, the damage done to the target the mere consequence of that objective.

In contrast, with mobbing, damaging the target is the objective, the abuse itself a strategy toward that objective. Academic mobbing is collective aggression against an individual, usually a faculty member, with the objective of eliminating them from the academic institution, stripping them of any ability to defend themselves (by way of destroying their reputation or branding them with false accusations of wrong-doing or criminal acts), defeating any legal claims they may have, and communicating to the group (the broader faculty) what happens to someone marked for elimination. It's an abusive tactic with the goal of not just eliminating someone who cannot be easily terminated from their position (such as protected by tenure or contract), but with the added goal of control over the group.

Whereas bullying can be initiated by anyone who is psychologically prone to aggression against those they perceive as weaker, mobbing is almost always initiated by someone in a position of leadership, and perpetrated by an ever-increasing circle of administrators, faculty, and staff who may themselves have no history of bullying or interpersonal aggression and importantly, do not view their actions as cruel, but as necessary if unpleasant. Far from "bullies," the majority of people who engage in mobbing are kind and humane people. The shunning they engage in is not viewed as abusive because it is a non-action—one which they are persuaded the target brought on themselves. The gossip they engage in is viewed as spreading news and bonding with other colleagues who share their experiences with the target and the drama that s/he has allegedly created. And the accusations they make are viewed as legitimate concerns—no matter how far-fetched and unfounded those accusations may be. By the time such accusations are made, the target has been the object of so much social distancing and so many rumors and acted in such seemingly disturbing ways—expressing their anger, anguish, and fears, demonstrating their confusion, exhaustion and desperation—that their every act and statement, past and present, is viewed with caution and distrust and often, reported to administrators.

In short, rather than being bullies, the majority of those who engage in mobbing have been persuaded by social cues that the person they are targeting is a threat to the organization, is deserving of the abuse they receive, and must be eliminated for the greater good of the group.

In an academic setting, what that means is that whereas a bullied faculty member may be mistreated and even shunned by one or a few of their colleagues, and this abuse may be ignored by administration and even influence the views of administrators over the targeted faculty member, that abuse is best understood in terms of the individual psychology of the actors. This is where such melodramatic characterizations of bullies as "psychopaths," "snakes," "evil," and other extreme labels may reflect a kernel of truth. The abuses are being perpetuated by mean-spirited people who take pleasure in the control they have over someone else, in the pain their actions cause, and in the superiority they feel over their victim. For these perpetrators, there will always be someone to kick around, as well as someone to recruit to their cause.

When administration communicates to the faculty and/or other administrators that a specific faculty member is undesirable, however, whether or not that administrator takes pleasure in bullying, mobbing is likely to commence. The reason the person in leadership wants the target out may be related to bullying—they've found a vulnerable victim—but more commonly is related to a threat they perceive from the target—a strong and challenging personality, a public challenge to their authority, a grievance that has been filed, or just being a member of a group perceived as different from the group—a different race, a different gender, or a different ideology.

While mobbing will initially be triggered by the acts and/or statements of an instigating administrator (usually a department head but may be senior faculty), over time the abuse will include increasingly aggressive and anti-social acts perpetrated by almost all faculty and administrators against the target. Investigations will likely be initiated against the target for specious violations of ethics or professional conduct, and overseen by investigators primed to view the target as guilty of the charges. The more damage these players inflict, the more everyone involved will view the target as damaged, thereby justifying and expediting their objective of expelling the undesirable faculty member.

Thus, mobbing is best understood not in terms of individual psychology, but in terms of the psychology of the group—as well as instinctive primate behaviors which have characterized our species' actions throughout millennia. Primates are one of the only species that will organize to abuse, expel or kill a member of its own species, and once they do so, almost all primates will engage in the aggression, even if they are otherwise passive and cooperative. While there are a few other nonhuman species which do so, our species is relatively unique in its aggressive instincts toward our own kind, and the rapidity with which otherwise kind and humane people will act cruelly and inhumanely toward each other once they believe their actions are justified, necessary, and will please their leader.

With these thoughts in mind, in this chapter I explore select animal behavior to show the patterned and predictable trajectory by which a group leader communicates to the group that one of its own is undesirable and the group obliges to drive the target out. As I do so, I explore not only the abusive behavior of the broader group, but the behavior of the target to show how specific behaviors of the target intended as self-defensive and corrective, instead lead to increased aggression and ultimately, greater damage to the target.

Moreover, I suggest that the bully paradigm has promoted stereotypes of the target as someone who is supremely qualified, did nothing to instigate the aggression, and was targeted because they are superior workers and morally superior people. These stereotypes may be true of some targets, but they do disservice to all targets because they prevent the target from reflecting on their own role in any conflict, how they are perceived by others, or on the quality of their performance. As such, they disempower targets who come to believe, falsely in many cases, that there is nothing they can do to quell the aggression or prevent future abuse at the next job. Even poor or annoying workers can be bullied and mobbed, but that does not justify the abusive treatment they receive. Telling them comforting lies, however, assures that they remain vulnerable to rejection and abuse wherever they go.

I then turn to the organizational context in which these behaviors are manifest in an academic setting to show that the individual psychology of the bully paradigm is deeply flawed in any effort to understand, much less address, group mobbing. Instead, I argue that the bully paradigm does more to promote mobbing in an organizational setting than it does to eradicate the problem. That is because once a universally abhorred category has been accepted, all that it takes to eliminate the target is to place them in that category and the group will feel justified in their actions. As such, efforts to address academic bullying and mobbing that rely on branding people as "bullies," "difficult employees," "bad fits," or the popular descriptors of "evil psychopaths" and the like, are unlikely to resolve the problem and far more likely to intensify the problem. By viewing the conflict inherent in mobbing as one of individual character, rather than patterned group behavior, whoever has the least power, challenges leadership, or has been negatively perceived by group "consensus," is the one who will be labeled the aggressor and threat to the group.

The Animal in Us All

The term "mobbing" was introduced by zoologist Konrad Lorenz in the mid-twentieth century to describe the group aggression he noted in birds when they collectively circled and attacked other birds, typically predatory or larger birds which had transgressed their territory (Lorenze 1963). Swedish psychologist Heinz Leymann applied the term to workplace aggression, noting the rapidity with which coworkers would join in aggression aimed at someone targeted for abuse (Leymann and Gustavsson 1984). Yet as the term moved from the zoological realm into the human realm, its roots in animal behavior remained buried. This loss is particularly unfortunate given how much we can learn from studying first, animal behavior, and then second, reflecting on our own primate behaviors.

In my own work I have discussed at length the many forms of animal behavior that reflect patterns of dominance and subordination regarding aggression against one's own species (e.g. Harper 2013/2016). Although most species will independently act aggressively against their own species, relatively few species organize and collectively do so as a group against one of their own. Among those that do are the birds that Leymann wrote about, but others include wolves and primates.

For example, naturalist R. D. Lawrence (1996) observed the pack behavior of wolves turning against members of their own pack when the alpha male instigates the harassment and/or shunning of a lower-ranking wolf. When this happens, not only do other wolves "follow the leader," but they will continue their aggression until the targeted animal displays signs of submission, such as exposing its throat, belly or groin to the pack. Moreover, if the victimized wolf fails to submit soon enough, the aggression escalates until the victim does submit. Lawrence provides an example of a female wolf which eventually had been collectively harassed for so long that she permanently displayed signs of submission such as walking in a crouched position with her tail between her legs.

It's not such a far stretch to recognize the parallels to workplace mobbing, where the target who accepts their defeat early on is likely to move on to employment elsewhere, or withstand the brutalities of probationary status and/or a few black marks on their record and perhaps a raise denied or promotion delayed. They are the ones who suffer the least psychological and professional damage. The longer they resist submitting or fleeing, however, and object to their treatment, the greater the abuse is likely to become, as allegations and humiliations mount and concerted efforts are made to dismiss the faculty member. If they do not succeed in expelling the faculty member, they usually succeed in reducing them to a permanent weakened status, with lowered self-esteem and less productivity, a human version of the defeated wolf forever walking with its head lowered and its tail between its legs.

The psychological beating a faculty member who is mobbed endures is great, and includes not only lowered self-esteem, but a diminished professional reputation, if not career destruction. Moreover, many, if not most, targets of academic mobbing were previously well respected by the very colleagues who have turned against them. To better understand how seemingly intelligent and moral faculty and administrators can engage in this behavior against a once-respected colleague, it is useful to reflect on our own animal behavior by examining other primates.

Rhesus monkeys provide, perhaps, the most intriguing example of mobbing behaviors. Primatologist Dario Maestripieri (2007) has observed what he characterizes as Machiavellian behaviors among these primates as they not only harass and shun their own kind, but engage in cunning and manipulative behaviors against a hapless monkey in order to advance their own social status and/or gain access to resources. In contrast to wolves, which must show submission early on in order for the abuse against them to stop, among the rhesus monkeys, submitting too quickly can encourage greater abuse. One reason for this difference, I would argue, is that among the wolves the aggression that demands early submission is aggression inflicted by the pack, whereas among the rhesus monkeys, the aggression that demands a swift counter-attack to bring an end to the abuse, is aggression that is inflicted by a single primate against another primate. Once the bullying monkey's aggression escalates, however, other monkeys often encourage and join in the abuse until the victim is killed. In other words, the bully monkey has gained status through his unchallenged abuse, and the victimized monkey has not only lost status, but demonstrated his weakness to the group—thus marking him as unfit for the group and someone who can be exploited for strategic gain—by jockeying for a higher social position within the group, taking the food, sleeping spot or mate of the weaker animal, or gaining favor with another aggressor.

Maestripieri further notes that the monkeys most likely to be targeted for this aggression are not only the ones who display submission at the first sign of a swift knock off a perch or swipe of a banana, but newcomers to the group. These newcomers are at risk from both senior members of the group, and other newcomers. That is because newcomers instinctively know their subordinate place to senior males and females—just as they know that in times of group conflict if they join in any aggression against another subordinate member, they can gain status with the senior members. Because females are typically the most subordinate members of the group, one of the few ways they can form coalitions with higher ranking members is by harassing newcomer females. Thus, the subordinate females are often the most aggressive when these primates collectively bully one of their own. The high-ranking monkeys may or may not have instigated the abuse, but they will watch from afar and grant approval and respect to those subordinates who have defeated a potential threat to the group, and thus protected their leader.

So how does a rhesus monkey survive such abuse? If they are being batted about by a single monkey, fighting back at the first sign of aggression will likely stop the attacks. The aggressor will know they picked on the wrong monkey. But if the aggression is collective and many monkeys join in the abuse, then it is imperative for the victimized monkey to change its behavior and display submission in order to survive—just as the wolves did—or leave the group altogether. If they fail to do so and continue to engage in battle, they are likely to be killed.

Because status in their society is based on forming coalitions, one of the common responses for rhesus monkeys under attack is to scream for help. But as Maestripieri points out, who they turn to for help is critical to their survival—and it is probably not a good idea to turn to the leaders of their group.

You might expect that everyone would ask for help from the king and the queen of their group, but that's not always a good idea, for a couple of reasons. First, like all royals, the rhesus king and queen are very good at feigning indifference when the requests for help come from somebody at the bottom of their society. Second, if they are really bothered by all the noise and insulted by being asked to get their hands dirty with fighting, they may intervene and attack the victim who's seeking help and not the aggressor (Maestripieri 2007:50).

As primates ourselves, then, we might consider these behaviors when addressing workplace aggression. Turning to administrators for help might be the recommended course of action by Human Relations departments and anti-bullying literature, but like the kings and queens of lower primate societies, the kings and queens of university administration may well resent calls for help when asked to get their own hands dirty. And turning to other subordinates for support may well misfire, as those subordinates discern the opportunity to score points with those with higher status. After all, while workers may unite against management on the shop floor of a factory, the university is not the shop floor—every faculty member is vying for strategic alliances with administration, just like the rhesus monkeys.

Moreover, fighting back too persistently and vociferously against the group engaged in mobbing (or against someone in a high-ranking position) is likely to be perceived as a threat that must be quashed, whereas responding with displays of subservience and weakness early on when one abusive member begins to bully can lead others to sense a weakness that encourages them to join in. The key to knowing how to respond and when to respond, how to submit and when to submit, is thus found in distinguishing between the aggressive instincts of a single member ("the bully") and the aggressive instincts of the group ("the mob"). Unfortunately, the literature on bullying and mobbing far too often conflates the two, and by failing to distinguish the strategic objectives of each, those who respond to mobbing by treating it as just another form of bullying writ large, are bound to end up on the losing side of the battle. Which brings us to the anti-bully paradigm and why it is so deeply flawed.

The Anti-Bully Paradigm Gone Wrong

With the publication of Gary and Ruth Namie's (2000/2003) bestselling book, *The Bully at Work: What You Can Do to Stop the Hurt and Reclaim Your Dignity on the Job*, the workplace bully became a topic of widespread discussion and relatively little debate. After all, who hasn't encountered the nasty coworker—if not manager—who takes pleasure in insulting, ignoring and sabotaging a worker they have singled out for harassment? Yet in bringing to light the prevalence of workplace bullying, the Namies, and many of those who came after, all too often conflate mobbing with bullying, using the terms interchangeably. In so doing, they have presented bullies as psychopathic individuals who select not the weakest in the group for their abuse, but the strongest. Depicting "bullies" as "evil," and their targets as inherently superior, characterizations such as, "Bullies are inadequate, effective and poorly developed people [and] targets are empathic, just and fair people" (Namie and Namie 2000:14), the individual psychopathology of the abuser is used to explain why certain people engage in bullying behaviors and the inherent goodness of the target explains why they were targeted.

This view frames the dynamics of abuse in terms of morality, which may be comforting to targets, but leaves them wholly unprepared for the cruelty with which otherwise kind and humane people will engage in once they join the mob. Moreover, by emphasizing the inherent goodness and professional and psychological superiority of the target, one is left to presume that poor workers cannot be bullied or mobbed, that morally ambiguous personalities cannot be bullied or mobbed, and that people who themselves have acted unfairly toward other workers cannot be bullied or mobbed. There are two fundamental flaws in this line of thinking.

The first is that the person who becomes targeted for abuse is left with the self-perception that their actions and reactions have played no part in the abuse. While the abusive nature of both bullying and mobbing is hardly justified and, I would argue, is always disproportionately cruel and unjust in comparison to any missteps of the target, with this view the target needn't reflect on the ways in which their actions or reactions may have contributed to the conflict, however unintended. For example, a poor worker who is mobbed by his or her coworkers because tenure or other forms of job security make it difficult to terminate their employment, is unlikely to recognize the ways in which their poor job performance has affected the workplace. True, once bullied or mobbed, it becomes especially difficult for anyone to perform well at work, but without the courage or encouragement to reflect on one's job performance, that job performance will remain poor—and subject the target to similar abuses wherever they work in the future.

Similarly, a worker with poor communication or social skills, or who persistently acts in ways that are perceived as challenging to leadership, will continue to do so. They will have no incentive to change how they communicate or address workplace issues, and if anything, they will find reinforcement for their behaviors because they have been led to believe if they were treated badly at work it was because of their superior work, their effectiveness and their goodness. This is not to suggest that those perceived as challenging are themselves necessarily the problem. Indeed, while some people might be rude, sexist, racist or otherwise difficult to deal with, others, such as women, gays, people of color, or faculty who ideologically differ from the larger group are commonly perceived as "lacking collegiality," "raising their voice," or speaking offensively regardless of how reasonable they are when raising questions or posing challenges to prevailing views. But even in these cases, to survive academic mobbing, it is in the target's best interest to reflect on how they are perceived by their colleagues—even if that perception is skewed. When confronting any threat to our survival by an animal or human, we are more likely to survive if we recognize the cues that might ignite the rage of that aggressor. The same is true for the threats we face by members of the academy.

Perhaps most important for the target of bullying and mobbing, is that they understand that their reactions, however normal and understandable, risk contributing to an escalation of the abuse. Because for every action there is a reaction, as targets struggle to survive and engage in self-defensive behaviors—such as filing complaints, seeking support from their colleagues, providing copious evidence in their defense, and firing off angry emails documenting and objecting to abuses—all of which are encouraged by many of those who write about bullying and mobbing—their reactions risk being perceived as threats, evidence of their instability, and their inability to withstand the stressors of the workplace. Just as the responses of subordinate wolves or monkeys are considered cues for their abusers to escalate their aggression, the primates of the workplace demand obedience and conformity of their colleagues. Failing to heed the nuanced social cues in the early stages of abuse may prove fatal to the worker who is encouraged to rally support and take action against "the bully."

A second reason that regarding targets as inherently good and superior to their abusers is problematic is that it presumes that those targets who are not necessarily kind, fair and good, deserve the abuse and hence, the abuse they receive is not bullying or mobbing. Just as all wars are justified in the name of self defense, so, too, is mobbing. Those who engage in it persuade themselves that their actions are necessary and of the target's own making. As the character assassination of the target intensifies, and the target displays their anguish, anger and confusion, colleagues shift their perception of the target from someone being treated unfairly, to someone who needs to go, if not "for their own good," then for the good of the group.

It is no surprise, then, that while condemning mobbing, those who advocate for the removal of "bullies" in the workplace persist in labeling the aggressor(s) "bullies," thereby dehumanizing them, encourage documenting any perceived adverse act or statement of "the bully," reporting them to supervisors, telling others of their experiences and soliciting similar accounts, and refusing to engage with them and even refusing to work with them.

In other words, the anti-bully paradigm suggests that the way to deal with an unpleasant colleague is to call them names, keep a close eye on them and document the slightest offense, file grievances or otherwise raise concerns about them, gossip about them, encourage others to view them in the same way, shun them and sabotage their work by not cooperating with them and excluding them from committees and other opportunities. These are mobbing tactics, and they are commonly considered justified by those who write about "bullies," because bullying is so destructive to both individuals and to the workplace.

Yet if "the bully" is being mobbed out of the workplace, how is s/he to know that their behaviors played a role in the conflict if everywhere they turn they are being told that the aggressors against them are the bullies and they are the ones who are inherently good, fair, superior and did nothing to bring on the abuse? The problem here is not only that the very abuse that is so damaging is considered acceptable if the target is "a bully," but that it creates a universally abhorred category in which to place the mobbing target, in order to justify the abuse. The faculty member who files complaints against the abuse or reports discriminatory actions can be characterized as "always complaining." As the abuse transforms to mobbing and others join in, it can be said that "everybody has a problem with them." As they react with anger, they can be described as "always angry." If they indicate they may take legal action or otherwise fight back through lawful means or through institutional processes, they can be characterized as "making threats." And as their productivity declines and their confusion, grief and anguish become visible to others after being abused and shunned for weeks, if not months or years, they can be characterized as "not doing their job," "mentally unstable," or other derogatory characterizations that describe the normal symptoms of abuse as evidence of unfitness. Once described in these terms, they can readily be labelled as "a bully" and their abuse and elimination unquestioned because "bullies" have to go.

Thus, by conflating bullying with mobbing, framing the problem as one of morality and not group behavior, and reducing the players to simplistic stereotypes of good guys and bad guys, the person with the least power, not the most aggressive, is the one most vulnerable to the bully label. Moreover, they are further disempowered by making them think they played no role and that the abuse against them is solely because of their moral and professional superiority, which sets them up for similar abuses in the future, and leaves them wholly unprepared for the colleagues who are good and kind but will inevitably join in the shunning and abuse as administrators make it clear that they want their target gone, tenure or contract be damned.

The Organizational Context of the University

Although bullying can arise wherever two or more people interact and mobbing can transpire in any group setting, whether the workplace, community, school, place of worship, club, neighborhood or even family, there are certain unique features of the university that make mobbing relatively common. These features include the tenure system, promotional opportunities, the job market for faculty, and the intellectual and ideological nature of university positions themselves.

Because the tenure system makes it so difficult to dismiss faculty, including tenure-track faculty who are productive and have documented success in teaching, service and research, when a faculty member is marked for elimination, they cannot just be fired. There must be cause, and if tenured, exceptional cause. Consequently, mobbing serves two purposes toward this end. By making it so unpleasant to remain, it is hoped that the undesired faculty member will simply leave. Cutting off access to resources, not providing raises or promotions, subjecting them to investigations, not including them in committees, discussions or social events, and similar tactics is a way to suggest it is time to leave.

And if they don't leave, mobbing serves another purpose. It establishes a paper trail of poor performance (whether legitimate or not), and the gossip and rumors that are encouraged almost always lead to accusations of ethical, professional or even legal wrongdoing which can eventually provide the cause needed to terminate their employment. It needn't be proven that a faculty member is indeed guilty of whatever it is they are accused of, as long as enough faculty and administrators can agree they probably are.

Another organizational feature of universities which make them all the more susceptible to mobbing behaviors is that there are limited opportunities for advancement. The promotions that are typically available to a faculty member are to move from Assistant Professor to Associate Professor to Professor. With the exception of the occasional endowed professorship, once a faculty member reaches full professor, there is nowhere to go but administration if one wants to advance in the university system, as well as increase the salary beyond the meager raises full professors typically receive.

As a result of these limited opportunities, there is greater competition for resources, and for those who do advance to administration, remaining there is typically the favored goal. Thus, any complaint or concern raised by a faculty member, or any challenge to their authority, real or perceived, can be viewed as a threat to their status at the university. Pleasing those in higher administration is the goal, not pleasing the faculty. To achieve that end, it is imperative that the trouble-making faculty member be dealt with swiftly and discreetly—and the more noise the faculty member makes about it, the more they will be characterized as the problem. Showing higher administrators that "the problem" (i.e., the faculty member) has been dealt with will cement their place in the administrative coalition—just as the rhesus monkeys learn to do.

The job market for faculty is another feature that makes academic mobbing relatively common. Because tenure-track jobs are so limited, and tenured positions even more so, to leave a tenured or tenure-track position willingly is not easy. It means, in most cases, selling the home, leaving the community, persuading a spouse to leave their work and friends and find something new, disrupting children from their school and friendships, and often starting on the tenure-track all over again. A bullied or mobbed faculty member is not going to pack their bags and move on at the earliest signs of harassment. They will likely stay and fight for their jobs—risking escalating the harassment and accusations against them.

Moreover, the tenuous job market for faculty is accompanied by decreasing resources once they are employed. Limited research funds, few raises, increasing course loads and other demands, have created a hyper-competitive environment in which faculty now work. Like a calculating rhesus monkey, cutting off the resources of a colleague can help another colleague to access them—and to advance. Even for those not so calculating, once administration has signaled displeasure with a faculty member, others quickly wise up to the fact that aligning themselves with administrative goals—getting rid of the problem colleague—will free up resources for themselves and increase their own opportunities for advancement.

Finally, the very nature of the job contributes to academic mobbing and its escalation. That is because there is a tendency to think that educated people, particularly those who teach in the areas of social science, humanities, social work, law, and the health sciences, are more moral and intelligent and thus less likely to engage in the petty and cruel tactics of mobbing. In so thinking, we do two things. First, we fail to recognize that they very well will do so, and are consequently unprepared for their betrayals when they do. Second, we fail to recognize our own aggressive tendencies which leave each of us vulnerable to engaging in such unnecessary and cruel behavior. By persuading ourselves that we are smarter than that, kinder than that, and above all that, when we do treat our colleagues badly, when we do gossip about our colleagues, and when we do report them to administration for something we object to, we persuade ourselves that we are doing so because they have it coming. We are not the problem. The person we want out is.

And, that, I fear, is the heart of the problem. Mobbing isn't something evil, psychopathic bullies do. It's something primates do. What sets us apart from the monkeys and apes below us in the primate hierarchy is our ability to think abstractly and give meaning to our lives and worlds and to the social relations we forge. So when we behave badly, we draw on our higher brain power to justify our actions. We persuade ourselves, and those around us, that we did what we had to do to eliminate a problem. And in a university setting, those primate intellects of ours are all the more clever and cunning and capable of defeating those who threaten our status with the group.

It has been said that one of the reasons academics behave so badly toward each other is because the stakes are so low. I would suggest that it is quite the opposite. Academics behave so badly because the stakes are, indeed, so high. To lose an academic job means losing a home, a community, and more. It means perhaps never working in the academy again. It means being branded as "difficult" or a "failure" by one's national colleagues. And it may mean that the many years that have gone into earning that doctorate, and the sacrifices made to relocate for a tenure-track job may have been in vein.

Because the stakes are so high, the resources so limited, and the competition so great, mobbing among academics is as easily ignited as is mobbing among monkeys. But as long as the focus is on bullies, the faculty marked for mobbing, and the faculty engaged in it, will fail to recognize their actions as anything other than good and necessary. No matter which side one is on.

CONCLUSION

As this chapter has suggested, academic mobbing is not the same as bullying, even if bullying is inherent in the mobbing process. Bullying is best understood in terms of individual psychology, whereas mobbing is best understood in terms of group psychology, and academic mobbing is best understood, as well, in terms of the organizational context of the university.

Mobbing serves an added purpose other than just eliminating an undesirable faculty member. Once a faculty member has been expelled from the university, the aggressive actions of the faculty and administration may well recede and greater bonding of the group may temporarily ensue, but the punitive tendencies of leadership will be strengthened, dissent suppressed, and allegiance to administration rewarded just as resistance is punished. This dissent may include ideological differences—anyone who expresses or pursues ideological or intellectual viewpoints that differ from the majority will soon learn that they are not safe in doing so. They will learn to conform, leave, or risk becoming targets themselves.

One of the reasons mobbing continues is that for all the damage it does to morale and to the intellectual and working environment, it also benefits those who engage in it. The consequences for the targeted faculty member may be severe, including career destruction, while the consequences for the faculty who engaged in the mobbing will include institutional awards accompanied by heightened competition, less respect for individuality and difference (regardless of any allegiance to diversity), greater expectation for conformity and obedience, and a greater likelihood that faculty who are promoted into leadership will be those who are most likely to perpetuate mobbing tactics against any future tenured or tenure-track faculty perceived as problematic.

In the end, a veneer of consensus and cohesion in a post-mobbing academic environment will conceal a divisive and competitive faculty who fear deviating from the norm. Concepts of diversity will appeal to those who welcome phenotypical diversity but reject any substantive diversity of thought, ideology, or communication styles. By conflating bullying with mobbing, the greater damage that mobbing does to both the target and the institution (which in many cases will pay significant financial settlements for their actions), is obscured.

Finally, the bully paradigm may well apply to interpersonal aggression perpetrated by a single individual, but it is a poor fit for understanding and addressing the collective aggression that ensues when administration signals, like the alpha apes before them, that one of their own is unwanted. When that happens, the bully paradigm will only serve the bully in administration who set the process in motion—by branding their target as the bully.

REFERENCES

Harper, J. (2013). *Mobbed! What to Do When They Really Are Out to Get You.* Tacoma: Backdoor Press.

Lawrence, R. D. (1986). *In Praise of Wolves.* New York: Henry Holt and Company.

Leymann, H., & Gustavsson, A. (1984). Psykiskt våld i arbetslivet. Två explorative undersökningar [Psychological violence at work places: Two explorative studies]. Stockholm: Arbetarskyddsstyrelsen.

Lorenz, K. (1963). *Das sogenannte Böse zur Naturgeschichte der Aggression.* Verlag Dr. G Borotha-Schoeler.

Maestripieri, D. (2007). *Macachiavellian Intelligence: How Rhesus Macaques and Humans Have Conquered the World.* Chicago: University of Chicago Press. doi:10.7208/chicago/9780226501215.001.0001

Namie & Namie. (2000). *The Bulloy at Work: What You Can Do to Stop the Hurt and Reclaim Your Dignity on the Job.* Naperville, IL: Sourcebooks, Inc.

Chapter 3
The Role of Passive Evil in Perpetuating Downward Academic Mobbing

Theodore W. McDonald
Boise State University, USA

Sandina Begic
Boise State University, USA

R. Eric Landrum
Boise State University, USA

ABSTRACT

Downward academic mobbing occurs when unethical administrators initiate a pattern of bullying, intimidation, and the commission of personal and career damage on undeserving faculty members (most often principled, tenured professors who question their decisions or call attention to unethical behavior such as policy violations and lack of academic due process). Once these unethical administrators succeed in framing a faculty victim as a target (often through innuendo, factual distortions, or outright lies), the victim's colleagues—many of whom have known and benefited from the victim for years—either fail to support the victim (a problem known as passive evil) or begin actively participating in the persecution themselves (often in pursuit of personal gain). The purpose of this chapter is to focus on the first instance (i.e., passive evil), and to discuss how passive evildoers' failure to stand up for victims of downward academic mobbing effectively encourages future acts of persecution—including against the passive evildoers themselves.

DOI: 10.4018/978-1-5225-9485-7.ch003

Copyright © 2020, IGI Global. Copying or distributing in print or electronic forms without written permission of IGI Global is prohibited.

INTRODUCTION

Downward academic mobbing occurs when unethical administrators initiate a pattern of bullying, intimidation, and the commission of personal and career damage on undeserving faculty members (most often principled, tenured professors who question their decisions or call attention to unethical behavior such as policy violations and lack of academic due process; Faria, Mixon, & Salter, 2012; Khoo, 2010; McDonald, Stockton, & Landrum, 2018). Once these unethical administrators succeed in framing a faculty victim as a target (often through innuendo, factual distortions, or outright lies), the victim's colleagues—many of whom have known and benefited from the victim for years—either fail to support the victim (a problem known as passive evil) or begin actively participating in the persecution themselves (often in pursuit of personal gain; Duffy, 2009; Westhues, 2005). The purpose of this chapter is to focus on the first instance (i.e., passive evil), and to discuss how passive evildoers' failure to stand up for victims of downward academic mobbing effectively encourages future acts of persecution—including against the passive evildoers themselves.

This chapter is organized into several sections. First, an overview of workplace bullying and academic mobbing is presented, including a discussion of the interchangeability of the wording regarding these constructs. The prevalence of bullying, the dynamics of bullies and their actions, and the effects of bullying on victims are presented. In the second section, passive evil as a phenomenon is explored, as well as the damage it causes to the victim. Third, the authors discuss how passive evil (particularly through the mechanism of selective moral disengagement) not only fails to stop the persecution of the initial victim, but also virtually guarantees that there will be future victims (including, quite likely, victimization against those who fail to stand up for themselves and others). In the final section, some ways of combating passive evil, and for protecting faculty members from downward academic mobbing in the future are discussed.

WORKPLACE BULLYING AND ACADEMIC MOBBING

Research on workplace bullying has been accumulating for over 50 years, dating back at least to Brodsky's (1976) book on workplace harassment (Duffy, 2009). The term 'harassment' did not survive long in the context that researchers currently describe workplace bullying, perhaps due to its longtime association with status-based offenses such as racial and sexual harassment (Duffy, 2009). What is now known either as workplace bullying or mobbing (or even as psychoterror, as Leymann [1993] once described it) is sometimes discussed with both of these terms interchangeably, as some researchers recommend (e.g., Namie & Namie, 2003). As described by Duffy (2009), the eminent sociologist Westhues (Westhues, 2005; 2006), spending much of his career studying academic mobbing, argued that the two terms should not be confounded, as he believed that the term bullying evoked an image of a stereotyped two-person conflict (such as a playground fight) whereas mobbing involves more than one perpetrator, and because mobbing is a more nuanced problem that requires a more nuanced solution than simply punishing the perpetrator (as mobbing involves multiple perpetrators and is often facilitated by a toxic organizational climate). In any case, as Pheko (2018a) observed, "bullying and mobbing can lead to similar consequences, such as a loss of dignity, lowered self-confidence and productivity, and an excessive amount of non-work-related stress and other related health issues" (p. 2). With apologies to those who prefer to differentiate between bullying and mobbing, for the sake of consistency with many authors who research these topics (as well as for simplicity), in this chapter the authors use the terms fairly synonymously, with the caveat that workplace bullying is considered a problem that occurs in all employment sectors, and downward academic mobbing refers to the similar processes occurring specifically in the higher education environment.

Because the authors use the terms bullying and mobbing as general synonyms, it seems prudent to give general definitions of both; in most cases, readers will see clear commonalities. A good, general definition of workplace bullying is "the persistent exposure to interpersonal aggression and mistreatment from colleagues, superiors or subordinates" (Einarsen, Hoel, & Notelaers, 2009, p. 24). In some sectors, the bullying practices are typically overt behaviors carried out by a single person, most often an administrator or senior colleague (with a clear power differential) against a less powerful coworker or subordinate (Pheko, 2018a), with an element of workplace exclusion involved (often forced, such as banishment of the victim from department meetings or social activities); another feature of workplace bullying is that it tends to escalate over time (Beckman, Cannella, & Wantland, 2013). A good working definition of mobbing is offered by Duffy and Sperry (2007; as cited in Duffy, 2009), who defined mobbing as:

The nonsexual harassment of a coworker by a group of other workers or other members of an organization designed to secure the removal from the organization of the one who is targeted. Mobbing results in the humiliation, devaluation, discrediting, degradation, loss of professional reputation, and, usually, the removal of the target of the organization with all the concomitant financial, career, health, and psychological implications that one might expect from a protracted traumatizing experience. (p. 245)

Many other researchers who use definitions of mobbing (e.g., those used by Metzger, Petit, & Sieber, 2015; Prevost & Hunt, 2018; Twale & De Luca, 2008) agree on these key features of the construct. In this chapter, it should be noted that the focus is on *downward* academic mobbing, which differs from a more general form of academic mobbing in that the former is always initiated by a superior (in most cases, an unethical mid-level academic administrator such as a department chair, director of a school, or a college dean), whereas the latter could be initiated by another faculty member, a staff member, or even a student.

With respect to downward academic mobbing specifically, McDonald et al. (2018), summarize the literature (relying particularly heavily on the work of Faria et al. [2012] and Khoo [2010]) on the critical elements thusly:

First, academic mobbing tends to be initiated by unprincipled administrators whose malfeasance was questioned or revealed though the expression of academic free speech. Second, the victims of academic mobbing tend to be productive, likable, principled tenured professors who publicly speak out about administrative wrongdoing. Third, academic mobbing involves manipulation of the language or misrepresentation of the facts regarding the victim's motivations, speech, or behavior. Fourth, the victim's colleagues are either poisoned against him or her, or choose not to support the victim due to fear of sharing his or her fate, indifference, or a lack of conviction (a pervasive problem in educational administration characterized by Samier [2008] as "passive evil"). Finally, the victim is left personally and professionally injured, while the perpetrator(s) goes unpunished and therefore perhaps empowered to pursue a new target. (para. 18)

Most often, faculty members who are targeted for mobbing have done nothing "wrong" in the legal or policy sense; they have not lied, cheated, plagiarized, sexually- or racially-harassed, or engaged in any other type of moral or academic turpitude (American Association of University Professors [AAUP], 2015b). What the faculty member has done, in almost all cases, is exercise his or her right to academic freedom by questioning or challenging unethical decisions made by administrators (AAUP, 2015a; AAUP, 2015c). In such situations, unethical administrators have no valid basis for punishing the victim, *so they create a reason*. Often, the 'reason' is so baseless as to be almost absurd if it was not so serious for and damaging to the victim; typically, victims are accused of "being uncivil," "not collegial," or violating some form of "shared values" (AAUP, 2015b). In short, the accusations are often deliberately nebulous, and because they are so ill defined and subjective they are almost impossible to definitively disprove or defend oneself against in any form of procedural or legal fashion (McDonald et al., 2018). When unethical administrators punish longtime, established, and accomplished faculty members through mechanisms so obviously unjustified and malicious (Faria et al., 2012; Khoo, 2010), they send a clear message to other faculty members who are newer, less accomplished, or with lower reputation capital: "*If I can do this to Professor Established imagine what I can do to you?!*"

Prior to proceeding to a presentation of the tenets of passive evil, it seems beneficial to summarize several features of downward academic mobbing sequentially. These features include characteristics of the perpetrators, characteristics of the victims, and the methods used by perpetrators to bully victims.

Researchers have identified a number of specific features of workplace bullies. Some of these researchers have focused on identifying personality traits of perpetrators, and there are definitely some distinct and common features. For example, Young (2017) reveals manager bullies to have a psychological profile of being competitive, demanding of respect, and having extrinsically-motivated narcissistic pride combined with Machiavellianism (i.e., being sneaky, cold, amoral). Other researchers (e.g., Glendinning, 2001) have reported similar findings, while identifying other undesirable traits such as being domineering, arrogant, and having a strong (though undeserved) sense of entitlement. The workplace bully has the goal of humiliation, intimidation, and punishment – all directed toward the target (Einarsen et al., 2009; Young, 2017). Interestingly, the bully's bad behavior increases when bystanders fail to comply, a colleague asserts his or her independence, social skill, or professional success, or if the targeted victim of the bullying exhibits personal vulnerabilities (Young, 2017).

A recent area of investigation has involved applying principles from the study of domestic violence to the study of workplace bullying. Scott (2018) published an article revealing that the personality traits and characteristics of workplace bullies were extremely similar to male batterers in domestic violence situations. Using what is known as the Duluth Model, she mapped workplace bully behavior onto a schematic commonly used for understanding domestic violence, and created the Workplace Power Control Wheel pertaining to workplace bullying. This wheel consists of eight spokes, including:

1. *Using intimidation (making workers feel uncomfortable or afraid)*

2. *Using emotional abuse (name calling, making workers think they are crazy, humiliating workers)*
3. *Using isolation (controlling whom workers communicate with, where they are allowed to go)*
4. *Minimizing, denying, and blaming (making light of the worker's concerns, denying abuse is happening, shifting the blame from the manager to the worker)*
5. *Using co-workers (making workers feel guilty for the work levels of other workers, or how the worker's supposed misbehavior affects other workers)*
6. *Using employer privilege (treating workers like servants, not involving workers in decision making)*
7. *Using economic abuse (threatening the worker's job, tenure, or work conditions)*
8. *Using coercion and threats (making threats to employee rights or privileges).* (p. 447)

There are at least two remarkable contributions from Scott (2018). The first is that she articulates that workplace bullying in general, and downward academic mobbing as a sub-case, *constitutes interpersonal violence*. It may not be physically violent; however, it creates all of the other levels of harm associated with domestic violence. Second, it lays out a sequence of behaviors that bullies/mobbers use to harm their victims. The Workplace Power Control Wheel seems to be a very valuable tool in demonstrating how bullies try to accomplish control and domination, and also why society should perhaps treat workplace bullying/mobbing as seriously as it treats domestic violence.

New work is just now emerging from researchers such as Pheko (2018b), who describes how bullies and those who engage in academic mobbing achieve their goals. Two tools of the trade that are not covered in the Workplace Power Control Wheel (Scott, 2018) but are common elements of the bullying/mobbing repertoire, are rumors and gossip. Rumors are "unsubstantiated and instrumentally critical pieces of information in circulation, which function to assist people in making sense and managing risks within concepts of uncertainty, danger, or a potential threat" (Pheko, 2018b, p. 452), whereas gossip is "evaluative talk arising in the context of social network formation, change, and maintenance about individuals who are not present" (Pheko, 2018b, p. 452). Four possible strategies have now been identified as to how rumors and gossip are used by those who engage in bullying and academic mobbing (Pheko, 2018b): (1) as a tool for maintenance of oppression and social dominance; (2) as an expression of envy and social undermining; (3) as weapons to humiliate subordinates by corporate/organizational psychopaths; and (4) as an attempt to widen the power gap. By understanding these uses, it is also apparent that these are the warning signals/red flags to be watchful for to differentiate between fun and engaging hallway conversation and more sinister gossip with latent, malicious motivations.

The victims of bullying seem a more heterogeneous lot, both demographically and psychologically, than their persecutors. Whereas some reviewers (e.g., Prevost & Hunt, 2018) suggest that predictors of academic mobbing include race (with racial/ethnic minority members bullied more often than Non-Hispanic Whites), gender (with females being bullied more often than males), and age (with younger faculty being more often mobbed than older faculty), other scholars (e.g., Khoo, 2010; Thomas, 2009) suggest that the people most likely to be bullied/mobbed are those whom bullies find the most threatening—particularly tenured professors and those whose "reputation capital is combined with academic freedom, and the combination is then used to criticize the actions of the administration of the institution (Faria et al., 2012, p. 721). Regardless of whether there is a victim/target "type," there is tremendous commonality in the physical and mental health consequences of bullying/mobbing. Prevost and Hunt (2018) provide an excellent summary of these consequences, and they are presented in Table 1.

Armed with an understanding of what downward academic mobbing is, who perpetrates it (and how), and how it impacts its victims, the authors now proceed with an exploration of the nature of passive evil, before presenting how passive evil perpetuates downward academic mobbing.

PASSIVE EVIL

Passive evil is a concept that gained particular interest after the Second World War when a number of academics such as Hannah Arendt began studying how many good people, including ordinary, non-ideological citizens of Germany during Hitler's Third Reich, failed to defend or protect their neighbors who were targeted by the Nazis for being members of a 'socially undesirable' group (such as Jewish persons) or being involved in activities (such as trade unionism) considered dangerous to the regime (Adams & Balfour, 2009; Davenport, 2013). Although Arendt (1963; 1978) is best known for her writings on the banality of evil, in which fairly ordinary, unspectacular persons such as Adolf Eichmann and Albert Speer came to commit extraordinary crimes during the Holocaust, she also wrote extensively on how

Table 1.

Summary of Reported Physical, Emotional, and Psychological Consequences of Academic Mobbing (Presented in Alphabetical Order)
Anger
Anxiety
Confusion
Damaged personal relationships/family issues
Depression
Despair
Destructive behaviors
Difficulty concentrating
Embarrassment
Fear (Afraid of tormentor, exposed as victim)
Foolishness
Hopelessness
Humiliation
Inferiority and withdrawal
Pain
Phobias
Pointlessness
Post-Traumatic Stress Disorder
Powerlessness
Reduced self-esteem
Reluctance acceptance/denial of experiences
Sadness
Self-blame
Self-doubt
Shame
Social isolation
Stress
Stress-related illnesses and health issues (digestive, sleep disturbances, change in eating patterns, increased smoking/drinking)
Suicidal thoughts

Note. Source: Prevost and Hunt (2018)

bystanders and witnesses, through their inability or unwillingness to confront evil or protect its victims, were guilty of the commission of evil themselves. Arendt (1978) conceptualized evil as a fungus, and maintained that people who fail to resist it become part of that fungus, passively following the externally-set order of a given system (be it an organization, an institution, or a society) rather than attending to their inner structures that, through introspection and self-reflection, would enable them to differentiate good from bad and right from wrong. Vuger (2017), drawing on Arendt's conceptualization and expanding it to other bureaucratized settings (such as workplaces), deftly demonstrated how the same processes of passive evil occur there; by identifying with the organizational system (and the evils it contains or allows) rather than with fellow individuals within it, people engage in acts of self-deception that make witnessing evil more bearable. How this relates to our discussion of downward academic mobbing is as follows: In practice, a person who acts in discord with the system (for example, whistle-blowing or calling attention to administrative malfeasance) is labeled as a dissident or an enemy of the system (in a philosophical sense, an Other) and as such any punishment that is within the established parameters of the system is considered appropriate, under the guise of protecting the system but without regard to the Other (Vuger, 2017).

What is clear in this work is that through inaction we implicitly (although perhaps unknowingly) risk becoming passive collaborators in the potential destruction of people who are dear to us and/or are members of our own communities, including our work community. In fact, both sadly and paradoxically, this is something that happened to Arendt in her own career; she was a workplace-mobbing victim who paid the price for speaking her truth. As discussed by Davenport (2013), after describing Eichmann as an ordinary man (albeit one who was a willing participant in a murderous bureaucratic machine) rather than a dispositional monster, Arendt was subjected to name calling, ostracism, banishment from her Jewish community of friends and fellow thinkers and threatened with the loss of her lecturership at the New School of Social Research. This is a textbook example of how quickly people can abandon an individual, through action and inaction (in the latter case, failing to speak up on behalf of the person being mobbed) when that individual is courageous enough to challenge the system or otherwise question the institutionally sanctioned way of thinking.

Researchers demonstrate through a rich literature that the line between active (whether banal or not) and passive evil is very thin, and often blurred. In any case, they are highly interrelated: Through passive evil, people enable active evil. As noted by Augustein (as cited in Welz, 2018), "people who look away do not stop the crime but join in it: through Weggucken [looking away] and Mitmachen [partaking] one tolerates evil, to say the least, or even causes it" (p. 65; bracketed translations added). Indeed, Welz (2018) asserts that thoughtlessness can be a root of evil: When people do not think about their actions or inaction, they engage in "absence of thought," which may lead to wickedness or allow it perpetuate. Welz (2018) argues that Nachdenken, or thinking about one's deeds, relationships, and events happening may be an antidote for the banality of evil. In our discussion of downward academic mobbing, such critical self- and other-awareness may be an antidote to the passive evil of silent acquiescence to administrative bullying.

Many people remember social psychologist Phillip Zimbardo for his classic study of destructive obedience in the Stanford Prison Experiment. Certainly, destructive obedience to malignant workplace norms is related to our discussion of passive evil in the context of downward academic mobbing, however another area of Zimbardo's scholarship, for which he is less well known, is even more relevant to this exploration. This area involves his investigation of institutionalized evil as it manifested itself in the administration of the Abu Ghraib prison in Iraq, as well as other workplace settings; these manifestations are described in detail in his (2007) book titled *The Lucifer Effect*. Zimbardo (2007) spends ample effort discussing the evil acts (e.g., beatings, torture, humiliation, rape) perpetrated on the Abu Ghraib prisoners, however he also focuses considerable attention on those who watched or were aware of what was being done, but said or did nothing to stop it. He also writes at length about the experience of Joseph Darby, who was the "whistle-blower" that provided evidence which sparked the investigation. Instead of being hailed as a hero for exposing human rights violations, Darby was shunned, pilloried as a traitor, and received death threats for his efforts (Zimbardo, 2007). This case may seem extreme, however Zimbardo (2007) argues that the institutionalized evil of inaction is common, involving perpetrators, victims, and observers "who know what is going on and do not intervene to help or challenge the evil and thereby enable it to persist by their inaction" (p. 317). Illustratively, he provides some examples in other workplace settings:

It is the good cops who never oppose the brutality of their buddies beating up minorities on the street or in the back room of the station house. It was the good bishops and cardinals who covered over the sins of their predatory parish priests because of their overriding concern for the image of the Catholic Church. They knew what was wrong and did nothing to really confront that evil, thereby enabling these pederasts to continue sinning for years on end (Zimbardo, 2007, p. 318).

Perhaps the foremost author on forms of passive evil that occur specifically in educational contexts is Samier (2008), who provided an excellent overview of the philosophical and ethical considerations in both administrative and passive evil in educational settings. She begins with several quotes on the consequences of passive evil, including one attributed to German Lutheran pastor and concentration camp survivor Martin Niemoller:

In Germany they first came for the Communists, and I didn't speak up because I wasn't a Communist. Then they came for the Jews, and I didn't speak up because I wasn't a Jew. Then they came for the trade unionists, and I didn't speak up because I wasn't a trade unionist. Then they came for the Catholics, and I didn't speak up because I was a Protestant. Then they came for me, and by that time no one was left to speak up (Samier, 2008, p. 2).

This quote is perhaps the best possible summary of the nature of passive evil, because it highlights the unthinking self-centeredness of it all. At its core, passive evil is acceptance of massive wrongdoing provided it does not directly harm oneself. However, as Samier (2008) articulated, there is much more to passive evil than that. It would be far too easy to think of passive evil as only unthinking self-centeredness. Engaging in passive evil requires choices. One of the choices is to deceive oneself to accept that the evildoers, as administrators or leaders of some supposedly morally legitimate bureaucracy (whether a government, a military, or a university), have the right to act as they do, even (or perhaps especially) when it harms undeserving victims. Another is avoidance, often of both the perpetrator and the victim. Several of the avoidance techniques articulated by Samier (2008) are paraphrased below:

1. Rationalizing that the perpetrator will not always be in his or her position and disregarding the personal and professional damage he or she will cause in the meantime ("She won't be here forever…it's best to just ride this out!")
2. Infantilizing the perpetrator as too emotional or hypersensitive, and therefore somehow excusing the damage he or she causes ("That's just how Jim is!")
3. Inflicting or focusing on suffering within oneself ("I've lost so much sleep over this!") but doing nothing to meaningfully address the problem or protect the victim
4. Avoiding the victim so as to not know about the (often gory) details of the persecution, as this enables one to feign ignorance about the seriousness of the situation and therefore feel morally uncompelled to act ("If only I had known!")

Samier (2008) makes it quite clear that engaging in passive evil is, in many respects, less passive than it seems. It requires an abdication of moral responsibility—a process social psychologist Bandura (1990; as discussed in Samier, 2008) referred to as "selective moral disengagement." Several key ways people engage in this process are known as moral justification, euphemistic labeling, and dehumanization. In the context of a downward academic mobbing episode, moral justification could involve justifying the punishment of a professor who complained about policy violations and lack of due process because he or she was "standing in the way of progress," or "reducing efficiency" or "being unreasonable" by demanding that policy be followed. In essence, it involves justifying the evil (as unfortunate as it may be) as necessary for "the good of the organization." In the same context, euphemistic labeling could involve stripping away the emotion from the mobbing as an act of interpersonal aggression, by referring instead to a sanitized euphemism such as "a disciplinary action." Dehumanization involves distancing oneself from the victim as a human being morally undeserving of maltreatment by discussing the act of mobbing in technical or economic terms (e.g., "He was just another cog in the wheel..."). In all cases, selective moral disengagement is a self-protective process that allows ordinarily caring people to commit passive evil.

Passive evil creates harm primarily through two separate but interrelated mechanisms. The first is that it causes irreparable, *additional* damage to the victim—in our case, the faculty member who has already been personally and professionally devastated through active evil (i.e., downward academic mobbing). Second, and much closer to the major thrust of this chapter, is that *it encourages further acts of mobbing* (Meiyun, Huawei, & Guoan, 2014). Because the personal harm caused by the passive evil has sometimes been described as being as great or greater than the mobbing itself, it warrants discussion here before embarking on the more targeted thesis. A number of researchers focusing on workplace bullying and downward mobbing from the perspective of the victim have noted the existential shock, epic disappointment, and sense of intimate, relational betrayal victims experience when their colleagues—many of whom they have known, helped, and cared for over the course of years—fail to support them, or even acknowledge what happened to them, after they have been bullied or mobbed (Hodgins & McNamara, 2017).

One common feature of downward mobbing, and one that perhaps encourages passive evil, is that the perpetrator deliberately uses victim isolation as part of the mobbing strategy (Hodgins & McNamara, 2017; Scott, 2018). Frequently, victims are banned from meetings, forbidden to communicate with colleagues, or in extreme cases have their workspaces physically relocated to secluded locations where they are unlikely to have contact with others in their workgroup. In such cases, it is perhaps more understandable that mobbing witnesses do not provide much social or material support. However, more often witnesses simply withdraw from or avoid communicating with the victim even though they are proximally near, depriving the victim of the types of supports that are known the mediate the harmful effects of bullying (and by doing so, magnify the negative health and emotional consequences of their victimization; Scott, 2018; Zapf, Knorz, & Kulla, 1996). Both the mobbing and the social isolation lead to what Lewis and Oxford (2005), based on interviews of 10 mobbing victims, characterized as a ripple effect—cascading, expanding waves of life disruption resulting from the damage inflicted on the victim. A quote from one of their respondents is particularly poignant: "They [employers] have dashed everything, they've just destroyed everything, and its had a terrible ripple effect, my daughters, my daughter in law, my son, my sisters, my friends, its affected" (Lewis & Oxford, 2005, p. 37). The same respondent later stated, "They've [employers] shattered everything that I have ever believed in, that I have ever worked to try and put right. The relationship with colleagues, the relationship with family, my whole reasoning, everything" (Lewis & Oxford, 2005, p. 40). What is left unsaid is that had the respondent's colleagues had the courage/or and moral fiber to protect him or her, the ripple effect that 'shattered' the victim's life and relationships may have been avoided or at the very least dramatically attenuated. Through their lack of fortitude and moral disengagement, they not only sanctioned the damage, they intensified it. Such, it seems, is always the case with passive evil.

HOW PASSIVE EVIL HELPS PERPETUATE FUTURE MOBBING

As noted in the previous section, the literature on passive evil seems quite clear that many people who engage in it do so because it is thought to be self-protective. The thinking seems to be that if one does not directly engage the active evildoer(s), then he or she will be safe from personal victimization himself or herself. Such thinking is clearly lazy, shortsighted and craven, however, it seems it would be at least somewhat justifiable (e.g., as an evolutionary survival mechanism) if it was often accurate. However, as the earlier quote attributed to Niemoller attests, feigning ignorance and bearing passive witness to evil is not often protective; it may delay personal victimization, but it certainly does not guarantee safety. It does, however, ensure that there will be more victims before the evil runs its course (if/when it ever does). In the next section of the chapter, the authors present the argument that selective moral disengagement and all other forms of passive evil perpetuate active evil through assuring the perpetrators that he/she/they can act with impunity.

One of the primary reasons that bearing silent witness to downward academic mobbing perpetuates further mobbing is that perpetrators—experiencing no negative consequences for their unethical behavior—come to see mobbing as a successful management strategy. In fact, they may not even recognize that their behavior is widely considered pathological. As Piotrowski and King (2016) noted, "many supervisors... consider their domineering and controlling management style as laudatory" (p. 301); this manner of thinking is referred to as 'moral inversion' (Adams, 2011). As such, administrative bullies engage in downward mobbing because it works: They disparage and damage the victim (often a model faculty member and the only one with the courage to stand up to them; Khoo, 2010) so as to silence him or her, cow the witnesses, and face no consequences for doing it (Parker, 2014). Thus, it seems an efficient strategy (and in particularly toxic organizations, may even be rewarded by equally destructive superiors; Lutgen-Sandvik & Tracy, 2011; Parker, 2014; Piotrowski & King, 2016). This type of efficiency must seem attractive to unethical, corporate-minded mid-level academic administrators, as the traditional university environment—valuing considerable shared governance that encourages faculty members to be meaningfully involved in decision making processes—likely seems "too slow" to them and, when administrators participate in such shared governance, they sometimes have to compromise or accept not being able to "get what they want." Thus, frequently downward academic mobbing is often initiated *precisely to intimidate the faculty as a whole* and *discourage them from engaging in their rights to shared governance*; in this respect, destroying a particular victim's career and personal health is not necessarily the goal but rather a convenient means to an end (Vega & Comer, 2005).

Another reason that faculty witnesses' engagement in passive evil perpetuates future mobbing is that if the faculty (often with their union and/or legal representatives) will not confront the bully, it is very likely that Human Resources (HR) staff and/or higher-level university administrators (e.g., vice presidents, provosts, and presidents) will not do so, either. One of the most disheartening findings in many published studies on downward academic mobbing is that university HR departments, in particular, are not only unhelpful to victims (either by failing to recognize the mobbing or mismanaging the cases brought before them) but in many cases *actually protect and assist* unethical administrators in their framing and abuse of targets (Barratt-Pugh & Krestlica, 2018; Catley, Blackwood, Forsyth, Tappin, & Bentley, 2017; Hodgins & McNamara, 2017; Parker, 2014). In his excellent commentary, Adams (2011) argued that modern organizations, especially those with hierarchical structures and diffused/fragmented roles, responsibilities, and sources of information, are particularly prone to administrative evil and the cannibalization of their workers (for further discussion of how organizational attributes relate to supervisory bullying, see also Roscigno, Lopez, & Hodson, 2009). To the extent that universities continue to be infused (or infected) with corporate values, and university employees are viewed simply as means of production (Adams, 2011), faculty can sadly expect more mobbing from their mid-level administrators, and less help and protection from HR professionals and their higher-level administrators.

Many universities make at least a pretense of protecting their employees from adverse treatment, however it is difficult to discern how much of this is 'window-dressing.' As noted earlier, there is a shameful lack of institutional action against administrative bullies (indeed, sources such as Barratt-Pugh & Krestelica [2018] and Namie [2017] report that less than 3% of reported cases involve any action against perpetrators). In those rare cases in which there is a genuine organizational intention to stop bullying, there is often little success in doing so—for when universities have policies against bullying, in the absence of willingness to enforce them, these policies themselves will be violated and therefore have no value at all (indeed, as McDonald et al. [2018] recently noted, one of the most common reasons that unethical mid-level administrators engage in downward academic mobbing is to punish faculty who protested the fact that the administrators were violating a policy in the first place). Barratt-Pugh and Kreselica (2018) argue that nothing less than an organizational culture change, which could (and should) be initiated from upper levels of university administration, is likely to serve as an institutional deterrent to downward academic mobbing. In a similar vein, Duffy (2009) noted:

In workplaces characterized by fear and mutual mistrust, low morale, high levels of competitiveness, lack of operational openness and transparency, poorly disseminated and understood organizational structure and policies, and limited opportunities for innovation, tacking on an antimobbing or antibullying policy to this already dismal mix is unlikely to result in the desired outcomes of preventing and reducing mobbing behaviors and their devastating impact on victims. (p. 249)

A third reason that passive evil leads to further mobbing is related to the last, though it goes considerably beyond. It has been established that organizations will typically not stop the bully (and may actually reward him or her). Some people who morally disengage and allow a colleague to be bullied may do so because they make one of the most common errors in bully perception—they assume the bullying is the result of a "personality clash" between two people (albeit an unbalanced one, with one person [the bully] with the power to harm, and the other [the victim] without) and that the bullying will end as soon as the victim is silenced, quits the place of employment, or succumbs to mental exhaustion (or takes his or her own life; as Pompili et al. [2008] demonstrated, bullied employees have a considerably elevated rate of suicide). They fail to understand that bullying is a process and a strategy, and that *bullies will not stop bullying under their own volition*. As discussed earlier, bullies tend to be competitive, domineering, amoral, arrogant, and entitled people (Glendinning, 2001; Young, 2017). They enjoy power and they enjoy abusing it, and they also enjoy abusing subordinates, whom they legitimately perceive as inferior to themselves (Glendinning, 2001). Because they enjoy what they are doing and they believe it makes them look powerful, they will continue their behavior until it is stopped by others. Because selective moral disengagement—as a form of passive evil—will not stop them, active resistance and a concerted effort by the victim and his or her colleagues is the only appropriate response.

CONCLUSION

Workplace bullying is, sadly, a highly common phenomenon. Bullying in academia—often known as downward academic mobbing—appears the most common manifestation of all workplace bullying. Given that bullying creates a toxic work environment, and causes adverse outcomes for targets (including mental and physical health problems, as well as early death), witnesses, and the workplace itself, it is important to combat it with all strategies available.

In this chapter, it has been made clear that up to the present, very little success has been achieved in combating downward academic mobbing. The main premise of the chapter is that much of the lack of success can be attributed to the passive evil perpetrated by faculty colleagues who observe unethical mid-level administrators bully and mob one of their own (in most cases, the most principled, accomplished, and courageous among them), and do nothing (or in some cases, due either to their own lack of scruples or in an effort for personal gain, join in the mobbing). This calls the question: How does one exhort colleagues, who clearly default toward selective moral disengagement, to act in defense of each other (or even—because it is clear that bullies will not stop and will typically find new victims in the future—in proactive defense of themselves)? Directly asking others to have courage is not likely to be an effective strategy. Other ways seem necessary, and in this final section of the chapter, several possible ways will be discussed.

One potentially promising avenue for combating academic mobbing is to communicate to faculty members just how prevalent—and how damaging—the problem is. It seems likely that many faculty members are not aware that the higher education sector is the one in which bullying and mobbing is most likely to occur. As noted earlier, many witnesses to bullying/mobbing make a fundamental error in perceiving bullying and mobbing to be isolated events, often occurring as the result of a "personality clash" between bullies and their victims, rather than understanding bullying as a frequently used management strategy adopted by toxic leaders to devastate dissenters and intimidate witnesses (thereby discouraging future dissent). If faculty members were able and willing to recognize this, it seems they might be more willing to defend victims and collectively confront bullies, if not out of moral strength or genuine compassion for the victim, at least out of a drive for self-preservation (i.e., to reduce the likelihood the bullies target them in the future). One way to communicate the prevalence and perniciousness of downward academic mobbing would be for local chapters of the AAUP and unions to hold highly advertised campus workshops on these topics. Excellent resources exist through organizations such as The Workplace Bullying Institute (WBI; www.workplacebullying.org), which offers online resources, support, intensive training, victim coaching, and other valuable services; one particularly attractive feature of the WBI is that its founders, Drs. Gary and Ruth Namie, are among the foremost authors on workplace bullying and, as they have both worked widely in academic settings, know mobbing in this sector well. The axiom "Knowledge is power" may not fully apply with respect to fighting passive evil (as passive evildoers are known to self-deceive and feign ignorance about what is happening around them), however, disseminating knowledge certainly seems a good place to start.

Trade organizations also have an important role to play in combating downward academic mobbing. "There is strength in numbers" is another axiom, and it seems to apply more fully in the present context. One of the ways academic bullies work is through systematically eliminating (Namie & Namie, 2011; Parker, 2014) whom they perceive to be dissenters—that is, they attempt to "pick them off" one at a time (from an efficiency standpoint, eliminating only one and intimidating all others is almost certainly the preferred outcome, however, if other dissenters emerge they are typically targeted in succession). Local AAUP and union chapters, if they act immediately and call attention at the first sign of mobbing, can fight passive evil by correctly characterizing the mobbing as "a methodological crusade of interpersonal destruction" (Parker, 2014, p. 171) and 'circling the wagons,' so to speak, for a common defense. Most trade organizations have legal defense funds, and many will help identify or employ labor/employment legal firms that specialize in fighting workplace bullying. Of course, it would be desirable to handle bullying/mobbing incidences within the university, however, as it has been demonstrated here, university HR departments and higher-level administrators have, at least historically, defended or abetted the bullies and ignored or disparaged their victims (WBI, n.d.). As a result, collective action among faculty members and the use of off-campus resources may often be necessary to stop/punish occurrences of downward academic mobbing.

One other way that faculty, perhaps working in unison with members of trade organizations, could work to decrease the prevalence of downward academic mobbing, is to be very active in the recruitment and selection of mid-level academic administrators (Sepler, 2015). Typically, these processes are dominated by higher-level administrators and HR personnel, who often exercise almost exclusive control over the search processes (e.g., use of a search firm) and the questions asked of candidates (Glendinning, 2001). Faculty members must (again, perhaps through their trade organizations so as not to make themselves individual targets for bullying) agitate for an active role in screening candidates and for the inclusion of language in the position description that makes clear that bullies need not apply. As Flynn (1999) noted (cited in Glendinning, 2001):

To begin with, make sure job descriptions include treating employees in a dignified and appropriate manner. Include behaviors that won't be tolerated, and hold them accountable for turnover. This not only makes the company's stance very clear, but it emphasizes the importance of treating people well. Once the job description includes behavior, HR can effectively reward or discipline managers through performance reviews. (p. 283)

During the interview itself, questions should be crafted that ask directly about mobbing behaviors, in an effort to ferret out potential bullies. Finally, faculty members should be involved in the process of checking references (Flynn, 1999), with a special focus on learning about how candidates handle conflict and their level of respect for meaningful faculty involvement in shared governance. Through these processes, faculty may be able to reduce the likelihood that bullies enter the university in the first place (Sepler, 2015).

A more systemic way to combat workplace bullying and mobbing is to address these problems at the legislative level. According to the WBI (n.d.), unlike some other countries, the U.S. does not have a national law providing legal protections against workplace bullying (several states, fortunately, are working on their own laws), and as such, according to Duffy (2009), victims "must rely on organizations to 'do the right thing' in the event of complaints of mobbing and bullying" (p. 242). As has been demonstrated, most universities have historically not "done the right thing," and regardless of whether they have internal policies against bullying, they have generally been consistent in "doing the *wrong* thing" by ignoring or further damaging victims and defending or abetting their bullies (WBI, n.d.). Compliance with a state or national law would be a stronger inducement to avoid bullying for unethical mid-level academic administrators than following an internal policy—especially given that most internal policies on employee behaviors do not specifically address bullying/mobbing (Duffy, 2009) and that unethical administrators seem almost compulsive policy violators themselves (McDonald et al., 2018). The Healthy Workplace Bill (WBI, n.d.), championed by the WBI and a host of others, may be the best step forward to compel universities to take bullying and mobbing seriously, as it has clear consequences, not only for employers but also for the individual perpetrators themselves (see Table 2).

Downward academic mobbing is a major problem; it appears to be the most common form of workplace bullying in existence. It is perpetuated largely by the passive evil of faculty colleagues who could collectively confront it, decreasing the future likelihood that it happens to others as well as themselves. Fortunately, bullying and mobbing can be stopped. It requires courage and character, however through the organizational, legal, and legislative strategies discussed here, perhaps future academic settings will be largely free of the toxic climate and personal and professional harm so many faculty members experience today.

Table 2.

Summary of Proposed Benefits of the Healthy Workplace Bill (HWB) for Employers and Workers, <u>as Well as What Negative Consequences it Will Not Cause</u>

What the Healthy Workplace Bill Does for Employers
1. Precisely defines an "abusive workplace environment" – it is a high standard for misconduct
2. Requires proof of health harm by licensed health or mental health professionals
3. Protects conscientious employers from vicarious liability risk when internal correction and prevention mechanisms are in effect
4. Gives employers the reason to terminate or sanction offenders
5. Requires plaintiffs to use private attorneys
6. Plugs the gaps in current state and federal civil rights protections

What the Healthy Workplace Bill Does for Workers
1. Provides an avenue for legal redress for health harming cruelty at work
2. Allows you to sue the bully as an individual
3. Holds the employer accountable
4. Seeks restoration of lost wages and benefits
5. Compels employers to prevent and correct future instances

What the Healthy Workplace Bill Does Not Do
1. Involve state agencies to enforce any provisions of the law
2. Incur costs for adopting states
3. Require plaintiffs to be members of protected status groups (it is "status-blind")
4. Use the term "workplace bullying"

Note. Source: http://healthyworkplacebill.org/bill/

REFERENCES

Adams, G. B. (2011). The problem of administrative evil in a culture of technical rationality. *Public Integrity, 13*, 275-285. doi:10.2753PIN1099-9922130307

Adams, G. B., & Balfour, D. L. (2009). *Unmasking administrative evil* (3rd ed.). Armonk, NY: M. E. Sharpe.

American Association of University Professors. (2015a). *Ensuring academic freedom in politically controversial academic personnel decisions. In AAUP policy documents and reports* (pp. 32–36). Baltimore, MD: Johns Hopkins Press.

American Association of University Professors. (2015b). *On collegiality as a criterion for faculty evaluation: 2016 revision. In AAUP policy documents and reports* (pp. 227–228). Baltimore, MD: Johns Hopkins Press.

American Association of University Professors. (2015c). *On the relationship of faculty governance to academic freedom. In AAUP policy documents and reports* (pp. 123–125). Baltimore, MD: Johns Hopkins Press.

Arendt, H. (1963). *Eichmann in Jerusalem: A report on the banality of evil.* New York, NY: Viking Press.

Arendt, H. (1978). *The Jew as pariah - Jewish identity and politics in the modern age.* New York, NY: Grove Press.

Bandura, A. (1990). Mechanisms of moral disengagement. In W. Reich (Ed.), *Origins of terrorism: Psychologies, ideologies, theologies, states of mind* (pp. 161–191). Cambridge, UK: Cambridge University Press.

Barrett-Pugh, L. G. B., & Krestelica, D. (2018). Bullying in higher education: Culture change requires more than policy. *Perspectives: Policy and Practice in Higher Education*. doi:10.1080/13603108.2018.1502211

Beckmann, C. A., Cannella, B. L., & Wantland, D. (2013). Faculty perception of bullying in schools of nursing. *Journal of Professional Nursing, 29*(5), 287–294. doi:10.1016/j.profnurs.2012.05.012 PMID:24075262

Brodsky, C. M. (1976). *The harassed worker.* Toronto, Canada: Lexington Books.

Catley, B., Blackwood, K., Forsyth, D., Tappin, D., & Bentley, T. (2017). Workplace bullying complaints: Lessons for "good HR practice.". *Personnel Review, 46*(1), 100–114. doi:10.1108/PR-04-2015-0107

Davenport, N. (2013). *Hannah Arendt: Battling the banality of evil*. Retrieved from https://www.spiked-online.com/2013/10/07/hannah-arendt-battling-the-banality-of-evil/

Duffy, M. (2009). Preventing workplace mobbing and bullying with effective organizational consultation, policies, and legislation. *Consulting Psychology Journal: Practice and Research, 61*(3), 242–262. doi:10.1037/a0016578

Duffy, M., & Sperry, L. (2007). Workplace mobbing: Individual and family health consequences. *The Family Journal (Alexandria, Va.), 15*(4), 398–404. doi:10.1177/1066480707305069

Einarsen, S., Hoel, H., & Notelaers, G. (2009). Measuring exposure to bullying and harassment at work: Validity, factor structure, and psychometric properties of the Negative Acts Questionnaire-Revised. *Work and Stress, 23*(1), 24–44. doi:10.1080/02678370902815673

Faria, J. R., Mixon, F. G. Jr, & Salter, S. P. (2012). An economic model of workplace mobbing in academe. *Economics of Education Review, 31*(5), 720–726. doi:10.1016/j.econedurev.2012.04.004

Flynn, G. (1999). Stop toxic managers before they stop you. *Workforce, 78*, 40–45.

Glendinning, P. M. (2001). Workplace bullying: Curing the cancer of the American workplace. *Public Personnel Management, 30*(3), 269–286. doi:10.1177/009102600103000301

Healthy Workplace Bill. (n.d.). *Healthy Workplace Bill*. Retrieved from http://healthyworkplacebill.org/

Hodgins, M., & McNamara, P. M. (2017). Bullying and incivility in higher education workplaces: Micropolitics and the abuse of power. *Qualitative Research in Organizations and Management, 12*(3), 190–206. doi:10.1108/QROM-03-2017-1508

Khoo, S. B. (2010). Academic mobbing: Hidden health hazard at workplace. *Malaysian Family Physician, 5*, 61–67. PMID:25606190

Lewis, S. E., & Oxford, J. (2005). Women's experiences of workplace bullying: Changes in social relationships. *Journal of Community & Applied Social Psychology, 15*(1), 29–47. doi:10.1002/casp.807

Leymann, H. (1993). *Mobbing: Psychoterror am arbeitsplatz und wie man sich dagegen wehren kann* [Mobbing: Psycho-terror in the workplace and how one can defend against it]. Hamburg, Germany: Rowolht.

Lutgen-Sandvik, P., & Tracy, S. J. (2011). Answering five key questions about workplace bullying: How communication scholarship provides thought leadership for transforming abuse at work. *Management Communication Quarterly*, *26*(1), 3–47. doi:10.1177/0893318911414400

McDonald, T. W., Stockton, J. D., & Landrum, R. E. (2018). Civility and academic freedom: Who defines the former (and how) may imperil rights to the latter. *The College Quarterly*, *21*. Retrieved from http://collegequarterly.ca/2018-vol21-num01-winter/civility-and-academic-freedom-who-defines-the-former-and-how-may-imperil-rights-to-the-latter.html

Meiyun, F. U., Huawei, M. A., & Guoan, Y. U. E. (2014). Bystanders in workplace bullying: Roles, behaviors, and influence mechanism. *Advances in Psychological Science*, *22*(6), 987–994. doi:10.3724/SP.J.1042.2014.00987

Metzger, A. M., Petit, A., & Sieber, S. (2015). Mentoring as a way to change a culture of academic bullying and mobbing in the humanities. *Higher Education for the Future*, *2*(2), 139–150. doi:10.1177/2347631115584119

Namie, G. (2017). *Workplace Bullying Institute U.S. Workplace Bullying Survey: September 2007 report*. Retrieved from http://workplacebullying.org/multi/pdf/WBIsurvey2007.pdf

Namie, G., & Namie, R. (2003). *The bully at work: What you can do to stop the hurt and reclaim your dignity on the job*. Naperville, IL: Sourcebooks.

Namie, G., & Namie, R. (2011). *The bully-free workplace: Stop jerks, weasels and snakes from killing your organization*. Hoboken, NJ: John Wiley and Sons, Inc.

Parker, K. A. (2014). The workplace bully: The ultimate silencer. *Journal of Organizational Culture, Communications, and Conflict*, *18*, 169–185.

Pheko, M. M. (2018a). Authethnography and cognitive adaptation: Two powerful buffers against the negative consequences of workplace bullying and academic mobbing. *International Journal of Qualitative Studies on Health and Well-being*, *13*(1), 1–12. doi:10.1080/17482631.2018.1459134 PMID:29667923

Pheko, M. M. (2018b). Rumors and gossip as tools of social undermining and social dominance in workplace bullying and mobbing practice: A closer look at perceived perpetrator motives. *Journal of Human Behavior in the Social Environment*, *28*(4), 449–465. doi:10.1080/10911359.2017.1421111

Piotrowski, C., & King, C. (2016). The enigma of adult bullying in higher education: A research-based conceptual framework. *Education*, *136*, 299–306.

Pompili, M., Lester, D., Innamorati, M., De Pisa, E., Iliceto, P., Puccinno, M., ... Girardi, P. (2008). Suicide risk and exposure to mobbing. *Work (Reading, Mass.)*, *31*, 237–243. PMID:18957741

Prevost, C., & Hunt, E. (2018). Bullying and mobbing in academe: A literature review. *European Scientific Journal*, *14*(8), 1–15. doi:10.19044/esj.2018.v14n8p1

Roscigno, V. J., Lopez, S. H., & Hodson, R. (2009). Supervisory bullying, status inequalities, and organizational context. *Social Forces*, *87*(3), 1561–1581. doi:10.1353of.0.0178

Samier, E. (2008). The problem of passive evil in educational administration: Moral implications of doing nothing. *International Studies in Educational Administration*, *36*, 2–21.

Scott, H. S. (2018). Extending the Duluth Model to workplace bullying: A modification and adaptation of the Workplace Power-Control Wheel. *Workplace Health & Safety*, *66*(9), 444–452. doi:10.1177/2165079917750934 PMID:29582701

Sepler, F. (2015). Workplace bullying: What it is and what to do about it. *Journal of Collective Bargaining in the Academy, 0*. Retrieved from http://thekeep.eiu.edu/jcba/vol0/iss10/42

Thomas, A. (2009). Internal grievance imperatives for universities. *African Journal of Business Ethics*, *4*, 25–36.

Twale, D. J., & De Luca, B. M. (2008). *Faculty incivility: The rise of the academic bully culture and what to do about it*. San Francisco, CA: Jossey-Bass.

Vega, G., & Comer, D. R. (2005). Sticks and stones may break your bones, but words can break your spirit: Bullying in the workplace. *Journal of Business Ethics*, *58*(1-3), 101–109. doi:10.100710551-005-1422-7

Vuger, D. (2017). Incubation of evil: Evil as the problem of human thinking and praxis. *Synthesis Philosophica*, *32*(1), 51–66. doi:10.21464p32104

Welz, C. (2018). Facing the problem of evil: Visual, verbal, and mental images of (in)humanity. *Scandinavian Jewish Studies*, *29*, 62–78.

Westhues, K. (2005). *Workplace mobbing in academe: Reports from twenty universities*. London, UK: Mellen Press.

Westhues, K. (2006). *The envy of excellence: Administrative mobbing of high-achieving professors*. Lewiston, NY: Edwin Mellon Press.

Workplace Bullying Institute. (n.d.). *Why U.S. employers do so little*. Retrieved from https://www.workplacebullying.org/individuals/problem/employer-reaction/

Young, K. Z. (2017, Spring). Workplace bullying in higher education: The misunderstood academicus. *Practical Anthropology*, *39*(2), 14–17. doi:10.17730/0888-4552.39.2.14

Zapf, D., Knorz, C., & Kulla, M. (1996). On the relationship between mobbing factors, and job content, social work environment, and health outcomes. *European Journal of Work and Organizational Psychology*, *5*(2), 215–237. doi:10.1080/13594329608414856

Zimbardo, P. (2007). *The Lucifer Effect: Understanding how good people turn evil*. New York, NY: Random House.

Section 2
Organizational Culture and Leadership Accountability

The organizational culture is analyzed, including individual, administrative and operationalized structural contributing factors.

Chapter 4
Narcissistic and Sociopathic Leadership and the World of Higher Education:
A Place for Mentoring, Not Mobbing

David B. Ross
Nova Southeastern University, USA

Cortney E. Matteson
Orange County School District, USA

Melissa T. Sasso
Nova Southeastern University, USA

Rande W. Matteson
Nova Southeastern University, USA

ABSTRACT

This chapter was designed to explore mobbing and bullying within higher education. This chapter per the researchers revealed the theoretical framework, the schema of people making versus bullying and mobbing, as well as differentiating between bullying and mobbing. Moreover, an array of examples of types of dark leadership and toxicity was provided. Furthermore, the researchers felt it was imperative to include the organizational culture applied to bullying and mobbing, in addition to the emphasis of counterproductive behavior. Also, the physiological and psychological impact on individuals under that leadership was provided as well as bullying and mobbing case studies. Preventative measures of bullying and mobbing within all levels was discussed and included a solution such as the TSTL survey created by Dr. David B. Ross. Lastly, a conclusion was provided.

DOI: 10.4018/978-1-5225-9485-7.ch004

Copyright © 2020, IGI Global. Copying or distributing in print or electronic forms without written permission of IGI Global is prohibited.

INTRODUCTION

Sticks and stones may break our bones, but words will never hurt us. This is a very well-known phrase that our parents and teachers would tell us when our classmates attempted to or succeeded at hurting us by means of bullying. From young, we were taught to ignore the venom that spewed from individuals whose sole objective was to harm us in any way, shape, or form. We all assumed that this form of misbehavior would end sometime in elementary or even high school, but who would ever imagine that this would continue to follow us as adults, and in the work-field, more specifically, the higher education field.

Many individuals write fables and comedy about bullying, mobbing, inflicting pain, and hurting people physically and emotionally. There must be a truth to this, as there is always a lesson to be learned with each story told. In comedy, we laugh at it to take our minds off of it, as it is a way of getting away from reality. Dating back to Plato's *The Republic*, it was known to be acceptable to laugh at others, in order to feel superior (Guardian News, 2007). More specifically, Plato felt that when individuals laughed at others' misfortunes, it was inappropriate. As time progressed toward the Middle Ages, individuals ridiculed those who were physically impaired, such as dwarfism, and a person who suffered from Kyphosis (i.e., roundback, a hunchback). This form of ridiculing continued into the Victorian Era where individuals laughed at those who were mentally ill and who were committed to psychiatric institutions (Guardian News, 2007). A certain Aesop fable, for example, can prove this point, such as the frog and the scorpion (Aesop's Fable, 2011). For instance, the scorpion needed to get to the other side of the river; however, he could not swim. The scorpion then befriended the frog, who did not trust the scorpion. After pleading with the frog for a long period, the frog finally gave in and agreed to take the scorpion to the other side with the understanding not to sting and kill the frog. Once the scorpion and frog arrived at the other side of the river, the scorpion stung the frog and killed him. The moral of the fable is to be careful of whom you trust as they could sting you and/or bully you into doing them a favor. This is the same in the workplace, where people will promise you one thing and bully you the next; this is frequent behavior as the workplace is full of competition and jealousy and will undercut you to seek favor (Aesop's Fable, 2011).

Although, it must be stressed that bullying and mobbing do not solely occur within the higher education field (Matteson, 2002; Sasso, 2017). A study conducted by Sasso (2017) illustrated narcissistic leadership in all fields, whereas a study conducted by Matteson (2002) focused on mobbing and bullying within the federal government.

Narcissistic and Sociopathic Leadership and the World of Higher Education

Based on the information given, let us take a look at a story that occurred within the National Football League. Richie Incognito, a professional sports player, along with two other teammates were accused of bullying behavior toward another player within their own team (Schefter & Walker, 2014). This behavior of harassment included racial insults and other forms of verbal abuse and bullying/mobbing, especially towards his family members, mainly his mother and sister. Incognito, who was later traded to another team, displayed a pattern in that he continued with his malfeasance for bullying another player. Years later, Incognito was named as an ambassador to an anti-bullying nonprofit group *Boo2Bullying* as he felt he could help with this epidemic as he has had experience as a person who bullied and was bullied (Rodak, 2018). There can be change among individuals regarding this type of behavior, which is enlightening, especially in many professionals who are seen as role models.

Within the professional sports profession, Burgess Owens, a former NFL player and motivational speaker, wrote a book on Liberalism and the Feminization of Young Males who are linked into the *Queen Bee Theory* where very dominate female structures have proven adverse outcomes to young males through various tactics, including the theory of shame/guilt to force compliance to their standards of behavior. Heim, Murphy, and Golant (2003) mentioned that the Queen Bee Syndrome is a characterized behavior that illustrates when a senior positioned individual distances themselves from their junior-positioned counterpart. Paradigm shifts in culture and society are clear as Owens (2016) made a statement that young men should be aware of the power and influences that surround them and their peers. Owens suggested young people look up to people of influence and are continually seeking examples of role models and mentors to help them along their journey in life. The researchers from this book chapter put forth the argument that absent scientific and data that is definitive human behavior is much a product of learning from others as opposed to being biologically influenced. Mixed up core values and learning poor behavior, such as bullying and mobbing, derails positive modeling or mentoring (Owens, 2016).

The researchers of this book chapter suggest higher education is not so much different in its overall concept to most private sector businesses and find each has a requirement to produce revenue and behavioral outcomes, or otherwise each will cease to exist. However, strategically, higher education aligns its mission and operational outcomes to many other types of structured organizations and each share similar concepts and struggles among all shareholders. In this chapter, the data will extrapolate information from a variety of sources to provide a foundation whereas the reader can adapt various modalities to construct improved leadership in higher education. Regardless of the origin, the organization or group within higher education that is infected with bullying and mobbing behaviors is so costly that we should demand a positive change. The public educational system in the United States obtains its funding from tax dollars and is by far one the most expensive programs of all social systems today. Private education and those institutions are largely funded by both private and some public monies via special programs. Therefore, it seems logical we conclude that these organizations should be accountable and structured and lead by authentic and competent leadership (Corsi-Bunker, n.d.).

For this chapter, the researchers will focus on mobbing and bullying within the higher education field. Readers will embark on a journey that starts with the description of the theoretical framework, followed by a literature review that will encompass bullying and mobbing, the myriad forms of toxic and dark leadership, the organizational culture and how it is applied to bullying and mobbing. Furthermore, the emphasis of counterproductive work behavior, the psychological and physiological impact on individuals under that type of leadership, applied relevant case studies, preventative measures of bullying and mobbing, and lastly the conclusion.

THEORETICAL FRAMEWORK

There are many theories to bullying and mobbing based upon the actions of the individual bully or the group/mob who bullies others (Duffy & Sperry, 2014; Heim, Murphy, & Golant, 2003; Namie & Namie, 2001). Various perspectives of relevant theoretical frameworks were investigated under which this chapter is presented. Since there are many concerns of bullying and mobbing in the workplace, these issues are detrimental to stress, health, workplace hazards, work productivity, and morale and unethical means of communication to ridicule and humiliate others. The following theoretical frameworks are discussed: (a) catastrophe theory, (b) social exchange theory, and (c) superiority theory. The theory based on the need to look at the phenomena of bullying and mobbing, which has a sudden shift in human behavior is the *Catastrophe Theory*. The catastrophe theory was created by Rene Thom who was a French mathematician in the 1960s, which was used regarding the evolution within nature, but also applied to social and biological sciences. This theory claims to be a method that deals with reality and the synthesis of two fundamental notions of science (e.g., idea of function, the idea of a dynamic system) (Thom, 1977).

George Homans who looked into social behavior and interactions of individuals designed the *Social Exchange Theory*. For this chapter regarding bullying and/or mobbing, the social exchange theory compares and contrasts an exchange between individuals and/or groups valuing the costs and benefits of that relationship (Ritzer & Smart, 2001). Many issues arise with the study of human interaction regarding this theory covers the costs versus the benefits; the costs are considered the negative aspects, while the benefits are the results of positive interactions (Cherry, 2018; Redmond, 2015). Expectations and comparison levels are vital by the influences of social expectations and any past involvements that were developed between individuals and/or groups. Evaluating the alternatives and the length of the relationship are also proven to be important if individuals want to reassess any interactions, especially with bullying and/or mobbing (Cherry, 2018; Redmond, 2015).

Under the philosophy of humor, where at times people use humor to ridicule others in a bullying/mobbing sense, the *Superiority Theory* plays a part in human interactions, especially when it is used to display power over others (Morreall, 2012). It is essential to recognize the elements of power being utilized when certain individuals feel they can control others; control is having power over people while influence is collaborating with others (Ross, 2008, 2017; Ross, Matteson, & Exposito, 2014). There are many other theories to investigate regarding the phenomena of bullying and/or mobbing in the workplace. Branch, Ramsay, and Barker (2013) found other theories that explain the unique characteristics, backgrounds, and experiences that influence certain behavior of people. These theories are noted as the *Affective Events Theory*, *Social Identity Theory*, and the *Social Rules Theory*.

The Schema of Peoplemaking vs. Bullying and Mobbing

There is little disagreement among scholars and human behavioral experts that almost any person can learn to become a bully (Duffy & Sperry, 2014; Namie & Namie, 2001). Although, an interesting topic that draws considerable discussion, there is no scientific data and research to make a substantial claim that human behavior is biological. Absent from this data, the researchers make the statement that human behavior is most probably learned. We can examine and complete investigations to pinpoint the exact schematic that a human follows and that rewires their brains. This is learned from a culture that believes that they are to act this way to get along with others. Sociopathic behavior is to fit into a culture no matter the negative behavior, which in turn can damage the other individual and motivate them to mistreat others. People making skills focuses that individuals want people to be productive in life, whether family or in organizations and have goals that meet and improve the organizational mission and vision. In her book titled *The New Peoplemaking*, Virginia Satir (1988) felt that communication is powerful and can create a nurturing situation for all stakeholders to succeed by assisting others. Virginia Satir designed a practical model that was focused on the entire person and that how that person can generate a transformational change within themselves, family, and the social life force that provides a drive for growth. In addition, people must be able to be responsible for all decisions and actions, understand that all people are of equal value, and it is acceptable to have differences as long as others respect one's individuality (Gomori, 2017; Yildirim, 2017).

A review of educational and business-focused educational and training programs specifically in concert with the large volume of textbooks and other learning modalities designed to develop people skills for roles as exemplary leaders can be deconstructed for a variety of reasons. Just because a person attends a prestige leadership program does not guarantee they have the necessary skills and temperament to lead. According to Harvard Professor Howard Gardner, as humans, a child can figure out how to manipulate its caregivers and situation(s) by the age of five. That same child continues to improve their ability to manipulate well into adulthood. Gardner has identified humans as having an ability to fluctuate behaviors through Multiple Intelligences when interacting among others (President and Fellows of Harvard College, 2017).

However, it is not yet accepted that we can say with complete certainty behaviors A+B+C equals a bully. Therefore, it is more probable to say the human that decides to use bullying as their method of operation, does so from a sum collection of their life's experiences and observations of other's behaviors. Given the choice or option on how a person chooses their style of behavior will require many years of critical review of countless amounts of data and human behavioral experiences. This process may be a waste of time because the individual chooses how to approach a situation using a dysfunctional form of situational leadership when they are unable to discern what style of leadership is appropriate for the particular situation for the desired outcome. Therefore, from a fallback position and levels of personal frustration can be explained for the use of bullying tactics. These choices may explain in part how the leader can fill a gap whereas critical thinking and sound leadership options may have become devoid of the inventory of choices for the leader.

These researchers from the book chapter assert based upon considerable research and review of data that a person who chooses to utilize mobbing tactics makes an intentional choice to act out their edicts via the process of autocratic directives. In other words, regardless of their backgrounds and educational training, they want to be in control regardless; therefore will take steps to assure they remain in control. We can describe the end game as trying to go along to get along among victims of mobbing because they may feel overwhelmed by tactics of the manipulative sycophant with few options. It is very probable for the researchers to suggest in our complex world today, that some people have not fully developed a layer of thick psychological skin and not let others' behaviors towards them cause them pain. Those who have difficulty in adapting to a conflict may feel helpless and choose to take their own lives seeking out some form of attention to stop the perceived mobbing behavior (Khoo, 2010). Completing psychological autopsies after the suicide become a difficult task that generally angers family members and close personal friends of the victim. The data can be misinterpreted and not reveal the most accurate reasons for the suicide. The World Health Organization records global suicide rates, according to the WHO, the United States has fewer suicides than Russia, Eastern Europe and Latin America (World Health Organization, 2019). Although death is not a positive outcome for those suffering from depression, it is possible the attention, media, and related conversations regarding mobbing suicides are somewhat exaggerated by special interests.

Bullying and Mobbing

The term *mobbing* was initially utilized by Konrad Lorenz, an Australian scientist who observed animal behaviors in the 1960s (Çubukcu, Girmen, & Donmez, 2015). Lorenz utilized the term mobbing as a way to describe how they engaged in activities to scare away their killers or any other unwanted animal. However, 20 years later, an individual by the name of Heinz Leyman witnessed comparable behavior on employees, therefore commenced utilizing the term mobbing to express the gravity of the violence that occurred among employees within workplaces (Çubukcu, Girmen, & Donmez, 2015). The term mobbing is more frequently associated among people in the United Kingdom and has only recently become interchangeable with the more common term of bullying. Bullies can come in all shapes and sizes, and from all educational and professional backgrounds, a GED to Ph.D. and beyond have all been identified as bullies.

Westhues (2004) proclaimed that individuals who are mobbed have a far more different experience than those who are bullied by a single individual. However, both bullying and mobbing are behaviors that are not in any way short-standing, as a study indicated that 21% of their participants endured bullying for more than five years while working in their institution (McKay, Arnold, Fratzl, & Thomas, 2008). In contrary, a study conducted by Zapf and Gross (2001) explored that the number of individuals was associated with the duration of the bullying. It was observed that the greater the individuals who partook in the situation, the lengthier the duration of the bullying. Therefore, as bullying commences, and the longer the duration, the greater it is that other colleagues will be sucked into the situation, hence the increased rate of bullying and mobbing rates among faculty in higher education (Keashly & Neuman, 2010).

It is common today to read about alleged toxic behaviors among people in various situations (Sasso, 2017). We can use as examples a person who makes a claim they have been mistreated and are the victim of mobbing. Until such time that all the facts are known, it may be a claim that people use to deflect some irresponsible behavior on their part. Taking the time to investigate the situation thoroughly and all the facts consume considerable time, and it could lead to finger pointing on both sides of the argument. The American Judicial System is proclaimed to be the best in the world. Its use today is stretched beyond its original design and intent. Frequent news stories are at times difficult and stressful to readers because they are abhorrent and can be classified as against social norms. At times, we can say human behavior is challenging to comprehend based upon their individual choices. We make the argument that these stories of human behavior are far outside what a child learns at an early age. Confused as to what is acceptable behavior from their family or role model is a clear juxtaposition of what any young person can comprehend. The negative influence in a child's life leaves a permanent impression in their minds, and they may not be able to replace those negative teachings with more positive thinking.

Aside from the dysfunction, economic and adverse outcomes associated with poor, learned behavior, a society most likely will have to take on more future problems because people fail to act and teach others to be responsible (Skousen, 2016). The courts have not fully embraced the legal tort action of mobbing. We do have many criminal statutes for laws that could be applied to certain types of mobbing behavior. Strong aggressive personalities can control many different outcomes associated with mobbing. The fear of a threat, real or perceived, could be debilitating to many people, regardless of age and intellect. We have read stories about victims of mobbing whom apparently were unable to adjust to the behavior and believed they had little if any options end up exacting revenge and violence towards those perceived to have harmed the victim (U.S. Department of Health and Human Services, 2017).

In regards to bullying within the workplace, Keashly and Neuman (2010) defined it as,

harassing, offending, socially excluding some-one or negatively affecting someone's work tasks. . . . It has to occur repeatedly and regularly (e.g., weekly) and over a period of time (e.g., at least six months). Bullying is an escalating process in the course of which the person confronted ends up in an inferior position and becomes the target of systematic negative social acts. (p. 49)

Research has indicated that bullying rates are rather high when compared to those in the general population, such as 2% to 5% in Scandinavian countries, 10% to 20% within the United Kingdom, and the United States with 10% to 14% (Keashly & Neuman, 2010). It was further illustrated that amongst university employees, that 63.4% of colleagues were deemed to be labeled as bullies by faculty. Whereas 52.9% of superiors were seen as bullies by their staff (Keashly & Neuman, 2010).

EXAMPLES OF TYPES OF DARK LEADERSHIP AND TOXICITY

Queen Bee Syndrome

Simply put, the Queen Bee syndrome is when a female does not want to assist other women (Heim, Murphy, & Golant, 2003). In fact, she will not only not assist women, but she will also go out of her way by destroying their hiring or coercing them to quit an existing position, to prevent other women from advancing in the work field as well as undermine them (McKoy, 2013; Rossbacher, 2013). This behavior occurs, as queen bees are threatened by women who are highly educated, successful, smart, as well as knowledgeable (McKoy, 2013). McKoy (2013) stated that queen bees tend to have, "supervisory, tenured, or higher ranked positions of power" (p. 200). According to Rossbacher (2013), the typical attitude that one can find in a Queen Bee is, being that it was difficult for them to advance in the work field, they will make it tough for other women who want to progress as well. The terminology, *Queen Bee*, was first coined in the 1970s by researchers at the University of Michigan as they discovered the workplace behavior that some women illustrate (Rossbacher, 2013). It was further revealed that research conducted by the Workplace Bullying Institute demonstrates that men (60%) are more prone to display bullying behavior and women (57%) are more likely to report being the victim of this unprofessional behavior. However, when females are bullies, their victims tend to be women (71%) (Rossbacher, 2013). Mckoy illustrated that forensic specialists, as well as other educators, see this behavior as a type of bullying or *women cruelty*.

Rossbacher (2013) stated that researchers, who are experts in this field, deem that academia may produce more bullies then many other professions. Some reasons include but are not limited to, (a) faculty members who are promoted to roles such as supervisors or administrators without requiring the necessary management training, (b) one's perception of having their tenure protected as well as the increasing number of adjunct faculty with less job security, and (c) decentralization that can pressure people from reporting or finding a resolution outside of the department they are working for (Rossbacher, 2013). Similarly, McKoy (2013) explicated that the queen bee syndrome is an "evolving plague in academia" (p. 200). As new women enter the work field of academia, they frequently believe that they will be assisted by other women in their organization and be offered professional as well as emotional support based on mutual understanding. However, that could not be further from the truth, as they are at the forefront of being attacked and stung by queen bees (McKoy, 2013).

McKoy (2013) stated that queen bees are known to have what is termed, *PICO*, which is when an individual possesses an analysis mentality and persona. The term PICO stands for, "power, influence, control, and over the top feelings of importance resembling a unique form of narcissism" (p. 200). It has been observed that in specific environments within higher education that queen bee supervisors will treat their male employees far more professionally and with more respect than women. Furthermore, evidence illustrates that an individual's gender in a leadership role is linked to their subordinates' physical as well as mental health (McKoy, 2013).

Sociopathic/Dark Triad Leadership

Perry (2015) indicated that sociopathic personality traits that are found in individuals who have managerial positions could easily wreck business organizations even though they were deemed as individuals who are greatly capable and therefore a strong desire to be successful. These traits are also found in chief executive officers, as well as lawyers and media (Perry, 2015). Of the numerous traits, three of them are referred to as *socially-aversive* and are also considered as *dark*. The dark triad is referred to the amalgamation of three socially evil characteristics and behaviors that consist of (a) Machiavellianism, (b) subclinical narcissism, and (c) subclinical psychopathy (Nahavandi, 2015; Perry, 2015). Recent research focuses on positive leadership and how this is the definition of leadership. However, it is also imperative to know that leaders who possess negative traits can still attain positive results. Interestingly enough, some of these negative leaders were also initially popular, such as Hitler. Nevertheless, comprehending these negative leadership styles and the characteristics and traits that they encompass, as well as how they add to destructive leadership is critical (Nahavandi, 2015).

Moreover, it is essential for the readers to comprehend that the terms sociopath and psychopath have been utilized interchangeably within literature, as the two are somewhat similar, however, the two should not be confused. According to Millon, Grossman, Millon, Meagher, and Ramnath (2004) both psychopaths and sociopaths are terms both utilized to refer to individuals who commit monstrous crimes. Often a writer will choose to utilize one term over the other due to the preference of word, and not based on the scientific differences. Psychopaths are thought to have some constitutional disposition to the syndrome. Whereas, sociopaths are biologically normal, however, acquire antisocial characteristics via inept or hostile socializing, more specifically poor parenting. Both sociopath and psychopath can be best observed as existing on a continuum (Millon et al., 2004).

Machiavellian Leadership

This personality is founded on Niccolo Machiavelli's work, entitled *The Prince* (Furnham, 2010; Nahavandi, 2015). Leaders who possess this characteristic are known as being more eager than other individuals to situate their self-interests and predilections above the interests of the group. Furthermore, they have no qualms in manipulating individuals for their gain (Nahavandi, 2015). Furnham (2010) moreover stated that Machiavellian leadership is comprised of a leader who is exploitative, competitive, as well as selfish. In addition, Gkorezis, Petridou, and Krouklidou (2015) study revealed that this form of leadership has led to both a direct and indirect effect of emotional exhaustion on employees.

Psychopathic Leadership

Nahavandi (2015) revealed that the psychopathic personality is considered as both a personality disorder and also have a normal form in which individuals are characterized by, "impulsivity, thrill seeking, low anxiety, and lack of concern for others or remorse" (p. 126). Moreover, Boddy (2017) illustrated that researchers stated that these are individuals who have a dysfunction of the amygdala. Furthermore, they are known corporate psychopaths are described to be immoral managers as well as abusive supervisors (Boddy, 2017). However, the disorder displays extreme characteristics as well as behaviors that comprise of violent and antisocial behaviors that are associated with criminal behavior (Nahavandi, 2015).

Narcissistic Leadership

Narcissism, as stated in Nahavandi (2015), can also be considered as both a personality disorder as well as have a normal form where individuals are characterized by, " a sense of entitlement, superiority, and grandiosity, preoccupation with status, and insensitivity to others" (p. 125). Sasso (2017) explicated that narcissistic leadership is a type of leadership that has been associated to, "ineffective and immoral leadership, counterproductive leadership, counterproductive work behavior, and low job satisfaction" (p. 1). That stated, subordinates who are employed under this form of leadership within organizations, are undergoing a diminution in motivation and morale, stress, and confronted with unsatisfying work conditions (Doty & Fenlason, 2013; O'Reilly, Doerr, Caldwell, & Chatman, 2013).

Sociopathic Leadership Within Higher Education

According to Brown and Moshavi (2002), the leadership role within a university is different from leadership within other forms of organizations. Interestingly, it has been equated to *herding cats* (Brown & Moshavi, 2002). Why leaders bully other employees is a question that has become one of prominence that academics have sought to answer since the 1990s. One of the many researcher's engaged in understanding bullying and mobbing is Swedish psychologist Heinz Leymann, who is well recognized for his work in bullying, suggests our workplace factors squarely in the discussion of the reasons why bullies exist (Farley & Sprigg, 2014; Thomas, 2016). Leymann found a myriad of reasons he believes people bully others in the workplace. Regardless of one's educational and professional experience, authority-power and lack of control can be described as factors that he suggests is at the root cause for the behavior (Farley & Sprigg, 2014; Thomas, 2016). Understanding the behavior of the sociopath is helpful to the conversation on bullying and mobbing in higher education (Thomas, 2016).

The sociopath is hidden and comes out to attack those who are or perceived to be weak and vulnerable (Wise, 2010). Not being about the organizations' mission and its people seems to be at the center of the discussion on bullying (Appelbaum & Girard, 2007; Chamberlain & Hodson, 2010). It is commonplace to find nepotism and favoritism among the ranks of managers and staff in any organization. The employee who is unable to identify the threats within their organization entirely is most likely going to fail or be held back at their job. It remains a mystery as to how an employee can become aligned to management if they are not liked personally by management (Farley & Sprigg, 2014).

It may not be accurate to suggest the workplace alone, itself, or its culture causes people to bully. It seems reasonable to step aside and say this complex topic is challenging to define entirely and to eliminate its existence. There are so many other people and social factors that influence individuals to become bullies; it is nearly an enigma to explain everything with certainty (Einarsen, 1999; Emamzadeh, 2018). One example can be that institutional competition and jealousy may be two reasons why people choose to bully. If we examine reward systems, most of those programs tend to require a person to complete a series of actions in order to be recognized and or promoted in the workplace. In other words, the organization somewhat encourages competition among employees, which can cause folks to do most anything to be recognized and become promoted (Farley & Sprigg, 2014).

Sometimes, getting to be recognized and climb the career ladder, takes a person who is driven and aggressive to the point of winning at all costs (Farley & Sprigg, 2014; Gould, 2018). Those who are not following a similar tact, may not get the eye of the higher-level managers and end up leaving the organization feeling bullied, rejected, or otherwise suffering from what they describe as being burnt out. The plethora of research suggests people that bully others have personalities that include; narcissism, low self-esteem, anxiety driven, fearful and are many times uncomfortable in social settings. These researchers suggest victims share some similar characters and are found to be vulnerable, suffer from low self-esteem, and are harboring negative emotions as well as lack confidence (Farley & Sprigg, 2014; Kane, 2018). Regardless of the causations of bullying, so far, the processes to both eliminate and resolve its wrath of destructive victimization still have considerable progress to make it in the future (Farley & Sprigg, 2014).

Flaherty (2017) indicated that students, professors, and support personnel in higher education could all share similar roles as bullies, victims, and advocates of bullying and mobbing behaviors. Bullying and mobbing can be identified in; for-profit, religious, military, and for-profit institutions of higher education. Understanding the schema is essential for people who may find themselves caught up in workplace conflicts. Considering higher education was sold as a haven for open dialogue, free critical thinking and unlimited learning opportunities it becomes questionable when the enterprise shifted away from those early descriptors. If the person being bullied flees the organization, they may encounter the same or similar behavior elsewhere and not find a suitable organization to work. Some may take on the identification of damaged goods, and their lives can spiral out of control leading to self-destruction (Flaherty, 2017).

Toxic Leadership

According to Chua and Murray (2015), toxic leadership is evident when leaders attack their employees' abilities as well as personalities. That stated toxic leadership characteristics consist of the leader attacking their employees' performance, not providing their employees with any credit for their ideas as well as utilizing their employees' ideas as their own. Furthermore, a toxic leader will have no problem in humiliating their employees in front of their colleagues. Pelletier (2012) further included that a leader is considered toxic if they bring on unremitting and persistent severe maltreatment to their employees. Moreover, Chua and Murray indicated that toxic leaders are notorious for being individuals who have a predisposed notion of detestation, considerably high levels of narcissism as well as charisma, a yearning to attain power in addition to negative life themes. In addition, Ross, Matteson, and Exposito (2014) illustrated via a plethora of research that toxic leadership affects the mental and physical health of subordinates; there is an increase in counterproductive work behavior (CWB) and tardiness, followed by transfers and resignation.

Chua and Murray (2015) revealed that subordinates of toxic leaders would more than likely fall in two categories, and that is conformers and colluders. Conformers are those who are deemed to be psychologically immature as well have low self-esteem. This, in turn, makes them believe that they deserve to be maltreated and disrespected by their leaders. Therefore, they want to attain approval by their leaders. However, colluders, on the other hand, are those who want to share and acquire equivalent beliefs of their toxic leaders, where they seem to excel in that environment that is produced by toxic leaders (Chua & Murray, 2015).

Organizational Culture Applied to Bullying and Mobbing

Those who are employed and can genuinely say that they work in a healthy and positive organizational culture are fortunate souls; as working in a toxic culture can prove to pose an abundance of heartache. Sasso (2017) revealed that researchers stated how toxic workplace environments are a worldwide social problem that unfortunately is affecting millions of subordinates. It has been illustrated that an employee's place of work can psychologically affect their well-being either adversely or positively. In addition, it can affect their job productivity (Sasso, 2017). Seago (2016) demonstrated that evidence shows how an organizations' culture can determine how prosperous an organization becomes. A corporate culture study was conducted at Duke University and results illustrated 91% of CEOs in addition to chief financial officers from North America indicated that culture is important to an organization. Moreover, 91% also showed that bettering their organization's culture would heighten the value. Finally, more than 50% concurred that culture has a significant effect on the organization's (a) ingenuity, (b) productivity, (c) growth and rate, and (d) the volume of profit it can make (Millage, 2016; Seago, 2016).

Moreover, Chamberlain and Hodson (2010) incorporated that organizational effects also comprise of (a) defective judgment, (b) absenteeism, (c) turnover in employees, and (d) low morale. It has also been illustrated that the effect of toxic cultures affects both the employees as well as the employees' families (Millage, 2016). A toxic work environment has various components to it and could affect a person's sociological, psychological, and physical well-being (Too & Harvey, 2012). It was also indicated that these sections could derive from numerous origins such as (a) the physical building itself, (b) the barriers that have been placed, (c) obstacles that prevent employees from face to face communication, (d) electronic contact, and (e) absence of personal privacy (Too & Harvey, 2012). There is evidence demonstrating that subordinates are affected when they cross paths with these properties individually. However, when united it has been witnessed that subordinates have a debilitating effect on subordinates well-being (Chamberlain & Hodson, 2010; Too & Harvey, 2012). Furthermore, it was demonstrated that toxic cultures are fabricated to guard the leader's selfish goals and offer the organization with no productive value (A Toxic Culture, 2016).

The Cause of Toxic Culture and Its Effect on Job Performance

Balthazard, Cooke, and Potter (2006) conducted a study, which looked at how organizational culture could affect behavioral norms as well as expectations, and more precisely focusing on behavioral norms associated with constructive, passive/ defensive, and aggressive/ defensive cultural styles. Singh and Kumar (2013) also analyzed what facets had an effect on internalization of dysfunctional norms among subordinates in their organization. Balthazard et al. (2006) study illustrated that constructive cultural norms are positively and substantially associated with participants who showed role clarity, job satisfaction, in addition to the quality of communication in the organization. Whereas expectations for passive and aggressive behaviors were negatively associated with role clarity, job satisfaction, as well as communication quality and are positively associated with behavioral conformity. Moreover, constructive norms are positively associated with the quality of services, excellent customer service, quality of the place of work, in addition to flexibility. Results from Singh and Kumar's 2013 study revealed that pervasiveness had five predictors and it was perceived leadership integrity that deemed to be the most important and most potent predictor of pervasiveness. The other four that followed thereafter were (a) strong growth, (b) job codification, (c) a hierarchy of authority, and finally, (d) serial versus disjunctive socialization tactics.

Emphasis of Counterproductive Work Behavior

Research indicates that counterproductive work behavior is present under dark leadership styles (Braun, Aydin, Frey, & Peus, 2016; Campbell, Hoffman, Campbell, & Marchisio, 2011; Grijalva & Newman, 2015; Meurs, Fox, Kessler, & Spector, 2013; Perry, 2015; O'Boyle, Forsyth, Banks, & McDaniel, 2012; Ross, Matteson, & Exposito, 2014). A study conducted by O'Boyle et al. (2012) had results that revealed that when there was an augmentation in the presence of Machiavellianism, that there was a decrease in subordinate performance and therefore an increase in CWB. This study further illustrated that there was a noteworthy positive association between narcissism and CWB. Similarly, Grijalva and Newman (2015) additionally demonstrated that narcissism is significantly associated with CWB as well as how cultures that are elevated in, in-group collectivism, have a weak connection with CWB and narcissism. Meurs et al. (2013) study was comparable as it revealed that organizational constraints and interpersonal conflict were positively correlated with CWB for organizations as well as individuals. However, narcissism was negatively associated with organizational constraints, and grandiose exhibitionism was positively linked to CWB in individuals.

We continue to find plenty of evidence that bullying and mobbing take place among working groups in all sectors (Matteson, 2002; Sasso, 2017). There is no absence or lack of examples of jealousy and workplace envy among colleagues and various tiers of managers and supervisors. As counterproductive as these activities are, along with our great strides in improving the efficiency within the workplace, this phenomenon has been recognized through public awareness, supported by ample research and yet the problem behavior remains a topic of prominence. Stepping back, we find little if any disagreement among scholars and practitioners throughout history that social networks are sensitive mechanisms and can result in various positive and negative outcomes all based upon the perception of the engaged actors. It is commonplace to find examples of retaliation by victims of bullying and mobbing and those actions can be described in many different forms. Subtle to violent reactions by mobbing or bullying victims are devastating to any person, organization, and mission with negative economic and operational outcomes.

It can be difficult to fully interpret and understand all the variables and complex dynamics within the workplace that can potentially and negatively impact staff. Handling these events in an appropriate, effective, and grounded approach takes considerable people making skills including knowledge, skills, and abilities on balance with the business model of an organization, always keeping the importance best as possible, workplace and personal relationships intact. Lastly, although it is only normal to engage in counterproductive work behavior due to bullying, one should also be cautious of individuals in today's world who dramatize and exaggerate the impact of being bullied, which in turn may be utilized as an excuse not to produce as they should in the workplace.

The Psychological and Physiological Impact on Individuals Under That Type of Leadership

Keeping thoughts as to what behaviors can undermine people, processes, and outcomes take being proactive as a forward and visionary leader, sadly, a rare trait in many organizations today. However, considering the devaluation and emotional damage as a result of bullying and mobbing their wise and prudent leader most likely would like to err on the positive side of being able to control for loss of productivity and damaged staff (Matteson, 2002; Sasso, 2017).

It is not difficult to find people who exhibit behavioral traits such as arrogance, egotistical, egocentric, conceited, boasting, bragging, taking advantage of people and situations for their gain or gaming the system, and of course, harming others by psychological and physical means. Some also fit the definition of bullies and people who choose to engage in mobbing behavior. Generally speaking, humans through life experience and positive role modeling are all able to adapt to most any situation and remain relatively intact emotionally, if they choose to do so. Here is the argument, being held hostage within an organization with few options becomes overwhelming for many people, and they feel as if there are no options to their situation.

Noll and Carter (1998) found that nearly everyone in the United States has been subjected to behavior similar to bullying and mobbing at one time or another in their lives. They found these incidents are easily recalled well into their adult years. Generally, the behavior tends to be observed by others who at many times emulate the same behavior and create additional bullies in order to be perceived to have the authority and hold power over others. Reasoner (2000) opined by stating humans gain strength by omitting behavioral nonsense and adding instead, authenticity, competence, a healthy self-esteem, realistic accomplishments, bouncing back from failures and adopting practices of efficacy grounded in integrity and self-responsibility. Otherwise, as Reasoner suggested anger becomes a negative precursor to violent behavior.

Although somewhat dated, the professional work of renowned Psychologist Dr. Murray Banks, was able to find creative means to advance the theory of Mental Hygiene as a means to control human behavior by introducing positive coping strategies on balance with negative life events. Banks, in high demand, traveled the world (Circa 1950-1970s) using humor and personal experiences to large crowds helping them to understand human behavior and why people do what they do, as there is always a particular reason for the conduct. Banks (1965) suggested human beings are vulnerable to criticism who can lead to life-altering consequences that are intended to destroy our self-esteem, self-worth, and leaving us in despair. Banks focused upon taking control of your situation and infusing humor into negative situations as argued and this approach allowed people from all walks of life to develop a personal Mental Hygiene model to cope with a variety of life's negative events, productively.

In recent times, Namie and Namie (2001) outlined bullying and mobbing with a definition that included a component of harassment, threats, belittling opinions, or public humiliation, name-calling insults, intentionally withholding information-praise, undue pressure at work, setting impossible deadlines as well as assigning meaningless tasks, reprisal and racism as a few examples. Wyatt and Hare (1997) align to Namie and Namie thoughts and found an abundance of research that suggests bullies and mobbing is grounded in narcissistic managers who had been shamed as children and later follow those same learned behaviors into adulthood. As a result, the workplace becomes a dark and fearful environment full of staff, which have developed feelings of worthlessness.

We find mobbing and bullying in all organizations including the United States government. Although many federal agencies including our most sensitive missions-organizations complete an in-depth pre-employment background investigation and use of a polygraph, there is no lack of bullies who mob coworkers and others in the workplace.

Dobson (2001) and Field (2002) offered a more micro perspective on the outcomes related to bullying and mobbing within the workplace. With a focus on national security, their research suggests the victim may carry the wounds and emotional scars for a lifetime and become vulnerable as unwitting sources of information and or traitors to adversaries and enemies of the United States.

Yes vs. No: Biological Conversation

The nature versus nurture conversation on human and animal-mammal and primate behavior dates back to some of the first accounts of recorded behavior and has been replicated to the current times. British medical researcher Michael Marmot along with Robert Sapolsky an American neurooncologist both conclude behavior is learned

(Marmot & Bell, 2010; Sapolsky, 2017). Physical telomers, cortisol, and science to this part are stressors that are transferrable to a fetus and dovetails to the works of Marmot of the Dutch Hunger Winter studies. The Dutch Winter Hunger research underscores the problem with mobbing behavior (intentional societal harassment) directed at pregnant women during World War II and their offspring were fearful in their mother's womb. Marmot was able to link by science that these children were medically harmed for life (Institute of Health Equity, 2019; Schulz, 2010; Wu Tsai Neurosciences Institute, 2019). Medically, we find ample evidence to support the claim that mobbing is harmful to our health (Sasso, 2017; A Toxic Culture, 2016). In the Frontline documentary titled *Social Determinants of Health*, the research was clear that we have become a product of our environment and that a person's status dictates your health and your ability to compete in the workplace. Generally speaking, the working class always remains the working class.

These researchers suggest it is a reasonable assumption that no perfect elixir exists to provide a perfect prescription to bullying and mobbing, however by presenting data and evidence along with suggestions, this part of the topic may enlighten public awareness and over time reduce the current problem.

Applied Relevant Case Studies

These researchers take the position that educators pursue higher education degrees and are exposed to a plethora of information and data that can be applied to both K-12 to university programs. Taking the recent academic scandal within the Atlanta Public School System, we learned that numerous administrators went along with an illegal scheme to fix grades and falsely make it appear that the student's performance was far better than reality. After an intensive criminal investigation by the Georgia Bureau of Investigation, numerous top tier administrators were sentenced to prison terms. It was clear that a large number of school staff were bullied into not reporting the conduct out of fear for losing their jobs (Cox Media Group, 2018).

Faculty expressed concerns that they have been unfairly identified as targets of bullying and mobbing within higher education settings. There are numerous case examples that both full time and adjunct faculty report as incidents of being victims of bullying and mobbing by their administrators, leaving them without many options.

Students are not immune from being the instigators using bullying and mobbing tactics to nullify a faculty member whom they perceive is driven by standards of excellence, and academic rigor otherwise is too demanding of their students in the class. One such example includes a faculty member who found himself unsupported by students who challenged the course rigor and his dean who was more focused upon control and the revenues of the University. In 2017, Dr. Peter Zeno was hired by the University of Connecticut to teach a section of *CSE 1010 - Introduction to Computing for Engineers* for the fall 2017 semester. Zeno quit after several conflicts arose between him and the CSE department, the last of which was a conflict over his decision to give the class extra credit work and two midterms instead of one (Debenedictis, 2017).

Another example involves the Penn State University, where numerous students were sexually battered, and others were threatened to remain quiet. The scandal led to the University President and coaching staff with long prison sentences. Former Federal Judge, Prosecutor and Street FBI Special Agent, and FBI Director Louis Freeh was retained to fully investigate the bullying behavior at Penn State, and those findings can be described as perverted and repulsive. One can understand it would take a strong person to become a whistleblower and expose what had been a long-standing practice among Penn State University staff (Burke, 2012).

Similarly, a conference was held at the American Association of University Professors' international conference on globalization, in which a session was based on a paper titled *Mobbing as a Factor in Faculty Work Life*. This story was written by Joan E. Friedenberg, a professor of bilingual education at Florida Atlantic University, as well as her co-authors, Mark Schneider, an associate professor of sociology at Southern Illinois University at Carbondale, and Kenneth Westhues, a professor of sociology at the University of Waterloo (June, 2009). It was based on how administrators and work colleagues ganged up on an exceedingly industrious tenured professor. This poor professor was falsely accused, removed from having an office, rejected from departmental meetings as well as committees, in addition to being accused of engaging in inappropriate activity with a graduate student. This professor was ultimately fired and instantaneously passed away from a stroke that stemmed from the stress of all that occurred (June, 2009).

This story was an amalgamation of real experiences of numerous professors who were targets of mobbing and believed that by combining a plethora of stories into one, allows her to communicate better, *the following of perplexity and trepidation that those who are victims of mobbing feel.* Mark Schneider further included that victims should not always assume that by advising an administrator that it will help, rather evidence has revealed that administration might find it simpler to be part of the mob rather than to stop it. This is due to administrators believing that it is far better to have one individual angry with them in comparison to a group. However, Ms. Friedenberg additionally stated that administrators should be aware that mobbing could have a *boomerang effect* on them as those who are targeted by bullying may engage in a substantial counterattack (June, 2009).

The final case study illustrates a 2013 Michigan State University student Evan Schrage, who found himself in conflict with one professor and he described the behavior as bullying. So, Schrage chose to expose the conduct. The professor was dismissed for his alleged conduct and Schrage became a student advocate against bullying in higher education settings (Swick, 2013).

As students suggest they at times feel bullied, depressed and or ganged up on (mobbing) in higher education, the problem seems to suggest a deeper behavioral problem of; incivility and being insensitivity in society is a starting point for meaningful conversations. In an exchange of finger pointing exercises, we still have more questions than answers to the problem. It would be easy to say people are weak and have not been exposed to the real world; therefore, they have not matured to a level of adulthood and developed healthy coping skills to navigate life's challenges.

However, to balance out the discussion, stakeholders should be cognizant that individuals from all walks of life have various and different perceptions of their upbringing and family structures; this includes their versions of the alleged bully and victim. These researchers find similar outcomes from bullies and victim's behavioral traits. In other words, nearly most of our population can offer personal stories related to their belief they have been mistreated in their lifetimes. Not discounting the trauma and psychological effects and resulting damages from being abused, it becomes difficult at times to thoroughly dissect all the events (assigning blame) that influenced many of these subjective stories with total accuracy in order to adequately address how to prevent and overcome these behaviors. Finding the right solution for the right time and place remains the challenge. Becoming angry and using violence is not the right choice (Marraccini, 2013).

PREDICTING THE FUTURE: PREVENTATIVE MEASURES OF BULLYING AND MOBBING

Within the Ranks as Well as Leadership

Ross (2008) revealed that when people are being influenced by others, there is a form of power, whether it be positive or negative that is used by them. Ross further explicated that various administrators utilize power in a fashion that constructed a culture of intimidation, fear, and coercion. Aldag and Joseph (2000) stated that power is seen as (a) relative, (b) dynamic, (c) latent, and (d) perceived. It was further indicated that there are three ways that one would utilize power, and that is, (a) power over, (b) power to, and (c) power from (Aldag & Joseph, 2000). Sasso (as cited in Stogdill, 1974) indicated that power is acknowledged as, (a) referent, (b) coercion, (c) reward, (d) legitimate, and (e) expertness. Sasso (2017) further revealed the plethora of bases of power that were further created by French and Raven and Daft, Dawson, and Raven. That said, Sasso revealed that a total of 14 power bases currently exist.

In regards to how power is utilized from administrators over faculty, students toward faculty and faculty over faculty is one that may leave a sour taste in our mouths. As previously indicated, various forms of mobbing and bullying are administration on faculty, students on faculty, as well as faculty on faculty. It was further illustrated that toxic leadership styles are a style which displays an organization's leader as a bully over their employees due to the psychological and physiological damage that occurs to those individuals who work under that form of leadership. Keeping this information in mind, it is imperative to discover various measures to prevent mobbing and bullying within the higher education field.

Administration on Faculty Bullying

Statistical data in regards to workplace bullying illustrate that approximately 80% of the offenders are bosses (Harvey, Heames, Richey, & Leonard, 2006). Research in the field of higher education and administration on faculty bullying is still very novel; therefore data is relatively scarce (Piotrowski & King, 2016). However, Simon, Hurst, Kelley, and Judge (2015) illustrated that as institutions of higher education seem to stick to a hierarchal organizational structure, forms of mistreatment or even abuse of employees can be incredibly intensified. Moreover, a majority of administrative and teaching staff in educational institutions are tenured employees; abusive supervision can increase over time and form a long-lasting, toxic environment (Simon et al., 2015).

In regards to preventing administration on faculty bullying/ mobbing, the institution can distribute *The Survey on Toxic Leadership* (TSTL) created by Dr. David B. Ross in 2016. The TSTL survey comprises of three components for the participants to complete. The first component is a 24-item survey that measure's a person's characteristic of narcissism, toxic leadership and, elements of power. The second component consists of six open-ended questions that bring up the overall leader's effectiveness. The final component of the survey relates to obtaining demographic information about the individuals of the study. This survey was used to measure toxic leadership and organizational culture in various professions to include education, which can be located in Sasso's 2017 study.

Student on Faculty Bullying

Ever since the *academic entitlement era* has come about, there has been a significant influx of students within higher education utilizing their power over professors such as written and verbal intimidation (Sasso & Ross, 2019). This is because students have the ability to, in essence, determine whether their professor will be able to keep their position, based on the end of semester reviews completed by their students, which are then reviewed by the administration and other evaluational procedures. As illustrated in research, students who do not attain the grade they feel they deserve, not earned, will automatically poorly rate their professor at the end of semester reviews (Keashly & Neuman, 2010; Sasso & Ross, 2019). Students can also bully professors via the Internet on professor rating websites. Therefore, professors fear of losing their position and are pressured to giving their students generous grades. However, in order to prevent this cycle from occurring, it is critical for administration to implement policies and procedures regarding grades and student intimidation towards faculty (Keashly & Neuman, 2010; Sasso & Ross, 2019).

Faculty on Faculty Bullying

As previously stated, studies have illustrated that bullying and mobbing are long-lasting and that for 21% of the participants that it can persist for more than five years. However, that same study also revealed that the percentage increased to 49% when it was focused on faculty on faculty bullying and mobbing (McKay et al., 2008). It is believed that the academic field is one that has a setting for this form of behavior due to tenure, which in turn allows for faculty to develop long-term relationships with each other (Keashly & Neuman, 2010). In addition, faculty use a mobbing technique when they feel threatened by their colleagues' achievements as well as other issues of jealousy and envy. Research further illustrated that the lengthier and more interactive the relationship is, the vaster the opportunity for bullying and mobbing like behaviors to occur (Keashly & Neuman, 2010).

According to Keashly and Neuman (2010), it is critical to partake in early action to prevent situations from intensifying into progressively toxic situations such as bullying and mobbing. Therefore, policies, processes, and procedures must be implemented to provide support to those individuals being affected. It was further included that there must be mechanisms and procedures set to tackle the underlying triggers of these toxic communications to prevent these conditions from occurring.

Therefore, the following are specific methods in faculty to faculty bullying and mobbing prevention, (a) skill development in negotiation and associated skills, (b) mediation, and (c) problem solvers. This takes form in (a) active conflict management strategies, (b) grievance and arbitration procedures, (c) informal processes, and (d) informal approaches.

CONCLUSION

Based on today's society and the increase of social media, the incivility of the community, as well as the media, has contributed to the increase of bullying and mobbing. Martin and Pena Saint Martin (2014) stated that mobbing had increased dramatically throughout the world.

It can be defined as a group systematically attacking a person's reputation for an extended period of time, using negative communication as a weapon. The intention is to destroy the target's value as a reliable individual, initially causing them to lose power and prestige, with the long-term goal of achieving their dismissal, resignation or general ostracism. Our aim is to demonstrate that this kind of behavior can also occur in the public sphere. (Martin & Pena Saint Martin, 2014, para. 1)

Case and point, when people view the mass media, journalists have reported on students who have been bullied in schools, especially based on heartrending school shootings. However, the news is selective in the issues that they report and promote based on interpretation, evaluation, and/or solutions. This is based on media framing, which is how the media decide which *slice* of the larger picture they want to endorse or refrain from giving it to the public (Knight, 2015). There is and has been an outcry from the public regarding bullying from high profile and sensationalized media cases (Knight, 2015). However, for every segment that the media reports that bullying is unacceptable in today's society, they engage in the same toxic behavior when the media feels others are not aligned with their opposing views. As a result, there could be an attack upon others' reputations on a continuous news cycle, especially if the viewers are not aligned with journalists' points of view, it is considered bullying. To extend that thought, mass media expands bullying to mobbing if people do not agree with networks ideologies, theories, and pundits.

There is a need for positive news rather than negative news regarding any ridicule and condescending actions towards others. This can start by media reporting on issues that represent how others help and mentor people. The mass media, which can be viewed 24/7 with such a large audience, has the ability and connections to place a positive reinforcement of mentoring and to illustrate the reasons for communities at large to also act civil to one another. Therefore, future research should focus on other fields where bullying and mobbing are evident. Based on much research on bullying and mobbing, researchers and other interested parties should focus on the recommendations of the studies to report and implement these positive actions. Russom (2009) reported that it is imperative to compare schools prevention programs as well as teachers perceptions of bullying in order to look upon information to curtail bad behavior. Changing the organizational culture and striving for a zero tolerance for negative behavior and microaggression in the workplace. Spending time and communicating policy change for others in the workplace to model appropriate behaviors by creating nonviolent, civil, and respectful working surroundings. In addition, there is a need for leadership to address the misbehaviors in the workplace for resolution, as well as address risk factors and behaviors that accompany this epidemic of bullying to develop better policies, education, and training (Bergloff, 2014; Gardner Gilkes Benevides, 2012; Pollack, 2015; Shaw, 2017). "Research supports that policies and practices embedded in the culture considerably lower the probability of workplace bullying" (Bergloff, 2015, p. 91). Gardner Gilkes Benevides (2012) who stated that mobbing is in all cultures and professions, recommended that leadership play an important role in changing this phenomenon of mobbing by looking at the well-being of all employees, acquiring self-awareness, and eliminating the bad behaviors. Furthermore, leadership needs to implement and develop better policies for supporting professional consultation, education, and training, but more importantly, actually monitor and evaluate the culture of the organization.

Bullying is also well known within the political culture, which also exacerbates bullying to the same level of intensity that the mass media portrays (Barber & Hamas, 2009). Every election cycle, candidates from their party bully each other on the campaign trail; in addition, some candidates join forces to ridicule one candidate that might have a higher poll number; this act of bullying expands to mobbing. This behavior that occurs in any political party is covered via the mass media who also add fuel to the fire as they feel they have power over people. UNESCO illustrated that mass communication has several functions, (a) providing news and information, (b) socialization, (c) motivation, (d) discussion and dialogue, (e) educational function, (f) the function of cultural improvement, (g) entertaining function, and (h) function of integration (Çubukcu, Girmen, & Donmez, 2015). This power that the mass media holds is influence over the general population. The mass media and their connections to politics have radically changed in how they report their news platform regarding the operations of government institutions and the communication style of political leaders. The new media have a heightened level of instability and unpredictability into the method of how communication within the political field is processed (Owen, 2017).

Much like the media, there is also a growing problem of celebrities bullying the general population, by, in essence forcing their political views on them. When the population goes against them, they engage in bullying-like behavior that leads to mobbing and eventually, death threats are made to those who go against celebrity views. Unfortunately, a myriad of individuals is also influenced by celebrities as much as they are to media. Therefore, they look up to these celebrities, which in turn, lead to toxic and unlawful behavior. Based on the information provided the researchers have witnessed this common trend of bullying and mobbing among various fields. That stated, it is critical that further research is conducted on mobbing and bullying across all professions and within all levels of power.

The professions that genuinely stick out are higher education, politics, and media as they have a direct connection to the community and thus would be beneficial for them to mentor and educate individuals as well as show a positive light in how we are to conduct ourselves. As professors are influential to their students, they should utilize most of their time mentoring rather than enforcing their views and agenda on their students and for that matter even on their colleagues at work. Whether it is on the professional level or a personal level, how we conduct ourselves at work can follow us at home. It is imperative to know that mobbing occurs on campus and we covered higher education, media, and politics because students in higher education obtain their information from higher education, media, and politics. In turn, they utilize the academic institution as a platform to express their beliefs and as a result, mob those who disagree with them.

REFERENCES

A Toxic Culture. (2016). *Internal Auditor*, 21-23. Retrieved from https://www.iia.nl /SiteFiles/IA/ia201612-dl.pdf

Aesop's Fables. (2011). *Online collection*. Retrieved from http://www.aesopfables.com /aesop4.html

Aldag, R. J., & Joseph, B. (2000). *Leadership and vision: 25 keys to motivation*. New York, NY: Lebhar-Friedman Books.

Appelbaum, S. H., & Girard, D. R. (2007). Toxins in the workplace: Affect on organizations and employees. *Corporate Governance, 7*(1), 17–28. doi:10.1108/14720700710727087

Balthazard, P. A., Cooke, R. A., & Potter, R. E. (2006). Dysfunctional culture, dysfunctional organization: Capturing the behavioral norms that form organizational culture and drive performance. *Journal of Managerial Psychology, 21*(8), 709–732. doi:10.1108/02683940610713253

Banks, M. (1965). *How to live with yourself*. Sorrento, FL: Murmill Associates.

Barber, C. M., & Hamas, S. H. (2009). The media harassment of public figures from the ethical perspective of Madrid journalists. *Latin Magazine of Social Communication, 64*, 880–893. doi:10.4185/RLCS-64-2009-868-880-893

Bergloff, L. M. (2014). *Correlation between self-reporting of exposure to workplace bullying behaviors and self-reporting of symptoms of anxiety and depression* (Doctoral dissertation). Available from ProQuest Dissertations and Theses database. (UMI No. 3708845)

Boddy, C. R. (2017). Psychopathic leadership: A case study of a corporate psychopath CEO. *Journal of Business Ethics, 145*(1), 141–156. doi:10.100710551-015-2908-6

Branch, S., Ramsay, S., & Barker, M. (2013). Workplace bullying, mobbing and general harassment: A review. *International Journal of Management Reviews, 15*(3), 280–299. doi:10.1111/j.1468-2370.2012.00339.x

Braun, S., Aydin, N., Frey, D., & Peus, C. (2016). Leader narcissism predicts malicious envy and supervisor-targeted counterproductive work behavior: Evidence from field and experimental research. *Journal of Business Ethics*. http://dx.doi.org.ezproxylocal.library.nova.edu/10.1007/s10551-016-3224-5

Brown, F., & Moshavi, D. (2002). Herding academic cats: Faculty reactions to transformational and contingent reward leadership by department chairs. *The Journal of Leadership Studies, 8*(3), 79–93. doi:10.1177/107179190200800307

Burke, T. (2012). *Report of the Special Investigative Counsel Regarding the Actions of The Pennsylvania State University Related to the Child Sexual Abuse Committed by Gerald A. Sanduksy.* Retrieved from https://www.scribd.com/document/99901850/Freeh-Report-of-the-Actions-of-Penn-State-University?ad_group=33330X911648Xa7c6ee68af263f4e6d6fe721c2d688f3&campaign=SkimbitLtd&keyword=660149026&medium=affiliate&source=hp_affiliate

Campbell, W. K., Hoffman, B. J., Campbell, S. M., & Marchisio, G. (2011). Narcissism in organizational contexts. *Human Resource Management Review, 21,* 268–284. Retrieved from www.wkeithcampbell.com/wp-content/uploads/2013/08/CampbellHRMR2011.pdf

Chamberlain, L. J., & Hodson, R. (2010). Toxic work environments: What helps and what hurts. *Sociological Perspectives, 53*(4), 455-477. doi:10.1525op.2010.53.4.455

Cherry, K. (2018). *Understanding social exchange theory in psychology: How it influences relationships.* Retrieved from https://www.verywellmind.com/what-is-social-exchange-theory-2795882

Chua, S. M. Y., & Murray, D. W. (2015). How toxic leaders are perceived: Gender and information-processing. *Leadership and Organization Development Journal, 36*(3), 292–307. doi:10.1108/LODJ-06-2013-0076

Corsi-Bunker, A. (n.d.). *Guide to the education system in the United States.* Retrieved from https://isss.umn.edu/publications/USEducation/2.pdf

Cox Media Group. (2018). *A timeline of how the Atlanta school cheating scandal unfolded.* Retrieved from https://www.ajc.com/news/timeline-how-the-atlanta-school-cheating-scandal-unfolded/jn4vTk7GZUQoQRJTVR7UHK/

Çubukcu, Z., Girmen, P., & Donmez, A. (2015). The investigation of mobbing events taking place at higher education institutions in Turkey considering the reflections on media. *Practice and Theory in Systems of Education, 10*(3), 245–256. doi:10.1515/ptse-2015-0022

Debenedictis, G. (2017). *UConn professor was 'bullied' out of a job in CSE department*. Retrieved from http://dailycampus.com/stories/2017/12/7/uconn-professor-was-bullied-out-of-job-in-cse-department

Dobson, J. (2001). *Discussion on the effects of bullying.* Retrieved December 12, 2018, from http://www.family.org

Doty, J., & Fenlason, J. (2013). Narcissism and toxic leaders. *Military Review*, 55–60.

Duffy, M., & Sperry, L. (2014). *Overcoming mobbing: A recovery guide for workplace aggression and bullying.* Oxford, UK: Oxford University Press.

Einarsen, S. (1999). The nature and causes of bullying at work. *International Journal of Manpower, 20*(1/2), 16–27. doi:10.1108/01437729910268588

Emamzadeh, A. (2018, September 27). *Workplace bullying: Causes, effects, and prevention: A recent article discusses and reviews causes and effects of workplace bullying.* Retrieved from https://www.psychologytoday.com/us/blog/finding-new-home/201809/workplace-bullying-causes-effects-and-prevention

Farley, S., & Sprigg, C. (2014, November 3). *Culture of cruelty: Why bullying thrives in higher education.* Retrieved from https://www.theguardian.com/higher-education-network/blog/2014/nov/03/why-bullying-thrives-higher-education

Field, T. (2002). *Tim Fields article on abuse.* Retrieved May 28, 2002, from http://www.shadesofsorrow.net/abuse/abusearticletimfields.htm

Flaherty, C. (2017). Worse than it seems. *Inside Higher Ed.* Retrieved from https://www.insidehighered.com/news/2017/07/18/study-finds-large-share-cases-involving-faculty-harassment-graduate-students-are

Furnham, A. (2010). *The Machiavellian leader. In the elephant in the boardroom.* London, UK: Palgrave Macmillan.

Gardner Gilkes Benevides, S. (2012). *Mobbing: A not so new phenomenon* (Unpublished thesis). University of Phoenix, AZ.

Gkorezis, P., Petridou, E., & Krouklidou, T. (2015). The detrimental effect of Machiavellian leadership on employees' emotional exhaustion: Organizational cynicism as a mediator. *Europe's Journal of Psychology, 11*(4), 619–631. doi:10.5964/ejop.v11i4.988 PMID:27247681

Gomori, M. (2017). *The Satir approach: Essence and essentials.* Retrieved from http://www.evolutionofpsychotherapy.com/download/handouts/Maria-Gomori-Essence-and-Essentials-Satir-handout.pdf

Gould, T. (2018, May 28). *Watch out for these 8 workplace bully personality types.* Retrieved from http://www.hrmorning.com/8-workplace-bully-personality-types/

Grijalva, E., & Newman, D. (2015). Narcissism and counterproductive work behavior: Meta-analysis and consideration of collectivist culture, big five personality, and narcissism's facet structure. *Applied Psychology, 64*(1), 93–126. doi:10.1111/apps.12025

Guardian News and Media Limited. (2007). *The truth about lying and laughing.* Retrieved from https://www.theguardian.com/science/2007/apr/21/weekendmagazine

Harvey, M., Heames, J. T., Richey, R. G., & Leonard, N. (2006). Bullying: From the playground to the boardroom. *Journal of Leadership & Organizational Studies, 12*(4), 1–11. doi:10.1177/107179190601200401

Heim, P., Murphy, S. A., & Golant, S. K. (2003). *In the company of women: Indirect aggression among women: Why we hurt each other and how to stop.* New York, NY: Penguin Group.

Institute of Health Equity. (2019). *About Professor Sir Michael Marmot.* Retrieved from http://www.instituteofhealthequity.org/about-us/about-professor-sir-michael-marmot

June, A. W. (2009, June 11). *Mobbing' can damage more than careers, professors are told at conference.* Retrieved from https://www.chronicle.com/article/Mobbing-Can-Damage-More-Than/47736

Kane, S. (2018, October 21). *Who is a workplace bully's target? Defend yourself against workplace bullies.* Retrieved from https://www.thebalancecareers.com/who-is-a-workplace-bully-s-target-2164323

Keashly, L., & Neuman, J. H. (2010). Faculty experiences with bullying in higher education: Causes, consequences, and management. *Administrative Theory & Praxis, 32*(1), 48–70. doi:10.2753/ATP1084-1806320103

Khoo, S. B. (2010). Academic mobbing: Hidden health hazard at workplace. *Malaysian Family Physician, 5*(2), 61-67. Retrieved from https://www.ncbi.nlm.nih.gov/pmc/articles/PMC4170397/

Knight, K. (2015). *Framing responsibility for bullying: An ethnographic content analysis* (Doctoral dissertation). Available from ProQuest Dissertations and Theses database. (UMI No. 1586807)

Marmot, M., & Bell, R. (2010). Challenging health inequalities-implications for the workplace. *Occupational Medicine*, *60*(3), 162–164. doi:10.1093/occmed/kqq008 PMID:20423942

Marraccini, M. E. (2013). *College students' perceptions of professor bullying*. Open Access Master's Theses. Paper 9. Retrieved from https://digitalcommons.uri.edu/theses/9

Martin, B., & Pena Saint Martin, F. (2014). *Public mobbing: A phenomenon and its features*. University of Wollongong. Retrieved from http://www.bmartin.cc/pubs/14Gonzalez.html

Matteson, R. W. (2002). *A qualitative study of bullying behavior in federal law enforcement: An examination of former officers perceptions regarding the problem* (Doctoral dissertation). Available from ProQuest Dissertations and Theses database. (UMI No. 3072568)

McKay, R., Arnold, D. H., Fratzl, J., & Thomas, R. (2008). Workplace bully-ing in academia: A Canadian study. *Employee Responsibilities and Rights Journal*, *20*(2), 77–100. doi:10.100710672-008-9073-3

McKoy, Y. D. (2013). The queen bee syndrome: A violent super bee. *Journal of Nursing Care Quality*, *2*(3), 200–200. doi:10.4172/2167-1168.S1.004

Meurs, J., Fox, S., Kessler, S., & Spector, P. (2013). It's all about me: The role of narcissism in exacerbating the relationship between stressors and counterproductive work behaviour. *Work and Stress*, *27*(4), 368–382. doi:10.1080/02678373.2013.849776

Millage, A. (2016). When toxic culture hits home. *Internal Auditor*, *73*(3), 7.

Millon, T., Grossman, S., Millon, C., Meagher, S., & Ramnath, R. (2004). *Personality disorders in modern life* (2nd ed.). Hoboken, NJ: John Wiley & Sons.

Morreall, J. (2012). Philosophy of humor. *The Stanford Encyclopedia of Philosophy*. Retrieved from https://plato.stanford.edu/entries/humor/

Nahavandi, A. (2015). *The Art and Science of Leadership* (7th ed.). Upper Saddle River, NJ: Pearson Education.

Namie, G., & Namie, R. (2001). *Workplace bullying*. Retrieved November 15, 2018, from http://www.bullybusters.org

Noll, K., & Carter, J. (1998). *Taking the bully by the horns*. Greensboro, NC: Unicorn Press.

O'Boyle, E., Forsyth, D., Banks, G., & McDaniel, M. (2012). A meta-analysis of the dark triad and work behavior: A social exchange perspective. *The Journal of Applied Psychology*, *97*(3), 557–579. doi:10.1037/a0025679 PMID:22023075

O'Reilly, C. III, Doerr, B., Caldwell, D., & Chatman, J. (2013). Narcissistic CEOs and executive compensation. *The Leadership Quarterly*, *25*(2), 218–231. doi:10.1016/j.leaqua.2013.08.002

Owen, D. (2017). *The new media's role in politics*. Retrieved from https://www.bbvaopenmind.com/en/articles/the-new-media-s-role-in-politics/

Owens, B. (2016). *Liberalism or how to turn good men into whiners, weenies and wimps*. New York, NY: Post Hill Press.

Pelletier, K. L. (2012). Perceptions of and reactions to leader toxicity: Do leader-follower 184 relationships and identification with victim matter? *The Leadership Quarterly*, *23*(3), 412–424. doi:10.1016/j.leaqua.2011.09.011

Perry, C. (2015). The dark traits of sociopathic leaders: Could they be a threat to universities? *Australian Universities Review*, *57*(2), 17–25.

Piotrowski, C., & King, C. (2016). The enigma of adult bullying in higher education: A research-based conceptual framework. *Education*, *136*(3), 299–306. Retrieved from https://www.researchgate.net/publication/303365811_THE_ENIGMA_OF

Pollack, J. M. (2015). *Understanding how organizational leaders describe the process of workplace bullying and enable capable guardians or mediators to prevent it* (Doctoral dissertation). Available from ProQuest Dissertations and Theses database. (UMI No. 10827825)

President and Fellows of Harvard College. (2017). *The John H. and Elisabeth A. Hobbs Professor of Cognition and Education Adjunct Professor of Psychology, Faculty of Arts and Sciences*. Retrieved from https://www.gse.harvard.edu/faculty/howard-gardner

Reasoner, R. (2000). *The true meaning of self-esteem*. Retrieved October 31, 2018, from http://www.self-esteem-nase.org/whatisselfesteem.html

Redmond, M. V. (2015). Social exchange theory. *English Technical Reports and White Papers, 5*. Retrieved from https://lib.dr.iastate.edu/cgi/viewcontent.cgi?article=1003&context=engl_reports

Ritzer, G., & Smart, B. (2001). *Handbook of social theory*. Thousand Oaks, CA: Sage;

Rodak, M. (2018). *Richie Incognito named ambassador of anti-bullying nonprofit group*. Retrieved from http://www.espn.com/nfl/story/_/id/24090452/nfl-offensive-lineman-richie-incognito-named-ambassador-anti-bullying-organization-boo2bullying

Ross, D. B. (2008). Historical lecture on power for advanced school policy. *Fischler College of Education: Faculty Articles*, 1-7. Retrieved from http://works.bepress.com/david-ross/29/

Ross, D. B. (2017). Eight fundamentals of power: Information for policy and leadership courses. *Fischler College of Education: Faculty Articles*, 256. Retrieved from http://works.bepress.com/david-ross/256/

Ross, D. B., Matteson, R., & Exposito, J. (2014). Servant leadership to toxic leadership: Power of influence over power of control. *Fischler College of Education: Faculty Presentations*, 1-37. Retrieved from http://nsuworks.nova.edu/fse_facpres/244

Rossbacher, L. A. (2013). From the chair of the women's network executive council. *Network News, 1*(3), 1–10.

Russom, A. (2009). *Teacher and administrator perceptions of bullying: Gender and occupational differences* (Unpublished doctoral dissertation). Nova Southeastern University, Davie, FL.

Sapolsky, R. M. (2017). *Behave: The biology of humans at our best and worst*. New York, NY: Penguin.

Sasso, M. T. (2017). *How narcissists cannot hold an organization together: A mixed method approach to a fictitious puzzle factory* (Doctoral dissertation). Available from ProQuest Dissertations and Theses database. (UMI No. 10819904)

Sasso, M. T., & Ross, D. B. (2019in press). Academic entitlement and the K-20 system: The importance of implementing policies to better the education system. In J. O'Connor (Ed.), *Strategic Leadership in PK-12 Settings*. Hershey, PA: IGI Global.

Satir, V. (1988). *The new people making*. Mountain View, CA: Science & Behavior Books.

Schefter, A., & Walker, J. (2014, February 15). *Incognito, others tormented Martin*. Retrieved from http://www.espn.com/nfl/story/_/id/10455447/miami-dolphins-bullying-report-released-richie-incognito-others-responsible-harassment

Schulz, L. C. (2010). The Dutch Hunger Winter and the developmental origins of health and disease. *Proceedings of the National Academy of Sciences of the United States of America*, *107*(39), 16757–16758. doi:10.1073/pnas.1012911107 PMID:20855592

Seago, J. (2016). Toxic culture. *Internal Auditor*, *73*(3), 29–33.

Shaw, S. J. (2017). *Teachers' perceptions of the manifestation of horizontal workplace bullying in the K-12 setting* (Doctoral dissertation). Available from ProQuest Dissertations and Theses database. (UMI No. 10666730)

Simon, L. S., Hurst, C., Kelley, K., & Judge, T. A. (2015). Understanding cycles of abuse: A multi-motive approach. *The Journal of Applied Psychology*, *100*(6), 1–10. doi:10.1037/apl0000031 PMID:26011719

Singh, S., & Kumar, R. (2013). Why do dysfunctional norms continue to exist in the workplace? *Journal of Organization and Human Beahviour*, *2*(2), 11–19.

Skousen, T. (2016, April 12). *Responsibility vs. Accountability*. Retrieved from https://www.partnersinleadership.com/insights-publications/responsibility-vs-accountability/

Stogdill, R. M. (1974). *Handbook of leadership: A survey of theory and research*. New York, NY: Free Press.

Swick, A. (2013). *Student exposes bullying professor*. Retrieved from https://www.leadershipinstitute.org/News/?NR=10102

Thom, R. (1977). What is catastrophe theory about? In H. Haken (Ed.), *Synergetics. Springer Series in Synergetics, 2* (pp. 26–32). Berlin: Springer;

Thomas, M. E. (2016). How to spot a sociopath. *Psychology Today*. Retrieved from https://www.psychologytoday.com/us/articles/201305/how-spot-sociopath

Too, L., & Harvey, M. (2012). Toxic workplaces: The negative interface between the physical and social environments. *Journal of Corporate Real Estate, 14*(3), 171-181. http://dx.doi.org.ezproxylocal.library.nova.edu/10.1108187/14630011211285834

U.S. Department of Health and Human Services. (2017). *How does bullying affect health and well-being?* Retrieved from https://www.nichd.nih.gov/health/topics/bullying /conditioninfo/health

Westhues, K. (2004). *Workplace mobbing in academe: reports from twenty universities*. Lewiston, NY: Edwin Mellen Press.

Wise, J. (2010, October 17). *How psychopaths choose their victims just as sociopaths are a special breed, so too are their victims*. Retrieved from https://www.psychologytoday.com/us/blog/extreme-fear/201010/how-psychopaths-choose-their-victims

World Health Organization. (2019). *Suicide data*. Retrieved from https://www.who.int /mental_health/prevention/suicide/suicideprevent/en/

Wu Tsai Neurosciences Institute. (2019). *Robert Sapolsky*. Retrieved from https://neuroscience.stanford.edu/people/robert-sapolsky

Wyatt, J., & Hare, C. (1997). *Work abuse*. Rochester, VT: Schenkman Books.

Yildirim, N. (2017). Virginia Satir's family education and therapy model. *International Journal of Social Science Studies*, *5*(72). doi:10.11114/ijsss.v5i12.2778

Zapf, D., & Gross, C. (2001). Conflict escalation and coping with workplace bullying: A replication and extension. *European Journal of Work and Organizational Psychology*, *10*(4), 497–522. doi:10.1080/13594320143000834

Chapter 5
Mobbability:
Understanding How a Vulnerable Academia Can Be Healthier

Naomi Jeffery Petersen
Central Washington University, USA

Rebecca L. Pearson
Central Washington University, USA

ABSTRACT

This chapter discusses mobbing as a predictable institutional disorder with significant community effect. Academic departments are particularly vulnerable as contexts where conflicting motivations and tacit power differentials may allow undetectable and infectious incivility, and while there are research tools to measure experience, there are few effective practical campus-based strategies to monitor these issues. The authors explore mobbing through the lenses of epidemiology, public health, and organizational psychology. As part of this exploration the terms "mobbable" and "mobbability" are proposed, connoting the degree of incivility tolerated in the workplace climate, people's and institution's vulnerabilities, and the potential for improved capacity surrounding mobbing prevention. Outlining a story of academic mobbing, the chapter highlights contributing factors at both personal and organizational levels. The authors close with practical suggestions for recognizing symptoms and opportunities.

DOI: 10.4018/978-1-5225-9485-7.ch005

INTRODUCTION

Situating and Defining Mobbability

Most professionals, whether within academia or outside it, would be unsurprised that individual incivility and aggression thrive in certain work settings; however, we might hesitate to consider and discuss the possibility of more organized mistreatment. People who have experienced this more insidious abuse, though, know it exists and understand its serious nature.

Fortunately, for those wishing to improve our own and others' working lives, mobbing is becoming more familiar as a concept. Khoo (2010) identified five phases through which a mobbing usually progresses: 1) a critical incident (conflict phase), 2) the mobbing and stigmatizing itself, then 3) personnel management, 4) incorrect diagnosis, and, finally, 5) expelling of the target (p. 63). However, its nuances require at least one more term to help discuss those persons and workplaces who may be inherently vulnerable.

In the absence of such language, the authors of this chapter propose the term *mobbable* to refer to both targets and those who engage in mobbing as being fundamentally susceptible, respectively, to experiencing or perpetuating this condition. The authors have not seen the word other than in its use as a proper name for the Facebook-based social media app with no academic definition. *Mobbability* is defined here as two possible states of being: A workplace's mobbability is seen in its cultivation of either a mobbing-friendly or an anti-mobbing organizational climate.

This chapter is written by two authors who share a common perspective, but approach the problem with different views of mobbing's victimhood. An epidemiologist may be seen as treating the environment itself as the patient, and this is the first author's view. Investigating and curtailing a mobbing outbreak, then, might entail teasing out particular aspects of the mobbed environment as symptoms to address. Such symptoms may include noticeable irritation or silence in meetings, apathy surrounding campus projects, or other signs that the campus is unwell due to an attack of severe but shrouded incivility. Soon after salient symptoms are identified, attention might be turned to the predicted sequelae in this multi-faceted patient: growing or lingering distrust of colleagues or administrators, lack of engagement in new, positive initiatives, and acknowledged inabilities to discuss desired or needed change on campus, no matter the focus or reasoning for such change.

The second author sees campuses themselves as hosts, with the agent being incivility, and the environment (in which both the agent and host exist) being academia as a whole. In this view, the campus that has contracted a mobbing virus, or that may do so, has characteristics that have made it vulnerable. Addressing those characteristics becomes the priority. The characteristics contributing risk prompt this chapter's focus: the social ecology of mobbing on campus.

This chapter is grounded in commitment to health and wellbeing, and a belief that mobbing is a threat on personal and corporate levels. The authors suggest the possibility of, and ways to create, a safe work environment fostering beneficial effects for individuals and consequently greater productivity and creativity to achieve institutional missions. They believe that mobbing can be predicted and prevented, which is an optimistic response to a disheartening reality: that mobbing may be an anticipated part of academic life, facilitated at the institutional level, whether or not those causing it are consciously aware of what they are fostering or their responsibility.

One of the authors comes from public health, focusing her work on the external factors outside of people's direct control. An important aspect of that work is teaching individuals what they must know in order to take control of their own health outcomes. The other author comes from teacher education, working intensively with individuals to understand, and plan to make, their professional lives as teachers. Both are university professors actively engaged in scholarship and service at the university level and have experienced varying degrees of mobbing that have heightened their awareness of its effects. Together they bring theory and research about public health, education, psychology, and leadership to their study of mobbing. Their outlooks converge with the lens of social ecology as developed by Bronfrenbrenner (as cited in Eriksson, Ghazinour, & Hammarström, 2018; Stokolz, 1996; Wold & Mittelmark, 2018), and Durkheim's assumption that social facts explain individual experience (Morrison, 2006).

As an avoidable condition, mobbing requires preventive action at many levels. The chapter emphasizes the authors' prevention-oriented views of mobbing as relevant to an epidemiological consideration, more specifically from a social epidemiological perspective, which "focuses particularly on the effects of socio-structural factors on states of health" (Honjo, 2004, p. 193). The authors believe that the story they tell will, regrettably, strike many readers as familiar or at least unsurprising, but they also believe that the insights they share will reassure all readers that mobbing does not have to be an inescapable part of university life.

Mobbings as Shared Cultural History

Mobbing is everywhere, and it is not new. In 1706, Matthew Henry noted the significance of Christianity's commandment to avoid bearing false witness: Speaking unfairly about something that has (perhaps mistakenly) gone wrong, thus worsening a situation, stands to cause harm to others (Henry, 1706). Centuries before, Luther further interpreted the commandment to mean one must view and report others with the most generous construction (Luther & Smith, 1529/1999), that is, look for the good. Thus we see the timelessness of issues surrounding incivility. A few iconic examples will place mobbing episodes in context as predictable tales: Stock characters make dramatic turns familiar.

Meet Desdemona, never suspecting that others would be motivated to harm her. Thanks to Iago's machinations, her maid was duped into a charade with a willing henchman to destroy Desdemona's reputation and marriage. Her husband Othello was the actual object of the malicious campaign, but she was the victim. She was mobbed. Also offered by Shakespeare is Hero. A virtuous young woman, Hero is victimized by her community after one person, Don John, acts to convince others (falsely) of her unfaithfulness to her fiancé, Claudio. In Hero's case, not even her father stands up for her or investigates the facts, determining that it would indeed be best if Hero were to die.

Finally, meet Laura Ingalls. In countless episodes of *Little House on the Prairie* (McWray, 1974), the snobbish Mrs. Oleson gossips at the expense of the hapless and virtuous, a useful trope for considering the common community dynamic of sacrificing safety and cohesion for personal ambition and vengeance. Note that Mr. Oleson provides a stock character as well: morally aware and sympathetic, but nonetheless passive and risk avoidant. The caution is that, rather than focusing on the episodic plot lines between characters, it is important instead to emphasize the health of a very small, geographically-bound population, operating under unspoken rules of civility, who must either coexist or leave.

The examples of Desdemona, Hero, and Laura help contextualize stories, occurring quietly around the world's academic workplaces, that may be ignored or dismissed while the target endures the gut-wrenching consequences. This book exists as testimony that such stories are not unique. However, the characteristics of mobbing make it nearly unfathomable to those who have been targets, let alone to those with no experience of it. Thus, the authors offer a discussion grounded in science and in our cultural myths and stories.

Discussing Mobbability: Abby's Story

The personal story shared here is admittedly anecdotal and not collected through formal qualitative methods. The authors spoke with a tenured professor to assemble an example of mobbing behavior in an academic setting. Names and identifying details have been changed or eliminated to protect her privacy.

You cannot find a more engaged faculty member than Abby. Her energy and enthusiasm are legendary. Her discipline is her passion, and she involves her students at a remarkable level with authentic research-based projects – not, though, without ruffling a few old guard feathers. She has initiated unique campus efforts, and been part of others. Her interests are multi-faceted, and she is a willing volunteer for most initiatives. This paints a portrait of a dynamic contributor to the mission of the university, but it also profiles her as a vulnerable target for mobbing.

When Abby became acutely aware of what was happening to her, she had no name for it. She confided in a colleague – herself a mobbing survivor – who recognized the experience for what it was, stated that neither her own story nor Abby's was unique on their campus, and suggested she read articles about mobbing. Abby found it illuminated her experience, and her contribution to this chapter is an effort to add to that literature.

As she shared her story, and discussed the research on workplace abuse with the authors, Abby realized that she probably had been somewhat conscious of the threatening dynamic: She remembered that, over the last couple of years, she had often asked for a commitment to openness. Using this chapter's proposed new language, Abby can be viewed as arguing for mobbability in its positive second meaning, asking her colleagues to engage with her in actively building an anti-mobbing setting for their work together. For her, the public health concept of comorbidity resonated (Valderas, Starfield, Sibbal, Salisbury, & Roland, 2009): Rather than staying healthy or regaining health after a minor episode, the individuals and the community had together become seriously ill, in a second way, from the turmoil and toxicity already affecting them.

As the authors analyzed Abby's story, they realized that vagaries in the organizational setting are among the requisite characteristics of mobbing. The authors believe vagueness – of protocols, lines of authority, or requirements both within and across units – forms a piece of the groundwork that allows certain individuals to be picked out as deserving of the "subtle, 'behind your back' aggression" that Jensen, Patel, and Raver (2014, p. 305) discuss as a typical characteristic of incivility and related employee victimization. Additionally, "high performers" are particularly likely to experience "ostracism, backstabbing," and other covert attacks (p. 298). These authors further note that this disproportionate risk is "irrational when viewed from a group effectiveness perspective" (p. 305), given that a unit's success depends on such superior performance. However, as Feather (1989) made clear, some employees are powerfully motivated to diminish an active, successful colleague and thus camouflage their own limitations of competence or character. In a susceptible setting, mobbing is a convenient strategy to achieve that purpose.

Chapter Objectives

Objective 1: Discuss mobbing as a predictable, and preventable, workplace health issue.
Objective 2: Share a literature- and theory-based analysis of a personal experience of mobbing.
Objective 3: Discuss the campus as a social ecological system.
Objective 4: Propose strategies for prevention.

BACKGROUND

Individual Motives and Perceptions

Mobbing is best understood as organized bullying, "with collusion or active participation of the management" (Segal, 2010, p. 2), and is considered by Zapf to be "a severe form of social stressors at work" (as cited in Vveinhardt & Štreimikienė, 2017, p. 53). Andersson and Pearson (1999) defined incivility as ''low-intensity deviant behavior with ambiguous intent to harm the target, in violation of workplace norms for mutual respect'' (p. 457). Such behaviors include ignoring and gossiping about coworkers – wherein the malicious intent may be difficult for the target, bystanders, and administrators to determine (Nielsen & Einarsen, 2018), but the combined effect is toxic.

The prevalence of workplace abuse is well known, but the mechanisms by which mobbing emerges and is tolerated are less understood. If individuals and the leaders in organizations can better anticipate the coordinated incivility that is mobbing, they can intervene to adjust vulnerable conditions and respond appropriately. It is therefore necessary to consider motives and perceptions on both individual and community scales. The roles of the bully, accomplices, and target are motivated by personal survival needs and ambitions which must be studied in the context of the workplace with its own institutional versions of survival needs and ambitions. Although a collective phenomenon, involved individuals are nonetheless agents who have their own logic for behavior.

Mobbing behavior has been studied as a manifestation of psychological deviance described as Machiavellian (Pilch & Turska, 2015), but this quality is now considered a component of the overall dynamic rather than the sole agent (Reknes, Einersen, Knardahl & Lau, 2014; Segal, 2010). The term 'Machiavellian' refers to the sixteenth century author who articulated the political strategy of sacrificing private morals for a perceived good, that is *the end justifies the means*. Preservation of power in the political context is paramount. In the case of the everyday workplace bully, Machiavellianism is more sinister because lack of empathy, or even outright cruelty, is more intimate. By contrast, the target tends to be more mission-driven and unlikely to sacrifice personal morality for any gain, public or private.

Popp (2017) presented a chilling picture of a "zero-empathy" employee, leading a group action that is rendered invisible by its stealth and ambiguity: Coworkers unable to consider the possibility that another "could intentionally visit this kind of evil on a colleague" make it even more effective (p. 5). He suggested that a trait of extreme indifference to others is not just a well-established phenomenon but is actually fairly common – with an estimated 1 in 25 people exhibiting zero empathy. He further attributed the bully's motives (for a rational, calculated campaign) not just to an act of self-preservation but to schadenfreude, pleasure in seeing others suffer.

According to self-determination theory (Ryan & Deci, 2000), all actions serve three fundamental needs: autonomy, competence, and affiliation. Mobbing tactics aggressively undermine the target in all three areas, triggering a depressive cycle. Indeed, depression is the most prevalent of conditions affecting the mobbing victim (Kostev, Rex, Waehlert, Hog, & Heilmaier, 2014), and its mechanism is worth understanding because it is context-specific: Vulnerable conditions and people's efforts to survive them are somewhat predictable.

The tenure and post-tenure review process is one such vulnerable condition. It is a potential intervention point for those wishing to reduce mobbing, because it is the process by which faculty are most exposed to hidden and easily misinterpreted action, and it has such consequential effects. When faculty are diminished by review decisions, ostracized, and stigmatized, not only are their professional trajectories placed at risk, but their standing among colleagues may be perceptibly damaged. Thus a spiraling effect occurs with mobbing begetting more mobbing, bringing attendant despair.

Mobbing is ambiguous on the surface and therefore difficult to detect. Targets are made more vulnerable because both they and others are oblivious to the real threat emerging. Oblivion can be due to several conditions:

- Individuals may be self-absorbed and thus oblivious to cues of others' perspectives and behavior, as well as naïve regarding significance;
- The culture may not encourage communication nor monitor awareness and behavior; and
- Mobbing behaviors may be intentionally camouflaged.

In academia, these are common conditions. In addition, the minority voice, the loyal opposition, the gadfly, and the odd duck are often perceived as threats, and are therefore vulnerable – paradoxically, given that such roles are recognized as essential elements of a vibrant culture (Dewey, 1939/1989). In any case, a psychologically traumatic chain reaction is activated once the victim perceives the threat.

As Gilbert (2006) has explained in a psychobiological model of depression, stress appraisal triggers changes in biological processes, potentially generating the need for support and efforts to avoid attack, and thus simultaneously inhibiting aggressive behavior. This increases doubt in oneself as exhibited in ambivalence, passive avoidance, and more compliant behavior which in turn increases feelings and perceptions of low status and personal worth (p. 155). The mobbing target's vulnerability may be seen as related to genetic predisposition to seek support and avoid risk (e.g. of abandonment and isolation), and to the escalating nature of perceptions once alerted to a pattern. The target will not, however, choose to seek support or avoid risk until alerted to threats: Feedback is needed to change the momentum of a current trajectory, as explained in cybernetic theory (Smith & Smith, 1966). Unfortunately, feedback in mobbing situations tends not to support the target to resolution, but instead often further undermines the sense of self and any thought that the events are unjust: As Khoo (2010) noted, administrators tend to diagnose the situation incorrectly, and any response on the part of the target is seen as further support that the target is actually the problem.

Ironically, a professional working hard to prove competence and earn respect may unwittingly pose a threat to others enjoying unearned status. Jensen et al report finding that, corresponding with "rational choice" theory, perpetrators "choose to inflict harm… in ways that minimizes [sic] danger to themselves" (2014, p. 297). As explained by Gilbert (2006) above, threat to status is existential – for it triggers fear of exposure and loss of privilege, explaining the compulsion to protect one's imperiled position. Mobbing is simply one strategy for undermining threats to status. The attack may be initiated by someone who is already identified as a bully, but it is perpetuated by onlookers and passive participants who willingly exploit new, or newly noted, opportunities to find advantage and avoid risk. As a more hidden variant of broader workplace abuse, mobbing is a preferred strategy among those whose status is threatened.

A manifestation of this cycle is a reduced commitment to the organization, compromising productivity by burnout, absenteeism, resignation and transfer – any of which burdens the organization to meet emergency needs and correct mistakes, but also destabilizes the workplace further by requiring replacements. It is therefore in the organization's interest to maintain adequate civility. However, the organization's more immediate interest is its own survival, and that of its culture. This more salient priority may mean institution-level prevention opportunities go unnoticed or are actively avoided, or that efforts are superficial and narrow in scope rather than effective systemic reforms.

Individual Perspectives of the Workplace

A micro view of individual effects must therefore be balanced with a macro view of the institution, with the administrator's leadership central to the organizational culture's mobbability. The bully role is shared by an instigator and accomplices, and thus the psychology of the individual bully, while necessary for initiating the campaign, is insufficient to explain it. The administration – another collective identity shared by chairs, deans, human resources staff, provosts, and other administrators – takes on a corporate role of responsibility for the overall workplace.

Bullies are focused on their positions within the work environment, thereby limiting their scope of concern to their immediate contexts of power. Bullies perpetually seek a dominant position, continuously promoting personal influence and reducing threats to their status. Because the scope is defined by the workplace, the bully can be far more vigilant about emerging trends and ever ready to take advantage of random conversations and policy changes. A bully's accomplices have varying degrees of power motive but may be characterized as having a concern for their survival, again within the workplace context. Aligning with the bully is a strategy to avoid being bullied, but also an investment in the bully's success by which associates may also benefit. Any concern for higher purpose may be used to rationalize an action, but will not be a governing motive.

By contrast, the target may see the workplace itself as a means to an end, serving to achieve a higher purpose. This clouds the perception of the immediate environment while focusing on the ideal. Targets will happily modify or even sacrifice the current workplace configuration in order to fulfill a noble mission. Thus, misalignment of priorities is revealed in the different stakeholders' motives. The distinct ecological roles hold different views of the workplace, depicted in the table below. This provides a framework for understanding the vulnerability of a workplace such as academia to the phenomenon of mobbability.

Considering, and Considering Assessment of, the Social Ecology of Mobbing

Humans do not operate in isolation from each other nor from their settings. Bronfenbrenner's Ecological Systems theory supports an investigation of the campus

Table 1. Intersecting stakeholder perceptions related to the workplace

Stakeholder Priority	View of Team Mission	View of the Institution
Target: mission first.	Applies to both end and means. Path of least hypocrisy.	A means to an end greater than the institution.
Bully: status first.	Applies to end, not means. Path of least risk or discomfort.	Personal status within the hierarchy is the goal.
Colleagues: survival first.	Applies to end, not means. Path of least resistance.	Survival within the institution is the goal.
Administration: risk management first.	Applies to end, not means. Path of least cost.	Sustainability of the institution is the goal.

as the context for individual interactions and effects. Originally conceived as a way of understanding children's development, his theory emphasized three levels of context: the individual's ability to influence the environment, the reality that people define their own experiences, and that "environments will not be randomly distributed," but will instead have *niches* (Darling, 2007, p. 204). The characteristics of a given "niche" may lead different individuals with different prior experiences and different understandings of their current situations to different endpoints. While the individual is compelled to navigate this system, the system is motivated to nurture individuals to keep itself going.

Higher education's structural social ecology has been blamed for the creation and maintenance of tokenism for faculty of color who work in predominantly white institutions (Niemman, 2016). White privilege is the systemic advantage whites have become accustomed to; there are other socially constructed defaults – race, gender, sexuality, and even ability – with unacknowledged advantage that are systemic in academic workplaces, no matter the efforts to eliminate their effects via policy. No amount of objective statistical data exposing ongoing multifaceted inequity and oppression will persuade the privileged person to change a system that is advantageous, and threats to its stability are resisted. Indeed, as cited in Porter (2018), Westhues noted that those who are perceived to be "different" in any way are particularly vulnerable. The same systemic context must be recognized as a component in the perpetuation of incivility that, taken further, becomes mobbing.

Several measures have been designed to detect individual experiences of incivility (Blau & Andersson, 2005), e.g. the Workplace Incivility Scale (Cortina, Magley, Williams, & Langhout, 2001) and the Uncivil Workplace Experiences Questionnaire (Martin & Hine, 2005). However, it is important to note that the focus of these measures is on capturing individual experiences of uncivil behaviors, rather than on the context surrounding such mistreatment (Donovan, Drasgow, & Munson, 1998). The Perceptions of Fair Interpersonal Treatment scale produced by Donovan et al., for example, does not capture practices that suppress disrespectful behavior (e.g., telling a coworker to stop their rude behavior) to maintain workgroup norms for civility (Hackman, 1992, as cited in Walsh et al., 2012). Walsh, et al. composed the Civility Norms Questionnaire-Brief (CNQ-B), a 4-item measure designed to assess workgroup climate for civility. *Climate for civility* is defined as employee perceptions of norms supporting respectful treatment among workgroup members. The CNQ-B is a promising instrument given the validation based on multiple large samples that encompass both within- and cross-organization perspectives on civility norms. However, this tool does not apply to mobbing, which is more subtle and may not appear disrespectful.

Using instruments such as those discussed above to detect mobbing, or a tendency to mob, begs the question of administrators monitoring for vulnerability. Any survey, though, of employee perceptions and experience may be powerful not for its wording but for the message that there is interest in their voice – and that expressed perspectives may contribute to institutional improvement. As is well understood in academia, assessment is largely intended to demonstrate gaps between what is and what should be or, put more positively, to demonstrate opportunities for change. Thoughtfully designed, context-specific assessment studies may well be a reasonable (and cost-effective) first step in a proactive administrative approach to preventing mobbing.

ACADEMIA AS A MOBBABLE SETTING

The academic community is a fertile ground for mobbing to emerge, given how pervasive the threats. It may be hidden from students, but campuses are innately competitive settings in which faculty and departments contend for limited resources. Additionally, faculty continuously struggle to demonstrate worth relative to that of others who are similarly faced with a recurring need to maneuver in order to gain and keep administrator approval. Consequential decisions are made in veiled circumstances: Multiple levels of peer review are based on documentation with ambiguous guidelines and idiosyncratic interpretation. Direct communication is typically limited, with narrow windows to counteract negative determinations.

It follows that faculty may benefit by learning to become advocates who can effectively ask administrators to emphasize, or reemphasize, the meaning and quality of teaching, research, and service. Faculty performance evaluation and review is particularly critical as an administrative decision-making realm: Administrators' interpretation of processes and criteria, substantive and meaningful fidelity to them (or its opposite, petty micromanaging), and resulting determinations can affirm faculty members' efforts to contribute strong, innovative teaching and engaged and impactful scholarship and service or, on the contrary, devalue those same efforts.

Armstrong (2012) reasoned that "the relatively nebulous leadership roles that many… hold… afford a good deal of responsibility but very little actual power" – accounting for "the ubiquity of faculty skirmishes, turf battles, verbal aggression, brooding, anxiety, and status insecurity" (p. 100). Such a context may encourage faculty to become guarded, even cagey, in their interactions, leading to a workplace culture in which private conversations – held among a few, and regarding other colleagues, their actions, and their motivations – become the norm. In contrast, open discussions, in which involved colleagues participate honestly together in dialog about situations, are rare. Because "negative communication" about a colleague is a hallmark of, and an intentional "powerful weapon" in, mobbing (Seguin, 2016, p. 1), this characteristic of academia – as a place where exclusive conversations about other people are often the rule – is concerning. Thus academia is a naturally mobbable setting, with recognizably mobbable people building important aspects of their lives in that setting.

Although this chapter's focus is on adults, the mobbing literature suggests similarities with school bullying, and even that mobbing origins may be in the settings children and youth inhabit. In a study of bullying in two London schools, Jamal, Bonell, Harden, and Lorenc (2015) challenged the simple explanation of a power differential between individuals, finding repeated aggressions more complex and "fluid with regard to the bully and victim role" (p. 731). Notably, these authors found schools' policies to be "complicit in the making of stable bully and victim roles, thus indirectly contributing to the reproduction of unhealthy relationships between students" (p. 731).

As Seguin noted, "the severity of mobbing in academic settings destroys [the] fantasy" (p. 3) that people (in particular, faculty themselves) hold about universities as distinctive places where faculty are respected for, and supported to produce, strong and meaningful work. Even on its own, this destruction, of a powerful and encouraging vision that what faculty do matters, harms both individuals and institutions. Less obviously, but no less importantly, students and the public – the purchasers of faculty work – are also harmed when faculty are disillusioned about the places in which they have chosen to engage in that work.

Thus, along with its impacts on targets, mobbing has serious implications for campuses. The authors argue too that mobbing also harms those who engage in it. In particular, faculty who may unwittingly be a part of a mobbing action are damaged as a result of violating their own integrity. Such broad and serious impact supports discussion of mobbing as a societal issue, namely a public health issue (Seguin, 2016). Mobbing in academia is faced by a specific population group – albeit a group that the general public may view as somewhat privileged. Thus, mobbing easily lends itself to an exploration via epidemiology and relevant theory from public health and other fields.

Parallels to Infectious Disease Control and Prevention

Mobbing has severe long-term consequences that damage quality of life, making chronic disease a fitting metaphor. However, thinking about mobbing as a communicable, or infectious, disease becomes relevant as well. Cholera is particularly apt as a way to understand mobbing as such an issue, and to consider prevention opportunities and strategies. When John Snow acted in 1854 to investigate and stop a deadly epidemic, his efforts in hindsight were truly heroic, as he faced strong resistance to his suggestion that community decisionmakers – the Board of Guardians of St. James' Parish in London – take away access to a primary source of local residents' drinking water. The suggestion was followed, with the pump handle removed less than a day after Snow approached the Board, and the epidemic ended (Chave, 1958).

A century and a half later, we look back on Snow's work and its significance to public health as self-evident. It would be astonishing to meet anyone who would deny the possibility of practical curtailment and prevention of known, suspected, or future outbreaks of waterborne disease. In the workplace today, we have a similar epidemic of staggering consequence.

Mobbing has been discussed as a "sophisticated, 'ganging up' behavior adopted by academicians" (Khoo, 2010, p. 61), a "pernicious and dangerous workplace injury," (Segal, 2010, p. 1), and a "violent and deliberative process in which the individual psychologies of the aggressors and their victim provide no keys to understanding the phenomenon" (Seguin, 2010, p. 1). The experience and its aftermath are extremely damaging. As a result of their colleagues' actions, mobbing targets may experience lasting "self doubts [sic], shame, worthlessness, humiliation, unhappiness, and desperation" along with stress-related physical health issues (Khoo, 2010, p. 64), e.g. post-traumatic stress disorder. Other serious consequences include job and income loss, engagement in lengthy legal battles, and sometimes permanent unemployment or underemployment (Segal, 2010). Seguin alerts us that mobbed professors may take extreme measures of escaping the pain, estimating that 12% commit suicide.

Looking closely, we can see that, like cholera, mobbing is caused by an invisible infection to which some populations are more susceptible than others. Similarly, both mobbing and cholera can be predicted in high risk contexts, and mobbing can be prevented with similarly diligent monitoring and practical – but provocative – interventions that, like Snow's, may challenge norms and be perceived as problematic by those with administrative power.

Similarly again to cholera, multiple factors converge to create mobbing-friendly conditions. A classic model of epidemiology is the Epidemiological Triad – where a health issue, in particular a communicable disease, is conceptualized as the result of the connections between *agent*, *host*, and *environment* (Centers for Disease Control and Prevention [CDC], 2012). The triad provides a useful framework for considering mobbability, for there is always a bully with accomplices, a target, and a workplace context. To use the model, the mobbing-focused epidemiologist would determine which element fits where. Each corner of the triangle (the perpetrators, the target, and the context itself) may develop symptoms. In regarding the three elements, the authors found their views diverging a bit, with both perspectives providing value to the discussion and, ultimately, coming together to form a coherent and more detailed picture of their analysis of epidemiology as related to mobbing.

Typically, an infectious disease epidemiologist's first focus is on the group whose obvious and acute ill health must be improved. This focus is made possible in large part because the methods of disease surveillance, whether active or passive, function well. Individual cases of the issue come to this professional's attention via local statistics built of self-reported illness, clinical care visits, or unanticipated mortality. Importantly, with dangerous or highly infectious diseases, a single record of unexpected diagnosis or potential diagnosis serves as a sentry for a population, alerting the epidemiologist that there is an acute community problem. Indeed, the term *sentinel event* is used in epidemiology to denote an observation that, according to The Joint Commission (2017), acts to "signal the need for immediate investigation and response" (Sentinel Event Policy and Procedures para. 3). Once such a sentinel event is noted, the epidemiologist then can inform and work with prevention specialists, primary and other care providers, emergency services personnel, law enforcement, and others who may interact with ill persons.

The epidemiologist's role is to investigate, and work to improve, less than optimal health outcomes for the community – whether in the face of a sentinel event like a cholera outbreak, which must be stopped, or more endemic issues, such as colds and flu, that are avoidable but not eradicated. Therefore, these more expected issues still demand consistent, usually systematic, and effective monitoring, with relevant intervention strategies planned and implemented to help maintain the community's disease experience at a low, manageable, and predictable level. Whether such interventions take the form of educational campaigns, health fair-style events, or free vaccine distribution at easily accessible venues such as supermarkets, all are aimed at controlling the spread of a predictably transmissible illness by helping the population recognize the signs. In civility terms, the citizens must be educated about the difference (and relationship) between malicious mobbing and routine gossip, alert to the significance that common negative communication must be seen as a symptom of a more severe disorder.

As discussed above, it is reasonable to anticipate a certain amount of incivility in the academic workplace environment. Thus, its most virulent variety, the stealthy aggression that characterizes mobbing, may well be seen as endemic to the faculty population. In parallel to such low level concerns as colds, then, prior to the emergence of, say, strep throat, it would be prudent for campuses to undertake practical prevention and control strategies before incivilities give way to mobbing.

Abby's Experience of Mobbing

When a person experiences the kind of workplace abuse seen in typical mobbings, it is likely that a first step is to confide in a trusted friend or colleague, in an effort to comprehend, define, or at least endure what has happened. As previously discussed, Abby's confidante led her to the literature on mobbing, which aided in understanding the incidents as being representative of a common set of experiences shared by many in academia.

The Campus Situation

Abby's personal experience of mobbing is grounded in an institution that was experiencing widespread demoralization with increasingly severe treatment by administration. Performance review processes, for those who have achieved tenure, emphasized stringent, unclear, and micromanaged requirements for documentation of scholarly efforts, rather than meaningful depictions of that effort; used selected negative student comments to make the case that an instructor might need remediation surrounding teaching (and did *not* use positive comments to bolster an opposing argument); and allowed university administrators to overturn decisions made by faculty peers on personnel committees. As noted above, until, at her confidante's suggestion, she explored the literature on mobbing, Abby had no name for what was happening to her. It has since become apparent that the organizational climate was itself vulnerable, both reflecting and contributing to the confluence of motives found in her colleagues, and that what Abby went through indeed reflected a sequenced experience of workplace abuse.

The Historical Context

When the mobbing happened, Abby boasted a record of highly productive service and scholarship, as well as effective teaching. Abby had worked collaboratively with colleagues, and hired new faculty whom she'd nurtured. She cultivated their cohesiveness, supported their innovations, and worked to emphasize equity. Abby's emerging leadership led to her increasing visibility across campus, and she continued her strong teaching, scholarship, and service; in hindsight, the context for Abby's mobbing exhibited classic vulnerability conditions.

The Phases and Events

Using Khoo's (2010) terms for phases of mobbing, the *critical incident* began when Abby was informed by her chair that junior colleagues had reported feeling intimidated, and that he was looking to make changes base on the reported situation. Thus the *stigmatizing* and *personnel management* were revealed. She thought the situation had resulted in an *incorrect diagnosis* and was horrified to be *expelled* from meaningful roles and work without proven – or even investigated – cause.

During conversation, the chair suggested mediation. Abby adamantly refused, stating that mediation would put her more at risk. Following her clear request that mediation not occur, a university staff member called Abby to offer mediation, stating that the chair had requested her to do so.

Abby realized that she was not going to be given an opportunity to defend herself, but decided to take the opportunity of an upcoming meeting to read a statement formally expressing her dismay at the situation and communication approach. Weeks later, further developments confirmed the mobbing, personnel management, and incorrect diagnosis phases. Abby's colleagues had contacted a Human Resources staff member, who told her that her colleagues had spoken to her of concern about Abby, noting that Abby's statement at the meeting had been perceived as somewhat "out of control." Upon reading a copy of the statement, though, this staff member commented that it did not appear to be problematic. The staff member admitted she had no training in handling this type of issue. Nonetheless, she recommended counseling for Abby, to help her through her "difficult situation." There was no suggestion of remedying the situation or the perceptions of others.

Taking a Levels of Prevention Approach to Mobbing on Campus

Reading through Khoo's (2010) descriptions of what actually happens in each phase, a target may well feel at once chilled and slightly comforted, as did Abby, when realizing that these events are indeed what has been recently lived through. For example, recognizing that "because of fundamental attribution errors, colleges and management tend to create explanations based on personal characteristics rather than on environmental factors" (p. 63) may help a mobbing target to begin taking note of components of the campus situation, and of administrative behavior and responses, that were previously only background noise. It will now become clear that such campus characteristics in fact contributed to the mobbing.

Although systemic change, and education for life within a system, is challenging, prevention of organizationally situated issues may be even more so: In contrast to more societally placed issues, the context is one in which policies and procedures quite directly affect professional lives and outcomes every day, and in which people may – or may not – be able to exert more control than they do (Wold & Mittelmark, 2018). Particularly in universities such as Abby's, in which shared governance is emphasized, faculty might be expected to be able to get involved in improving this aspect of institutional health and professional quality of life. However, the larger context of the organization itself may not support that involvement. Thus, faculty may themselves need instruction and assistance regarding taking more control of their own working lives.

In a highly structured organization like a university, recourse is limited to officially adopted policies to determine whether complaints are justified. The authors' faculty union and the formally recognized department chairs' group drafted a statement of principle on unprofessional conduct, making it clear that it was not policy. That it was even drafted, though, acknowledges that the union had reason to view the local faculty community as being at some risk of negative, severe, and potentially communicable outcomes grounded in interpersonal behaviors. It is particularly concerning that those producing the statement felt it necessary to remind faculty to be particularly aware of what is said in front of students. This admonition suggests an awareness of the potential damage that such negative communication, a hallmark of mobbing, carries. The statement raised the specter of personnel action or even litigation but did not specify responsibility for proactive monitoring. It is noteworthy, though, that the statement was solely a statement on unprofessional conduct – as opposed to a manifesto for a contrastingly civil level of professional conduct.

Mobbing as a Preventable Chronic (and Communicable) Condition

Obscured – but aggressive – incivility results in long-lasting harm to individuals both personally and professionally, as well as to institutions and the public. The authors regard such workplace abuse as a common and predicable phenomenon that can be detected and also prevented. The critical nature of this issue, with its far-reaching implications for well-being among faculty in institutions of higher education, prompts this chapter to address it, and the authors view the language of public health issues, in particular diseases, as contributing the most to a practical, action-oriented exploration of potential prevention. The authors propose universities first as risky contexts with respect to the dangerous experiences of mobbing, and thus as having potential for self-improvement: hence, the two-sided definition of mobbability.

As with other societal issues and norms, such as poverty (Gans, 1972) or the "celebration of self-sufficiency and fear of parasitism" (Sennett, 2003, p. 74) that arguably serve a function for one group or another, that characteristic – of serving a purpose – may make preventing mobbing more challenging: Necessary organizational change, already difficult, may be viewed as problematic by those with power to make it. Prevention-oriented change is complex, whether efforts are aimed at improving individuals' knowledge, attitudes, and behaviors linked to preventable outcomes such as illness and premature death, or instead at societal norms and values that make such outcomes more likely.

When moving to a societal story of mobbing, both public health theory and the science of epidemiology become relevant. Epidemiology is the basic science of public health, concerned with the "study of the distribution and determinants of health-related states or events in specified populations, and the application of this study to the control of health problems" (CDC, 2012). Using epidemiology allows researchers and practitioners to count and compare populations with respect to their experiences of preventable illness, injury, and death, and to describe the patterns and progression of specific health issues. Analyses and resulting findings support public health professionals, medical care providers, and other relevant personnel to determine and enact strategies to prevent these issues and thus improve population outcomes.

As discussed above, literature estimating mobbing's pervasiveness and severity exists. This literature paints a picture of risk, symptomatology, natural history, and immediate and long-term sequelae: in essence, a picture of disease or disorder.

Most disease is preventable to some degree, even if prevention demands organized societal effort at the level of governmental agencies or other institutions. This chapter contributes by suggesting that colleges and universities use the basis provided in literature to consider ways to strengthen their campuses by understanding – and proactively addressing – the risk that these workplaces carry as mobbable settings.

GUIDELINES FOR INTERVENTION AND PREVENTION

Managerial considerations such as predicting individual vulnerability to contributing to mobbability are beyond the scope of this chapter, but certainly potential as part of an approach for campuses wishing to build an actively anti-mobbing culture. For example, it would be possible to pre-screen for certain psychological tendencies, such as degree of empathy, preference for power over cooperation, susceptibility to coercion, or awareness of group dynamics.

This chapter suggests less arguable – if no simpler – possibilities, however. It would be practical and reasonable for supervisory roles to include responsibilities to monitor and intervene in hostile working conditions, or even to work to establish organizational structures that empower faculty, and support and promote productive collaboration, while deemphasizing detachment and competition. More research might investigate the promise of different tactics to do so.

Higher education could learn from the knowledge base of K-12 education, which has already addressed the problem of bullying with strategies including school-wide discipline policies as well as curriculum. It is such a recognized problem that the Bullying Prevention Steering Committee, an interagency effort co-led by the Department of Education and the Department of Health and Human Services, works to coordinate policy, research, and communications on bullying topics and host a website, Stopbullying.gov, to promote interventions. While this demonstrates federal leadership, the Southern Poverty Law Center also reported a disturbing increase in hate crimes and anxiety in the nation's schools after the 2016 presidential election, confirming the powerful influence of administrative leadership to help or harm a culture of safety, mutual respect, and civility (Costello, 2016). *Teaching Tolerance*, a project of the Southern Poverty Law Center, includes professional development for cultivating positive school climate with an anti-bias curriculum (Pettway & Phillips, 2018). Their guidelines (Teaching Tolerance, n.d.), adapted below, are instructive for higher education faculty as well, as we consider how these recommendations compare to current situations, and they offer a multi-tiered system of support addressing the social ecology of multiple perspectives and intersecting events. These guidelines also reflect circumstances that might have aided Abby had her institution made use of them.

Do Not Confuse Bullying With Conflict, or Victimhood With Incompetence

This guideline addresses the importance of accurately interpreting events: "Bullying is a form of victimization, and addressing it as a 'conflict' downplays the negative behavior and the seriousness of the effects. Educators should strive to send the message that 'no one deserves to be bullied,' and to let the bully know the behavior is wholly inappropriate." Higher education can adopt a parallel practice of recognizing the difference between academic debate and mobbing-level incivility, and producing institutional guidance to help faculty engage each other more productively and positively.

Monitor and Intervene

The message to the K12 teacher is to physically intervene in a verbal altercation, standing between the bullied student and the bullies, and blocking eye contact. In a mobbing, the interaction is covert, so intervention is not the same as simply stopping the aggressive behavior at the time of the incident. Time is clearly important, as a systemic malady will fester and re-emerge if untended, just as the workplace climate can become more civil if cultivated. In academia, the administrator who is not monitoring civility is providing tacit approval for survival tactics (Reknes et al., 2014).

Refer to Rules of Civility

The teacher is further advised to establish authority to intervene and to use the occasion as a teachable moment: Describe what occurred and announce that bullying is always unacceptable. Thus maxims are communicated with the intention of establishing behavioral norms. In academia, codes of conduct and criteria for evaluation focus on evidence of scholarship, teaching, and service, with accountability for civility only occurring when formal complaints are lodged. Then formal policies, when existing, are invoked (Khoo, 2010). It is thus helpful if teams are expected to draft their own working norms, if only to provide a formal focus for people to raise issues of incivility. The targeted colleague can then recognize how civility has been violated, instead of feeling disenfranchised or relying on external (and often incorrect) feedback that the problem is an individual one, with the target at fault. Note that referring to rules against bullying is not the same as emphasizing principles of civility.

Support the Targeted Individual

Here the teacher or administrator must be adept in psychology in order to preserve the person's dignity and address fear of retaliation. The target must believe the leader is accurately diagnosing the situation and focusing on the resulting climate of fear and mistrust. As Khoo (2010) noted, personnel management is a key phase of mobbing, so administrators must be cautious to see how any decisions regarding the faculty's status and responsibilities are perceived. Support also includes increasing supervision, acknowledging the likelihood of recurring incidents. Clearly, the point is to reinforce the perception that the leader is guided by principle and will intervene to maintain a civil society. If the response is tepid, the bullying is likely to escalate (Popp, 2017).

Schools and workplaces are cautioned not to use peer mediation: "It can be very upsetting for a child who has been bullied to face his or her tormentor in mediation. Giving both parties an equal voice can empower the bully and make the bullied student feel worse. In addition, there is no evidence that peer mediation is effective in stopping bullying (Stopbullying.gov)."

Offer Guidance to Bystanders

This is a crucial element: It recognizes the role of the pawns in the game. Counteracting the subterfuge means confronting complicit participation, whether as unknowing or active carriers of the contagion, indicating they are responsible for cultivating the environment. The unit itself must be seen as a victim as well, that each person is either helping or harming. However, leadership training is apparently necessary, given that without it, human resources officials are unlikely to be effective (Reknes et al, 2014), again, as Abby experienced.

Notify Colleagues and Parents

Transparency is thus established as part of civility, when the leader lets the bully know he or she is being watched. This is the most challenging step. It violates the assumptions of confidentiality about personnel issues. However, it is important to let stakeholders know that the events occurred and were recognized for what they were: a symptom of a weakened community. Announcing that recent events warrant reinforcing the need for collegiality would be enough to alert the workplace to the value placed on civility (Schiel, 2015), and also weaken the perceived power of those engaging in mobbing.

Follow Up and Intervene as Necessary

The last positive action recommended is to monitor situations closely, and continue to exhibit proactive leadership. All stakeholders need support and opportunities to express their feelings and recognize their own behavior. The bully may need to be redirected to use his or her power and influence positively; the accomplices need to see other opportunities for alignment with more positive individuals; the target must not feel abandoned or ignored. In other words, one intervention does not function as a vaccination to prevent future incivility. Effective intervention must happen, must resolve situations, and must be ongoing to prevent others.

FUTURE RESEARCH DIRECTIONS

This chapter reports an exploratory and reflective effort; empirical studies may reveal faculty and other academic staff's perspectives surrounding institutional risk factors and vulnerabilities, as well as their attitudes toward various types of intervention. Future research is also needed to determine whether conclusions regarding the bullying of children in schools are generalizable to adult workplace contexts. Another area of potential investigation is the comparison of different university policies regarding peer interaction and the ability of such policies to define civility as an environmental factor. Yet another research agenda concerns the training and evaluation of administrators to accurately identify and intervene in incivility trends. The theoretical framework of this article used public health and social ecology to interpret events; further research may synthesize these parallel efforts using psychology to interpret motives and behaviors. Comparisons of different career groups and different cultures will be of interest.

CONCLUSION

Mobbability refers to the vulnerability of an academic workplace to the emergence of subtle bullying tactics by a group of colleagues targeting an individual. Vulnerability increases when there are no explicit norms of collegiality and when leadership is weak. Stability, cohesiveness, effectiveness, and safety of workplaces is threatened by mobbing; it is similarly strengthened by policies that clearly identify mobbing and other bullying tactics as inappropriate and counter to institutional missions.

REFERENCES

Andersson, L., & Pearson, C. (1999). Tit for tat? The spiraling effect of incivility in the workplace. *Academy of Management Review*, *24*(3), 452–471. doi:10.5465/amr.1999.2202131

Armstrong, J. (2012). Faculty animosity: A contextual view. *Journal of Thought*, *47*(2), 85–104. doi:10.2307/jthought.47.2.85

Blau, G., & Andersson, L. (2005). Testing a measure of instigated workplace incivility. *Journal of Occupational and Organizational Psychology*, *78*(4), 595–614. doi:10.1348/096317905X26822

Centers for Disease Control and Prevention. (2012). *Principles of Epidemiology in Public Health Practice*. Retrieved from https://www.cdc.gov/ophss/csels/dsepd/ss1978/SS1978.pdf

Chave, S. (1958). Henry Whitehead and cholera in Broad Street. *Medical History*, *2*(2), 92–108. doi:10.1017/S0025727300023504 PMID:13526540

Cortina, L. M., Magley, V. J., Williams, J. H., & Langhout, R. D. (2001). Incivility in the workplace: Incidence and impact. *Journal of Occupational Health Psychology*, *6*(1), 64–80. doi:10.1037/1076-8998.6.1.64 PMID:11199258

Costello, M. (2016). *After election day, the Trump effect: The impact of the 2016 presidential election on our nation's schools*. Montgomery, AL: Southern Poverty Law Center.

Darling, N. (2007). Ecological systems theory: The person in the center of the circles. *Research in Human Development*, *4*(3), 203–217. doi:10.1080/15427600701663023

Dewey, J. (1989). *Freedom and culture*. Amherst, NY: Prometheus. (Original work published 1939)

Donovan, M., Drasgow, F., & Munson, L. (1998). The Perceptions of Fair Interpersonal Treatment Scale: Development and validation of a measure of interpersonal treatment in the workplace. *The Journal of Applied Psychology*, *83*(5), 683–692. doi:10.1037/0021-9010.83.5.683 PMID:9806012

Eriksson, M., Ghazinour, M., & Hammarström, A. (2018). Different uses of Bronfenbrenner's ecological theory in public mental health research: What is their value for guiding public mental health policy and practice? *Social Theory & Health*, *16*(4), 414–433. doi:10.105741285-018-0065-6

Facebook. (2018). *Mobbable*. Retrieved from https://www.facebook.com/Mobbable/

Feather, N. (1989). Attitudes toward the high achiever: The fall of the tall poppy. *Australian Journal of Psychology*, *41*(3), 239–267. doi:10.1080/00049538908260088

Gans, H. (1972). The positive functions of poverty. *American Journal of Sociology*, *78*(2), 275–289. doi:10.1086/225324

Gilbert, P. (2006). Evolution and depression: Issues and implications. *Psychological Medicine*, *36*(3), 287–297. doi:10.1017/S0033291705006112 PMID:16236231

Henry, M. (1706). *Exodus* (Vol. 1). Commentary on the Whole Bible. Retrieved from https://www.ccel.org/ccel/henry/mhc1.Ex.xxi.html

Honjo, K. (2004). Social epidemiology: Definition, history, and research examples. *Environmental Health and Preventive Medicine*, *9*(5), 193–199. doi:10.1007/BF02898100 PMID:21432303

Jamal, F., Bonell, C., Harden, A., & Lorenc, T. (2015). The social ecology of girls' bullying practices: Exploratory research in two London schools. *Sociology of Health & Illness*, *37*(5), 731–744. doi:10.1111/1467-9566.12231 PMID:25655642

Jensen, J., Patel, C., & Raver, J. (2014). Is it better to be average? High and low performance as predictors of employee victimization. *The Journal of Applied Psychology*, *99*(2), 296–309. doi:10.1037/a0034822 PMID:24219126

Khoo, S. (2010). Academic mobbing: Hidden health hazard at the workplace. *Malaysian Family Physician*, *5*(2), 61–67. PMID:25606190

Kostev, K., Rex, J., Waehlert, L., Hog, D., & Heilmaier, C. (2014). Risk of psychiatric and neurological diseases in patients with workplace mobbing experience in Germany: A retrospective database analysis. *German Medical Science*, *12*, 1–9. PMID:24872810

Luther, M., & Smith, R. (1999). *Martin Luther's Small Catechism (R. Smith, Trans.)*. Project Gutenberg. (Original work published 1529)

Martin, R., & Hine, D. (2005). Development and validation of the Uncivil Workplace Behavior Questionnaire. *Journal of Occupational Health Psychology*, *10*(4), 477–490. doi:10.1037/1076-8998.10.4.477 PMID:16248694

McWray, K. (Producer). (1974). Little House on the Prairie [Television series]. Hollywood, CA: National Broadcasting Company.

Morrison, K. (2006). *Marx, Durkheim, Weber: Formations of modern social thought* (2nd ed.). London: SAGE.

Nielsen, M., & Einarsen, S. (2018). What we know, what we do not know, and what we should and could have known about workplace bullying: An overview of the literature and agenda for future research. *Aggression and Violent Behavior, 42*, 71–83. doi:10.1016/j.avb.2018.06.007

Niemann, Y. (2016). The social ecology of tokenism in higher education. *Peace Review, 28*(4), 451–458. doi:10.1080/10402659.2016.1237098

Pettway, A., & Phillips, H. (2018). *The Teaching Tolerance social justice standards: A professional development facilitator guide.* Southern Poverty Law Center. Retrieved from https://www.tolerance.org/sites/default/files/2018-11/TT-Social-Justice-Standards-Facilitator-Guide-WEB_0.pdf

Pilch, I., & Turska, E. (2015). Relationships between Machiavellianism, organizational culture, and workplace bullying: Emotional abuse from the target's and the perpetrator's perspective. *Journal of Business Ethics, 128*(1), 83–93. doi:10.100710551-014-2081-3

Popp, J. (2017). Social intelligence and the explanation of workplace abuse. *Journal of Workplace Rights, 77*(2), 1–7.

Porter, S. (2018). *How academic mobbing works.* Retrieved from https://stephenporter.org/how-academic-mobbing-works/

Reknes, I., Einarsen, S., Knardahl, S., & Lau, B. (2014). The prospective relationship between role stressors and new cases of self-reported workplace bullying. *Scandinavian Journal of Psychology, 55*(1), 45–52. doi:10.1111jop.12092 PMID:25271332

Ryan, R., & Deci, E. (2000). Self-Determination theory and the facilitation of intrinsic motivation, social development, and well-being. *The American Psychologist, 55*(1), 68–79. doi:10.1037/0003-066X.55.1.68 PMID:11392867

Schiel, T. (2015). Grappling with collegiality and academic freedom. *Academe, 101*(6).

Segal, L. (2010). The injury of mobbing in the workplace. *Conflict Remedy.* Retrieved from https://conflictremedy.com/the-injury-of-mobbing-in-the-workplace/

Seguin, E. (2016) Academic mobbing, or how to become campus tormentors. *University Affairs.* Retrieved from https://www.universityaffairs.ca/opinion/in-my-opinion/academic-freedom-and-the-faith-based-university/

Sennett, R. (2003). *Respect in a world of inequality*. New York: Norton.

Smith, K., & Smith, M. (1966). *Cybernetic principles of learning and educational design*. Holt, Rinehart, Winston.

Stokols, D. (1996). Translating social ecological theory into guidelines for community health promotion. *American Journal of Health Promotion*, *10*(4), 282–298. doi:10.4278/0890-1171-10.4.282 PMID:10159709

Stopbullying.gov. (n.d.). *Misdirections in bullying prevention and intervention*. Retrieved from https://www.stopbullying.gov/sites/default/files/2017-10/misdirections-in-prevention.pdf

Teaching Tolerance. (n.d.). *Bullying: Guidelines for teachers*. Retrieved from https://www.tolerance.org/professional-development/bullying-guidelines-for-teachers

The Joint Commission. (2017). *Sentinel event policy and procedures*. Retrieved from https://www.jointcommission.org/sentinel_event_policy_and_procedures/

Valderas, J. M., Starfield, B., Sibbald, B., Salisbury, C., & Roland, M. (2009). Defining comorbidity: Implications for understanding health and health services. *Annals of Family Medicine*, *7*(4), 357–363. doi:10.1370/afm.983 PMID:19597174

Vveinhardt, J., & Štreimikienė, D. (2017). Demographic, social, and organizational characteristics on the levels of mobbing and single cases of harassment: The Multicomplex approach. *Economics and Management*, *20*(3), 52–68.

Walsh, B., Magley, V., Reeves, D., Davies-Schrils, K., Marmet, M., & Gallus, J. (2012). Assessing workgroup norms for civility: The development of the Civility Norms Questionnaire-Brief. *Journal of Business and Psychology*, *27*(4), 407–420. doi:10.100710869-011-9251-4

Wold, B., & Mittelmark, M. (2018). Health-promotion research over three decades: The social-ecological model and challenges in implementation of interventions. *Scandinavian Journal of Public Health*, *46*(20_suppl), 20–26. doi:10.1177/1403494817743893 PMID:29552963

ADDITIONAL READING

American Association of University Professors. (2016). *On collegiality as a criterion for faculty evaluation (2016 Revision).* Retrieved January https://www.aaup.org/report/collegiality-criterion-faculty-evaluation

Asghar, R. (2013, July 5). How to screen out the sociopath job candidate. *Forbes.* Retrieved from forbes.com/sites/robasghar/2013/07/05/how-to-screen-out-the-sociopath-jobcandidate/#28466ddd60dd

Bonita, R., Beaglehole, R., & Kjellstrom, T. (2006). *Basic epidemiology.* Retrieved from http://whqlibdoc.who.int/publications/2006/9241547073_eng.pdf

Carter, S. (1998). *Civility.* NY: Harper Perennial.

Einarsen, S., Hoel, H., Zapf, D., & Cooper, C. (2011). *Bullying and harassment in the workplace: Developments in theory, research.* NY: CRC Press/Taylor & Francis.

Gibbon, S., Duggan, C., Stoffers, J., Huband, N., Vollm, B., Ferriter, M., & Lieb, K. (2010). Psychological interventions for antisocial personality disorder. *Cochrane Database of Systematic Reviews*, (6): CD007668. PMID:20556783

McGregor, J., & McGregor, T. (2013). *The empathy trap: Understanding antisocial personalities.* London, England: Sheldon Press.

Moulton Sarkis, S. (2018). *Gaslighting: Recognize manipulative and emotionally abusive people – and break free.* NY: Da Capo Press.

Namie, G., & Lutgen-Sandvik, P. (2010). Active and passive accomplices: The communal character of workplace bullying. *International Journal of Communication*, 4, 343–373.

Popp, J. (2015). *How sociopaths destroy good teachers: The invisible threat to education.* Lewiston, NY: Edwin Mellen Press.

Westermair, A. L., Stoll, A. M., Greggersen, W., Kahl, K. G., Hüppe, M., & Schweiger, U. (2018). All unhappy childhoods are unhappy in their own way: Differential impact of dimensions of adverse childhood experiences on adult mental health and health behavior. *Frontiers in Psychiatry*, 9, 198. doi:10.3389/fpsyt.2018.00198 PMID:29875707

KEY TERMS AND DEFINITIONS

Academia: Higher education as a workplace employing faculty to produce scholarship, teaching, and service to the immediate institution as well as to professional fields.

Civility: Patterns of behavior resulting in positive relationships ranging from peaceful coexistence to productive collaboration. Usually associated with formal manners and restraint of impulsive and destructive words or actions.

Climate for Civility: Employee perceptions of norms supporting respectful treatment among workgroup members.

Comorbidity: Coexisting conditions in intersecting components contributing to ill health.

Epidemiological Triad: The intersection of agent, host, and environment to produce unhealthy environmental conditions (e.g., epidemics of contagious disease).

Mobbability: The degree of incivility tolerated in the workplace climate rendering units and individuals vulnerable to strategic campaigns to discredit, stigmatize, and ostracize.

Sentinel Event: Signals the need for immediate investigation and response.

Social Ecology: A model for conceptualizing social issues as part of an interdependent system.

Target: Individual or group victimized by coordinated negative campaign to strategically discredit, stigmatize, and ostracize. Akin to the concept of host in the epidemiological triad.

Zero-Empathy: An employee with extreme indifference to the experience of others.

Chapter 6
Neoliberal Technocracy and Opposition Exams for Hiring Tenured Full-Time Professors in a Mexican Public University

Silvia Karla Fernández Marín
National School of Anthropology and History, Mexico

Florencia Peña-Saint-Martin
National School of Anthropology and History, Mexico

ABSTRACT

In this chapter, the introduction of technocratic neoliberal policies in Mexico, starting in the mid-1980s, and their repercussions in higher education are analyzed. Special focus is set on its negative consequences for hiring tenured full-time professors at public universities. A case study from a public university is used to demonstrate how suppressing candidates and arbitrarily favoring others through sham dealing are almost part of the formal procedures now. This case was used because access to all the documentation was granted, and it was possible to interview in depth a female candidate who was suppressed twice. Unfortunately, experiencing suppression, workplace bullying, and mobbing for some candidates is almost the norm now. Also, when suppressed, they are left in a powerless position with almost no resources to confront injustice.

DOI: 10.4018/978-1-5225-9485-7.ch006

INTRODUCTION

Starting in the mid-1980's, the introduction of technocratic neoliberal policies in Mexico, along with their repercussions on higher education, has negatively impacted the dynamics of hiring tenured full-time professors through opposition exams in public universities (Valenzuela, 1991). Such dynamics are the central focus of this text.

Based on the neoliberal economic system, structural adjustment measures were imposed with the goal of "freeing" the economy, such as: reducing the public budget by selling off and cutting back on State enterprises; curbing the general population's salaries while disproportionately increasing those of government officials; as well as strategies indirectly fostering precarious work, self-employment, underemployment, etc. (Tello, 2019). "Cutbacks" to State intervention led to an increase in national and foreign private sector investments, especially in profitable areas of the economy such as health, education, petrochemicals, etc. Borders were opened, based on the belief that trade would be regulated through competition, putting national products at a disadvantage with respect to their international counterparts (Tello, 2019).

Such policies impacted social dynamics through multiple recursive relationships between national and international areas and contexts. Some of the most relevant transformations in this respect include: the redistribution of socially produced wealth through the concentration of enormous fortunes in the hands of a few, a rise in poverty, and a decline in a majority of the population's standard of living.

Preexisting inequalities were deepened as the State redefined its relationships and commitments to society by eliminating subsidies on basic consumer goods and defunding public health, education, and housing. While many state services were transferred directly into private hands, the private sector also began to intervene in these areas through so-called public-private associations (Pérez del Castillo, 2018). This led citizens to shoulder many of the costs for which the State relinquished responsibility, triggering a process of privatization of life that contributed to the impoverishment of the vast majority. Interpersonal relationships in the job market, in social life, and in the private sphere were also modified. Competition and individualism were enhanced, which explains, in part, the significant rise in violence during recent years (Vieyra, 2015).

Ultimately, these measures exacerbated poverty and extreme poverty, deteriorating standards of living through a combination of low salaries, underemployment, unemployment (the product of short-term contracts without social benefits, the subcontracting of workers, outsourcing, precarious jobs, and self-employment) and lack of institutional social benefits (de la Garza, 2011). In this way, large sectors of the population were excluded from access to goods, services, and rights that had been previously enjoyed by the population during the import substitution economic era. The uncertainty prompted by such technocratic measures in economic, social, political, and other sectors, led to a continued rise in social discontent and, ultimately, to the rejection of this model at the polls last July 1, 2018, leaving the country to face a transitional situation which is not yet clearly defined, despite the current president, in charge since December 1, 2019, declaring the end of neoliberalism in the country (*Proceso*, June 13, 2019).

Neoliberalism in Mexican Higher Education

During the neoliberal era, the fields of education and work were especially affected. The former, because it was employed to reproduce the ideology of that system through policies that privileged individualism and competitiveness over solidarity, collegial decisions, and teamwork. The latter, because it was the arena where a struggle took place to avoid unemployment and to obtain benefits or incentives at all cost, without any regard for the other. Workers had been subjected, for thirty-six years, to these dynamics both in the classroom and in the workplace focused on quashing or suppressing potential competitor(s) in organizations, businesses, trades, and institutions. The university setting combined both spheres: education and the labor dynamic. This led to a redefinition of the university, in tune with neoliberal policies, that promoted an organization culture privileging individualism and competition (Ibarra, 2001).

Likewise, in the academic communities of public institutions of higher education (IHE), competition and individualism were institutionalized through incentives for performance and productivity. The National Researchers' System (*Sistema Nacional de Investigadores,* SNI. Retrieved on February 11, 2019, from: https://www.conacyt.gob.mx/index.php/el-conacyt/sistema-nacional-de-investigadores; which gives economic rewards for high research productivity), created in 1984 (*Diario Oficial de la Federación,* July 29, 1984), was a fundamental part of this policy. Researchers could only apply to the SNI if they had a full-time affiliation at a university or research institution and held a PhD. In addition, a peer review committee determined whether the researcher applying for such grants had enough academic merit. This extra money, along with the prestige accompanying it, made belonging to the system a generalized goal in academic communities.

Among other processes, the transformation of the public IHE occurred because the State ceased to consider them places of university education and producers of specialized knowledge, to instead conceive them as enterprises that offered services that had to respond to market demands (Ibarra, 2011). As a result, it triggered an ongoing process of evaluation of full-time professors, universities and graduate programs with performance indicators determined by technocratic bureaucrats, outside of academic communities. This, along with a decrease in student enrollment and labor supply for professionals who wished to enter as tenured full-time professors, disrupted their internal dynamic. Voices critical of these policies remained, as did honest teamwork and solidarity. At the same time, groups seeking power and resources to fulfill the now requisite standards through unethical strategies, began to be organized.

These latter strategies generally had a double purpose: to benefit members of these groups and to boycott those who represented competition or who affected their interests in some way. The list of actions stemming from the pursuit of these goals is long, but the most common can be mentioned: agreed sham co-authorships of publications; occupying positions on councils and committees with academic personnel on the team to ensure that the group's or members' interests were not affected; assigning graduate students to team professors (supervising graduate students is one of the major evaluation criteria today to be approved as a member of the SNI); rejecting or blocking students from signing up to work with those professors that represent competition. Another method is to use opposition exams to hire tenured academic personnel to consolidate groups, despite sometimes not having the best candidates. This latter strategy is the focus of interest of the present work.

Obviously, implementing the negative strategies mentioned above often unfairly affected third parties, sometimes in obvious ways, but sometimes undetected. Because of these dynamics, the development of professional careers has been boycotted, interrupted, or hindered. In addition, they contributed to creating toxic academic environments. Thus, excellent research projects have been deprived of funding or not awarded the amount they deserved; students who, based on their own merit, should have entered graduate programs are rejected; well-structured and grounded articles are rejected for publication; degree exams for well-founded theses and dissertations are postponed or boycotted; dissertations and publications that deserved prizes are denied to graduate students or researchers; student theses supervised by professors not aligned with power groups are expelled or unfairly failed, and so forth.

Opposition exams for the entry of tenured academic personnel do not escape these negative dynamics, although they are based on regulations established to guarantee equity and fair conditions among the candidates who apply. Groups with formal or informal power often manipulate exams, boycotting those who do not serve their interests and guaranteeing the hiring of their allies. These processes take place within regulated procedures and frameworks. However, their results often convert the biased and arbitrary academic acts committed into legal procedures, so injustice is extremely difficult to prove and defend.

Given this increasingly frequent panorama, the goal of this paper is to identify the mechanisms of manipulated opposition exams used to suppress those who, albeit possessing a high professional level, do not suit the convenience of power groups. It will also explore the defenseless situation in which they later find themselves and how it impedes their struggle against injustice.

Among the many cases of workplace bullying strategies that have been documented in Mexican universities (Peña & Fernández, 2016), the fraudulent suppression of candidates with high qualifications who aspire to a tenured position has not received the attention it deserves. This happens often, and in recent decades it has become a common practice that many full-time professors at different universities have witnessed and experienced. We believe these cases should be documented and exposed to guarantee the fairness of opposition exams in the future, so that the best candidate be granted the position, thus strengthening institutional interests rather than those of certain groups. For the analysis of this type of institutional violence, it is necessary to define several concepts.

BACKGROUND

Suppression of Dissent

One of the lines of analysis this paper will follow is Brian Martin's conceptual definition of the suppression of dissent. In this case, it refers to the suppression of candidates with academic merits that is carried out against those who do not coincide with the interests created by formal or informal power groups, which includes, but in fact goes beyond, merely punishing dissent, as Martin proposes:

Action taken in an attempt to stop or penalize a person who makes a public statement or does something that is seen as a threat to a powerful interest group, such as a government, corporation or profession. Typical actions include ostracism, harassment, censorship, forced job transfer, reprimands and dismissal. Suppression is action against dissent that does not involve physical violence. (Martin, retrieved on January 15, 2019, from: https://documents.uow.edu.au/~bmartin/dissent/intro/definitions.html)

Martin enumerates the most common methods employed for this purpose in academic contexts: censorship of writing; blocked publications; blocked citations; blocked promotions; blocked or withdrawn research grants; forced work transfers;

reprisals; denial of research opportunities; taking legal actions; ostracism; harassment; dismissal; blacklisting, and the spreading of rumors. Not being accepted as a tenured full-time professor after being rejected through rigged opposition exams should be added to this list.

According to Martin and Peña (2011, 285), suppression of dissent

... implies attacks on dissidents and the disgruntled, as well as against the ideas and behaviors that challenge orthodoxy or the interests of power groups... Less frequently, the efforts to achieve the social elimination of someone are based on personal reasons, such as having an aversion to someone, wishing to get revenge for personal or professional envy, or for prior conflicts or disagreements. Annulation may also be attributed to "collateral damage" ...

As Brian Martin (2012, 246) sees it, there are three forms of suppression:

1. Direct, when a person makes a public statement or does something that is seen as a threat to the powerful interest group. The group most commonly is a government, industry or profession, but could be, for example, a trade union, church or environmental organization. As a result, action is taken to stop or penalize the person or activity; 2. indirect, "because of the way in which powerful interest groups control major institutions. This applies particularly in employment and education. Individuals who find the institutionalized ideas irrelevant to their own have their own ideas suppressed through lack of opportunity. They can also experience direct suppression if they attempt to bring about change"; and 3. Self-censorship, because people are worried about risking their jobs, promotion prospects or ability to live without threat in their community, or because they fear direct suppression. Self-censorship makes overt suppression unnecessary.

The reasons for which opposition exams lead to the suppression of a candidate who should have been given a position, predominately fall into three categories: the individual has threatened a power group in some way, there is a desire to suppress or weaken the group that the candidate belongs to because it represents a threat or competition, or the position is devised for a candidate who is already part of the power group. Of course, antagonism toward an applicant is also possible, as well as other specific motives, but they are less common. The suppression of the candidate takes place through another concept, known as administrative sham dealing.

Sham Dealing

According to Osborne (2009, 1) "... sham dealing types of managerial actions have the appearance of genuine dealing but are characterized by a deceptive misuse of legitimate processes." She considers sham dealing an additional form of workplace bullying. It involves unfair treatment but under the pretense of a fair, legitimate, and genuine administrative process, which it is not. Sham dealing is a common process in higher education institutions because they must prove their actions are legal and fair, even if they are not. Often, those who carry out peer reviews and tenure track opposition exams, among other processes, pretend that they do them in an unbiased way. In deliberately skewed opposition exams for full-time tenured positions at public universities, the unfair suppression of candidates takes place through sham dealing.

Sham dealing and suppression of dissent, among many other strategies, are part of the violence that exists in institutions of higher education, which in turn forms part of mobbing processes (Westhues, 2006). Theoretically, aggression (Lorenz, 2016) and violence (OMS, 2002), while linked, are different events. Aggression, a survival strategy, is defined as the possibility of reacting in a way that defends our survival or our kin´s. Violence is characterized by intentional behaviors that harm someone or have the power to harm them in a deliberate way. Thus, violence is present only in the human species.

In higher education, physical violence is usually legally forbidden. In many institutional legislations, it even constitutes a reason to fire its perpetrators. However, repeated communicational behaviors to diminish an individual, that are continuously carried out during long periods of time, are in fact considered psychological violence and are emotionally very harmful (moral harassment, Hirigoyen, 1999). They can destroy or damage lives and carriers, stop promotions, cause loss of prestige, isolate individuals, etc. However, they are very difficult to prove and claim and, hence, often used in workplaces, including IHE, to attack somebody, usually without facing any consequences. Violence in IHE is usually attached to struggles for power. For those interested in these kind of issues in academic contexts, it is strongly recommended to visit Dr. Kenneth Westhues' web site: http://www.kwesthues.com/mobbing.htm (retrieved on June 11, 2019).

Suppression of Dissent in Universities under the Neoliberal System

Among other processes, the commercial opening of Mexico interfered with the academic life of universities, especially that of public, tuition-free institutions. Its relationship with the labor market was modified by a tendency to value teaching know how, through the training of future workers in their classrooms. This resulted in many study plans being redefined by public policies, now organized through the development of "competitions".

At some universities this led to the formation of opposing groups in permanent struggles. One line of thought defended the universality of education, the right to it, and freedom of thought, favoring knowledge generated in supportive teams and with trans-disciplinary views, over technical approaches. Others fell in line with the demands of the neoliberal system, of competitive individualism, and of perspectives based on linear cause-effect frameworks. Suppression among academics, students, and administrators also arose from this polarization grounded in public policies. Between the two factions, a struggle to ensure their own stance ensued. Of course, for the hiring of new tenured academic personnel, both sides tried to make opposition exams strengthen their own visions, falling into the temptation to suppress those who did not share their own positions or who contravened their political interests, instead of fostering plurality.

Opposition Exams

Starting in the late 1970s and early 1980s, professors' academic promotions and the hiring of new tenured track professors in IHE were gradually regulated. As a result, the Autonomous Metropolitan University (*Universidad Autónoma Metropolitana*, UAM) approved the Academic Personnel Entry, Promotion, and Retention Regulations (*Reglamento de Ingreso, Promoción y Permanencia del Personal Académico*, RIPPPA; *Universidad Autónoma Metropolitana*. Retrived on February 21, 2019, from: https://www.uam.mx/legislacion/ripppa/). These regulations state that they "come from Section 3, Subpart VIII of the Mexican Constitution (*Diario Oficial de la Federación*, February 5, 1917), in which universities and institutions of higher education are granted jurisdiction. The RIPPPA establishes the public publishing of opposition exam announcements along with the requirements and stages of the process. Given that the UAM is a federally funded institution, it also follows the Federal Law of Transparency and Access to Information (*Ley Federal de Transparencia y Acceso a la Información*, *Diario Oficial de la Federación*, May 9, 2012). However, administrators and professors who make decisions in this regard, on many occasions implement sham dealing to favor or suppress specific candidates based on their own convenience and interpretations of these regulations.

METHODOLOGY

In order to fulfill the proposed objective of understanding the process that those who "are not hired" go through in opposition exams for extra-academic reasons, the experience of a single informant with a high academic level is analyzed here as a case study (Martínez P.C., 2006). This case is particularly illustrative because before the first exam she applied for, she was already hired as a non-tenured professor at one of the five campuses of the UAM, a public institution in the metropolitan area of Mexico City. Given that her epistemological stance in the social sciences was complexity, she clashed with the logical positivist views of the department head, who was also the leader of the group in power. Our perspective for the case analysis is not psychological, but rather anthropological. That is, we see the case as attached to the general social dynamics of a particular historic moment, rather than to the individual characteristics of the perpetrators or the victims (Piñuel, 2001).

The subject of our case was a target of repeated actions of suppression on behalf of her boss throughout a long period. Sometimes, he was backed by other professors, so it can be said that she was also, at times, a target of mobbing. That is, she was attacked intentionally by an organized group with the intention of suppressing her (Leymann 1996, 7).

Psychological terror or mobbing in the workplace involves hostile and unethical communication, which is directed in, a systematic way, by one or a few individuals, mainly towards one who, due to mobbing, is pushed into a helpless and defenseless position, being held there by means of continuing mobbing activities. These actions occur on a very frequent basis... and over a long period of time...

Thus, when she registered as a candidate in an opposition exam for a tenure-track position, sham dealing was used during the whole process to push her out, while the candidate who coincided with the power group officially "won" the position. Four years later, she participated in another opposition exam at a different UAM campus, in which she was also suppressed. She concluded that the negative result of the second opposition exam was influenced by the first suppression because she lodged a formal complaint before local authorities and external legal bodies after the results of her first exam. This made her be seen as a "problematic" person, leading to a suppression in the second exam, despite her very high academic qualifications. As usual, though, because the whole process followed all the expected legal procedures, "proving" her suppression is almost impossible, as many others facing such unfair and violent behaviors face.

The selection of her case was also based on the fact she has the complete documentation of these two exams and agreed to provide it to us. Her first opposition exam took place in 2013, the second in 2017; hence, the two cases occurred at the same institution, in two different campuses, to the same person. She also agreed to in-depth interviews, which made it possible to reconstruct the negative, deviant and paradigmatic evaluation processes she went through "with greater advantages for the aims of research" (Martínez, M., 2006, 86). One in-depth interview was conducted to reconstruct the administrative process she experienced, checking the relative documents too. Two additional semi-structured interviews were constructed, based on a list of items that attested to her experience. Given that she had been a target of workplace bullying by her boss and mobbing, at times, as an untenured professor, the first semi-structured interview was aimed at recovering that experience based on Martin (2012) and Martin and Peña (2011) and the strategies they list. Also, the description of the sham dealing that involved her case was recorded.

In-depth interviews generally pursue "… the singularity of the vital experience of each one of the informants, the subjective meanings that for them are the cause of a specific social event" (Izcara, 2014, 145).

The second semi-structured interview was planned to raise questions on the connections she experienced between neoliberalism, technocracy, and the suppression strategies she was the target of. The main goal of the open questions was to obtain information "… on the problems and needs of individuals and suggestions for resolving them; opinions on situations, things, and people; a description of events or phenomena; and knowledge of the attitudes, expectations, customs, experiences, etc., of which we have little information" (Cortés, 2012, 105).

The first semi-structured interview included ten questions with three alternative responses, two of which were close (yes or no), while the third one was open (how or why). The second semi-structured interview was composed of nine questions with the option for an open answer. The items were designed to facilitate the codification of the responses into symbols that could be translated into explanations in line with the research goal. In the first questionnaire, there were fewer question items: blockage, reprimands, denial, legal actions, ostracism, and harassment, dismissal, blacklisting, rumors, while she was an untenured professor. Three ideas were eliminated from Martin's list (2012) because they were not pertinent for this case. The second interview had nine questions, related to: consequences of competition and individualism, transformation of universities, formation of groups, use of academic spaces, causative factors, incompatible ideas, poor performance, double standard, and sole recourse.

New topics arose in fieldwork that were also considered in the analysis and interpretation, seven of which emerged based on Martin (2012) and Martin and Peña (2011). The application of the interview guide examining neoliberalism, technocracy, and elimination strategies resulted in ten new topics. The data gathered were categorized according to the items in the interview guides, as well as those that arose during its development. Given the interviewee's high academic training, concepts and categories were employed in the construction of guides.

The interviews were transcribed directly on a computer; no sound recording was made. The informant requested anonymity and approved the analysis and the results presented in this paper. The interviews were conducted in three sessions, beginning with the reconstruction of the whole process (two hours, reviewing the documentation too), and followed by an initial inquiry based on Martin (2012) and Martin and Peña (2011), which lasted an hour, addressing the specific subject of the research. The next session was conducted in an hour and a half. The instruments were confirmed by cross-checking with the second interview, because we were concerned that the interviewer might falsify or hide some aspects regarded as compromising.

The validity of the instruments was subjected to constructive criticism by the authors and another colleague doing research on the subject, without being a co-author of the present text. The strategies recommended by Izcara (2014, 47) were followed in order to obtain a high degree of "suitability of the results to social reality."

The guide for the first session, based on Martin (2012), included the questions: Did they censor your writing? Did they block publications? Did they block citations or references to your publications? Did they block promotions? Did they block or withdraw research grants? Did they force you to accept a work transfer? Did they reprimand you? Did they deny you research opportunities? Were you the focus of legal actions that affected you? Were you subjected to ostracism and harassment? Were you dismissed? Did you form part of the "blacklist"? Did they spread rumors about you that affected you? The second part's questions appear implicitly in the respective Analysis and Interpretation section, one per paragraph.

RESULTS

From the interviews, it can be concluded that our informant was subjected to sham dealing, based on the description of the position's profile, which was tailored for a specific candidate and would have been difficult for her to fulfill. The same happened with the designation of the evaluating Committee, which acted under unofficial agreements. Sham dealing continued with the biased assignment of productivity points on her curriculum vitae, according to a tabulator; points were unfairly subtracted to suppress her. The dynamic of the exam itself was also based on sham dealing. In other words, the entire process she went through deployed a sham dealing of the tacit rules to suppress her while making the entire process appear to be fair and legal. Not uncommonly many candidates are suppressed in this same way, ending up defenseless because through sham dealing the whole process appears as fair and legal.

This also occurs because neoliberalism diminished budgets and constrained positions for new full-time professors, instead of creating the necessary positions to meet the needs of the students enrolled. Therefore, the struggle to be a full-time professor in IHE is harsh.

Opposition Exams as a Process of Suppression

At the UAM, the profile to be filled by a new professor is prepared by the department chair, at times, informally, in coordination with the Division director. Also, professors affiliated with the department in question can participate; personal and power relations commonly exist among them as a group. The RIPPPA establishes it is in the Division Council where the needs for new academic personnel are determined annually. Nevertheless, the profiles and justifications for hiring new tenure-track professors are made in the departments and then sent to the Councils. As a result, academic profiles became a sort of composite sketch designed to fit the candidate to be favored or suppressed, when the reason to create a new position should be academically and not politically motivated. This is a tacit rule that, in our experience, is often replicated at other educational institutions.

The RIPPPA was made to prevent these practices, so it also stipulates the participation of external advisors from the department for which the new position is considered. However, in a single discipline in the Mexican academic world, everyone knows each other, so the department chair can easily negotiate who the external advisors will be.

Section 121 of the RIPPPA establishes that job announcements must contain, in addition to general elements, the profile and "specific activities to be carried out, the area of knowledge and the discipline." However, this information is also manipulated though sham dealing by skewing the candidate profile. For instance, if the goal is to hire a loyal Z in department X of the Division of Social Sciences and Humanities, the activities to be carried out must specify: a) the plan and study programs of the

BA where the new position is needed, and b) the lines of research in the department to be taken into account, since full-time professors are also researchers. However, if Z is weak in any of the two requirements, in the opposition exam greater weight is given to the candidate's strengths.

Once the profile is approved by the Division Council, the vacancy is published in the *Órgano Informativo* (a gazette which is distributed free-of-charge on all UAM campuses) as well as on the university website. After reviewing the documents submitted by the candidates to guarantee that they fulfill the profile requirements, approved applicants are notified that they passed on to the next stage. The oral exam that follows consists of making a critical analysis of a Teaching-Learning Unit of the BA involved (*Unidad de Enseñanza Aprendizaje*, UEA; this is, a BA course) in a maximum of five pages, and 2) writing an essay of a maximum of 20 pages on one of the research topics published in the announcement. Likewise, candidates are notified of the place, date, and time for the oral exam, usually in the Dean's building office in Southern Mexico City (*Rectoría General*).

The notification that the Committee sends to the candidates states that if the work is not submitted by the due date or if the applicant does not appear at the oral exam within 30 minutes of the specified time, the candidate will forfeit the right to continue being evaluated. However, this is not always respected; if the loyal Z does not meet one or both conditions, whoever supports that individual on the Committee justifies the omission, for example, by claiming the papers were mislaid or blaming Mexico City's traffic. This also constitutes sham dealing, because it produces unequal evaluation conditions among the candidates.

Furthermore, biased exams lobbying in favor of or in opposition to a candidate take place throughout the process. In an unofficial way, the groups pressure the Committee on the suitability of their candidate or the defects of the one to be suppressed. At this stage, the department chair who wrote the academic profile description and who first lobbied on the Division Council has advantages.

On oral evaluation day the candidates are presented before a minimum of two representatives from the university and at least two outside advisors (the evaluation Committee) who decide the course of the examination. How long the presentation of each applicant will be for each of the two stages, the number and quality of questions for each phase, as well as other procedures that "they consider appropriate for the position to be filled" (RIPPPA, ART. 116). The members of the Committee have a wide margin of action, depending on the power of each one in relation to the groups they are connected to or defend. The situation can be critical if there are disputing groups supporting different candidates, which has happened.

Once the oral evaluation is finished, the candidates must wait for the Committee decision. According to the RIPPPA, the Committee should offer academic arguments that justify its decision. However, its members do not always do so; sometimes they do not present academic reasons or grounds, but rather only communicate the result. For instance, they might say it was Z who obtained the highest point rating in the curriculum vitae, without proving it. In the oral opposition exam and the evaluations carried out through the critical analysis of the program and essay, the evaluation of the applicant's teaching capacity, as well as their written and public defense of the research topic, they do not always provide objective, measurable, quantifiable elements to compare candidates' performances and make clear the reason for their decision. These proceedings also constitute a sham dealing that violates the rights of candidates who are not in the final selection, who at least have the right to know the academic reasons for the results. Our informant claimed that she went through all this sham dealing because, as a candidate, on both occasions she was suppressed on purpose.

Although UAM legislation considers an Appeals Commission in which applicants not in agreement can request to review the results; most applicants find it to be a waste of time, although there have been few cases, mostly of union affiliates, that have been won through this method.

Even at this stage, power groups continue to follow the lobbying that began with the profile description and continued through all stages until the signing of the contract with their candidate as an academic employee of the institution. They even lobby the Appeals Commission to make them reject or accept the requests, depending on the interests and the political strength of the power groups.

In our informant's experience, after the first exam, the Appeals Commission did not seriously consider her reason to review the process and the final decision was not changed. She filed her case at a Federal Bureau; however, she never got a resolution. Juggled between various lawyers and offices, as time passed her case was abandoned. This is an indirect proof of the difficulties to prove unfairness.

On the Suppression Process

The categories or items that arose in the application of data-gathering instruments are different from the original ones. The initial data confirmed our informant had been subjected to suppression as an untenured professor and as a candidate for a tenured position, while the latter focused on recognizing and describing her experience in the neoliberal economic-political model. Her response highlighted the importance of feelings, cognitive perceptions, health, legislation, and ethical behavior, not originally considered. This enriched the analysis and interpretation of the results, which are presented in three sections: the first two respond to each of the two instruments applied while, in the third, discussion is carried out. In the explanation of results, we decided to include textual extracts of the informant's words in order to illustrate them through her own voice. Of her own volition, the key informant narrated the two opposition exams in which she participated in each of her responses, despite the four-year interval separating the two events.

As already stated, the questions on the questionnaire were designed based on Martin (2012, 246), following the thirteen most common suppressive tactics, as mentioned in the Methodology section.

In the first three questions, the informant responded to the category: blocking. Through her account, three more items emerged that have to do with the consequences of blocking her: self-esteem, feelings, and health. The first is a cognitive perception "of self-worth" (FIA, n/d), the second is composed of mental images (Damasio, 2005, 32), and the third is "a state of complete physical, mental, and social wellbeing" (the classic definition of the World Health Organization. Retrived on December 15, 2019, from: https://8fit.com/lifestyle/the-world-health-organization-definition-of-health/). Understood in this way, we interpreted that she suffered negative physical and emotional consequences from the blocking she was subjected to as an untenured professor. She also experienced direct blocking in the first opposition exam, with the same consequences. Concerning the second exam, she did not refer to direct blocking, although she stated: "… in the evaluation they arbitrarily did not take into account my research publications…" alluding to a form of intentional indirect blocking.

As for reprimands, the informant described a category that reaffirmed her cognitive perception and was akin to an earlier question: undermining her self-esteem through circumstances that were intentionally created. As she was an untenured professor, the aim of the opposition exam was to prevent her from obtaining a tenure track position. This was a major reprimand affecting her career and her personal life. In the first exam, reprimands were direct, both in public and in private: "--- obviously, when the day of the exam came too… " and veiled on the second occasion: "… during the recess before my presentation, in front of the Committee and the other candidates, one of the evaluators, without it being called for, told me: calm down…" In both cases, the intention was to produce a symbolic effect of discomfort that would suppress her.

As for the strategy of denial of opportunities, no additional item was revealed by her. She recognized that as a non-tenured professor, she was subjected to this type of suppression, closely related to *blocking*:

Neoliberal Technocracy and Opposition Exams

They gave me excuses for excluding me [from joint research projects] by saying that my research topic [workplace bullying] was not in line with theirs. Nonetheless, I argued in academic and scientific terms that it was feasible to develop an innovative and interesting approach. So, I set out to research and present it.

The topics she alluded to were a book chapters about "citizen observatories" (which were ultimately published, but only after her protests derived from a first suppression) and "civil disobedience" (" ... the book was published, but they did not take into account most of my contributions and my personal chapter was not even included ... "). In these situations, she observed simulation as sham dealing. Through a gradual *crescendo piano, piano*, little by little, they eliminated her from the group's collaborations. In the two opposition exams they could not prevent her from applying, but the fact that she was not chosen for the positions even though she had a more substantial curriculum, constituted a major unfair denial of opportunities for her.

Asked if she was the object of unfair legal actions against her, she responded affirmatively: both as a non-tenured professor, and for the first opposition exam. Judicialization of politics is common now; that is, using laws to suppress through sham dealing. It was used recently in Brazil to incarcerate Lula da Silva and to dismiss Dilma Rousseff as president, as examples.

Yes, both, when I was an untenured professor, and when I was in the process of the first opposition exam. In the first situation, close to the deadline to approve the first untenured contract's extension for another year, I was called to a meeting where I was notified, I would not be rehired because I was not welcome in the department where I was affiliated. The way and action were irregular, given that rehiring is a decision that should be made by the collegial academic organ of the Division of Social Sciences and Humanities, not by personnel authorities. Faced with this, I filed a complaint with this organ, which resulted in my rehiring, given that I had excellent student evaluations for my teaching, and my academic research production was greater than and more recent than that of the rest of the professors in the department of affiliation.

As for the second case [the first opposition exam], the department head went to the area in charge of evaluating candidates and requested I not be the final selection. It was sham dealing because this was illegal, the department chair used this unwritten rule.

In the second opposition exam she did not report that legal actions had been carried out against her. The category that emerged from the first exam was applying unwritten rules against her (sham dealing involves using formal regulations in a tricky way to make them appear as fair and legal, and this case even goes beyond that).

When speaking of ostracism and harassment as a suppression strategy, she experienced them "... when I worked with short-term contracts as an untenured professor...". The department chair's groups harassed her and made her feel an unwanted colleague at some events. These strategies were extended to the first opposition exam and its result, all as part of the same mobbing in which the department chair and some professors, students, and administrators participated. As for the second occasion, she said that instead of open aggressions, indifference and discrimination were applied to her for not belonging to the group formed by all the other candidates:

Most of the other applicants came from the same group, they knew each other from before ... I was the only one with a postdoc, which intimidated them, in addition to the fact that I was the only non-sociologist... which resulted in attacks on my professional training on the part of some of the members of the Committee, although the profile for applicants was for sociologists or related fields.

Regarding dismissal, it happened to her when she was hired as a non-tenured professor: "... *de facto* yes, although *de jure* no...", she stated, referring to when she was arbitrarily not rehired. What she described in the legal actions item was a deceitful way of manipulation against her legal processes. In response, the interviewee reacted by filing internal recourses in the Appeals Commission of the University and, afterwards, external recourses in a federal agency. Her reaction generated animosity on the part of department's academic members and authorities, who influenced her suppression in the first opposition exam. Her experience led to an additional category, invisibility:

... To the surprise of some academic authorities, both for the result, and for the way it happened [referring to the fact I was not chosen in the opposition exam], I was hired two additional terms, but I was invisible to the department authorities, for other academic and administrative colleagues and even for some students who were sympathetic to the group that was suppressing me. During this period, I can state I was the target of workplace bullying.

Addressing the strategy of blacklisting for suppression, the informant claimed that when the attempt was made to not rehire her: "... there was a letter where the department chair had collected signatures of some of my colleagues to persuasively argue against me, in case I raised objections...". She did not get a copy of this letter. She found out about its contents through a university authority. Hiding the document from her was a violation of her human rights (no one can be accused without knowledge of it), and a symbolic tactic to intimidate her from defending herself from the arbitrariness of not hiring her, despite having the right to do so. As for the second opposition exam, an additional topic not originally considered arose, which was, in addition to reprisals: discrimination:

I suspect that at least two of the members of the Committee were aware of my claims concerning the results of the first exam [which took place four years earlier]. I decided to challenge these results at the Appeals Commission, and because it did not proceed, I later presented a suit against the University at the Federal Board of Mediation and Arbitration (Junta Federal de Conciliación y Arbitraje). That surely put me on a blacklist. Don't you think? I believe this unfair retribution could also be described as discrimination against those who defend themselves from their decisions.

By suppressing her, she was eliminated as the potential dissident and troublemaker she represented if chosen for the new full-time position.

Finally, as for the strategy of spreading rumors about her, the interviewee expressed that indeed this applied to her when she was temporarily hired:

... that was one of the mechanisms they concocted to carry out workplace bullying against me. They branded me as a homophobic harasser, a "cougar woman" (an English expression alluding to older women who prey on young men), although paradoxically, they also accused me of seducing ... a man older than me.... [They used to call her] an easy professor [giving inflated grades to students], when the truth was that, with good teaching plans, with detailed evaluation categories, with affable interactions with students, etc., they worked well and I had no need to fail them. (She found out about these rumors through students who respected her and were non-silent witnesses).

No additional category emerged. As a method to suppress dissidents, according to Martin (2012), spreading rumors in workplace bullying is one of the characteristic strategies of harassment of a group against an individual (mobbing, Leymann, 1996).

On Neoliberalism, Technocracy, and Suppression Strategies

As with the results of the application of the first instrument, in this section the items explored, including those not originally considered that arose in the responses.

She was questioned as to whether neoliberal policies of privatization of state enterprises, the privatization of many of its services, the cancelation of subsidies on basic consumer goods, etc., led her to suffer the consequences of competition and individualism as a non-tenured professor or in any of the opposition exams. Considering these analytical categories, she responded:

... in the case of the opposition exams, it translated into fights for tenured positions, fights with oneself and with others, some of them close to those in power, and therefore, they had greater possibilities of obtaining the desired end. In other words, positions are given based on influence and personal relationships, more than academic merits; mechanisms that did not end with the old regime, but, rather, were bequeathed to the new regime: the neoliberal system, in harsher conditions.

In addition, two new items arose: emotions and behaviors, stemming from neoliberal policies:

... which made some [persons] aggressive and others fearful, some more cautious and others bolder. Ultimately, that influenced the emotions and behaviors that affect academic expectations and even pocket money.

As for whether this was the result of the transformation of universities being seen now as enterprises that offer services and that must continuously be evaluated with quantitative performance indicators, she noted:

... there is no longer "a spirit that speaks for [the human] race," paraphrasing the motto of the UNAM (Autonomous National University of Mexico, Universidad Nacional Autónoma de México. The original motto is: For my race the spirit will speak ("Por mi raza hablará el espíritu"). Instead there are only individual interests in getting more points, getting tenured position for allies. All ultimately translate into prestige, power and money...

She affirmed this applies both to individuals and institutions, where the categories evaluations and resources aroused:

Neoliberal Technocracy and Opposition Exams

... for example, for getting prize bonuses, grants, public or private financing for projects, expansion of their campus or increasing student enrollment, etc. Institutions are in demand for their professors to produce, produce, produce ... And if they do not catch up, they are left out of the game, they become the subject of suppression, mobbing or they are pressured in some other way to force them to fit in. The very institutions are pressured with toxic propaganda favoring prestigious private universities, for example, by the media and now in social networks.

When asked if she believes that as a result of this, groups have been formed that are organized to meet the standards now demanded through questionable strategies, she answered:

[Now] the strategies they employ are more aggressive and justified by that ideology of competition and individualism. Ethical environments seem to be absent, through which the contributions of those who are not in the group and those who do not become involved and commit to the interests of the power group are overlooked, blocked, are seen as toxic, and are harassed.

About the utilization of academic spaces to benefit power groups in order to compete with an advantage for resources by, for example, using opposition exams for the entry of academic personnel that consolidates them, she responded:

Not only do power groups use academic spaces for themselves, these are now another resource, as are evaluators in the tenured full-time opposition exams ... So, academic spaces, understood as courses, plans, and programs, collective work groups (such as research areas, academic teams, etc.), as well as the facilities and human, material, and non-material resources, are all deployed to benefit the group(s) that hold power. At times, even struggling between them. It is not surprising that many universities have become toxic workplaces with very difficult relationships where nobody feels comfortable working.

As an additional category toxic workplace was mentioned, as well as the notion that academic spaces are now a new kind of resource to struggle for and control for themselves.

Of the three possible causative factors provided, she was asked if any of them was applicable to her case: 1. She had threatened the power group voluntarily or involuntarily, 2. There was a desire to weaken the group she formed part of, 3. The position had been intended for a candidate who was already part of the power group in order to consolidate it. She answered by adding a new category:

I think the three causative factors, in differing degrees of influence, applied to the first opposition exam in which I participated... As for the second ... my intuition is that all these arguments, used as rumors, served to not give me the position.

She was also asked if she considered she was indirectly denied because her ideas were not compatible with those of the group in power or because they implied a change that would harm them. She averred that in the first examination:

... I can say that not so much for my ideas, because I was always willing to adapt, but rather, perhaps, for the way I worked, because they considered me a workaholic ... As for the second examination, there I do think that my ideas, my theoretical position of complexity and transdisciplinary approach had an impact on my suppression.

Her description of herself as a workaholic (work addict), mentioned with the English colloquial term, together with the questioning of her epistemological focuses, are disqualifying strategies characteristic of the job harassment that she claimed to have experienced when she was hired as an untenured professor.

She was asked if her work performance or else her personality were elements that contributed to her suppression, which she denied:

On the contrary, in the first examination I can say my performance was very highly evaluated, both in teaching and in research, also my personality was open, flexible. But I was "condemned" to fail even before the exam. They did not like my profile, which led to their mobbing towards me, including suppressing me at the exam. As for the second exam, I don't think that on the day of the evaluation this had been considered, for there were many candidates and all of us were nervous, some more than others. As I said before, a main variable in my suppression on this occasion was that I defended myself after the first exam, even filing against the University in legal offices. This was sham dealing because only academic criteria should be considered, which was not the case.

An additional element emerged: the lack of objectivity in the proceedings of the second examination, because "two of the evaluators knew me." She only knew their names from having coincided in academic settings, but it is possible they had an animosity over the suit filed in court.

Concerning if she experienced double standards in being evaluated among all the candidates, she responded:

... at least four other professors, also hired as non-tenured professors, participated in the many different opposition exams that took place at the same time. But, unlike me, they were awarded the full-time positions they applied to. This, I believe, is because some were loyal to the department chair and others were condescending to him. In my case, I put academic ethics over my personal interest as an untenured professor and I think that was the fundamental element that worked against me and that ended up in my being suppressed.

Therefore, it appears, there was indeed a double-standard in evaluating her.

To conclude, she was asked if she thought the opposition exam was the *only resource* to eliminate her or if there could have been any additional elements. For each of the two opposition exams she presented the response was different:

The first opposition exam was seen by the department chair and his group as an opportunity to suppress me, because for almost all of the two previous years they had subjected me to mobbing. In the second exam, apparently the exam itself was the sole criterion used to evaluate me, because I was no longer working in the university when I applied for the position. However, as I said before, at least two of the Committee members knew about my case against the University in legal bureaus. Therefore, they used the opposition exam as a resource to suppress me too.

Mobbing (workplace bullying carried out in an organized way by a group) arose as an underlying topic in her case, given that in other responses she also mentioned it.

In this case, suppression using sham dealing as a result of the first opposition exam can be interpreted as the final stage of a long process of mobbing (Leymann, 1996) she was subjected to for more than two years (between October 2011 and November 2013). In addition to being unemployed as the result of an unfair process, the victim was emotionally and physically affected. Suppressing her from the group was the original aim, because she was not formattable (paraphrasing Hirigoyen, 2013) to epistemological positivism, to conservative ideology, and to the unorthodox academic practices which characterized the power group. As such, the opposition exam was the "cherry on the cake" and the ideal situation to give the final blow to her suppression, canceling her dissidence with respect to the rest of the group in question.

To confront the workplace bullying experienced as a non-tenured professor, which culminated in her not being rehired, she filed her case in the Divisional Council, with success. However, her participation as a candidate for a tenure-track position as full-time professor was used to remove her from the Department once and for all through sham dealing. Although she challenged the result in the Appeals Commission and in federal courts, the case became bureaucratized in hearings and different attorneys and it never had a legal resolution, proving the difficulties to deal with these negative events in workplaces.

However, four years later, the fact that the legal measures taken to express her inconformity became a non-explicit reason to not give her the tenure-track position she applied for, again, through sham dealing, despite having a curriculum that proved she was the most qualified candidate. These acts show that candidates who are suppressed in rigged situations find themselves affected in their life´s courses, emotional and physical health and end up in a condition of major vulnerability, with very few resources to successfully confront both workplace bullying and sham dealing given the huge bureaucratic apparatuses of universities and in official legal institutions.

CONCLUSION

In Mexico the impact of neoliberalism has had diverse effects on the daily life of the population at all levels, principally due to social polarization, given that wealth has been concentrated in the hands of a small number of individuals, while the vast majority has endured an ongoing process of impoverishment, loss of rights, contraction of earnings, and a rise in the prices of basic products. Recently, on July 1, 2018, this model was overwhelmingly defeated at the polls, with 30 million citizens voting against the candidates that guaranteed this *status quo* and in favor of the sole candidate who promised to redirect national policies toward a vision that considers the needs of the population. The new president was appointed on December 1, 2018. In general, 35 years of neoliberalism have exacerbated individualism and competitiveness. It will take time to reverse this trend and achieve solidarity and sincere and honest teamwork at universities.

Institutions of higher education did not escape this dynamic. There, diverse groups clashed for power, prestige, and money: some defending the universality of education, the right to it, freedom of thought, knowledge, and wisdom generated in collegial and inter or transdisciplinary, over technical approaches; others, defending the neoliberal system of competitive individualities based on linear cause-effect postulates.

Within these two major blocks, for academic reasons mini groups are formed, dissolved, accommodated, or unmotivated. Results from individualism and competition have become widespread and have also led to opportunism. This has also led to internal violence in the form of workplace bullying, mobbing, and suppression of dissent among academics, students, and administrators, whether by differentiated sectors or between them. An example of the resources employed as "weapons" against "academic enemies" are the opposition exams discussed here. Recently the Mexican Ministry of Labor has issued a technical legal regulation (*Diario Oficial de la Federación*, October 23, 2018) that provides recourses to confront so-called psychosocial factors, including workplace bullying. These regulations represent a hope because they did not exist in the country before. We also hope that the new government realizes that all these dynamics are a major problem for workers and require urgent recognition and solutions. Now, with severe employment shortages, struggles to get a tenured track position as full-time professor are harsh, and suppressing excellent candidates to favor others for political reasons using sham dealing has become a common practice. So far, suppressed candidates are powerless to prove and confront injustice. It is of crucial importance to trace the dynamics of these tainted opposition exams as a result of the individualism and competition that have been established in virtually all personal interactions at public Mexican universities today. Those students who "fail" admission exams or drop out, often for economic reasons, as well as those academics facing suppression through biased opposition exams, etc., are made invisible afterwards by the system itself, even though in many occasions they end up in an emotional crisis. It is important to make these processes visible in order to deal with them properly.

REFERENCES

Cortés, M. T. (2012). *Metodología de la investigación*. Trillas.

Damasio, A. (2005). *En busca de Spinoza. Neurobiología de la emoción y los sentimientos*. Barcelona: Crítica.

De la Garza, E. (2011). *Trabajo no clásico, organización y acción colectiva, Tomo I*. Universidad Autónoma Metropolitana, Unidad Iztapalapa.

Hirigoyen, M. F. (1999). *El acoso moral en la vida cotidiana*. Barcelona: Paídós Ibérica.

Hirigoyen, M. F. (2013). *El acoso moral en el trabajo. Distinguir lo verdadero de lo falso*. Barcelona: Paidós.

Ibarra, E. (2001). *La universidad en México hoy: gubernamentalidad y modernización*. Universidad Nacional Autónoma de México, Universidad Autónoma Metropolitana, Unidad Iztapalapa, Unión de Universidades de América Latina y el Caribe.

Izcara, S. (2014). *Manual de investigación cualitativa*. Fontamara.

Leymann, H. (1996). El contenido y desarrollo del mobbing en el trabajo. *European Journal of Work and Organizational Psychology*, 5(2), 165–184. doi:10.1080/13594329608414853

Lorenz, K. (2016). *Sobre la agresión. El pretendido mal*. Siglo XXI Editores.

Martin, B. (2012). Suppression of Dissent: What It Is and What to Do About It. *Social Medicine (Social Medicine Publication Group)*, 6(4), 246–248. Retrieved from http://www.socialmedicine.info/index.php/socialmedicine/article/view/582/1241

Martin, B., & Peña, F. (2011). *Mobbing* y anulación de la disidencia / descontento: Tras las huellas de sus interrelaciones. *Medicine and Society*, 4(4), 284–296. Retrieved from http://www.medicinasocial.info/index.php/medicinasocial/article/view/633

Martínez, M. (2006). *Ciencia y arte en la metodología cualitativa*. Trillas.

Martínez, P. C. (2006). El método de estudio de caso. Estrategia metodológica de la investigación científica. *Pensamiento y Gestión*, 20, 165–193.

OMS Organización Mundial de la Salud (2002). *Informe mundial sobre la violencia y la salud: resumen*. Ginebra: Organización Mundial de la Salud.

Osborne, D. (2009). Pathways into bullying. *Proceedings of the 4th Asia Pacific Conference on Educational Integrity*. Retrieved on September 14, 2018, from http://ro.uow.edu.au/apcei/09/papers/18/

Peña, F., & Fernández, K. (2016). *Mobbing en la academia mexicana*. Mexico City: Ediciones y Gráficos Eón, Red PRODEP Salud Condiciones de Vida y Políticas Sociales & Escuela Nacional de Antropología e Historia.

Pérez, G. (2017). Los desafíos sociales de la democracia en México. *Estudios Políticos*, *41*, 27-53. Retrieved on June 13, 2019, from http://www.scielo.org.mx/pdf/ep/n41/0185-1616-ep-41-00027.pdf

Piñuel, I. (2001). *Mobbing. Cómo sobrevivir el acoso psicológico en el trabajo*. Santander: Editorial Sal Terrae.

Tello, C. (2019). Austeridad, gasto público y crecimiento económico con justicia social. *Economía UNAM*, *46*(16), 54–60. Retrieved from http://www.economia.unam.mx/assets/pdfs/econunam/46/07Tello.pdf

Valenzuela, J. (1991). *Crítica del modelo neoliberal: el FMI y el cambio estructural*. Universidad Nacional Autónoma de México.

Vieyra, P. (2015). ¿Un nuevo tipo de individualismo? Las peculiaridades del individualismo mexicano. *Sociologica*, *30*(85), 65–100. Retrieved from http://www.scielo.org.mx/pdf/soc/v30n85/v30n85a3.pdf

Westhues, K. (Ed.). (2006). *The Remedy and Prevention Mobbing in Higher Education*. Lewiston, NY: Edwin Mellen Press.

ADDITIONAL READING

Cran, B. (2018). The academic mob and its fatal toll. *Quillette* (March 2). Retrieved August 15, 2018, from: https://quillette.com/2018/03/02/academic-mob-fatal-toll/

Martin, B. (n/d). "Tactics against bullying at work". Retrieved April 15, 2015, from: http://www.bmartin.cc/pubs/07bullying.html

Seguin, E. (2016). Academic mobbing, or how to become campus tormentors. *University Affairs* (September 19). Retrivied November 14, 2018, from: https://www.universityaffairs.ca/opinion/in-my-opinion/academic-mobbing-become-campus-tormentors/

Soh D. (2018). Who Will the Evergreen Mob Target Next? *Quillette* (April 20). Retrieved October 18, 2018, from: https://quillette.com/2018/04/20/will-evergreen-mob-target-next/

Torres, J. (2013). Sobre el desprecio moral. Esbozo de una teoría crítica para los indignados. *Espiral, Estudios sobre Estado y Sociedad*, 20(58) 9-35.

Westhues, K. (2004). *Administrative Mobbing at the University of Toronto: The Trial, Degradation and Dismissal of a Professor during the Presidency of J. Robert S. Prichard*. New York: Edwin Mellen.

Westhues, K. (2006). The Unkindly Art of Mobbing. Retrieved September 16, 2016, from: http://www.kwesthues.com/unkindlyart.htm

KEY TERMS AND DEFINITIONS

Mobbing: It is communicational violence in which the aggressors gang up on someone; occurs through organized repetitive hostile attacks that go on through time.

Neoliberalism: A set of policies imposed by the World Bank and the International Monetary Fund almost worldwide based on openness of local economies to international trade and investment, reduction of worker´s wages, preventing workers from unionized, cutting worker´s fringe benefits; cutting public expenditures, privatization of State own enterprises, cutting State´s expenditures in social services, such as education, health, etc.

Qualitative Methods of Research: Methods originated in ethnography based in face to face interactions between researcher and informants to gather social data.

Sham Dealing: Unfair and biased administrative dealing of procedures and complains using regulations to pretend that a fair and genuine process is going on. It is considered a strategy of mobbing, workplace bullying, suppression of workers and other negative and arbitrary acts.

Suppression: Negative actions taken to stop a person who says or does something that threats a powerful group.

Universidad Autónoma Metropolitana: A public Mexican university located in the metropolitan area of Mexico City, created in 1974 and considered one of the best. It has five campuses: Azcapotzalco, Cuajimalpa, Iztapalapa, Lerma (in the State of Mexico) and Xochimilco.

Workplace Bullying: Victimization of workplace members through systematic negative acts. Workplace bullying can be carried out by a single individual.

Chapter 7
A Remedy for Improving the Culture in Higher Education:
Toxic Leadership to Servant Leadership

David B. Ross
Nova Southeastern University, USA

Melissa T. Sasso
Nova Southeastern University, USA

Rande W. Matteson
Nova Southeastern University, USA

Gina L. Peyton
Nova Southeastern University, USA

ABSTRACT

The purpose of this chapter is to examine how servant-centered leadership should align with the values of higher education institutions than other forms of leadership. Servant leadership follows a value system, ethical philosophy, rather than a standard set of leadership practices. This chapter explores adult education and leadership-power philosophies, the historical perspective of leadership and management, followed by literature of servant leadership and toxic leadership. In addition, crises of higher education were discussed as well as the need to remedy a toxic culture toward servant-centered environment and that institutions of higher education must be the proactive educators. The researchers concluded that in order for an academic institution to thrive, the utilization and implementation of servant-centered leadership is paramount. It is also equally critical to teach students the philosophy of servant leadership so they in turn can give back to their communities.

DOI: 10.4018/978-1-5225-9485-7.ch007

INTRODUCTION

To lead and educate, you must serve. Servant leadership is the systematic process of developing the needs of servants ahead of those leaders found within private or public institutions. Servant leadership is positively needed in higher education, especially based on the institutions' purposes, accountability, practices, and core values of integrity, humility, empathy, and trustworthiness (Dean, 2014). In higher education, faculty, staff, and administration must model positive behavior as well as mentor and produce community-focused students. If promoting insignificant core values and teaching inadequate and unsuitable behaviors, the environment of higher education could become toxic (Ross, Sasso, Matteson, & Matteson, 2019). The principle behind effective leadership is based on the interplay of responsibility, respect, care, and working with people, compared to working against people, causing an environment of bullying, terror, and targeting behaviors. Ultimately, leadership is about character and substance. Using the distinct characteristics of servant leadership to promote and foster the development of successful individuals is one of the fundamental concepts of servant leaders. Honest and caring concern for others leads to empowerment and emotional support, which inspires the members to embrace the needs of the organization and creates a learning environment. This is the type of environment that is conducive to producing optimal performance from their employees and students.

Although many times leadership roles and responsibilities are misunderstood, leadership is firmly grounded in doing the right thing; servant leadership serves to balance out that misinterpretation. Employee and student attrition is a direct result of problematic leadership in higher education. Today, more than in the past, leaders are tasked with enormous responsibilities that demand both competent and effective leadership skills. Making an effective leader involves careful thought and skill development. The collective evidence strongly suggests that environments created through servant leadership will produce employees who challenge themselves to become creative, dedicated, loyal, and productive to the needs of their institutions' stakeholders, rather than a toxic culture within any organization. For this chapter, higher education needs to remedy an environment of toxicity and mobbing so all stakeholders can flourish in a learning community. Faculty must be treated fairly and with respect in order to transfer their wisdom and disciplines to students. These students, in turn, can then transfer this learning as well as character building to their communities and families.

Adult Education and Leadership-Power Philosophies

Just as adult education has many philosophies of transferring knowledge from faculty to students, leadership has many philosophies of transferring knowledge and experiences through two power perceptions: either influence or control. In higher education, faculty have different philosophies of the learning process and varying grading policies, types of assessments, discussions and dialogues, expectations, assignments, and research. There is a challenge in adapting to each learner's style as students respond differently to intrinsic and extrinsic motivation, whether the environment is the traditional, teacher-dominated classroom or the independent, and the non-hierarchical format (Hur, Glassman, & Kim, 2013). The *progressive style* of adult education supports critical thinking to stimulate or instigate thought for professional dialogue by seeking expertise and knowledge from all parties, and content from such courses that are applicable to the real world (Cox, 2015). This is an essential portion of a higher education vision by transferring learning through experiences that are positive, not toxic. Higher education can succeed if servant leadership is part of the vision and curriculum; if not, then it threatens the universities' abilities to prosper (Farnsworth, 2007). Cox (2015) mentioned that the *humanistic style* of adult education is intended to promote and facilitate learning while meeting and/or serving the needs of the learners. Faculty and other leaders in higher education who promote the *behaviorist style* of adult education is with hopes that students learn positive behavior skills as well as other characteristics and to implement those skills to other communities and workplace environments (Cox, 2015).

Different philosophies of leadership can be witnessed in various organizations. Management, which is a status quo environment, looks at short-term goals, whereas leadership is more about long-term goals. Leadership involves decision-making; in higher education, for example, classrooms can be arranged in management versus leadership format. Hur, Glassman, and Kim (2013) admonished that a grade is a nominal goal for a student to receive based on their work. From a leadership perspective, students should focus on a lifelong learning approach that is more collaborative in nature, rather than a separation of individual thought. "A more modern take might be individuals engaged in activity more for long-term sustainability than for short-term achievement" (Hur, Glassan, & Kim, 2013, p. 305). An effective faculty member or leader of an organization must continually reward and influence their students-employees based more on intrinsic values than extrinsic values. People want to be rewarded based on influence and develop that sense of belonging. Otherwise, the willingness to participate, learn, and be part of the organizational structure will weaken job performance and participation. Rather than using power to influence people, those who utilize a coercive style of power could lead to control and belittling others, causing a toxic environment (Matteson, 2002; Sasso, 2017).

Whether it is a faculty member or an individual with a titled position of an organization, power could be used to influence or control people. These philosophies have different levels of influencing or manipulating others. The influence point of view is based on shared power and a servant leadership approach. The power of control is an entirely different approach with an opposing position of narcissistic characteristics. Using power through exploiting others by virtue of one's entitlement, authority, arrogance, and self-absorption can destroy any organization and the mission of its existence; this narcissism is toxic to any organization (Matteson, 2002; Sasso, 2017).

Daft (1991, 2014) has determined that there are five elements of power used by leaders within an organization to influence the behavior of employees: legitimate, reward, coercive, expert, and reverent. Legitimate power focuses on a leader's title. Greenleaf (1970) personifies a servant leader as inspired by a vision, chosen by their supporters, and who have foresight, awareness, and listening, rather than coercive and manipulative characteristics. Leadership is the actual utilization of power, which brings about change in employee behavior. If a leader has expert and reverent power, employees will share in the leader's point of view and vision. If the leader has legitimate and rewards power, the employee will agree to carry out the instructions even if they do not agree with the given information. When a leader uses coercive power, it usually generates resistance, causing the employees to disobey orders, sabotage efforts, or to ignore any instruction from the leader deliberately. Daft (2014) stated there is a need for power: to influence or control others, to be responsible for others, and to have authority over others. An eminent need for power is often associated with those at top levels of positions within an organization.

Three components of leadership are prominent: people, influence, and goals. Daft (2014) observed that leadership involves the use of influence, and this influence is used to attain goals. Influence in leadership implies that the relationship among people is dynamic and designed to achieve a goal. Therefore, leadership is designed to have an effect on employees toward the attainment of the organizational goal. This necessitates that leaders be involved with their employees in the pursuit of the organization's objectives. Leadership is a dynamic function, which includes human resources and involves the use of power. The element of power is essential in influencing employees, whether or not the leader has the ability to generate compliance. These viewpoints fit into the framework for all organizations, especially in higher education and with servant leadership philosophies.

Winter (1973) explained that power has its roots in a Latin term described as to be able, forming his theory of power from observation of abilities. Winter refers to Freud's description of leadership as the differentiation of the ego and the world in terms of the awareness of power and ability. This description is an illustration of a person being influenced by external forces. Winter also related power to the ability as contrasted with the environment; there are three conditions necessary in a useful definition of power. First, one or more persons must have an effect on the behavior of others. Second, that person(s) must have an ability to produce an effect, signifying they can accomplish something whenever they want to. Third, social power can be an action, as one person could affect the behavior or emotions of another person when and if he or she wants to. Winter also described social power as the ability or capacity of some person producing intended effects, consciously or unconsciously, on the behavior or emotions of another. Winter described good power as leadership, guidance, and authority. Leaders and faculty within higher education should utilize these philosophes to promote a positive change rather than an environment of destructive leadership. A destructive leadership style is an intentional style of a twisted belief and value system that causes adverse outcomes and errors, as well as behaviors (Mulvey & Padilla, 2010).

Leadership and Management: A Historical Perspective

There was a monumental shift in the understanding and application of leadership and management that occurred throughout the 1980s and 1990s. During the industrial era, organizational effectiveness was based on the practice of scientific management made famous by Frederick W. Taylor (Hatch, 2013; Taylor, 1914). Organizational structures were generally bureaucratic with the traditional separations of work units and a rigid hierarchical structure (Locke, 1982). Leadership models during this period included the *great man theory* that proposed that leaders were born, not made (Borgatta, Bales, & Couch, 1954; Cawthon, 1996). This was superseded by the *trait theory*, which was similar in that it outlined the traits that were common to a good leader, but unlike the great man theory, it believed those traits could be environmentally dependent (Van Seters & Field, 1990). This was the common management and leadership thinking during most of the 20th century. A few management authors and theorists began to challenge the early industrial models as early as the 1940s. The statistical process control and quality management approach of W. Edwards Deming and the writings of Peter Drucker challenged some of the traditional notions of both management and the functions and practice of leadership (Bowman & Wittmer, 2000). Although these writings were available by the middle of the 20th century, some of the concepts did not come into widespread practice until later in the century.

Leadership theory was also evolving in 1939, at which point Kurt Lewin and colleagues categorized different leadership styles; namely autocratic leadership, democratic leadership, and laissez-faire (History of Leadership Studies and Evolution of Leadership Theories, 2012). These styles are still used in leadership literature and evaluations today, although some sources vary the category to authoritarian, participative, and laissez-faire leadership. Beginning in the 1960s and 1970s, leadership theories became more progressive. The behavioral theory of leadership had now completely divorced itself from the notions that leaders were born; instead of stating that the leadership traits from the trait theory were learned behaviors (May, 2010). This notion opened up an entirely new mindset. If leadership is a set of learned behaviors, then those behaviors can be taught and developed. Another newer leadership model contradicted the great man's premise that there is only one style of leadership; the new thinking was that leadership is adaptive to different circumstances, thus its name the *situational leadership theory* (Graeff, 1997).

Significant changes in organizational structure and the concepts of leadership were taking place. Organizations were moving away from the traditional hierarchical, line, and staff organization model to other models such matrix organizations, cross-functional teams, or the use of temporary interdisciplinary teams (Denison, Hart, & Kahn, 1996; Joyce, McGee, & Slocum, 1997). These structures could no longer be supported by the traditional management archetype. Since the late 1980s, management and leadership thought, and corresponding literature began exploring revolutionary leadership models where a temporary project team may include a junior person in the lead role with support from more senior people. The concept that leadership could be shared with each person, a valued leader in an organization would be heresy in the leadership paradigms of just a few decades earlier.

The new model of participative management, leadership opportunities were spread throughout organization structure. Managers and employees at all levels were invited and expected to participate in traditional management functions such as problem-solving and even strategic planning. The use of self-managed teams required team members to develop and utilize leadership skills such as goal setting, facilitating communication, and evaluation (Manz & Sims, 1987). Many organizations began training employees on how to perform the management and leadership functions with which they were now engaged (Porter & Parker, 1993). The new management leadership trends began treating leadership as a function and not a position. New organizational structures supported, encouraged, and even necessitated decentralized leadership and decision-making and leadership functions being performed throughout the organization. These new organizational and leadership models were proving to be more nimble and responsive to changing environments, and thus more successful.

Leadership and management can be evidenced in any organization. Covey (as cited in Epler, 2014, p. 13) stated, "all things are created twice. There is a mental or first creation, and a physical or second creation to all things." Covey (1989) described leadership and management as *creations*. Leadership is described as the first creation with an understanding that it is not management. Leadership deals with the top line: The tasks that a manager or employee can accomplish. Management, on the other hand, is noted as the second creation and is a bottom line focus: The processes of how a manager or employee can best accomplish a specified task. While management's function is *doing things right*, leadership's function is *doing the right thing*. In most organizations, professions, and personal experiences today, leadership is demanded first, and management is demanded second (Covey, 1989; Epler, 2014).

Covey (1989) illustrated some critical differences between leadership and management. He has the reader envision a group of managers and leaders fighting their way through a jungle of heavy undergrowth. The managers are sharpening cutting tools, writing policy and procedures, developing programs, improving technology, and setting up schedules, while the leaders are surveying the entire situation. As the group makes its way through the jungle, a leader realizes they are in the wrong jungle and points this out to the managers. The managers want to proceed because it seems as though the group is making progress, and it would not be doing the right thing by leaving the wrong jungle. The moral of this dilemma is that some managers are so caught up in trying to progress; they neglect to do the right thing. Norton (2005) inferred that an organizational structure could improve if the leader implements his or her beliefs, values, and expertise.

Leadership styles are generally classified by management decisions where a leader involves the employees to be part of the decision-making process. Bolman and Deal (2003, 2009) identified two operating frameworks that deal with people and structure: The caregiver and the analyst. Two other frames of leadership are needed, which "decode a world dominated by passion and power" (Bolman & Deal, 2009, p. 14). The two frames, known as political and symbolic, are not dominant with leaders who do not like to deal with conflict and the political games within an organization. If an organization is well-structured and operated efficiently, leaders hope the political games and nepotism will disappear. The symbolic frame is more difficult to understand.

They don't see it-or if they do, they don't get it. Great leadership cannot flourish without directly addressing political and cultural issues. Too many leaders don't even know which game they're playing. They try to play it safe and stay on the sidelines. That's why today's organizations need more wizards and warriors. (Bolman & Deal, 2009, p. 15)

A warrior can lose focus of the goals based on their obsession and do not see the big picture; whereas, a wizard is more symbolic by understanding values, wisdom, and rituals. An organization that does not have wizards can become toxic (Bolman & Deal, 2009).

Servant Leadership

The philosophy of *servant leadership* is to place the needs of the organization and people first and help others increase their knowledge, skills, and abilities so that they can contribute to the organizational mission and vision. The following characteristics help a servant leader focus on the needs of their people: healing, stewardship, serving others, listening, foreseeing the future, compassion, conceptualization, ability to persuade, knowledge of what is going on around them, sense of group closeness, and desire to help people grow (Barbuto & Wheeler, 2007). When people are pleased with their workplace environment and treated well by their peers and leaders, they are productive and committed to the organization. Servant leadership has a pay it forward philosophy as well. If an employee is happy, they pass this behavior on to others.

A significant issue for effective leadership in the future is to place the internal customer (the employee) first. This effort builds a confidence level within an organization in several ways. Employees feel part of a group, develop a sense of team within the group, and learn that they possess many talents. The leaders' philosophy of giving empowerment to the people helps build trust and respect between the leader and follower (Berraies, Chaher, & Ben Yahia, 2014; Yin, Xing, Li, & Guo, 2017). By involving everybody and focusing on the employee, the employee takes pride in his or her work, feels part of a team, and develops a strong commitment to the organization. Strict forms of management are being removed from organizations and replaced with a new model of employee participation in decision-making.

Servant leadership models are successful in higher education and any other global organizations. Servant leadership, particularly in higher education, builds collaboration, trust, empathy, ethics, and various conditions (e.g., cultural, demographic, economic, sociological) to meet the needs of all stakeholders. If this leadership model is applied to the context of higher education, it can be a long-term process, not a tactic to deceive employees. Instead, it creates a buy-in approach to fixing past organizational issues of high attrition, mistrust, poor performance, union conflicts, and low morale. The theory and concepts behind servant leadership are in sharp contrast to the notion that managers and leaders serve as power brokers and standardize discipline. In 1970, Greenleaf coined the term, servant leadership as the idea that places servants first, shifting from the *tough love style* leadership paradigm. Today, the visionary leader recognizes that a lack of business and political acumen along with a misunderstanding of the organizational culture and demands can result in poor productivity, as well as damage to the employees and the organization.

Servant leadership focuses on the leader serving the people under them (Greenleaf & Spears, 2002). Servant leaders are entirely different from traditional leaders, but only because they have observed the value among corporate boardrooms and public sector agencies and have grown to recognize that both sectors are pleading for change. Servant leaders do not hide behind their subordinates, but rally among coworkers from the front lines in a similar fashion to one of the original pioneers of servant leadership. Private and public institutions have significantly improved their organizational cultures and services through developing and supporting a vertical and horizontal culture of servant leadership. Relationships are essential in developing functional organizations or groups of people focused upon common goals. The lack of understanding this organizational restructuring will not promote effective change. Leadership is an art and involves a multitude of variables that require attention.

The importance of relationships is another principle foundation of servant leadership. Interpersonal relationships are critical elements within any organization as they afford a basis for how effectively the organization and its people function, perform tasks, and react to the external environment (Baron, 1996; Flum, 2015). It seems safe to assume that numerous scientific studies were undertaken by researchers and supporters of servant leadership, including Stephen Covey, Margaret Wheatley, Kenneth Blanchard, James Collins, Peter Senge, and Max DePree, corroborate the measures of organizational performance outcomes through well-designed skills and are more interested in building positive relationships.

Focusing on the needs and wants of a group, the organization can improve relationships. No one feels threatened, and retaliation becomes an embarrassingly outdated concept. Individual leaders and managers do not become the focus. Relationships can be developed through compassion; this trait is the ability to consider an employee's circumstances while performing job tasks. Leaders can be approached with questions and concerns that may not be directly related to job functions, and suffer vicariously through the employees. This compassion leads to more significant personal and organizational relationships; a leader understands that personal affairs may influence the employee, yet considers this when delegating job functions. This, in turn, leads to greater attachment and confidence with the leader, and employees feel more comfortable addressing concerns with their leaders that are external to the work environment. The mutual association that can be created when the group knows its needs come prior to their leader is astronomical. When the leader reframes the previously held notions of power and authority brokers as being the dominant member of the organization, the organizational relationship will significantly improve as individual needs are met. A persuasive leader influences others to perform; if one follows based on a desire rather than a need, a personal relationship of loyalty and fellowship will be established (Barbuto & Wheeler, 2007).

Toxic and Chaotic Leadership

Leadership has been researched for decades. Leadership also has another angle, which is the toxic side of operating an organization. Poor leadership includes *the chaos theory*, *toxic leadership*, and the increase of narcissism permeating the 21st century. Bolman and Deal (2009) stated that a person could avoid the toxic side of leadership by gaining a sense of self, build on strengths and weaknesses through feedback and reflection, and look for trust within their organization. A toxic leader causes isolation; this type of leader is unaware of his or her faults. Trust is also a virtue that is lacking in a toxic environment. There is a cost to distrust within an organization, which is a trend occurring in the past decades; particularly within the political arena. Covey (2010) demonstrated the media reports of many scandals of corporate or political leaders that have violated the public trust. Covey stated that "as trust goes down, speed goes down, and costs go up" (2010, p. 10). To rid distrust and toxic leadership within organizations, there needs to be a change in direction. For organizational leaders to be influenced and inspired by their people, building and modeling trust is vital. In addition, transparency is crucial to building trust and collaboration.

"Toxic leadership is a multidimensional construct that includes elements of abusive supervision along with narcissism, authoritarianism, self-promotion, and unpredictability" (Dobbs, 2014, p. 15). Research has found that toxic leadership impacts various organizations and sectors. These areas include (a) physical and mental health of employees, (b) increased dysfunctional group behaviors, (c) increased absenteeism and tardiness, (d) reduced productivity, and (e) resignation or transfers. In addition, toxic leaders possess the following characteristics: unethical or bad behavior, self-promotion, abusive and tyrannical supervision, downward hostility toward others, engage in destructive and demotivational behaviors, and narcissistic and authoritative tendencies (Dobbs, 2014; Schmidt, 2014).

Schmidt (2014) found that specific organizations with rigid hierarchical structures like the military had characteristics of subordination and abusive control. Bandura (1973) found people who considered leaders to have strong authority also had a high rank. In some situations, there necessitates autocratic leadership; however, the term subordinate within other industries can lead to arrogance, hubris, abuse of power, mistrust, and performance issues. "Military experience is a powerful way to test and develop oneself as a warrior" (Bolman & Deal, 2009, p. 16). Bolman and Deal (2009) consider a warrior as a leader who can build a stable organization; they recognize conflict and strive for reaching the goals of the organization. Leadership style(s) become fluid and represent a juxtaposition opportunity for meaningful dialogue among organizational stakeholders in most industries, except for these few autocratic missions like the armed forces.

It is unlikely that observations would not produce levels of arrogance, hubris, and bullying within any organization. An argument for the skewed "feel good" human brain neurotransmitter behavior suggests that pleasure is sought and many times obtained from those in titled positions of authority because they lack practical skills as leaders and managers. If a manager-leader lacks confidence in his or her own skill sets, the more prone he or she may be to the use of abusive tactics to control operations and people. This abuse can increase with longevity within the company. It is rare to find authentic leaders who are secure with their skills and are willing to embrace-promote and encourage more creative thought provoking staff who can take the organization to a more advanced position of critical thinking in a regulatory-driven and competitive business.

It is unlikely a perfect *organizational fit* exists; however, there is an expectation of a humanistic approach to leadership of most organizations and is more dominant than symbolic, political, and structural approaches (Bolman & Deal, 2003). Given the current issues with unemployment and underemployment conditions in the United States, it would be reasonable to postulate that people want and need jobs to support their families and become employed full time in a job with fair benefits. It would not be uncommon to find employees who are willing to accept and be mistreated by organizational managers-leaders who choose to abuse their position of authority and power to exploit others they feel are inferior to their organizational fit. One of the most damaging types of abuse is the marginalization of employees over non-merit factors or feelings of jealousy for those who have developed more advanced levels of critical thinking, and are viewed as threats to those in current leadership positions.

Drawing from *Maslow's Hierarchy of Needs*, people want to feel a part of the mission of the organization and not be excluded from improving skills and contributing to the overall goals and outcomes. However, there are ill-prepared and toxic people at all levels who hinder productive outcomes stifling healthy and productive ones.

People who remain in this environment perpetuate dysfunction within an organization. Global leaders must be sensitive to the needs of people in their organizations. An aloof and distant autocratic manager, who seeks to impress and gain favor from upper-level management, has diminished the organizational culture and its human assets. The sycophant approach to leadership and management is a clever con game causing extensive damage that stagnates performance and morale within the organization. If treated correctly, most staff members are willing to engage in any task to advance the mission and goals of the organization. Servant leadership, as applied to the workplace, suggests employees demand authentic leadership and loyalty as it can be applied to groups of diverse populations seeking common goals.

The crisis in institutional leadership also impacts productivity, motivation, morale, trust, and confidence. In some workplaces and the organizational structure and environment, there is an inclusion of mobbing, also called workplace bullying (Davenport, Schwartz, & Elliott, 2005; Duffy & Sperry, 2014; Namie & Namie, 2003). If this type of behavior infiltrates the organization, the *so-called leader* with no true leadership qualities would be the main contributor to the crisis. A person who is ineffective as a leader uses the chaos theory to control and bully people. With this type of philosophy, a so-called leader promotes a lack of knowledge of organizational direction so people will rely on this so-called leader for answers and directions. This *control tactic* creates a great crisis in the organization.

Crisis Within Higher Education

The culture of an organization is like a river. It can be fluid, strong, and consistent, serving as a lubricant while guiding its members in the right direction. In contrast, a river can become stale and toxic, silently killing those who drink at its shore. — Ron Kaufman

The education field is one that, in essence, molds today's future. We generally look at the current population of K-12 teachers as those who will shape our youth and determine what is to become of them in the workforce. They are the ones who introduce and teach our children about the plethora of fields that exist and have them thinking from a young age, what it is that they might want to be when they grow up. However, one must not also forget the impact that professors may also have on our young adults who are just as quickly moldable, manipulated, and observant when entering college. That stated, it is critical for professors to conduct themselves as professional adults within their institution as students will pick up on any *negativity* that may be produced amongst faculty and staff as well as administration within the institution. Stanley, Meyer, and Topolnytsky (2005) revealed that employees are the liaison amid the organization and their stakeholders. Furthermore, it was revealed that disgruntled employees tend to speak negatively about their employers as well as illustrate cynicism (Sasso, 2017; Stanley et al., 2005). This, in turn, takes us to the importance of ensuring that the organization is lead via servant leadership and not toxic leadership, as toxic leadership is destructive to not only the individuals within the organization but also to the organization itself (Sasso, 2017).

According to research, human capital is a crucial, maintainable, as well as a competitive advantage that organizations have, as they symbolize innovation, future leadership, as well as a foundation of bravery (Chaleff, 2003; Johnson, 2009; Kellerman, 2008). It was similarly stated by Tanzharikova (2012) that there is an essential relation between education, human capital, and economic growth of the country. However, when employees feel disgruntled and become cynical at work, they begin to speak negatively about their employer, which in turn unfavorably affect the customer's experience (Meyer & Schwager, 2007; Verhoef, Lemon, Parasuraman, Roggeveen, Tsiros, & Schlesinger, 2009). In this case, the customer refers to the students within higher education. That being said, toxic leadership within education not only affects the staff and faculty but the students as well. It is crucial to keep in mind that in today's day and age, higher education is experiencing a significant decline in student enrollment (Sasso & Ross, 2019). Therefore, it is of even greater importance for professors to illustrate and bring on an engaging and positive presence to the institution, where students feel secure and optimistic about their program and future degree.

Let us take a look at this scenario. Imagine a professor, in the middle of their lecture, stopping the class to allow students to *vent* about their issues with the academic institution. Better yet, imagine if this same professor then chimed in with the students about their disgust of the institution. How do you suppose that would make the students feel, knowing that professors from that same institution share the same negative feelings? How do you suppose that would help the institution's reputation or enrollment?

Bourne (2016) identified that many viewpoints, styles of leadership, which are designed as a leader who has power over others, should change in a direction, so educators and leaders of organizations employ a more power-with approach. This leads to higher performance as the leader is recognized as influential, not toxic. Greenleaf (2009) felt that the public sector have less persuasion and an increase in coercion, which leads to a society of oppression and corruption. In higher educational institutions, the environment must be welcomed by all staff, faculty, and administration, as there could be a decrease in enrollment as well as other university-based challenges. Universities must meet the needs of the student as "people are demanding an educational product that fits within their budget, time – work schedule, and that what is traditionally offered by higher educational organizations is not meeting the outside demands of the social or business world" (Bourne, 2016, para. 3). Farnsworth (as cited in Bourne, 2016) explicated that to address a decline in admissions, there must be a new approach to higher education leadership in the United States to meet potential students' opportunities they will face in the global markets.

Rosenbach, Taylor, and Youndt (2012) noted that there are many definitions of leadership being studied and observed, yet leadership remains little understood except to recognize that leaders are not born; leaders are made, and this also holds true within the higher education field. Theories of leadership can be measured by its effectiveness in higher education. Leadership has many traits, whether they are behavioral theories where leadership is learned or acquired, or based on the trait theory that people are born leaders (Mehta, 2012). There is no specific best-fit style of leadership as many theorists base leadership on decision making, goal structure, structuring of group tasks, power, personality, and situations (Mehta, 2012). "Leadership effectiveness can be achieved by ensuring a fit between the leadership style and the demand of the situation" (Mehta, 2012, p. 24).

One measurement of poor leadership is attrition; poor leadership leads to attrition. Leadership can be further explained as a process of social influence within diverse organizational environments in which there is a set of common traits for every situation. Rosenbach, Taylor, and Youndt (2012) explained that understanding leadership is necessitated by organizational and environmental dynamics and the increasing complexities of higher education. With higher education becoming increasingly diverse, leaders have more pressure and responsibility to deal with the challenges presented by employees. The faculty and staff of today's workforce need to be influenced by effective leaders who can protect their interests while pursuing the goals of the organization.

Attrition is an indicator of problematic leadership. Considering the competing result of scarce resources to recruit and retain good employees, attrition issues become one of the most sobering matters facing institutional leaders today. Employees can find themselves negatively impacted by the culture of the organization and miserable from being exposed to the degradation that runs rampant within their jobs. There is a high demand for control and expectations from the organizational leaders, and employees are bound to fail. Poor supervisory practices account for a significant number of employees who feel dissatisfaction and hold negative feelings. If a leader lacks certain elements of power, they have found to be tyrants and "on other occasions to be more aggressive or abusive than others" (Lee-Chai & Bargh, 2001, p. 119). Raven and Kruglanski (as cited in Lee-Chai & Bargh, 2001) mentioned that coercive power and tactics are used by people who lack confidence and other levels of power, such as expertise and informational power. Four areas which can be identified as problematic and noteworthy are (a) disruption in the work setting; (b) lack of communication with policies and procedures; (c) abusive, tyrannical, and inept leadership; and (d) organizational failure.

High attrition rates can become fiscally monumental. Large attrition is not unique to most organizations. A considerable amount of turnover occurs in state and federal agencies where costs can easily exceed thousands of dollars and higher to recruit and train individuals for employment, excluding relocation and other costs. It takes several years to train an individual in their field of expertise adequately. There is a drain of qualified people and the loss of productivity, lower morale, and safety issues surrounding high turnover rates. In addition, the number of complaints and the potential for civil liability increases the argument for a review of the servant leadership model.

To help curtail attrition, servant leadership certainly offers any organization an opportunity to develop into a learning organization, becoming a healthier, comfortable, and empowering place to work and be recognized for achievement and growth. To create a healthier professional environment for all stakeholders (i.e., employees, supervisory levels), there is a need for equity, equality, respect, core values, open communication, continual training, and other incentives to develop an internal self-confidence. An organizational structure should foster a sense of camaraderie and encourage growth for everyone to pursue a standard set of goals, which leads to a strong sense of belonging and personal motivation to remain employed within the institution. Moreover, the personal empowerment of these employees is further supported by working in a learning environment where the culture supports ownership in the organization through active participation of managers and leaders who are open to new ideas and change (Marquardt, 2011).

Aside from ownership within the organization, most employees desire the opportunity to be treated in a fair and balanced manner by the agency leadership. A few of those examples include regular promotions, mutual respect, educational opportunities, and consistent increases in annual pay and benefits. Employee attitudes can range from disempowered to empowered. A disempowered employee places recognition in the hands of the organization; whereas an empowered employee is responsible for his or her own sphere of influence. No matter what an individual's position is in any organization, the recognition process affects an individual's ability to reward and recognize others (Berraies, Chaher, & Ben Yahia, 2014). "Empowerment implies that employees throughout the organization have the authority to do whatever is necessary to meet requirements and satisfy customers and are trusted to make the best choices without having to wait for approval from management. It is a process of power sharing" (Schultz, 2014, p. 44). This influences employees to develop self-esteem and job satisfaction, thus increasing the organization's productivity and therefore, the value of the organization. It is leadership that fosters the growth of new ideas.

Servant Leadership in Graduate Programs

Bourne (2016) in his review of *Leadership as a Service: A New Model for Higher Education in a New Century*, stated that the author Kent Farnsworth stretched the concept of educational leadership to encompass obstacles facing higher education and a rationalization for a new model in all educational leadership, focusing on higher education and the institutions. Comparing a couple of philosophies of servant leadership by Steven Covey and Robert Greenleaf, Bourne identified Farnsworth's expertise as a professor and president of the higher education system, which gives merit to his philosophy to justify servant-centered leadership in both the public and private sectors. Greenleaf (2009) commented that trustees of higher education must change their model to be that as servants since these institutions build societies that give opportunities to people. There are many topics that should be discussed and incorporated in any university curricula to include (a) new leadership, (b) leadership as a pursuit to serve, (c) empowering toward service, (d) redesigning higher education, (e) organizing for service, and (f) barriers to leadership as service (Bourne, 2016). Farnsworth (as cited in Bourne, 2016) commented that he had become an advocate for servant leadership from the readings of Steven Covey and Robert Greenleaf. In support of servant-centered leadership, it should be the focus and vision of higher education as a "new direction in educational leadership will come through a complete commitment to service" (Bourne, 2016, para. 4).

Any curriculum designed for higher education leadership should have a servant-centered leadership component to include listening, empathy, healing, awareness, persuasion, conceptualization, foresight, stewardship, commitment to the growth of others, building community, and a calling to make a difference in others' lives

(Crippen, 2010). Crippen (2010) introduces the need for servant leadership to be taught in the K-12 school system, as a teacher is a leader who prepares students for the community. "Once you assume the mantle of teacher, you become a leader in your classroom and then in your school and learning community. Such leadership situations provide an opportunity to contribute to the moral ethos of that learning environment" (Crippen, 2010, p. 27). Courses in higher education, whether structured as face-to-face, online or blended, must improve student satisfaction and their commitment to learning. Sahawneh and Benuto (2018) explained for online courses, students would benefit from servant-centered leadership as students are isolated from the university, faculty, and their colleagues, unless faculty are engaging and influential, as well as offer servant leadership characteristics of emotional healing, commitment to building a strong community.

There are many benefits to incorporate servant leadership within higher education institutions. A discussion should take place to integrate servant leadership into higher education and organizational leadership graduate programs. Students in this field need to learn how to lead their organization with integrity, honesty, and humility. Servant leaders "put the needs of their followers before their own needs" (Hackman & Johnson, 2013, p. 358). They are humble stewards, and "scholars of leadership have increasingly emphasized that effective leadership emerges from inspiring, motivating, and mentoring followers" (Chin & Trimble, 2015, p. 128). With the uprising of mobbing and bullying in higher education institutions, graduate students need to understand how to incorporate servant leadership into their organizations to help promote harmony and avoid a toxic environment.

For example, students in a graduate course could identify and evaluate a case study associated with a mobbing/bullying situation in a higher education setting. By evaluating the case study, the students can review the administrative leadership to identify the effectiveness. The student could then identify the characteristics of servant leadership and provide examples of ways to intervene and correct the situation through a positive, ethical climate. Similar to the above example could be to review case studies where servant leadership was successfully implemented. Through research, students can identify effective techniques and skills on how to implement servant leadership and ways to promote a pleasant and safe environment.

Another example could be to require the graduate students to conduct a Strengths, Weaknesses, Opportunity, and Threats (SWOT) analysis on their organization regarding the leadership related to servant leadership. By description, servant leadership is the type of leadership that "promotes service, values, and characteristics include a strong service ethos, integrity, humility, morality, empathy, and trustworthiness; one leads by serving others and by inspiring and enabling others to exercise leadership responsibilities" (Dean, 2014, p. 274). As a result of conducting a SWOT analysis, students will have a better understanding of servant leadership and how it can benefit a higher education institution.

After the SWOT analysis, linking it to servant leadership, students can apply the information by creating an Anti-bullying Training Program at the higher education institution. As indicated by Chin and Trimble (2015) "training is effectively and appropriately used to create awareness and help people develop knowledge and skills, which could result in behavior change" (p. 240). Behavior change is what higher education institutions require to avoid the toxic environment associated with mobbing and bullying. Creating a calm, pleasant work atmosphere should be a high priority for leaders. Hackman and Johnson (2013) stated that "individuals working under servant leaders indicate that they are more satisfied, believe their needs are met, declare they will stay with their organization, think their organizations are more effective, put forth extra effort, and report that they are justly treated" (p. 358). Creating this type of environment would help to eliminate the negativity and preserve an encouraging work setting. Faculty and other higher education personnel must contribute to the well-being of others (Bourne, 2016).

CONCLUSION

Failure is not the end to success. The autocratic method of leading with a divide and conquer bully mentality fill employees with fear and destroys the organization. The opportunity to move ahead and develop an optimum performance model in higher education through a process of learning from missed clues and missteps becomes an inspiration to the institution's leadership.

Servant leadership is not intended to be passive in organizational edict when required, but most relationships respond well to employee nurturing to reframe the intended organizational goals through individual participation. True leaders work as part of a team and foster individual as well as group success. A leader must be willing to be a pupil, willing to listen, admit to, and learn from employees' mistakes, and accept constructive criticism. Regardless of how much education or experience a leader in higher education has, he or she should know how to incorporate listening skills into his or her leadership style.

Servant leadership is inspirational and promotes a culture of integrity, trust, and a real concern for others grounded in mutual respect. It sets the institutional foundation to serve the students, faculty and staff, and public and community through effective and competent leadership, which entices public servants to want to learn and become empowered to serve. The demand for great leadership is within every one of us.

Activities can be quantified, and we can assess a value to the task. Many critical questions arose during the research and analysis of this chapter. Aside from the obvious costs associated with employee attrition, other costs include the brand value and reputation for a College/University. There are the costs to replace personnel, recruitment, retirement, medical and physical healthcare, loss of clientele, and the organizational intellect. Organizations that breed a toxic culture drive people to leave and transfer their intellect to the competitive market as there is no opportunity for people to become long-term employees.

Change is not an option-it is an inevitability. And the tremendous changes in the culture that surrounds and impacts higher education have created both crisis and opportunity. As presently organized and delivered, higher education is no longer sustainable, technologically, or pedagogically. (Farnsworth, 2007, p. 2)

Those organizations that constantly seek recognition by having organizational culture style surveys produce data; however, it is not clear whether the responses are truly unbiased and accurately represent how employees feel working within the organization.

It is a commonplace for employees to mistrust organizational managers and leaders based upon prior experiences as well as colleagues who have experienced personal challenges. During the frequent transition of managers and leaders within an organization, there is a fear in the ambiguity of the future style of organizational leadership under the new administration. This confusion seems to benefit the new administration when people guess about how old traditions will be changed during the new administration. Leaders in higher education must know what it takes to lead. Throughout history, leadership theories have evolved to reflect events occurring within the societies of the current time. According to Goffee and Jones (2003), three dominant qualities seem to be fundamental to all successful leaders, and that has also been a historical continuum in leadership theories. Successful leaders are inspirational leaders, and they must know how to engage people (e.g., students, faculty) and encourage their commitment to the goals of the institution. According to the Goffee and Jones, the four common characteristics found in inspirational leaders include: (a) approachability and humanity and the ability to reveal weaknesses, (b) reliance on intuition and soft data to make certain decisions data, (c) they must demonstrate empathy with their employees, and (d) dare to be different and express their uniqueness.

Leadership is not only about the personal development of one person, but rather the formation of a learning organization. Leadership becomes an organizational and societal issue. A characteristic of a successful leader is encouraging people and supporting the accomplishments of tasks without being directed or micromanaged. The visionary leader who pursues creative approaches to leadership will find success in positive and measurable ways. This has been amply demonstrated by Harvard University, Starbucks Coffee, and Southwest Airlines representing a few examples of flagship organizations among a growing number of leaders who have embraced the demand for accountable and goal focused servant leadership. Today more than ever, leaders in higher education must encourage people to become critical thinkers in order to focus upon new and creative ideas. Employees in an organization or students in a classroom have competing interests with sometimes scarce resources, but still must be led to perform at an optimum level and beyond. For an organization to be effective, real, and valued input is encouraged by its people.

Leadership decisions may not appease everyone when implementing change. Drucker's research on positive humanistic leadership and organizational management is one of the many pioneers responsible for the paradigm shift away from the outdated autocratic style of leadership. According to Drucker (1998), "one does not manage people as previously assumed. One leads them" (p. 166). Servant leadership is not about oppressing or rejecting the ideas and values of others because of personal conflict, differing opinions, or insecurities. To step aside from the power-control image of a leader, the servant leader reframes the partnership with coworkers and promotes others to rise above their current status and values them by selecting the right people for tasks. A servant leader utilizes positive reinforcement to facilitate personal growth in the organization.

Deming (2000) observed that leaders must become empowering by tapping the potential of an organization's most valuable resource: The people who are dedicated and committed to the organizational mission, vision, and core values. "The greatest waste in America is failure to use the abilities of people" (Deming, 1986, p. 53). Among the many components that make up an organization are people and teams of people. They are not only important; they are unique, emotional beings who are subject to cultural conditioning. To understand people, a leader needs to know and be aware of their interactions with each other, the system in which they work and learn, and their motivations (Deming, 2000; Marquardt, 2011). When an employee is motivated, he or she is more consistent in performance and eager for constant improvement. Building teams and relationships in higher education are needed to keep the institutional goals on a positive path. Without motivation, communication, collaboration, and social relations, there could be a disruption in the flow of the organization (Levi, 2010).

The cost of public institutional services is measurable, and output is found to increase significantly because of the subtle power of coaching and the persuasion process used by the servant leader. The servant leader also benefits from this process by understanding ethics and power along with awareness of the value of organizational trust and its integrity and the coming together style of servant leadership. To become a servant leader, leaders must provide positive reinforcement and influence so that people can perform at an optimal level.

REFERENCES

Bandura, A. (1973). *Aggression: A social learning analysis*. Englewood Cliffs, NJ: Prentice Hall.

Barbuto, J., & Wheeler, D. (2007, October). Becoming a servant leader: Do you have what it takes? *NetGuide, 2000*. Retrieved November 1, 2014, from http://www.ianrpubs.unl.edu /epublic/live/g1481/build/g1481.pdf

Baron, R. (1996). Interpersonal relations in organizations. In K. Murphy (Ed.), *Individual differences* (pp. 334–370). San Francisco, CA: Jossey Bass.

Berraies, S., Chaher, M., & Ben Yahia, K. (2014). Employee empowerment and its importance for trust, innovation, and organizational performance. *Business Management and Strategy, 5*(2). Retrieved from https://pdfs.semanticscholar.org/3942/e29369ff7e50dc18c5fe0e26c1c1d43e46d6.pdf

Bolman, L. G., & Deal, T. E. (2003). *Reframing organizations: Artistry, choice, and leadership* (3rd ed.). San Francisco, CA: Jossey Bass.

Bolman, L. G., & Deal, T. E. (2009). Battles and beliefs: Rethinking the roles of today's leaders. *Leadership in Action, 29*(5), 14–18. doi:10.1002/lia.1306

Borgatta, E. F., Bales, R. F., & Couch, A. S. (1954). Some findings relevant to the great man theory of leadership. *American Sociological Review, 19*(6), 755–759. doi:10.2307/2087923

Bourne, P. A. (2016). Leadership as a service: A new model for higher education in a new century. *Review of Public Administration and Management, 4*(3), 196. doi:-7844.1000196 doi:10.4172/2315

Bowman, J. S., & Wittmer, D. L. (2000). The unfashionable Drucker: Ethical and quality chic. *Journal of Management History, 6*(1), 13–29. doi:10.1108/13552520010316592

Cawthon, D. L. (1996). Leadership: The great man theory revisited. *Business Horizons*, 1–4.

Chaleff, I. (2003). *The courageous follower: Standing up to and for our leaders*. San Francisco, CA: Berrett-Koehler.

Chin, J. L., & Trimble, J. E. (2015). *Diversity and leadership*. Los Angeles, CA: Sage.

Covey, S. M. R. (2010). How can workplace learning and performance professionals instill trust in an organization's leaders? *T+D, 64*(10), 10-11.

Covey, S. R. (1989). *The 7 habits of highly effective people.* New York, NY: Simon and Schuster.

Cox, T. D. (2015). Adult education philosophy: The case of self-directed learning strategies in graduate teaching. *Journal of Learning in Higher Education, 11*(1), 17–22.

Crippen, C. (2010). Serve, teach, and lead: It's all about relationships. *A Journal of Scholarly Teaching, 5,* 27-36. Retrieved from https://eric.ed.gov/?id=EJ902861

Daft, R. L. (1991). *Management* (7th ed.). Chicago, IL: The Dryden Press.

Daft, R. L. (2014). *Management* (11th ed.). Mason, OH: South-Western, Cengage Learning.

Davenport, N., Schwartz, R. D., & Elliott, G. P. (2005). *Mobbing: Emotional abuse in the American Workplace.* Ames, IA: Civil Society.

Dean, D. (2014). Servant leadership for higher education: Principles and practices. *Review of Higher Education, 37*(2), 274–277. doi:10.1353/rhe.2014.0010

Deming, W. E. (1986). *Out of the crisis.* Cambridge, MA: Massachusetts Institute of Technology, Center for Advanced Engineering Study.

Deming, W. E. (2000). *Out of the crisis.* London, UK: The MIT Press.

Denison, D. R., Hart, S. L., & Kahn, J. A. (1996). From chimneys to cross-functional teams: Developing and validating a diagnostic model. *Academy of Management Journal, 39*(4), 1005–1023.

Dobbs, J. M. (2014). *The relationship between perceived toxic leadership styles, leader effectiveness, and organizational cynicism.* Available from ProQuest Dissertations and Theses database. (UMI No. 3575052)

Drucker, P. (1998). *Managing and leadership.* Retrieved November 1, 2014 from http://web.mit.edu/mbarker/www/ideas/drucker.html

Duffy, M., & Sperry, L. (2014). *Overcoming mobbing: A recovery guide for workplace aggression and bullying.* New York, NY: Oxford University Press.

Epler, D. (2014). Identify your key goals and roles. *Strategic Finance, 96*(1), 13–15.

Farnsworth, K. A. (2007). *Leadership as service: A new model for higher education in a new century*. Westport, CT: Praeger.

Flum, H. (2015). Relationships and career development: An integrative approach. In P. J. Hartung, M. L. Savickas, & W. B. Walsh (Eds.), *APA handbook for career intervention* (pp. 145–158). doi:10.1037/14438-009

Goffee, R., & Jones, G. (2003). *The character of a corporation – How your company's culture can make or break your business* (2nd ed.). New York, NY: Profile Books.

Graeff, C. L. (1997). Evolution of situational leadership theory: A critical review. *The Leadership Quarterly*, *8*(2), 153–170. doi:10.1016/S1048-9843(97)90014-X

Greenleaf, R. K. (1970). *The servant as leader*. Westfield, IN: Robert K. Greenleaf Publishing Center.

Greenleaf, R. K. (2009). *The institution as servant*. Westfield, IN: Robert K. Greenleaf Publishing Center.

Greenleaf, R. K., & Spears, L. C. (2002). Servant leadership: A journey into the nature of legitimate power and greatness (25th anniversary ed.). New York, NY: Paulist Press.

Hackman, M. Z., & Johnson, C. E. (2013). *Leadership: A communication perspective* (6th ed.). Long Grove, IL: Waveland Press.

Hatch, M. J. (2013). *Organization theory: Modern, symbolic and postmodern perspectives* (3rd ed.). New York, NY: Oxford University Press.

History of Leadership Studies and Evolution of Leadership Theories. (2012). Retrieved from hubpages.com: http://ecoggins.hubpages.com/hub/The-History-of-Leadership-Studies-and-Evolution-of-Leadership-Theories

Hur, E. H., Glassman, M., & Kim, Y. (2013). Finding autonomy in activity: Development and validation of a democratic classroom survey. *Educational Assessment, Evaluation and Accountability*, *25*(4), 303–320. doi:10.100711092-013-9173-y

Johnson, C. E. (2009). *Meeting the ethical challenges of leadership: Casting light or shadow*. Thousand Oaks, CA: Sage.

Joyce, W. F., McGee, V. E., & Slocum, J. W. (1997). Designing lateral organizations: An analysis of the benefits, costs, and enablers of nonhierarchical organizational forms. *Decision Sciences*, *28*(1), 1–25. doi:10.1111/j.1540-5915.1997.tb01300.x

Kellerman, B. (2008). *Followership: How followers are creating change and changing leaders*. Boston, MA: Harvard Business Press.

Lee-Chai, A. Y., & Bargh, J. A. (2001). *The use and abuse of power: Multiple perspectives on the causes of corruption*. Philadelphia, PA: Taylor & Francis Group.

Levi, D. (2010). *Group dynamics for teams* (3rd ed.). Los Angeles, CA: Sage.

Locke, E. A. (1982). The ideas of Frederick W. Taylor: An evaluation. *Academy of Management Review*, *7*(1), 14–24. doi:10.5465/amr.1982.4285427

Manz, C. C., & Sims, H. P. (1987). Leading workers to lead themselves: The external leadership of self-managing work teams. *Administrative Science Quarterly*, *32*(1), 106–128. doi:10.2307/2392745

Marquardt, M. J. (2011). *Building the learning organization: Achieving strategic advantage through a commitment to learning* (3rd ed.). Boston, MA: Nicholas Brealey.

Matteson, R. W. (2002). *A qualitative study of bullying behavior in federal law enforcement: An examination of former officers perceptions regarding the problem* (Doctoral dissertation). Available from ProQuest Dissertations and Theses database. (UMI No. 3072568)

May, F. (2010). *Thesis project in management science: The power of a lollipop, from theory to action*. Retrieved from Thesis.fr: http://www.theses.fr/s90114

Mehta, M. (2012). Situational leadership and personal effectiveness: Managers in Indian development organizations. *Foundation for Organizational Research & Education*, *30*(1), 23–34.

Meyer, C., & Schwager, A. (2007). Understanding customer experience. *Harvard Business Review*, *85*(2), 116. Retrieved from http://zurichhpdelivered.com/internet/zna/SiteCollectionDocuments/en/media/FINAL%20HBR%20Understanding%20Customer%20Experience.pdf PMID:17345685

Mulvey, P. W., & Padilla, A. (2010). The environment of destructive leadership. In B. Schyns & T. Hansbrough (Eds.), *When leadership goes wrong: Destructive leadership, mistakes, and ethical failures* (pp. 49–72). Charlotte, NC: Information Age Publishing.

Namie, G., & Namie, R. (2003). *The bully at work: What you can do to stop the hurt and reclaim your dignity on the job*. Naperville, IL: Sourcebooks.

Norton, M. S. (2005). *Executive leadership for effective administration*. Boston, MA: Pearson.

Porter, L. J., & Parker, A. J. (1993). Total quality management: The critical success factors. *Total Quality Management*, *4*(1), 13–22. doi:10.1080/09544129300000003

Rosenbach, W. E., Taylor, R. L., & Youndt, M. A. (2012). *Contemporary issues in leadership*. Boulder, CO: Westview Press.

Ross, D. B., Sasso, M. T., Matteson, C. E., & Matteson, R. W. (2019). *Narcissistic and sociopathic leadership and the world of higher education: A place for mentoring, not mobbing*. Hershey, PA: IGI Global.

Sahawneh, F. G., & Benuto, L. T. (2018). The relationship between instructor servant leadership behaviors and satisfaction with instructors in an online setting. *Online Learning*, *22*(1), 107–129. doi:10.24059/olj.v22i1.1066

Sasso, M. T. (2017). *How narcissists cannot hold an organization together: A mixed method approach to a fictitious puzzle factory* (Doctoral dissertation). Available from ProQuest Dissertations and Theses database. (UMI No. 10819904)

Schmidt, A. A. (2014). *An examination of toxic leadership, job outcomes, and the impact of military deployment*. Available from ProQuest Dissertations and Theses database. (UMI No. 3627674)

Schultz, J. R. (2014). Creating a culture of empowerment fosters the flexibility to change. *Global Business and Organizational Excellence*, *34*(1), 41–50. doi:10.1002/joe.21583

Stanley, D. J., Meyer, J. P., & Topolnytsky, L. (2005). Employee cynicism and resistance to organizational change. *Journal of Business and Psychology*, *19*(4), 429–459. doi:10.100710869-005-4518-2

Tanzharikova, A. Z. (2012). The role of higher education system in human capital formation. *World Applied Sciences Journal*, *18*, 135–139. doi:10.5829/idosi.wasj.2012.18.120022

Taylor, F. W. (1914). *The principles of scientific management*. New York, NY: Harper & Brothers.

Van Seters, D. A., & Field, R. H. (1990). The evolution of leadership theory. *Journal of Organizational Change Management*, *3*(3), 29–45. doi:10.1108/09534819010142139

Verhoef, P. C., Lemon, K. N., Parasuraman, A., Roggeveen, A., Tsiros, M., & Schlesinger, L. A. (2009). Customer experience creation: Determinants, dynamics and management strategies. *Journal of Retailing*, *85*(1), 31–41. doi:10.1016/j.jretai.2008.11.001

Winter, D. G. (1973). *The power motive*. New York, NY: The Free Press.

Yin, K., Xing, L., Li, C., & Guo, Y. (2017). Are empowered employees more productive? The contingency of how they evaluate their leader. *Frontiers in Psychology*, *8*, 1802. doi:10.3389/fpsyg.2017.01802 PMID:29163249

Section 3
Accounts from the Ivory Tower Arena

Personal storytelling as a means through which to describe, explain and interpret academic mobbing as competently insidious.

Chapter 8
My Campus Administration, Faculty Association, Senate, and Me:
A Case Study in Academic Mobbing

Peter Wylie
University of British Columbia – Okanagan, Canada

ABSTRACT

This chapter recounts recent experiences of the author with the University of British Columbia (UBC), its Faculty Association (FA), this association's relationship with the author's campus administration at UBC Okanagan campus (UBCO), and the relationship of the campus administration with the senate of the campus. The chapter is a case study of academic mobbing. The author's targeting, exclusion, and ostracism is fully documented in the chapter and fully explained by the concepts of academic bullying, harassment, and mobbing. It is a case study of where an elected union representative of faculty members and an elected senator was targeted, excluded, and ostracized by the powers that be in the union and university administration, working in collusion and complicity.

DOI: 10.4018/978-1-5225-9485-7.ch008

Copyright © 2020, IGI Global. Copying or distributing in print or electronic forms without written permission of IGI Global is prohibited.

INTRODUCTION

This chapter recounts recent experiences of the author, a tenured associate professor close to normal retirement age, with the University of British Columbia (UBC), its Faculty Association (UBCFA, or simply, FA), this association's relationship with the author's campus administration at UBC Okanagan campus (UBCO), and the relationship of the campus administration with the senate of the campus. The chapter is a specific and personal case study of academic mobbing, defined as "an insidious, non-violent and sophisticated kind of psychological bullying that predominantly takes place in college and university campuses" (Khoo, 2010, p. 61). The chapter is one of a series of works the author has written and published in recent years on the institutional analysis of UBC, especially UBCO and the FA (Wylie, 2017, 2018a, 2018b, 2018c, in press). A comprehensive account of some early in time aspects of this case study is published elsewhere (Wylie, 2018c) and hence is not repeated in this chapter.

The inquiry draws on narrative and self-study methodology requiring a close, critical process of inquiry and reflection (Clarke & Erickson, 2003). Self-study is paired with narrative (Hendry, 2010, p. 73). Care however was taken to anonymize as much as possible, other than the actual institution. The chapter explores how administrative managers at the campus, who *de facto* control the senate, deny and explain away inconvenient information, and how the FA supports them do it. The article demonstrates a turn on 'don't shoot the messenger' wisdom, as sweetheart unionism, defined as "collusion between management and labour" in terms "beneficial to management and detrimental to union workers" (Dictionary.com, 2018) and an all-administrative academic governance (Ginsberg, 2011), goes out of its way to muzzle and sideline critics and whistle blowers. The analysis is partially grounded on a particular theory of human reception of *inconvenient data*:

We habitually avoid or ignore evidence that contradicts long-held views and tend to believe only the things reported to us by people we like. We reject inconvenient data as lies and propaganda. We are massively susceptible to peer pressure. We also fiercely resist admitting error. (Behr, 2010)

The objective of the chapter is to generate conversation, dialogue, feedback, input and future inquiry into the issue of academic mobbing, in the spirit of critical engagement as well as insight into new courses of action.

BACKGROUND: ACADEMIC MOBBING

Although the case study of this chapter is primarily a personal account of events, it is of course useful to locate it within the professional literature on academic mobbing. Estimates put mobbing at 15-20 per cent of all participants in the workplace in the United States (Davenport, Schwartz and Elliot, 2011; Hoel and Salin, 2003). Of the 100 or so academic mobbing cases known in Canada and the United States to one expert in the field, around two dozen were from Canadian institutions (Westhues, 2005). Others characterize such phenomena as "low incidence, high severity" (Gunsalus, 2006, pp. 124-25). Yet others argue that the phenomenon is pervasive (MacDonald, Stockton and Landrum, 2018). One commentator cites that an estimated 12 per cent of mobbed professors end up committing suicide (Seguin, 2016, para. 14). One infamous example is that of Justine Sargent, a McGill University neurologist, who committed suicide with her husband in 1994 (Cran, 2018).

The academic mobbing "process begins when a small group of instigators decide to cast someone out on the pretext that he or she is threatening their interests" and "negative communication frames the target as someone who is impossible to work with and who threatens the organization." The target is characterized as a "troublemaker," as someone who "doesn't listen to advice," who is "detrimental to the organization," even who "is mentally ill." Mobbing includes a range of oppressive tactics; "depriving the target of the right to have a voice, excluding them from committees and positions of responsibility, not responding to [their] emails, etc… the targets end up becoming completely ostracized – their reputation, credibility, authority, influence and contributions to the organization are nullified. As in a totalitarian situation, any attempts to defend themselves are perceived as additional proof of their "deviance." The target becomes a "non-person." Also is the fact that "university administrations and human resource departments are involved in most mobbing campaigns" (Khoo, 2010, pp. 61-63; Seguin, 2016).

Tenured professors engaging in academic freedom, particularly when it calls attention to or challenges administrators' mismanagement, is argued to be the most common reason for academic mobbing: "The most common trait of mobbing is that targets [are] blowing the whistle or having knowledge about a serious breach of ethics or wrongdoing by a powerful person in the workplace…people who speak out against unethical behaviour and are intolerant of hypocrisy are often targets" (Khoo, 2010, p. 63). It is argued that academic mobbing is largely practiced by "unprincipled" or "corporate-minded" administrators particularly to intimidate and dissuade faculty from publicly questioning their actions or decisions (MacDonald et al., 2018, para. 11).

McDonald et al. (2018) argue that almost all scholars who study academic mobbing agree in several key respects:

First, academic mobbing tends to be initiated by unprincipled administrators whose malfeasance was questioned or revealed though the expression of academic free speech. Second, the victims of academic mobbing tend to be productive, likable, principled tenured professors who publicly speak out about administrative wrongdoing. Third, academic mobbing involves manipulation of the language or misrepresentation of the facts regarding the victim's motivations, speech, or behavior. Fourth, the victim's colleagues are either poisoned against him or her, or choose not to support the victim due to fear of sharing his or her fate, indifference, or a lack of conviction...Finally, the victim is left personally and professionally injured, while the perpetrator(s) goes unpunished and therefore perhaps empowered to pursue a new target (MacDonald, et al., 2018, para. 12).

These characterizations fit perfectly the author's personal treatment at the hands of the UBCFA and UBCO senior administration since assuming an executive officer position with the FA and an elected senator role, both in July 2017. The author's targeting, exclusion, and ostracism by university and union administrators is fully documented in this chapter and fully explained by the concepts of academic bullying, harassment and mobbing of a principled tenured professor.

Despite a history of research and case studies, and a burgeoning professional literature, it must be noted at the outset that the FA and UBC managers do not acknowledge the existence of academic mobbing as a phenomenon. Nor can one find references to academic mobbing among the extensive official resources at UBC given to "bullying and harassment." Indeed, there is a double denial: once in denying that administrators, association officers, or faculty and staff members stoop to mobbing, and twice in denying that the phenomenon even exists.

THE START OF THE AFFAIR

The author began their FA role as 1st vice-chair of the Okanagan Faculty Committee (OFC), an executive officer position on this standing committee of the FA, in July 2017, and was also elected as a faculty representative of the joint Faculties to the campus senate in July 2017, for an additional 3-year term (having also served 2014-17). The academic mobbing campaign against the author by both the FA and the

UBCO campus administration, in collusion and conspiracy, was first triggered by an email the author sent on August 2, 2017. This was to the UBCO acting provost, copied to the FA, and a day later to the campus principal, as a result of discussions the author had, in their official role as executive officer of the FA, with a faculty member. This member who had approached the author had four graduate students, two PhD and two MA, approved by them for their graduate program admission for 2016-18, one in 2016-17 and three in 2017-18, all of whom they had agreed to supervise, rejected for admission, apparently by their director and associate dean. This was over their head, as the faculty member was neither consulted on nor informed of their rejection by either the director or associate dean. The author, in his FA executive role, queried this to the administration. In the meantime, the author was also helping this same member on their workload and other matters, because they were getting no help from the professional staff of the FA.

After six weeks of no response from the administration, on September 12, 2017 the author received a formal letter from their provost. The letter was not copied to others. In this letter, the provost (of all people) stated, amongst other things, that the author, as an elected executive officer of the FA, must *"cease and desist from any further involvement in the workplace affairs of faculty members"* as they *"do not have the authority to act on behalf of the FA"* and their statement that they were the elected 1st vice-chair of the OFC executive representative of UBCO faculty members was a *"willful misrepresentation of [their] status"* and that they had no authority to be *"involved in labour relations matters concerning members of the FA"* and the author was *"inappropriately engaging with FA members."* The provost also suggested that it might be a good idea if the author was to avail themselves of the psychological testing resources of the University. A good example of the collusion and complicity between FA and UBCO senior administration, and the author's academic mobbing where a "small group of instigators decide to cast someone out on the pretext that he or she is threatening their interests" (Khoo, 2010). But what were these interests? Was it just to protect the sweetheart unionism deal?

On October 10, 2017 the author received a further formal and threatening letter, this time from their UBCO campus principal and deputy vice-chancellor (DVC) of UBC, that stated, in part: *"I am restating the provost's clear direction that you are to cease communicating with University administration on matters related to labour relations and interfering in these matters, Sincerely."* The UBCO campus senior administration and the FA in complicity and collusion were turning up the heat on the author's academic mobbing, bringing in the principal of the campus this time. The FA and the administration appeared to be making a mountain out of a molehill, so what was the hidden agenda? Had the author turned over a rock and the administrators and the FA did not want to let the can of worms exposed beneath, out?

A week after receiving the threatening letter from the principal, the author received a formal letter on October 17, 2017 from the vice-president of the FA stating to them that they were: *"inappropriately engaging with FA members"* saying *"you do not have the authority to become involved with labour relations matters concerning members of the bargaining unit"*. Also that *"if you are approached by any members seeking assistance, you must refrain from providing advice."* Finally, in a letter to the author under the signature of both the FA vice-president and the chair of the OFC, dated February 1, 2018, the author was told: *"You are not to deal with members' concerns should they come to you, or you go to them…you do not have the authority…to deal with the University administration on any matters affecting the Faculty Association or any of its Membership…we consider this matter closed."*

The discussion in this chapter of this portion of the case study is necessarily brief as it is comprehensively covered in another of the author's recent papers to which to reader is hereby referred (Wylie, 2018c).

CONTINUATION OF THE AFFAIR IN SENATE

Concurrently, given the reception the author had received trying to act in their official role as elected executive officer of the FA, the author tried instead to raise the issue as an elected senator of the member's graduate students being turned away without consulting nor informing them, first at the September 28, 2017 senate meeting. At this meeting, the principal of the campus stated that the matter was one of labour relations that could not be commented on in senate as it was currently under discussion with the FA. Later however, and more revealingly, in mid-January 2018, the author, as an elected faculty officer of the FA elected to investigate the concerns of Okanagan campus faculty members, was asked by another faculty member, to bring another matter to the attention of the FA. The matter was this member's removal from their position of graduate program coordinator in their Faculty on September 8, 2016. This was, they felt, due to their principled opposition to "the improper suspension of admissions into the faculty graduate program in October 2015." This was, coincidentally, the same program, the Interdisciplinary Graduate Studies (IGS) program of the Faculty of Management (FoM), that the other faculty member had their students turned away from in July 2017, by their Faculty director and associate dean. This, in mid-January 2018, was the first the author had heard of this alleged suspension of admissions, dated from October 2015, apparently made without having the suspension approved by senate, without informing faculty or students, and without posting the suspension on any University website. Adjudication of admissions to the FoM graduate program had also been removed at this time from the authority of the senate-constituted committee of the Faculty, formerly chaired by this member, and placed in the hand of the director and associate dean of the FoM. The member was also concerned that their removal might affect his tenure denial reconsideration, another matter the author was helping the member with, as their elected faculty executive officer representative of the FA.

No administrator of UBCO, if they were aware of a suspension of admissions as of October 2015 and on senate, such as the dean of the FoM in question, who would have been the person to have made such a decision to suspend admissions, if any such decision was made (and from the administrative email evidence provided to the author, it appears it was made), and presumably the then dean of the College of Graduate Studies (CoGS), nor the provost or principal and DVC, informed senate of any suspension of admissions at the September 28, 2017 meeting, even though that would have been a sufficient explanation as to why the faculty member's students had been turned away. In fact, rather, both the UBCO provost and the FA president had already told the author, as had the UBCO principal and DVC, and as the vice-president of the FA, and chair of the OFC of the FA, were soon to tell the author, all in formal letters, to take their nose out of where, in their collective view, it did not belong, and to butt out. What was going on here, why were they all protesting so (too) much?

After discussion with their fellow executive officers of the FA, it was decided by the author that the alleged suspension of admissions was a matter for senate, the academic governance body of the University, and its admissions committee, rather than the FA. By the end of February, the author had determined to bring the matter to senate. Hence, as the faculty member's elected senator, elected to represent the UBCO joint Faculties, the author first offered the associate dean of CoGS and the director of the FoM the opportunity to meet with them to discuss the matter. However, neither demonstrated any interest in that, and the associate dean of CoGS denied the fact that there was a suspension of admissions, even though they had been in fact intimately involved in arranging it in October 2015 -- the member in question who had contacted the author about the matter had provided the conclusive documentary administrative email evidence proving that there had been such a suspension in October 2015, for a, so far, uncertain period. The director of the FoM did not reply to the author's enquiries, as an elected senator, suggesting a meeting to discuss.

The author requested that the matter be added to the agenda of the March 29, 2018 senate meeting. On March 21, 2018 the senate agenda committee refused to allow the matter to be added to the agenda. The committee suggested that the author take the matter up with CoGS and the FoM, which they of course had already done, and the senate secretariat knew that, and so presumably, did the agenda committee, as it was advised by the secretariat. Moreover, as an elected senator, the author was bringing the matter to senate -- are senators instead supposed to bring matters to the attention of other bodies on the campus, rather than to senate? The committee told the author that they could give notice of motion regarding the matter at the March 29, 2018 meeting, for addition to the agenda of the April 26, 2018 meeting. Therefore, the academic mobbing was extending itself to those senior administrators controlling the agenda of the campus senate, in charge of academic governance on the campus.

At the March 29, 2018 senate meeting, the author attempted to give this notice of motion for the April meeting, regarding the illegal suspension of admissions and the overriding of senate-approved procedures for adjudication of student applications in the FoM IGS program. The notice of motion was merely to the effect that student application fees collected by UBC while the secret suspension of admissions was in place be returned to the students. The notice of motion was disallowed by the chair of senate (the president of UBC) and secretary of senate, on the basis that the author did not provide an "exact wording of the motion." This was in violation of Robert's Rules under which the senate operates. Senate has no such special rule for the making of notices of motion. However, after the meeting was abruptly adjourned by the chair, cutting off the author's attempts to make the notice of motion, another member of senate was allowed, ex-post to the meeting, to give a notice of motion on the matter. Also at this March 29, 2018 meeting, the dean of CoGS denied loudly, by abruptly standing up and screaming at the top of their voice, on the author requesting the notice of motion, and hence interrupting the author without leave to do so, that there was no suspension of admissions into the IGS program in the FoM.

On April 19, 2018 the senate agenda committee refused to allow the author's background evidence, material to the other member's motion, to be added to the senate materials, for senate consideration. It told them if they wanted the material documentary evidence proving the suspension to be considered by senate, they would have to give a notice of motion at the April 26, 2018 senate meeting for consideration for the May 2018 meeting. On April 19, the author asked why this was, and the excuse given this time was that the agenda committee thought that the matter of any alleged suspension of admissions into the IGS in the FoM was a matter for the FA, not senate. This was of course preposterous, as senate has an admissions committee, and the FA has nothing to do with student admissions, but here we went round the academic mobbing merry-go-round. The UBC administration was making a concerted effort to suppress the information the author had asked as an elected senator to be discussed, trying all it could to stop it from being made public, not allowing the author's motions at senate, not allowing them to file the material evidence in senate, and their senior administrators not answering the author's requests for information as an elected senator, and refusing to engage in discussion of the matter.

Therefore, on April 23, 2018, the author made the material documentary evidence public themselves, by circulated the background evidence material (a 2-pager) to all members of senate for which they had email addresses, by email. There is of course nothing in the senate rules forbidding that. However, one senate member, an associate dean, and hence member of the senior administration, complained on the floor of senate at its meeting on April 26, 2018 that the author had illegitimately sent an email to senate members, that the material should be disregarded, and that the motion should be put to a vote without senate discussion. This was in clear violation and attempted infringement, censorship and suppression of the author's academic freedom, by a member of the senior administration, and an affront to academic freedom and the principle of senate debate. The dean of CoGS at the meeting referred to the author's circulated documentary material evidence as "vexatious." This was also in direct attack on the principle of the free expression of ideas, opinions and facts at UBC. The denials of the administration were getting louder and more vociferous, as the academic mobbing of the author intensified and widened.

Also at the April 26 Senate meeting the dean of CoGS informed senate that there was no suspension of admissions because they testified that there were offers made in the FoM IGS to students for entry in the three academic years 2015-16 to 2017-18, but that none of these offers resulted in any admissions, as all of the offers were declined by the students. Senate accepted this explanation, based on no official data, but just on the unsubstantiated word of the dean, and hence voted down by large majority, the motion and any further action on the issue. With the motion to return the student applications fees so defeated, the author then made a notice of motion for a future senate meeting worded: *"That senate conduct a full investigation, by whatever means deemed most suitable, into the management of the IGS program in the FoM, 2010-18."* Soon after the meeting a freedom of information (FOI) request was put in to UBC to reveal the offer letters and refusal letters of the students, 2013-18. It was later decided by the senate secretariat, on the author's suggestion, that the further motion be postponed for senate discussion until after the FOI request had been dealt with.

RESPECTFUL ENVIRONMENT AND ACADEMIC FREEDOM COMPLAINTS

The acting dean of the author's Faculty contacted them on July 31, 2018 to say:

I am writing to inform you that four complaints have been received by the Dean's Office alleging that your conduct breached UBC's Statement on Respectful Environment for Students, Faculty, and Staff in your April 23, 2018 communications to Senate and others. In accordance with UBC Respectful Environment Statement (RES), I am the responsible Administrative Head of Unit and request two meetings with you: The first is to provide you with copies of the written complaints and explain the investigation process and protocol. The second is to afford you the opportunity to respond to the complaints. As this is a formal process, you are entitled to representation and I encourage you to invite a FA representative to accompany you at the investigation meeting. A member of the Human Resources (HR) team also will be present during the meeting.

Dates for the meetings were suggested for August, the month of the author's scheduled vacation. The author finally obtained the complaints on August 14, and found that they were made by three deans and a director, three complaints on April 26, the day of the Senate meeting, and one on May 1. This certainly appeared to have been an organized effort on the part of the four UBCO senior administrators, and unexplained was the more than 3-month delay between HR at UBCO receiving these complaints, April 26-May 1, 2018, and the author being informed of them, on July 31, 2018, and being given them finally to read, on August 14, 2018. On August 12, before the author had received the complaints, they wrote to the president of UBC to say:

In April 2018 I raised at senate a significant issue of academic governance on the UBC Okanagan campus [and] on Jul 31, 2018 I received an email from my acting dean regarding this. I am concerned that the RES of UBC appears to be being used in an attempt stifle academic debate on campus, even in senate it appears, in a hope to silence criticism of the administration, and the raising of important issues of academic governance. In my view, senators, as do all members of the UBC community of scholars, need to be free to raise significant issues of academic governance as they see them, especially in senate, the academic governance body of the university, and need to be free to criticize the administration.

The four complaints were from the associate dean of the FoM, the director of the FoM, the associate dean of CoGS, and the dean of CoGS. The first complaint, from the associate dean of CoGS, in charge of the IGS program on campus, dated April 26, 2016, 12.29 PM (3 hours prior to the senate meeting of that day) claimed that the author's material documentary evidence emailed April 23, 2018 constituted a form of *"harassment against [them]"*, and that the author's material evidence should be *"severed"* from being presented to senate. This was in stark violation of this associate dean's duty as a senior administrator of UBC to protect and promote academic freedom at UBC. The author had sent this administrator one highly respectful email on this matter on March 7, 2018, to which they had curtly, disrespectfully and dishonestly replied to on March 8, in a one-line blanket denial.

The second complaint, dated April 26, 2016, 1.44 PM (2 hours prior to the Senate meeting of that day) was from the director of the FoM, who argued that the author's material evidence sent to senators on April 23, 2018 was *"harassing, exclusionary or defamatory"* of them and that the author was involved with *"secretive work with others"* -- the professor who had their students turned away and the professor removed as IGS coordinator -- to *"defame, exclude and harass [them]"* making *"false claims"* about their *"actions and character."* The author had sent this director one highly respectful email March 7, 2018 on the matter, to which the director did not bother to reply, even though they knew the facts the author was referring to. They now claimed that the author was making it *"impossible"* for them to carry out their *"work as director, their own research, and to enjoy their family life."*

The third complaint dated April 26, 2016, 1.52 PM (1.5 hours prior to the senate meeting of that day) was from the associate dean of the FoM who spoke of the author's alleged *"repeated breaches"* of the RES now involving an *"abusive, vexatious attempt [by the author] to diminish this associate dean's standing within UBC and the wider public"* and that *"the responsible authority [CoGS] has answered in plain terms that no such suspension has occurred."* But the author had the factual and irrefutable documentary evidence that it had occurred. This associate dean asked for *"anticipated and immediate administrative action"* against the author *"by the University administration"* and characterized the author's inquires on the matter as an *"apparently endless and evidently groundless vendetta against administrators."* In the author's view this complaint was an affront to academic freedom at UBC, and a violation of this UBC senior administrator's duty to protect and promote academic freedom at UBC.

The fourth and last complaint was dated May 1, 2018, from the dean of CoGS. It also spoke of *"continuous breaches"* of the RES claiming the author's *"abusive, distressful campaign to diminish [their] reputation"* on the part of the author and that the author was "*bullying and harassing*" them." The dean stated: *"[the associate dean of CoGS] has stated there was no suspension of IGS in FOM and I clearly stated such at March senate."* But unfortunately both of these statements, providing no evidence, were lies, as confirmed by the material evidence. This dean also asked for *"action"* to be taken against the author by the University. So, all hell appeared to have broken loose, with a line-up of senior administrators ganging up to have the author presumably at least disciplined, perhaps suspended, or even fired. Quite, in the author's view, an attempted cover-up and suppression of information and material evidence, violation of academic freedom, and academic mobbing.

In early September 2018 the author filed formal complaints to UBC, and asked the FA to bring a grievance, over the attempted suppression of the author's academic freedom by UBC, as revealed by the RES complaints. The author also brought a counter-compliant under the RES against named individuals for their disrespectful treatment of the author in the affair. In late October, after much toing-and-froing, the author was informed by UBC that they had hired an "external investigator" to investigate the various complaints and counter-complaints.

FREEDOM OF INFORMATION DATA RELEASED

Official applications, offers, and admissions data for the IGS 2013-18 were finally provided to the author in early October 2018, along with redacted letters of all admission offers and all student letters declining offers, as a result of the FOI inquiry. Remarkably, these data were apparently fully available in March 2018 when the author first made enquires for them, because in an email to the provost and others dated March 16, 2018, from the director of the FoM, an email the author was only inadvertently copied on in mid-November 2018, it was stated: *"... [the dean of FoM] has the admissions data and decisions on every applicant over this period, if needed."* So the director of the FoM had, in March 2018, direct access to these data, and was willing to provide them to the provost, but not to the author, the elected senator enquiring into the matter. This associate dean chose not to reply to the author's email to them of March 7, 2018, enquiring of these data. The author was only inadvertently copied on the email from the director of the FoM to the provost of March 16, noting that the data on admissions were fully available at that time, but apparently, not to the author.

Therefore, the author only received these data six months later via long and torturous FOI requests. Once provided to the author in October 2018, the official data showed that there were no offers of admission into the FOM IGS made in the

3 academic years 2015-16, 2016-17, 2017-18. The former dean of CoGS had told the April senate meeting that there were offers made in these three academic years, all rejected by the students. Not so as it turned out, according to the actual factual evidence. The last two offers made were made in the 2014-15 academic year, in July 2014 and March 2015, both declined by the students, and both well before admissions were suspended in October 2015. Other confirmed facts from the material evidence that the author already had was that there was a suspension of admissions to the FOM IGS from October 2015 until at some date in 2018, as confirmed by the former FoM IGS coordinator, who had been removed, because, as they thought, of their principled opposition to the suspension, and the administrative email evidence of October, 2015. This was without Faculty Council or senate approval, without informing students and faculty, and without posting the suspension on any UBC website. Also as confirmed by the factual email evidence and the former FoM IGS coordinator, there was a violation of senate-approved procedures in the FoM that took approval of IGS admissions away from the senate-constituted IGS coordinator and committee of Faculty Council they chair and into the hands of the director and associate dean. All applications October 2015-February 2018 were hence ultimately rejected by the director and associate dean.

The suspension of admissions decision appears to have been made by the dean of the FoM, and no students were admitted to the program after April 2015, until at some point in early 2018. Again, the former dean of CoGS at the April 2018 senate meeting said there were offers made and rejected during the last three academic years (2015-16, 2016-17, and 2017-18). The two offers made and rejected for 2015-16 were both made in the 2014-15 academic year, well before admissions were suspended in October 2015 (one in July 2014 and the other in March 2015). There were no new admissions offers made after March 2015.

As a result of receiving this confirmation of the facts in early October, the author asked that their further motion be now added to the agenda of the October 25, 2018 senate meeting: *"That senate conduct a full investigation, by whatever means deemed most suitable, into the management of the IGS program in the FoM, 2010-18."* The senate agenda committee this time agreed to allow the motion and (finally!) agreed to allow the author's material documentary evidence to be included in the senate materials, for senate discussion. Perhaps it was realized that the administration could no longer to deny and supress everything. At the October 25 senate meeting, the author reiterated their belief that this matter was in their view a serious issue of academic governance and institutional integrity, and asked: Did this matter constitute fraud and misrepresentation, the offering of something to prospective students under false pretenses? The author also asked: What explains the denials of UBCO senior administrators since the author's first inquiries in early August 2017, to date? The author reiterated their belief that UBC needed a fact-finding investigation into how and why this had been allowed to occur in violation of both academic governance and institutional integrity at UBC.

The author's motion was defeated at the October 25, 2018 senate meeting by a vote of 15-16. All of the elected student senators voted for the motion, all of the unelected, ex officio administrators on senate against, with elected faculty members split, some of course, as in any faculty member cohort, like-minded with respect to the administrators. The dean of the FoM of course voted against and this was the deciding vote on whether there should be an investigation into their actions or not. Debate went on for over an hour, the other business of senate was done in the first 20 minutes. Actually, as it had turned out, there was no need for an investigation, as all of the facts were already transparent. How long could the senior administration continue to ignore the facts to protect the dean of the FoM?

The author filed their written response to the four complaints of the deans and director in October, 2018. They stated that no amount of bluster and bombast from these deans and director could change the indisputable fact of the secret suspension of admissions. With the facts confirmed by the former IGS Coordinator of the FoM, who was in best the position to know, by the actual documentary email evidence, and by the official offers and admissions data, were these deans and director living in some alternate reality, preferring to peddle alternative facts? Quite an attempted campus-wide senior administrative cover-up and suppression of information, material evidence, academic freedom, and the facts, right up to the provost and principal, and the FA. Also, of course, an academic mobbing of the author for uncovering and prosecuting the facts, and then all and sundry ganging up to have the author presumably disciplined, suspended or even fired. The author was as mindful as ever, of course, of a core value of UBC, as written in its most recent strategic plan, of: "Academic freedom: A unique value of the academy: a scholar's freedom to express ideas through respectful discourse and the pursuit of open discussion, without risk of censure" (University of British Columbia, 2016, p. 9).

UNIVERSITY INVESTIGATION

There remained the matter of the investigation into these matters as a result of the RES complaints against the author by the four deans and director, the author's RES counter-complaints, and the author's complaints regarding administrative infringement of their academic freedom and academic freedom generally at UBC. The University had hired a lawyer as the "external and independent investigator" in October who had worked for many years for the FA's legal counsel firm, so the author suspected it was hardly going to be an independent investigation. The author was denied a copy of the terms of reference of the investigation, and had no say in them. The author met for a full-day meeting with the investigator on November 7, 2018. At this meeting the author supplied the investigator with their list of important witnesses, the two most important being one, the professor who had their graduate students turned away in July 2017, and two, the professor who was removed as graduate program coordinator because of what they felt was their principled opposition to the secret suspension of admissions. The author also provided the investigator with all of the, now extensive, documentary material evidence and admissions and offers data.

The report of the investigator was received by UBC on December 13, 2018, and the author was provided with a copy on January 31, 2019. The investigator completely ignored all of the documentary material evidence provided to them by the author at their meeting of November 7, evidence which conclusively and fully substantiated the author's case. The investigator completely ignored the evidence that demonstrated conclusively that the FoM had all of the admissions data and admissions offer letters that conclusively and fully substantiated the author's case in March 2018, and offered them then to the provost, but not to the author, the elected senator asking for them. The investigator completely ignored the offers and admissions data finally provided to the author in October, the data that completely and conclusively substantiated the author's case, saying these data were outside of the investigation's terms of reference. The investigator completely ignored the evidence of the October 25, 2018 Senate meeting debate that also conclusively and fully substantiated the author's case, saying the meeting occurred after they were hired and hence outside of the terms of reference given to them by UBC. The investigator failed to interview three of the four dean and director complainants, and only interviewed the fourth briefly via Skype. They failed to interview any of the people on the important witness list the author provided to them at their November all-day meeting. The investigator's failure to interview the professor who had their students turned away, and the professor who was removed as graduate program coordinator, the two central figures in the entire matter, was of course both outstandingly egregious and totally irresponsible.

The investigation, reporting to UBC administration, was hence a massive failure of total bias, irresponsibility, and brazen indifference to the actual evidence, facts, and truth. The investigator also refused to acknowledge that the dean of CoGS had deceived (lied to) senate at the April 26, 2018 senate meeting, as the subsequent evidence, facts, truth, admissions offers data and letters of offer to students, 2015-18, conclusively showed. They also failed to acknowledge that the senate secretary and chair of senate (the president of UBC) had failed to adhere to Robert's Rules in senate in denying the author's request for a notice of motion at the March 29, 2018 senate meeting, as Robert's Rules provided to them, conclusively showed. The investigator ignored this clear and conclusive evidence and fact, and made up their own alternative fact and truth in stating: "*It did not occur.*"

The investigator somehow managed to conclude, entirely unsubstantiated by any evidence whatsoever, that the author had acted with malice and was vexatious. The author was deemed by the investigator to have been malicious and vexatious because they "*had a desire to show [they] were right, and the administration was wrong.*" Of course, the investigator's baseless pronouncement was just what the University administration had ordered. It appears we cannot have faculty members and elected senators being right, and the administrators being wrong. The truth was that the author was engaged in an honest pursuit of the truth, as an elected senator, doing their job, truth that was eventually fully revealed in the release to the author of the admissions offers, data and letters in early October. Both the professor who had their students turned away and the one removed as IGS coordinator had to take sick leave for stress and anxiety over the matter. The investigator makes light of these facts by calling the author's enquiries malicious and vexatious. The FA had told both of these professors, after their returns from sick leave in February 2018, that there was no suspension of admissions, merely a "restriction" that faculty members had been fully informed of. Both of these statements were patently false, alternative facts, but were repeated verbatim by the investigator in their doublespeak and doublethink "findings of fact".

Thus the investigation initiated by the University turned out to be a sham, a kangaroo court Star Chamber, without due process, ignoring the clear material evidence, a continued attempted administrative cover-up of the actual facts and truth, an unsuccessful complete whitewashing of UBC administration, a massive personal and professional defamation of the author, an elected senator, and an totalitarian exercise in misinformation and denial of the truth. The author asked the FA to file a grievance on their behalf under the Collective Agreement statement on Academic Freedom. The FA of course denied this request, as per its sweetheart unionism deal with the University. The investigator's report was merely then the continuation of the pack of lies, disregard of conclusive material evidence, obfuscation, and academic mobbing the author had received from the University administration and the FA since their first enquiries into these matters in early August 2017.

The UBCO administration (deans, directors, provost and principal) and the FA could now continue to get away with their longstanding and concerted campaigns of fear, bullying, harassment and intimidation of regular UBCO faculty members, elected senators, and elected executive officers of the FA, such as the author, by being fully supported by an entirely biased, ridiculous, baseless and defamatory "independent investigation". The author had the facts, evidence and truth on their side, the administration and the FA, unfortunately, only falsehoods, lies and deceit, in an effort to keep everyone ignorant of what is really going on behind the scenes. IS UBC thus the Ministry of Truth, where power is the only truth and those with the power can make the truth into whatever they chose, with the actual truth rewritten in kangaroo courts of University-controlled "external investigation?"

One of the rationales for dismissing the author's claims given by the investigator was that the converse finding *"would show that Dr. Wylie was right and UBCO administration was wrong"*. Notwithstanding the fact that this would confirm the facts and the truth. But UBC and the FA did not want that, as the facts and the truth were detrimental to UBC and the FA. The investigator found fault with the author that they *"preferred to believe the hearsay evidence of two faculty members rather than the deans and director."* How about the factual evidence of the emails by the deans and director in October 2015 suspending admission, provided to the author by one of these two professors? The investigator even more remarkably stated: *"[The author] has no evidence of a suspension of admission."* Now we were really into alternative facts territory. To the investigator there were no facts or falsehoods, right or wrong, truth or lies, just as they stated *"matters of opinion and opposing views."* The one and only complainant interviewed by the investigator (and not in person), the dean of CoGS, remarkably stated: *"[The author] did not set out to gather and consider all available, relevant evidence."* Of course, this is exactly what the author did do, as an elected senator, for over a year. They also stated: *"[The author, an elected senator] undermined my role as dean."* Obviously a no-no in UBC's version of shared governance. Therefore, the "investigation' failed to acknowledge the conclusive material evidence, failed to interview any of the author's witnesses, failed to interview the complainants, and made entirely unsubstantiated accusations of malice against the author. Just what the University had ordered.

The executive director of the FA in March 2019 wrote to the author to say:

"[T]here are potentially very serious consequences to you that may arise out of the investigation and that if there is an underlying medical condition that could possibly be a contributing factor to the conduct which is the subject of concern, it would certainly help mitigate any potential consequences."

The author replied that personally they failed to understand how an elected senator exposing and seeking minimal redress for students for a minor bit of fraud and misrepresentation in a fairly minor program in a fairly minor corner of the campus can result in very serious consequences to that elected senator, as the author was merely asking that the student application fees October 2015-February 2018, when admissions to the program were secretly suspended, be returned to the students. About 10 students were involved, with the application fee of $100 per student.

The author in February 2019 received this further advice in the matter from the executive director of the FA:

The facts that UBC will act on are contained in the findings of the reports. What you are being asked to provide, if you wish, is any mitigating information that you would like the Dean to consider before [they make] a decision on the matter. Mitigating information is information which could excuse or explain the conduct in question, or information which could be relied upon to reduce any possible discipline that may be contemplated by the University. Mitigating information could include an apology, a medical reason for the conduct, an explanation that the conduct was an aberration which arose out of a misunderstanding and is unlikely to happen again in the future, that sort of thing. You are not being provided with an opportunity to redo the investigation and challenge the findings of fact that was arrived as a result of the investigation process. The one matter that our counsel found unusual was that [the investigator] did not interview any of the complainants or respondents except [the author] but instead relied on the notes that were provided to [them] from the interviews that [the Dean and HR] conducted. [Counsel] indicated that this action was somewhat unusual and unexplained for a person tasked with conducting an investigation. The investigator's consideration of the material facts before them was appropriate and their application of the applicable law was sound. Legal counsel did not find any substantive grounds upon which we might challenge the investigation process or its outcome. We will therefore not be filling a grievance on this matter.

Therefore, the above is further confirmation of the author's hypothesis that UBC and the FA are in cahoots and collusion in their Kafkaesque and Orwellian world. The FA in the author's view does not, in good faith, as a union with monopoly representational rights, fairly represent its members vis-as-via the employer and pays only lip service to but does not defend the principles of collegial shared governance and academic freedom at UBC. Also, of course, the author finds it strange that if someone has a commitment to seeking the truth and the facts at UBC, such as themselves, and with all due diligence carries out responsibly their role as a faculty member and elected senator, their only defence and excuse for such behaviour can be an abnormal mental condition. Very 1984 and Communist China.

THE GROWIING MOB

The spread of the author's academic mobbing then continued apace. On March 31, 2019 the author's former dean sent the following email to the author, copying it at the same time to over 300 faculty members at UBCO, over 50 percent of the voting FA members:

Evidently, Peter, you were seeking validation of your efforts as chief agitator and primary critic of the [University]. Perhaps it is time for some self-reflection, given your state of perpetual unhappiness. Why not resign your tenured faculty position (with its wonderful salary, great benefits, and permanency) and move on to something else more rewarding? Who at UBCO is keeping you chained to your misery?

This author takes such an unprovoked, personal and malicious ad hominin attack as indicative perhaps of the depths of administrator-ex-administrator disrespect for regular tenured faculty members. This former dean's venom is perhaps good evidence of what is said about the author behind the scenes as the academic mobbing campaign against them intensifies. The same day, March 31, 2019, a member of the author's own academic department filed another RES complaint against the author, to the HR department. In it they state:

Wylie…show[s] a significant degree of bias toward a negative assessment. Wylie is of course entitled to his views and opinions…He is not however, in my opinion, entitled to publicly berate the administration by questioning their abilities, their legitimacy or their aptitudes in performing their appointed duties…some means [should be] be investigated which will curtail Wylie's ability to [send] unsolicited, biased and negative messages about the inadequacies of the Faculty and administration... Perhaps IT could investigate ways to shut down his capacity for these email[s].

FUTURE RESEARCH DIRECTIONS

The in-coming president of UBC stated in an email to faculty at UBC in July 2016:

We will become a stronger and better university if our most outstanding faculty take ownership of our academic standards and academic governance…You are the real experts on UBC. You have ideas about how the university can be improved…I will work with the Board of Governors, Senates, central administration, deans, heads and director and faculty members at large to continuously improve UBC's governance, guided by principles of transparency, openness and accountability. It is critical that the faculty have reason to trust, respect and view as competent the people in leadership roles at the university. Together, we can improve UBC one step at a time (University of British Columbia, 2016).

And as the Universities Canada Statement on Academic Freedom states: "Evidence and truth are the guiding principles for universities…faculty must be…free to examine data, and therefore be guided by evidence" (Universities Canada, 2011). Except, it appears, if faculty are examining the administration of the University itself, where, if so, the first casualty is the evidence, facts and truth. The administration instead then choses to rely on deceit, lies and the covering up of the evidence, facts and truth, and academically mobs the whistle blower. There is no doubt in the author's mind, after a fairly cursory perusal of the professional literature, that the academic mobbing issue is pervasive in universities across the world as universities take on an increasingly corporate and vertically hierarchical organizational model rather than the collegial, shared governance, horizontal organizational model (MacDonald et al., 2018, Ginsberg, 2011). The author is quite sure that their experience is not an isolated incident. The larger picture of the mobbing and bullying of regular faculty members by their administrative and union officials needs to be recognized, as the lack of respect for faculty and shared governance has become pervasive, and as faculty unions and administrations increasingly collude and conspire against individual faculty members in sweetheart unionism deals. This case study in this chapter is not an isolated squabble but just one instance of a large, pervasive problem, that is getting larger in the author's view. Future research and comparative study is needed to explore just how pervasive this problem is becoming.

CONCLUSION

This in the author's view is a clear case of academic mobbing. The case fits perfectly with what is argued that almost all scholars who study academic mobbing agree is its primary characteristics; it is initiated by administrators whose malfeasance was questioned or revealed though the expression of academic free speech; the target tend to be tenured professors who publicly speak out about administrative wrongdoing; it involves manipulation or misrepresentation of the facts regarding the victim's motivations or behavior; the target's colleagues are either poisoned against him or her, or choose not to support the victim due indifference, or a lack of conviction, and the target is left personally and professionally injured, while the perpetrator(s) goes unpunished (MacDonald et al., 2018, para. 12). To this the author would add that the kangaroo court investigation procedures of the university are merely an extension of the academic mobbing process.

Perhaps has UBC and the UBCFA adopted the advice given to Forrest Gump by his mother that if you can't say anything nice, don't say anything at all? UBC claims to set its 'respectful environment' policies on not the Golden Rule Maxim, but its own new Platinum Rule: "Treat others in the way they would want to be treated". This is perhaps as characterized elsewhere as "The New Critiquette"; are we not allowed to engage in vigorous debate and conflicting views, must we be nice and agreeable at all times, like Stepford faculty, staff, and students? Is there no place for "reasonable hostility"; does the way one says something now count for more than what one has to say (Petrina, 2012, p. 41-42)?

Should an elected FA executive representative of faculty members and an elected senator be allowed to be targeted, excluded and ostracized by the powers that be in the union and university administration, working in collusion and complicity? Regarding senate, if faculty members, especially elected senators in senate, cannot express opinions or raise concerns and questions over issues of academic governance without administrators taking these as personal, how can substantive debate and discussion materialize or academic governance proceed? If administrators personalize issues by singling out faculty members and senators for retribution, with the FA idle and negligent, what faculty members and senators will want to bother participating? If faculty members, especially elected senators, cannot speak up and ask questions or make critical comments without fear of reprisal or retaliation from university administrators, what value is academic freedom? Senior university administrators such as directors, deans, provosts and principals are supposed to work for their faculty members and students, and their members of senate, not the other way around. The faculty and students, and their elected senators, are the university, not the senior administrators. The author is an elected senator, a representative of those who voted for and elected them, and of those who didn't. Administrators are supposed to respond to elected senator's requests for information, discussions, meetings, and inquiries. The university is its faculty and students, and its elected representatives, not its administrators. The administrators are hired by the university (its faculty, staff and students) to manage the university; they are supposed to work for us, not us for them.

REFERENCES

Behr, R. (2010, September 21). Almost everything you know is wrong: Review of Being wrong: Adventures in the margin of error. *The Observer.*

Clarke, A., & Erickson, G. (2003). Teacher inquiry: A defining feature of professional practice. In A. Clarke & G. Erickson (Eds.), *Teacher inquiry: Living the research in everyday practice* (pp. 1–6). London, UK: Routledge Palmer. doi:10.4324/9780203417669

Cran, B. (2018, March 2). The academic mob and its fatal toll. *Quillette.*

Davenport, N., Schwarz, R. D., & Elliot, G. P. (2003). *Mobbing and Emotional Abuse in the American Workplace.* Civil Society Publishers.

Dictionary.com. (2018). *Sweetheart contract.* Retrieved from https://www.dictionary.com/browse/sweetheart-contract

Ginsberg, B. (2011). *The Fall of the Faculty: The Rise of the All-Administrative University and Why It Matters.* New York: Oxford University Press.

Gunsalus, C. K. (2006). *The College Administrator's Survival Guide.* Cambridge, MA: Harvard University Press.

Hendry, P. M. (2010). Narrative as inquiry. *The Journal of Educational Research, 103*(2), 72–80. doi:10.1080/00220670903323354

Hoel, H., & Salin, D. (2003). Organisational antecedents of workplace bullying. In S. Einarsen, D. Zapf, & C. L. Cooper (Eds.), *Bullying and Emotional Abuse in the Workplace: International Perspectives in Research and Practice.* Taylor & Francis.

Khoo, S. B. (2010). Academic mobbing: Hidden health hazard in the workplace. *Malaysian Family Physician, 5,* 61–67. PMID:25606190

McDonald, T. W., Stockton, J. D., & Landrum, R. E. (2018). Civility and Academic Freedom: Who defines the former (and how) may imperil rights to the latter. *The College Quarterly, 21,* 1.

Petrina, S. (2012). The new critiquette and old scholactivism: A petit critique of academic manners, managers, matters, and freedom. *Workplace, 20,* 17–63.

Seguin, E. (2016). Academic Mobbing, or how to become campus tormentors. *University Affairs.*

Universities Canada. (2011, October 25). *Research Statement on Academic Freedom*. Retrieved from https://www.univcan.ca/media-room/media-releases/statement-on-academic-freedom/

University of British Columbia. (2016, July 12). *Invitation to engage from Professor Santa Ono* [email]. Author.

University of British Columbia. (2018). *Shaping UBC's Next Century: Strategic Plan 2018-2028*. Vancouver, BC: Author.

Westhues, K. (2005). *Workplace mobbing in academe: Reports from twenty universities*. London: Mellen Press.

Wylie, P. (2017). Memorandum of misunderstanding? Public accountability and the University of British Columbia, Okanagan Campus, 2004-17. *BC Studies*, *195*, 65–96.

Wylie, P. (2018a). The all-administrative campus: University of British Columbia, Okanagan. *Workplace*, *31*, 10–21.

Wylie, P. (2018b). Exclusionary and extractive campus management: The University of British Columbia, Okanagan. *Workplace*, *31*, 22–30.

Wylie, P. (2018c). My campus administration, Faculty Association and me: Academic mobbing and sweetheart unionism. *Workplace*, *31*, 31–41.

Wylie, P. (in press). The University of British Columbia's International Student Initiative: Implications for provincial public higher education. *Critical Education*.

ADDITIONAL READING

Aronowitz, S. (2000). *The Knowledge Factory*. Boston, Mass: Beacon Press.

Cebekhulu, E., & Mantzaris, E. (2006). Labour pains and university mergers: The case of UKZN. *Alternation (Durban)*, *13*(1), 182–202.

Faria, J. R., Mixon, F. G. Jr, & Salter, S. P. (2012). An economic model of workplace mobbing in academe. *Economics of Education Review*, *31*(5), 720–726. doi:10.1016/j.econedurev.2012.04.004

Gravios, J. (2006, April 14). Mob Rule. *The Chronicle of Higher Education*.

Harper, J. (2013). *Mobbed! What to do when they really are out to get you*. Backdoor Press.

ICES. (2014). Academic bullying and mobbing: Introduction to the special issue. *Workplace*, *24*, 56–57.

Sachs, B. (2010). Enabling employee choice: A structural approach to the rules of union organizing. *Harvard Law Review*, *123*(3), 655–728.

The Walrus. (2018, September 17). L'Affaire Galloway.

Thorne, A. (2013, September 23). *Can civility and academic freedom coexist?* Retrieved from http://www.thefire.org/can-civility-and-academic-freedom-coexist

Westhues, K. (2006). The unkindly art of mobbing. *Academic Matters: The Journal of Higher Education*. OCUFA, August, p. 18-19

Yale Law Journal. (1966). Union authorization cards. *Yale Law Journal, 75(5), 805-844.*

KEY TERMS AND DEFINITIONS

Academic Freedom: The freedom of faculty members to honestly speak their mind and opinions, including the freedom to criticize their university and union.

Academic Mobbing: The concerted attempt by university managements and faculty unions to ostracize a faculty member seen to be threatening their interests.

All-Administrative University: A university that is governed by its managerial cadre rather than its elected senate or other representative bodies.

Collusion: University management and faculty union working together in unison rather than in opposition.

Complicity: University management and faculty union united in turning blind eyes to violations of faculty member rights.

Faculty Association: A union of faculty members purportedly representing their collective interests vis-a-vis the university employer.

Investigation: An internal university procedure operating on the legal principles of a Star Chamber or kangaroo court.

Respectful Environment Policies: Attempts by university management to suppress academic freedom in the name of fostering a harmonious environment.

Senate: The elected academic governance body of a university in law but typically not in practice.

Chapter 9
Sins of a Syndicate:
Arresting Malicious Mob Assaults Against Academics

Denise M. McDonald
University of Houston – Clear Lake, USA

ABSTRACT

This chapter presents a fictitious and satirical story, which explores how individuals and groups of privilege in a university structure exert their power (through intimidation and other oppressive actions) on targeted individuals who are perceived as challenging or disruptive to the power group's existing control. The story is presented as an allegory of the 1920-1940's mafia.

INTRODUCTION

Criminal organizations generate power and control by instilling fear in others through domination, oppression, coercion, manipulation, bullying, extortion, threats, and violence. Many organizational structures in society, such as businesses and universities, operate in a similar fashion where privileged groups wield unchecked authority resulting in strategic intimidation of members. Academic environments are analogously afflicted with hegemonic challenges where underserved individuals are suffocated and choked into silence or are manipulated into adopting complacent, cooperating or consenting stances. Satirical storytelling, framed in a 1920-1940's mafia power construct metaphor, lends well for exploring organizational mob mentality within an academic environment, while retaining anonymity. This chapter, through

DOI: 10.4018/978-1-5225-9485-7.ch009

Copyright © 2020, IGI Global. Copying or distributing in print or electronic forms without written permission of IGI Global is prohibited.

fictitious narrative, expresses the author's experiential observations of faculty and administrative authorities' calculated attacks on and silencing of targeted vocal academics viewed by those in power as disruptive discontents in higher education.

Ratting Out

Divert the bright light for interrogation purposes, it's not necessary. I confess. I am driven by urges to write viciously and fictitiously. I cannot deny that I was once a non-believer in the spoils of fictitious prose; as it countered the research writing expectations in academia (of which, as a junior faculty at the time, I was beaten into submission through brutal and bloody initiation processes). So be forewarned, I must now come clean and admit, use of metaphors, analogies, idioms, alliteration, assonance, allegory, and satire cathartically intensify my empowerment as a renegade writer. Also, I plead guilty to plundering, pilfering, and pillaging words that tickle my own fancy and fantasy. Lastly, I am neither a criminal nor victim in this testimony. Rather, I am an appalled bystander who has observed severe crime scene offenses and abhorrent assaults on innocent, undeserving others who became targets of an academic syndicate's mobbing and robbing hit list. With this deposition, I request witness protection services (as through the aftermath of public or media exposure, retaliation by offenders is highly suspect).

LITERATURE

Auto-Fictitious Storytelling

Telling fictitious stories based on real-life ostracizing experiences, eloquently and poignantly reveals organizational power-structure inequities (Boje, 2008; Gabriel, 2000; Sole & Wilson, 2003). Fictionalizing situations sanctions the confrontation, challenge, and denouncement of power groups as flaccid and impotent oppressors. Through fiction, targeted victims have a fair, toe-to-toe, facing-off opportunity to punch back at offending archetypical assailants through the safe space of cleverly veiled anonymity. Ultimately, fictionalized storytelling empowers individuals to reshape and justify their professional identity from their perspective and on their own terms; where on some level, victims become victors (McDonald, 2016). Lastly, fictionalization sanctions latitude and liberty in broadening a writer's perspective through transforming the *strange as familiar* and the *familiar as strange* (See Caine et al., 2017; McDonald, in press).

Metaphor as My Meaning-Making Muse

Metaphors generate creative thinking through a disequilibrium process, which guilefully forces different perspectives to be acknowledged, scrutinized, rejected, revised, accepted or adopted. They provide structure and inspiration for individual interpretation of experiences, thoughts, ideas, and even casual ponderings (Lakoff & Johnson, 1980). In this paper, a Mafia construct serves as the heuristic metaphorical frame for artfully investigating how power corrupts and crushes concerted efforts toward constructive and continued change within a university setting.

A Summons for Satire

In dealing with hardships, humor heightens one's hardiness when taking professional hits from others (Dwyer, 1991). Satire allows transposition of difficult experiences in a dysfunctional and constrained environment into a liberating reflective process. Therefore, satire serves as a survival strategy in which I have been drawn to the dark side of the policing force in upholding justice. Word play generates "fighting words" for swinging truthful punches at tormentors. It is a strategy for blindsiding bullies or unmasking muggers and thugs, where skilled literary footwork is difficult to dodge and must be faced head-on. Lastly, perhaps playful writing, singed with seriousness such as allegory and satire, is timely. Perhaps the story will resonate with other academics as an alternative approach for taking productive action in establishing scholarly voice within a system designed to extinguish and silence it (Clair, 1998; Sue, 2015).

Heart of Hegemony Organizational Power Constructs

Institutional belongingness is critical to any progressive organization where members must believe their contributions are valued by others for positive and impactful actions to occur (Brown & Humphreys, 2006; McDonald, Craig, Markello, & Kahn, 2016). Social interactions validate or deny members' sense of acceptance within a group, which influence organizational dynamics (Humphreys & Brown, 2002; Tennant, 2005). Often, organizational power groups operate to exclude potential outliers who question and critique or perhaps reject the status quo, where differing perspectives are systematically stalled or eliminated. Herein lies the issue where advancement of new and creative ideas and projects of which the power group does not initiative are lost (that is, until those in power can buy time to bribe others in usurping targets' propositions and designs) (Fleming & Spicer, 2003).

Workplace Bullying and Mobbing

Bullying and mobbing, as evidenced through social exclusion, ostracism, episodic shaming, harassment, imposed stigmatization, ungrounded insults, smear campaigns, silencing of communication, slanderous gossip, deliberate public undermining, incivility, interpersonal conflicts, attempted subjugation, intent to harm reputation, systematic mistreatment, escalated or embellished conflicts, psychological aggression, squashing differing stances or enactments of social norms, marginalization of initiatives and ideas, and other forms of rejection are common phenomena in the workplace (Baumeister & Dewall, 2005; Caponecchia & Wyatt, 2012; Einarsen, Hoel, Zapf, & Cooper, 2011; Glasø, Nielsen, & Einarsen, 2009; Lipinski & Crothers, 2014; Nielsen & Einarsen, 2018). Generally, aggressive attacks result from power imbalances inflicted on targets by oppressors/aggressors. Emotional strain, as a result of bullying or a mobbing assault, reduces the stricken target's commitment and affective attachment to a work group; thereby, negatively impacting interpersonal interactions and the overall productivity of an organization. Targets feel defenseless and over time, hopeless. These types of oppressive actions and destructive consequences can occur in academia; and thereby, diminish one's scholarly identity through negative and tormenting social interactions (McDonald et al., 2016; Sargent & Schlossberg, 1988).

BACKGROUND

This fictitious story is contextualized through description of the setting framed within a loosely aligned 1920-1940's mobster organizational structure with prototypical characters.

Plea Deal

In the academic justice system, politically grounded offenses are judged to be notoriously atrocious. In academia, faithful faculty who uphold integrity amongst reprehensible associates are part of a select force known as Faculty Against Institutional Roughness (FAIR). The story you are about to read is fictitious. Names, gender, titles, affiliations, institutions, and events have been fabricated to protect the innocent. None of what you are about to read actually happened (but evidential truth is identifiable). This is just one story.

Disclaimer

The reporter requests that readers suspend disbelief long enough to acquire a plausible understanding, beyond a reasonable doubt, how although fictional, these types of offenses can occur in a real life situation or scenario (Chakraborty, 2017; Warwick, 2016).

Turf and Territory of Dispute

This institution was experiencing a turbulent turf war where territories were under dispute. Mobsters had infiltrated the organization, causing chaos and conflict amongst academic citizens. Other than the boss, within the Syndicate (i.e., mob family) there were bootlickers (kiss ups) and bootleggers (fakes/fakers and profiteers) of various scheming skills and underhanded talents. Unfortunately, the institution also housed complicit "Good Ole Guys and Dolls" as Associates, as well as "Targets" who became victims in territorial power wars. Additionally, there were a couple of advocates (with backbones) who, based on observed egregious assaults, openly championed the integrity of Targets and served to defend their honor and position within the institution. They were known in the institutional underground as the FAIR Advocates. Lastly, there were also many everyday academic citizens who attempted to avoid Syndicate attacks by going through daily routines as invisibly as possible. Much of the environmental climate was significantly comprised of these types of characters. This form of social dynamics advanced the emergence and fortification of a mobbing mentality.

Syndicate Members

Shameron "Sham" Bamboozle

Shameron had a rough childhood. Initially abandoned by an unnamed father and shortly thereafter by his mother, Sham was raised by his obsessively doting grandmother. In his eyes though, he grew up never having his "bag of candy" like other kids in his neighborhood (so he stole from them). His bully persona developed early on as he sought social recognition from others but could never effectively justify his importance as a leader or garner appreciation by peers. Therefore, as an academic, he implemented similar processes to muscle his way into acceptance throughout his tenure by lying, disparaging colleagues, stealing peers' accomplishments, fabricating questionable accolades, and oppressing those that he could intimidate.

Moving through multiple institutions with each unearned promotion, Dr. Bamboozle succeeded in fooling others into believing his manufactured accolades; and thus, landed a top administrative position at this institution. In a very short period of time, floozies flocked to his side and hand-selected henchmen man-handled heated issues on his behalf; all strategic efforts in promoting his illicit agenda and cementing unquestionable power constructs for shooing away any opposition. Disgracefully dishonest, he shrewdly accumulated his posse of proscribed professors and deftly proceeded to achieve power-seeking goals. To upstanding faculty, who viewed Sham as an inept middle-aged Italian with a bad comb over, he was donned the "Provolonist" (aka – the Big Cheese).

Mugs Baloney

Sham came to the university armed with his right-arm man, Mugs (i.e., with cheese comes baloney). Quickly, without question or condition and before anyone could blink, a position of administrative power was created for Mugs (i.e., one totally new to the system). In the eyes of many faculty, Dr. Baloney was full of it since his entry at the institution (as there is little known about his supposed academic accomplishments). He mostly operated in Sham's shadows and no one had a clear understanding what he actually did or when he would appear...as he emerged only at the bidding of the Provolonist. But, many suspected that Mugs was brought on board to cook the books of the university budget as he would quietly show up for administration budget meetings. Additionally, during myriad public hearings of funding and expenditure discussions, he would spin convoluted lies about university funding without blinking or flinching. No one dared gamble their safety by challenging his claims of how money was appropriated and spent (although many felt multiple muggings of their own budget lines). Questioning this aspect of university operations would make one a target. Additionally, Dr. Baloney received assistance from his wife, Emily "Em" Bezzle, in validating fabricated expenses sanctioned by and dispensed to Syndicate members. Regarding her post, claims of nepotism had been silenced through the Syndicate. There was an unspoken understanding, a code of silence, which had to be honored (to survive). Academic citizens knew not to throw the die against Mugs because of his strong connection to Sham; otherwise, they staked safe standings within the institution; or worse, risked their probable demise.

Bill "The Bully" Scheister

Known by his initials, BS functioned as an unethical used car salesman at the behest of the Provolonist. Dr. Scheister aggrandized everything of which he was a part and would attempt to sell a jalopy of an idea, falsely inspiring others to believe they would make lemonade from lemons discriminately disseminated to them. Basically, these arduous and time-consuming lemons were all busy work projects that no one in administration wanted to do, but Syndicate administrators would quickly take credit on their CVs for the lucrative lemonade stands that others had run without support or assistance.

Interestingly, BS wasn't the smartest academic by any means, but through shameless shrewdness always managed to interact at peak opportune times with the most powerful institutional members. He maneuvered through the university as a grifter and artful dodger, stealthily taking advantage of power acquisition and self-promotional opportunities as they emerged; exploiting all angles on all turfs. Therefore, he readily procured inclusion in key programmatic initiatives that invariably became nationally recognized or granted some feather in the university's cap. Serendipitously, he would thereby garner acknowledgment, accolades, and awards through association rather than smarts or the sweat of strenuous struggles. He was a *playa* at the highest echelon; and thus, quickly drew attention from the Provolonist who observed his talent and ultimately recruited Dr. Scheister to be part of his horde of hellions, henchmen, hoodlums, and heels (i.e., his evil, alter universe version of a warped 4-H club).

Because of his speculative skills and ability to read a room for power posturing of provocateurs, Dr. Scheister's main role was to serve as the Provolonist's "hunch"man and conspiracy consigliere. BS stalked Sham at every turn, never daring to step in front of him or ever lead the way. He pointed Sham in the direction to proceed, waited, and then followed. BS intuitively knew that the Provolonist's ego was his divining rod and the driving force for all actions taken; and therefore, he straggled safely behind, ensuring never having to take a bullet to protect this lackey (and lacking) leader. There was no misconstruing BS's commitment to his pseudo Goodfather/Godfather figure in this mob family; his act of allegiance to the Provolonist was completely self-serving, not fixed out of an abiding sense of loyalty.

Connie Anne Blyde

The first syllable of her first-name says it all. She is a con. Seductively deceiving, this initially charming (and harming) academic sought to draw every last drop of blood from any and all colleagues or competitors who threatened her institutional power or ambitions for attention and promotion. She slyly played the hierarchy game of kissing the rings of administrators, but interactions with subordinates involved a range of coercive actions that, as warranted, included magnetism (to reel in the unsuspecting), manipulation (used on those who questioned her intentions), and meanness (channeled against the astute and intuitive who clearly saw the self-promoting, insincerity, and superficial nature of her actions). Outside the Syndicate, one of Dr. Blyde's main goals was to craft an image as the consummate colleague. However, spreading rumors and initiating adverse innuendos about targeted others was her *modus operandi*. Other than her own shielded cluster of corrupt colleagues and fearful followers, all respectable and decent faculty attempted to avoid her. No one wanted to end up in Connie's sights for any pre-emptive strikes. Her hits effectively brought faculty to their knees when facing the barrel of her gossip gun, as it essentially dropped them into a professional grave. Previous bullet-ridden victims cursed her name in their last breaths when exiting the institution. Alas, and at last, those targets are now in a better place.

Additionally, as a backstabbing senior faculty snitch, she was highly skilled at covertly throwing shade on targets to demean, discredit, defame, disparage, and denigrate their reputations or standings within the university. With an inherent deficit perspective of all others, she was genius at identifying one's weakness(es) and exploiting for her own selfish purposes. Through power, intimidation, and indoctrination tactics, she often preyed on junior faculty as foot soldiers for tendering her footwork of slanderous smear campaigns on tough or tricky targets. For example, she has established associations with Willie Weisel (who willfully operates as a back-up snitch when called upon) and Veronica Vixen (a vexing sociopath, whose stilettos sinisterly stomp, slice, and stab sufferers with spontaneous strikes). Additionally, more calculated hits against others were often coordinated with close allies, Drs. Baloney and Scheister, who collaboratively spun facts into falsities. From Connie's perspective, there was force in (and enforcement with) numbers. So, strategic grooming of novices and palling around with simpatico associates who shared complementary power aspirations were essential tactics for her egotistical end goal of rising through the Syndicate ranks.

Sins of a Syndicate

Addie Hocker

As a low-level henchwoman for the Provolonist, Dr. Hocker mostly served as a Syndicate impromptu plant on contentious committees. She also generated and chaired erroneous committees intended to either promote Syndicate objectives or muddle and obstruct processes which did not enhance individual or collective Syndicate members' interests. There was always a particularly selfish objective in mind, with devious means-to-an-end processes implemented (usually resulting in significant collateral damage to innocent or uninvolved bystanders, of which she had no concern or empathy). Most of Addie's operations were undercover (and historically "under cover" with top Syndicate members); therefore, well-endowed with Syndicate protection, little evidence emerged for tracing back to and invoking accountability measures on her blatantly biased actions against targets and academic citizens. She was untouchable (i.e., with the exception of Syndicate cronies' welcomed "goomah" groping) and was an intimate associate with Willie Weisel (well-known Syndicate side-line snitch).

Tomás "Rat a tat tat, tit for tat" Gunn

The Provolonist jokingly anglicized his name as "Tommy" when relying on him to pull out the big guns of retaliation, vengeance, retribution, blood for blood, and blow for blow actions against targets or the silencing of identified potential marks within the academic citizen populace. So, if or when any drastic retaliatory actions needed to be taken, Dr. Gunn was the merciless rat to do it. His work was all pro bono, as he displayed indifference and psychopathic enjoyment in bringing down others (that included, against members within the Syndicate if needed). He was considered a Syndicate associate, but mostly functioned as a rogue or independent contractor in the system; thereby, responding and reporting to the highest bidder.

4H Club (aka - Horde of Hellions, Henchmen/ Henchwomen, Hoodlums, and Heels)

All Syndicate members as well as some complicit "Good Ole Guys and Dolls" and wannabe associates swore allegiance to this clandestine club (consensually or through forced measures). Members controlled the masses with gruesome public assaults or covert debilitating actions on antagonists, which impeded academic adversaries (and supported their mantra - Eradicate the Radicals). As a unit, members would collaboratively drive fear through smear campaigns, and hits or attacks on: targets' intellect (pummel their *head*), emotions (strike close to the *heart*), abilities or expertise (cut-off their *hands*), and general well-being (poison their *health* through harassment). Syndicate 4H Club members met secretly to plot and deal with exploitive tactics in manipulating the masses. Their behind-the-scene schemes spawned scaring strategies and scarring situations to be executed upon targeted academics. Faculty, forever fearful of the unknown, unforeseen and uninformed new situations, dreaded worst-case scenarios that the 4H Club members triggered with a quick flick of a finger (invariably, the middle one).

Complicit "Good Ole Guys and Dolls"

Patsy Stakes

Upon joining the university in an administrative role, Dr. Patsy Stakes hoped for a smooth running institution. Unfortunately, she was often duped by mobsters who infiltrated meetings and positioned her to unquestionably defend and unwittingly support the Syndicate's violations of policy actions. She was their clueless and naïve patsy for situations with much at stake.

Dud "Lee" Doo-Riot

Most colleagues believed that Lee's heart and intentions were in the right place, but his nearsighted, overzealous ballyhooing and nervous over-reaction to some circumstances incited divisive hysteria and hullabaloo amongst faculty. His lack of competence in communicating with colleagues caused divisiveness, which predictably generated extended discussions amongst opposing factions. Over time, the central issue of which he was involved would become a dud (extinguished) through his erroneous rants. At these propitious points, the Syndicate would effortlessly sweep in for the kill and take control. Dr. Doo-Riot was totally oblivious to how his actions deleteriously impacted those around him; apparently believing, he was doing right by his constituents. On the contrary, Doo-Riot's diddlings served as a catastrophic catalyst for Syndicate shenanigans where they tapped his ruckus and racket for their own racketeering.

Oxy Morono

As a know-it-all senior faculty with a long tenure at this university, Dr. Morono swore an apolitical, unbiased, bipartisan posture on all polemic debates and disputes (claiming history demonstrated his commitment to the greater good). However, multiple committee meeting minutes revealed that his words did not match his actions as he consistently and unequivocally supported and promoted Syndicate perspectives, initiatives, and directives. It can be surmised that institutional myths generated by the Syndicate became steeped in organizational values and legitimized in the social system through progressively perpetuating propaganda and practices (of which, Oxy was a pawn). Additionally, resistance from non-dominate circles became difficult to realize the longer the power-seeking group retained authority, as over time the Syndicate, as a power group generated multiple strategic measures built into the system, crafted to guarantee longevity of their reign (such as, pulling puppet strings of pansies). Dr. Morono, blindly engulfed in this process, served as a converted convict for the Syndicate.

Howard "the Coward" Capon

Howard cowered to all administrative authority and would never even *whisper* a critical comment about systematic issues; although, it was suspected he was fully aware of the Syndicate's self-serving, ill-intentions to others and consciously chose to turn a blind eye. As the Syndicate's power and influence grew, he became increasingly complicit and collusive with their goals and actions. Bottom line – Professor Capon protected his own skin and placed his needs before all others. Additionally, he used unsuspecting colleagues to shield himself from becoming inflicted as an unintended target during Syndicate skirmishes, dealings, and deeds.

Targets

Kharma Barter

Kharma functioned as a highly conscientious faculty member known for being exceedingly skilled at policing policy issues. A stickler for details, through her sleuthing and gumshoe activities, she often caught mistakes in the system (most notably, those meant to be concealed or never discovered). Dr. Barter was also very vocal in publically snaring and sharing systematic errors made as well as identifying the most obvious perpetrators of those blunders and offenses. Dr. Patsy Stakes was often called in to "deflect and protect" the Syndicate against push back from Kharma's claims of policy violations that she had unearthed. Also, various members of the 4H Club, through an ongoing fashion, continually chipped away at her credibility and deliberately denigrated her accomplishments and commitment to the university. Additionally, obvious arbitrary measures to limit Dr. Barter's opportunities for leadership within her department occurred without due process of investigation.

Frank Frette

A nationally renowned, well-cited scholar, Dr. Frette voiced glaring system errors that unjustly disadvantaged faculty (the Syndicate selected). Frank's frank delivery of organizational critique was harsher than the actual message content (where even academic citizens cringed in fear of retribution by vicarious association with him and his stances). Unfortunately, his raucous declarations of the dysfunction of a constrained environment ratcheted him to the top of the Syndicate's target hit list. The Provolonist as well as Drs. Baloney and Bylde had the biggest axes to grind with Frank. Through their "leadership" directives, Frette experienced stifling and unjustified actions against his academic identity, pedagogical practices, and scholarly endeavors. The most significant example was denial of his promotion to full professor (although documentation and multiple metrics indicated he was the most cited scholar in his college). Syndicate members were planted on his promotion committee to negatively spin and critically question validity of Dr. Frette's accomplishments (and were surprisingly successful in doing so). Additionally, as a perceived adversary, Frette was intentionally isolated and marginalized for challenging the Syndicate's sovereignty. In the Syndicate, he was named Public Frenemy #1.

FAIR Advocates

Alfie David

An upstanding, well-respected faculty member and colleague, Alfie sought involvement in all progressive actions for increasing quality programs within the university. His committee work and stances often occurred against the tide of Syndicate's sinful swells and surges. Additionally, as a promoter of social justice for others, Dr. David willingly tackled goliath issues of inequality inflicted upon targeted colleagues. In fact, he voluntarily served on many grievance committees as an advocate for faculty who suffered injustices committed by Syndicate members. As part of this service, he wrote extensive, factually detailed, lengthy letters of support on behalf of a grievant. This service was extended during grievance committee meetings through articulately argued apexes of arbitration. Surprisingly, the Syndicate did not view Dr. David as a significant threat to their operations; rather, from the organization's perspective, he was an annoyance at best. Also, the Syndicate recognized that directly targeting Alfie could rouse questions (and potential counter actions) from the general academic citizen population; therefore, covert attempts were employed to tamp down or neutralize his deeds when necessary. Fortunately, not all Syndicate shots at countering his good actions were effective.

Grace Ace

Dr. Grace Ace served as an informal mentor to all who sought her insight and wisdom for advice or direction. Her actions and interactions with others generated trust and she had been adoringly dubbed "Ace of Hearts" as colleagues believed her gracious good intentions trumped cards played by swindlers at committee card tables. She was often an unexpected *ace in the hole* during critical competitive contests. Unfortunately, house odds favored the Syndicate; so, she played her hand strategically when laying bets. As a committee member, Dr. Ace offered a quietly strong and prudent voice when sharing her position on important university decisions. Generally, in most gaming situations, arguments to counter her perspectives would fall short; unless, Syndicate members would somehow foresee her probable perspective and formulate pre-planned punctures as arguments against her position. By and large, Syndicate members could not improvise (from surprise), which gave Dr. Ace an occasional advantage in vital decision-making situations.

Mercy Tran

Dr. Tran, always true to her word and transparent in her professional goals, reliably fulfilled commitments for the betterment of all within the university. Since acquiring tenure, her energy and efforts were all service-driven; therefore, she was on a multitude of committees on all levels at the university. She conscientiously communicated with colleagues the myriad perspectives of committee discussions and diligently honored peers' input during decision-making negotiations. Her even-handed diplomacy was above reproach and well-respected by faculty. The Syndicate viewed her as "one vote" to which they paid little attention. On multiple occasions, her input and "one vote" championed greater-good initiatives, much to the chagrin of Syndicate "good fellas" who usually snubbed her or disregarded her influence.

Victor Inoalot

Dr. Inoalot was the most senior member at this campus and the sole remaining founding faculty of the university. He knew the campus history; all its quibbles, quirks, quarrels, quandaries, and quiddities. As an elder, his eidetic memory of policy changes over the years was often called into question by Syndicate members as reconstructed remembrances and faulty fabrications or façades with minimal accuracy of factual features or fine details and inferred flipped facets of fidelity. They would also spin strawman spats to shroud situations in stupefaction, which would stunt, stymie, stump, and spoil Dr. Inoalot's subsequent sermons for statutes of sincere civility during squabbles, scuffles, and skirmishes. Dr. Inoalot vied for viable victory during all vitriolic altercations and arguments; alas, to no avail. His plea for polemical peace was punctured at every point, but his resolve for rectifying wrong-doings was respected and revered by faculty and relished by institutional rebels and rogue comrades.

Academic Citizens

The bulk of remaining faculty are unassuming academic citizens (e.g., John Smith, Jane Doe, James Hoffa, and others) who go about their daily responsibilities and generally avoid controversy when possible. The Syndicate controls most of their activity through unquestioned systematic measures.

THE STORY

An Offer You Can't Refuse

Money allotments for the next year's institutional initiatives were discussed at the University Budget committee meeting chaired by the Provolonist Bamboozle. He had specific ideas for how funds would be parceled out and disseminated, including a significant portion allocated for a new surveillance software program to be implemented by the campus police department. This agenda item was added at the very last minute, as throwing in surprises to keep faculty off kilter was one strategy the Provolonist used to control his goals and keep his edge for strategic moves. This budget line was not an essential need for the campus, but served an important purpose for Bamboozle. He wanted campus police in his back pocket and ratifying this expensive luxury for their convenience (i.e., watching more screens rather than patrolling the campus) was an attractive perk that would garner support and keep the police force indebted to him. During the meeting, a few faculty committee members (i.e., Drs. Ace and Tran) politely imparted the opinion that the expense and extensiveness of the surveillance did not appear warranted for the institutional population size. Basically, considering all the other needs for students and faculty, committee members shared multiple points how this budget line was not comparatively prudent. Dr. Frette was the loudest in voicing contention. He countered the Provolonist's budget line suggestion by outlining several other initiatives which served greater university needs regarding the shifting student demographics (e.g., a Student Success Center to support first-generation college students and English as a Second Language [ESL] learners). Reacting to this challenge, Provolonist Bamboozle glared at Frette with obvious anger and quickly cast a subtle glance for back-up to his associate, Mugs Baloney, who dutifully pulled up a chart with multiple, convoluted lines of dollar figures. This dense document could not be discerned for discrete data upon which faculty could make a sound decision. The Provolonist's follow-up strategy after his "surprise" tactic was always to confuse by spinning the topic with erroneous lines of data. Most faculty were complicit with many of Bamboozle's kerfuffles, but not all, and apparently not during this budget meeting. Dr. Barter chased Frette's comments with other key points and bravely noted how this add-on budget line offered no evidence for effectiveness. She added that a last-minute presentation felt coercive to faculty, especially just prior to voting. The Provolonist argued that surveillance software offers additional security for all and is something no community member should refuse. He then attempted to incite fear by spouting national incidents of scary safety hypothetical issues. Committee members listened with earnest, but consensually agreed with Drs. Frette and Barter, that high expense and questionable need were not reasonable. Discussion completed, votes were cast and remarkably, the surveillance software was not supported for funding, but the support initiative for first-generation college students and ESL learners passed. This upheaval to the Provolonist's agenda immediately placed Drs. Frette and Barter on his hit list. He had assumed that placement of key cronies on the committee (i.e., Baloney, Scheister, Blyde, and Hocker) would ensure a positive outcome of voting for foundationally cementing his agenda initiatives and power within the system. But, several committee members who were FAIR Advocates refuted the need for surveillance over a student center based on strong stances for social justice (Drs. David and Tran), practical need (Drs. Ace, Frette, and Barter), and historical evidence (Dr. Inoalot). Notably, Frette and Barter were the ones who most persuasively argued their points; turning the table of committee members' perspectives and disrupting the Provolonist's goals. Shortly afterwards, 4H Club members received covert directions by the Provolonist to retaliate against the perceived disloyalty of Drs. Frette and Barter by discrediting and assaulting their reputations in all manners possible (i.e., personal and professional). Provolonist Bamboozle was notorious for callously going after faculty members who disputed his position on any topic; especially, if defeated initiatives prevented him from receiving behind-the-scenes padding of his palms from external contractors, which was the obvious situation in this police software case. From this point forward, Frette and Barter became targets of the institutional mob; and unfortunately, they had no clue of events which would unfold as a result of standing by their principles.

Hola a Mi Pequeño Amigo

The first crony called upon to go after the targets was Tomás Gunn. As the trigger man, he strategically planned to shoot holes in their respective reputations; beginning with Dr. Barter who was expected to go up for promotion. Apparently, the Syndicate found Dr. Barter to be a challenging foe on key university committees and hoped to clip her wings of influence by stalling her at the Associate Professor level.

Dr. Barter had submitted all the required documents for promotion and appeared well prepared for the review based on her record of service, teaching, and publications. In fact, her scholarship was touted by a prestigious research organization through a significant researcher award in her specific field. Her Promotion and Tenure (P & T) documents were available for review by all faculty within her program, including Dr. Gunn (who was not on the P & T committee). He evaluated her vitae and from a deficit model of analysis, outlined arguments which scrutinized and diminished her publication lines. He spun her multiple publications with students as opportunistic, although publishing with students was the norm for many faculty and previously encouraged by the College Dean (a least for select faculty supportive of the Syndicate). He noted the research award was granted to a collaborative trio, not just Dr. Barter; thereby, insinuating her contribution was marginal at best since a more senior member must have arguably led the research work and she just rode on that collaborating colleague's coattails. These points, and several others, were secretly presented in a hurtful dossier titled "little friend" to Syndicate members on Dr. Barter's P & T committee. Undeniably, P & T became a process for determining Syndicate loyalty amongst academics (i.e., for candidates under review, as well as elected or selected members who served on the committees). The Syndicate played a part in all P & T processes by planting henchmen and heels on specific committees to serve particular roles, which ensured decisive outcomes for the benefit of the Syndicate's existing power. Syndicate plants could (and would) spin faculty qualifications as faulty to keep any rising malcontents and dissidents suppressed; and conversely, those with similar accomplishments going under review, but viewed as faithful followers of the Syndicate, would receive embellished ratings. As a fraudulent process embedded in the system, the Syndicate members' spinning of facts on various committees helped establish, reinforce, cement, and increase their organizational power.

Doling Out Deals to Dolls

Dr. Barter's P & T committee, comprised of faculty in her department, included two planted Syndicate members (i.e., Drs. Blyde and Hocker) with the directed charge by Dr. Scheister, the third Syndicate member and "coincidentally" committee Chair, to surreptitiously utilize Dr. Gunn's dossier to the fullest extent and spin a negative review letter. In exchange, the Syndicate "dolls" would receive favor from the Provolonist for future promotions or lucrative leadership opportunities of notable recognition. Blyde and Hocker had established reputations as the Syndicate's go-to girls for gritty work in clobbering colleagues. They historically negotiated "deals with the devil" for acquiring power and viewed this as an opportunity with multiple benefits. They would crush a colleague they viewed as "in their way" of gaining service credit, recognition, and leadership positions within the department, college, and university. Additionally, they would earn valuable favor from the Syndicate (sort of like a "get out of jail free" card if needed in the future).

Hard Hits of Hegemonic Henchman's Hearsay and Heresy

During P & T committee meetings, Drs. Blyde and Hocker mentioned key points from the secretly supplied "little friend" dossier and improvised on sharing other adverse points regarding consideration of Dr. Barter's promotion (of which, nearly all points shared were not aligned within policy or a fair review process). They slyly imparted hearsay comments that Dr. Barter was not collegial with others *and* when asked or directed by superiors, she would not amend instructional activities or curriculum design of courses based on her view of intellectual freedom. Blyde asserted that Barter's stance on this issue was not based on intellectual freedom; but rather, she was obviously committing heresy against the program and college. Dr. Hocker supplied additional negative comments, which inferred that Barter's research was too dependent upon collaborators or doctoral students' work. At this point, Dr. Barter's promotion was no longer a "shoo-in;" instead, the Syndicate's copious covert conduct cemented the committee's rejection for her promotion. These types of committee actions underscore how the Syndicate tactically fitted and applied cement shoes to sink opponents into the swamp of hegemony.

Roweled Rebel

Unfortunately, letters from administrators paralleled the paucity of praise and pattern of prejudice. Dr. Barter was bloodied and decisively punched out of contention for promotion. Not to be down and out by the Syndicate's upper cut to her chin, Barter roweled as a rebel and did not throw in the towel. Rather, to advance for a second round in this bout, she rallied, went rogue, and tactically reviewed every syllable of the committee's letter, as well as the comparably critical letters from administrators up the chain of command. In an earnest effort to win her deserved promotion title, all gloves were thrown off during her intense training for the next round. Dr. Barter diligently recorded egregious errors in the letters; most of which were extreme with an enormous amount of evidence regarding policy and process encroachments in each essay. After consulting with Dr. David, Dr. Barter punched back at the Syndicate by writing and entering an essential grievance letter, which placed her back in the ring. Somewhat prepared for this second round of action, the Syndicate sent in a well-conditioned crony for combat on the grievance committee. With the grievance process in full swing and Dr. David as her trainer and ring-side coach, all bets were off for subsequent rounds in this brawl.

Pulling Out the Big Guns

In many ways, Dr. Barter's halted promotion and impaled reputation by the Syndicate pales in comparison to harassment Dr. Frette faced on a daily basis. Spearheaded by Dr. Connie Anne Blyde, the Syndicate relentlessly spewed assaults to break him down with ongoing, hard-hitting false accusations. This perfidious propaganda ploy propelled Frette into a precarious position of perpetual pain from the pounding and pummeling of persnickety peers (including Good Ole Guys and Dolls, such as, Drs. Patsy Stakes and Oxy Morono). A hostile and toxic environment generated against Dr. Frette destroyed his trust in colleagues. For example, Syndicate member Blyde took an ardent lead in steamrolling Frette's reputation by coaching junior faculty to file unwarranted charges against him. His only defensive move toward these formidable and unjustified assaults was to pivot their propaganda platform against him by catching them commit multiple policy violations within the system. Of course, although there was a fertile field of groundless assaults and faults against him, Frette's substantiated stances proved futile to the Syndicate's network of nasty and noxious gangsters and goons. The Syndicate's "good fellas" were formidable *foul fellows*. Few targets found forgiveness or could free themselves from these fiends' frightening and irrefutable retaliation schemes. Woefully, Dr. Frette was no exception.

Dirty Rat Who Killed My Druthers

Frank was completely deflated by continual ostracism and unjustified assaults. With his passion for academia broken, his commitment to the institution dissolved. For example, Dr. Blyde called on Dr. Gunn to single-handedly, with precision, shoot down and kill Dr. Frette's particular initiative for establishing a new online degree plan. Additionally, Blyde deliberately sabotaged, disrupted, and damaged his service work and university engagement through slanderous, behind-the-scenes comments to colleagues, which disparaged him as a peer or egregiously denigrated him as an ingrate. At one of his lowest points, when his closest colleagues Kharma, Alfie, and Grace confidentially shared their concern about his well-being, Frank confided "Connie Ann Blyde is the dirty rat who killed my druthers for contributing to committee work. She not only gets away with obvious drive-by personal shootings, bullified battering, and vicious violations of policies aimed at harming me, she also seems to be supported and applauded by administration…or they turn a blind eye to her offenses against me. I have tried, but it does not seem to matter what I do to better this situation. I need to hide-out for a while."

Self-Induced Solitary Confinement

Ultimately, Dr. Frette retreated into a protected shell of seclusion and sheltered in his office sanctuary. Additionally, to eliminate as many interactions as possible with Blyde, Frette taught mostly online and deliberately chose office hours at unique times when Blyde and her grifter group were not on campus. This strategic action eliminated most awkward interactions, but apparently not all. Blyde relished in blindsiding Frette; so, when she could not harass him face-to-face, she developed a pestering pattern of cryptic and confounding communications to stymie him and provoke agonizing anxiety. Based on historical interactions with Blyde; markedly when not fully informed, Frette assumed the worst and rightfully so. Blyde's veracity vacillated daily and there were just too many variables of vitriolic and venomous unknowns. These factors made Frette fretful and sometimes frantic with fear. Frette responded cautiously to all her messages, but Blyde collected and selected certain clauses from chosen communications and cunningly cut content from the comprehensive context of Frette's correspondences. Blyde charted and constructed these compilations into a contrived catalogue of cacophonous ca-ca. Dr. Frette's refuge within the confines of his campus office was virtually raided. He had no haven for hiding away from hegemonic heavy-weights. Chased like a cursed criminal, Frette collapsed and crashed.

Bulleted Blasphemy

At this vulnerable juncture for Frette, Blyde used her notorious notes to write a blistering letter about him addressed to his Dean. The Dean, Howard "the Coward" Capon, was somewhat complicit to Syndicate stabbing strikes against identified targets; especially, if collusion with their forces solicited Syndicate favor or prevented him from being considered a mark. Blyde's critical letter bulleted fabricated incidents of policy violations she claimed Frette had allegedly committed. There was no trial, investigation, data collection or due diligence on behalf of Frette. Although Blyde lied, the Dean never questioned Blyde's perspective as potentially faulty, biased, or incomplete. In fact, Capon blindly believed (as other bad behaving bullies) every syllable in the letter; and therefore, backed, buoyed, and buttressed Blyde's maligning manifesto of Frette's faults and frailties. Forced to be a fugitive, Frette fled to his ruined refuge (as there was nowhere else to retreat).

Unleashing the Hounds

Blyde rarely tackled challenges alone; for assistance in pacifying prey, she would swiftly rifle through her list of predatory peers to call in the big dogs (and throw them a bonus bone). Stories of her vicarious vindictive ventures often emerged as cautionary dogged tales/tails. Dr. Ace became a source for one of those stories regarding how Frette was placed on a hunting expedition hit list. It was well known that junior faculty members often sought advice from Dr. Ace, especially regarding policy violations, unethical episodes of coercion, or downright wrongdoings they experienced at the hands of Syndicate members. In confidence, one first-year faculty member, Dr. Jane Doe, who chaired the elections committee, shared with Dr. Ace that Dr. Morono, her Department Chair (and Blyde's close colleague) commanded her to change the anonymous voting results for an important university-level committee position. The tallies revealed Frette had received the most votes. In the moment of that inappropriate directive, Dr. Doe, like a deer in headlights, professed fleeting feelings of fight, flight or freeze, in which she ultimately froze. After what felt like an eternity, she unflinchingly stared directly at Dr. Morono (while slowly backing away) and simply said, "I can't do that." Knitting his brow, Dr. Morono scowled like a mongrel, flashing his fangs but suppressing his bark. As an untenured neophyte faculty, Dr. Doe feared she was now in the Syndicate's cross-hairs and would be shot down, skinned, and butchered (or buried in a shallow grave, perhaps like Dr. Hoffa, who suspiciously went missing, never to be heard from again). She worried that the Syndicate would unleash the hounds and she would become the next faculty fatality with her position ultimately mounted on the wall as a trophy of victory in immobilizing the meek and preying on the puny. Despite spiteful intent, Frette retained the committee position, as Doe did not acquiesce to Morono's maneuvers. This was just one scary story, which revealed how Syndicate members coordinated their pack to sniff out, spot, corner, and snuff out live game, such as Drs. Doe and Frette.

Back-Alley Allies

In another unnerving story, Dr. Doo-Riot, a Syndicate sycophant, strategically staged sinister strikes behind the scenes. Sanctioned by Bamboozle (who Doo-Riot, an ego-stroking extraordinaire, constantly kissed-up to), and soliciting assistance from Dr. Stakes (who was his pliable patsy), at a general policy meeting Doo-Riot suggested a new process for including "collegiality" as a construct rated on yearly faculty reviews by department peers. Doo-Riot believed a tug of thugs would garner support of this initiative; and thereby, could provide contrived controllable data necessary to oust troublesome faculty who disrupted Syndicate operations. This was obviously a conscious, unconscionable contract to convict colleagues who were on the Syndicate's hit list. Appalled, Dr. Tran commented, "This is a dangerous, back-alley process that has dire consequences. It allows for and provides validity to subjective ratings of colleagues, which have nothing to do with their skill sets. It could potentially polarize peers and promote campaigns against others with unorthodox views. As academics, we may not like someone, but we must be able to professionally work together and respect pluralistic perspectives." This incident revealed the Syndicate's unethical, covert, and crude approaches used to corner, disarm, reduce influence, and ultimately remove dissenting faculty from the university (most notably, the Syndicate's top target, Dr. Frette). Academic citizens across the university, who previously wanted to remain invisible, came out of the shadows and voted to not support the suggested initiative. However, everyone became increasingly wary when walking the campus corridors, as anyone could become a mark. Protection against trumped-up persecution was vital for all, but academic citizens were not sure how to shield themselves, enforce safeguards, and prevent assaults. New leadership was necessary and critical, but effective policing of policies had not occurred. Back-alley deals amongst allies to covertly commit attacks continued, much to the chagrin of conscientious colleagues.

Family Secrets

The Syndicate had not-so-secret secrets, which proved to be their weaknesses and undoing. At some point, all Syndicate heels ultimately revealed their Achilles Heel. For one, Provolonist Sham Bamboozle's paranoia and blind ego would never permit him to openly admit being wrong about anything, acknowledge mistakes or apologize. Unwittingly, this made him vulnerable to retaliation from those he targeted, as flagrantly flaunted flaws were prime sources for planning punishment on policy abuses and pre-arranging reprisals of retribution regarding wrongs he perpetrated on others. Additionally, his position of power also prevented his posse from opposing his perceptions, disagreeing with him on precarious points, and openly partaking in productive sharing of their own unique thoughts. A leader who is "never wrong" will never get truthful input from those he intimidates, including intimates tight in the Syndicate family, as well as outsiders. So, Sham's suspicions of all others helped him identify potential opposition, but worked against him within his own group of confidants and supporters who he equally distrusted.

Forfeiture or Curse?

The Syndicate operated as a family, where membership was viewed like a marriage. In the Syndicate's case, marriage in a dysfunctional family, which wedded power-seekers to other power-seekers (a volatile in-house space to find oneself) and wielded destruction and devastation to all dissidents outside the domestic circle. Family membership involved unconditional forfeiting of principles or members would suffer the curse of 'domicide' for deviation from the designated doctrine of the Syndicate. The cult conditions of the marriage also played into the Syndicate's demise, especially regarding family quibbles as some would butt heads for power or attempt to throw each other under the proverbial bus (of business) when things went wrong. Finger pointing actions often resulted in amputations of those very fingers, sending a morbid mafia message. The family was self-destructing and apparently wanted to take everyone down with them. The Syndicate's familial marriage vow: Forfeiture or curse, for better or worse (ended up worse).

Sins of a Syndicate

Exhortation of Extortion

From Bill "The Bully" Scheister's (aka – BS) perspective, skilled manipulation of faculty fears and coerced compliance to his caprices demonstrated power. Institutional power was realized through fueling his favorites with freebies and acquiring as much complicity and passivity of academic citizens as possible. Scheister conducted multiple extortion efforts, beginning with squeezing faculty regarding summer salary. He called an impromptu meeting, which few faculty members could make at the last minute (strategy borrowed from Bamboozle). During this meeting, he claimed that due to budget shortfall and other funding issues, summer courses could not be offered (i.e., with a handful of exceptions for his select few favorites). Further, he suggested faculty find other means in which to increase their salary, perhaps like grants (of which, the university would receive the highest percentage of funds and would cushion his own budget). In faculty minds, cutting summer courses was counterintuitive to climbing out of financial constraints, as offering courses in the summer yielded additional university income through enrollment. Dr. Inoalot quickly countered and challenged BS's BS with an extended historical explanation for how this type of budget issue had been sufficiently addressed in the past. Dr. Tran added her concern about junior faculty who relied on summer pay. BS just coolly shrugged and replied, "Well, that is the way it is going to be." Faculty felt extorted. Their livelihoods were in his hands and he knew it. He was manipulating their financial concerns to his advantage, asserting his authority, and enforcing their complicity in his decisions on future actions. He had hoodlum alums from other colleges echoing the same stance, so everything he spouted was taken as a real deal dire situation. Upper administration got wind of this blowhard and the nonsense he was spewing. Inexplicably, within a very short period of time, BS changed his tune and harmony returned regarding summer course loads.

Criminal Minds

Shenanigans saturated the university setting and spawned suspicious situations, which soured the Syndicate's standing in the system. Inappropriate activities drew notice from system administrators who began to question the soundness of decisions and the lack of inclusion of others in decision-making processes.

Take the Cannoli

Syndicate members, always clear in their goals, would freely steal others' best and brightest ideas to stage as their own. They snatched the sweet rewards of recognition to satisfy their appetites, rarely being challenged by colleagues who cowered in their company. FAIR advocates finally called several Syndicate members on their academic thievery. Through multiple grievances, these offenders would now receive their just desserts.

Collateral Damage

Unfortunately, system administrators were not aware of all the underground, behind the scenes assaults and mobbing of faculty that was occurring. The Syndicate's greatest injury was to the overall institutional climate, which twisted into a cesspool of distrust, caution, and faculty seeking safety within mediocrity. Fear driven, many faculty members were copping out of contributing their full attention to campus campaigns. Ultimately, their energy and efforts became collateral damage. A few righteous upper-level administrators noticed low morale and began probing faculty for input on what was happening. Several Syndicate members were identified as culprits in creating an atmosphere of distress and anxiety amongst faculty. Due to administrator queries, offenders now face grievances against their egregious deeds.

Usual Suspects

Sham Bamboozle, Mugs Baloney, Bill Scheister, and Tomás Gunn attracted critical attention from system officials, which resulted in an undisclosed investigation of their shady handiwork with university funds. In the past, the system turned a blind eye, now they went full force in hiring a Private Eye to unearth and uncover all corrupt actions (although offenses to faculty were not prioritized). Intense investigations found fault with the felonious four. Extensive data findings of adverse acts and corrupt collusion committed by the four administrators were collected. A mass exodus was expected, as none wanted detrimental charges brought against them.

"Soon-to-Be" Departed

Despite Provolonist Bamboozle's mob of Syndicate members entrenched in the institution who provided protected, his operational exploits finally caught up with him as well as the offenses of his horde of hellions, henchmen/henchwomen, hoodlums, and heels. Bamboozle was facing his demise at the university, as his departure was eminent. The system wanted to keep the Syndicate situation under wraps so that negative publicity would not impact the university's prominent image and solid student enrollment. Academic citizens were unaware of the clandestine dragnet operation occurring.

Lock, Stock, and Smoking Barrel

High-level, upper administration (within the institution, and more broadly in the university system) went gunning for Sham Bamboozle. They locked in on crafting an airtight stock of testimonies and other documents which outlined Bamboozle's ongoing false statements, violations of policies (including making up new ones without a shared governance review), and his many fraudulent escapades against others (the smoking barrel). There was no viable defense of charges brought against him.

No Contest Exit

Bamboozle was provided an opportunity to claim *no contest* on the myriad serious sins with which he was charged; therefore, Sham could avoid shame. Academic citizens never received any information publicly, but most did not care, as long as he left the community (for good). He was to leave quietly, and no charges would be formally filed. If he fought, he would lose his case and forfeit his position, of which he was well aware. Attempting to fight the case and stay at the university would result in being imprisoned with a demotion, which would stall his career indefinitely. Exiting was an appealing deal (without appeal). He quickly and quietly departed without incident. Back on the streets, he surprisingly found another institutional turf in which he could continue to reorganize and build a smaller Syndicate (i.e., if his reputation did not precede him). Leaving, he did the institution a favor; no one will dispute.

New Sheriff in Town

Interestingly, shortly after the Provolonist's apparent "getaway" (Mugs followed), a top administrative leader was hired from the system to clean up chaos in the academic community. Several complicit "Good Ole Guys and Dolls" who intuitively saw the new sheriff in town as a law-enforcing (i.e., policy implementer), wisely chose a quiet exit from the institution (many claimed early retirement or other professionally acceptable and valid, face-saving reasons for leaving). Remaining Syndicate members stood ground in hopes that this administrator would follow the same old pattern of accepting the norm of "this is the way it is and the way things have been done." Fortunately, she was not having any of it, so that would not be the case. A dragnet process of "cease and desist" was initiated as a measure to apprehend low-level offenders. Many Syndicate members found their improper actions of the past, which violated policy, were arrested in their tracks. Some negotiated for leniency, claiming they would be law-abiding from this point forward. A few others required being escorted off campus. A handful remained, still lurking in the shadows, waiting for an opportunity to strike. Amongst the academic citizenship, internalized oppression still lingers, but hope has emerged through open discussions where voices are heard and acknowledged. With corruption exposed and conditionally eliminated, perhaps Drs. Kharma and Frette will now experience their overdue due process and some semblance of justice.

CASE BRIEFING

Syndicate members operated through lies and dishonesty, shrewdness, unethical power-seeking actions, and aggrandizement of their own nominal efforts, where individual self-serving needs were prioritized over the greater good. During my 20+ year tenure, academia has shifted in its structure and design where historically-honored humanistic values such as provision of platforms for pluralistic views, altruistic actions, and philanthropic performances have taken a back seat (actually, thrown in the trunk) to polarized and polemic propaganda by players in power. Perhaps it has always been that way, but from my experience, ideologies closely rooted in principles of fairness, honesty, and justice amongst academics have been increasingly sidestepped, swung aside or swept away. I optimistically yearn for positive change where the scales of justice can provide balance to a once negatively weighted academic environment.

SUMMATION

This fictitious story metaphorically illuminates oppressive hegemonic offenses on academics; notably, how power-groups quash and squash targeted colleagues' educational values, academic professional goals, and scholarly identities. I view this piece of writing as a meta-narrative (i.e., a story about a story), which explores hegemony within institutional processes, structure, and organizational members. The fictitious and satirical retelling of events I have observed, lived, and experienced as an outsider may not be considered realistic or epistemologically sound research by some readers (See Barone, 2007). However, all stories serve a purpose; and hopefully, as a positional counter story, this one will resonate with broad-minded academics (See Olson & Craig, 2009; Milner, 2008). Additionally important, this story is authentic to my voice, writing style, and perspective as a socially conscientious researcher who seeks pluralistic forms of truth-telling as modes for upending injustices. Lastly, I believe "truth is no stranger to fiction" (McDonald, 2016, p. 4) and I must confess fictitious writing is meaningfully liberating, allows for personally sharing (in more depth) the affective dimensions of experiences within a protective space, stimulates creative and imaginative examination of social environments, challenges conformity, opens normative boundaries, and produces an enlightened and embodied understanding of complex experiences through disrupting, dismantling, and problematizing dominate ideologies, biases, and scripts (Caine et al., 2017; Clandinin & Connelly, 1995; Clandinin & Rosiek, 2007). There are no answers, solutions or resolutions to the power issues unmasked in this story, but exposing injustices and how they are inflicted on others (albeit, fictitiously), is one step forward in righting wrongs and perhaps commencing constructive change.

REFERENCES

Barone, T. (2007). A return to the gold standard? Questioning the future of narrative construction as educational research. *Qualitative Inquiry, 13*(4), 354–379. doi:10.1177/1077800406297667

Baumeister, R. F., & Dewall, C. M. (2005). The inner dimension of social exclusion: Intelligent thought and self-regulation among rejected persons. In K. D. Williams, J. P. Forgas, & W. von Hippel (Eds.), *The social outcast: Ostracism, social exclusion, rejection, and bullying* (pp. 53–73). New York, NY: Psychology Press.

Boje, D. (2008). *Storytelling organizations*. London: Sage Publications.

Brown, A. D., & Humphreys, M. (2006). Organizational identity and place: A discursive exploration of hegemony and resistance. *Journal of Management Studies*, *43*(2), 231–257. doi:10.1111/j.1467-6486.2006.00589.x

Caine, V., Murphy, M. S., Estefan, A., Clandinin, D. J., Steeves, P., & Huber, J. (2017). Exploring the purposes of fictionalization in narrative inquiry. *Qualitative Inquiry*, *23*(3), 215–221. doi:10.1177/1077800416643997

Caponecchia, C., & Wyatt, A. (2012). *Preventing workplace bullying: An evidence-based guide for managers and employees*. London, UK: Routledge Taylor & Francis Group.

Chakraborty, S. (2017). Using narratives in creativity research: Handling the subjective nature of creative process. *Qualitative Report*, *22*(11), 2959–2973.

Clair, R. P. (1998). *Organizing silence: A world of possibilities*. Albany, NY: State University of New York Press.

Clandinin, D. J., & Connelly, F. M. (1995). *Teachers' professional knowledge landscapes*. New York: Teachers College Press.

Clandinin, D. J., & Rosiek, J. (2007). Mapping a landscape of narrative inquiry: Borderland spaces and tensions. In D. J. Clandinin (Ed.), *Handbook of narrative inquiry: Mapping a methodology* (pp. 35–75). Thousand Oaks, CA: SAGE. doi:10.4135/9781452226552.n2

Dwyer, W. (1991). Humor, power, and change in organizations. *Human Relations*, *44*(1), 1–19. doi:10.1177/001872679104400101

Einarsen, S., Hoel, H., Zapf, D., & Cooper, C. L. (2011). The concept of bullying and harassment at work: The European tradition. In S. Einarsen, H. Hoel, D. Zapf, & C. L. Cooper (Eds.), *Bullying and harassment in the workplace: Developments in theory, research, and practice* (pp. 3–40). Boca Raton, FL: Taylor & Francis.

Fleming, P., & Spicer, A. (2003). Working at a cynical distance: Implications for subjectivity, power and resistance. *Organization*, *10*(1), 157–179. doi:10.1177/1350508403010001376

Gabriel, Y. (2000). *Storytelling in organizations: Facts, fictions, and fantasies*. Oxford, UK: Oxford University Press. doi:10.1093/acprof:oso/9780198290957.001.0001

Glasø, L., Nielsen, M. B., & Einarsen, S. (2009). Interpersonal problems among targets and perpetrators of workplace bullying. *Journal of Applied Social Psychology*, *39*(6), 1316–1333. doi:10.1111/j.1559-1816.2009.00483.x

Humphreys, M., & Brown, A. D. (2002). Narratives of organizational identity and identification: A case study of hegemony and resistance. *Organization Studies, 23*(3), 421–447. doi:10.1177/0170840602233005

Lakoff, G., & Johnson, M. (1980). *Metaphors we live by*. Chicago: The University of Chicago Press.

Lipinski, J., & Crothers, L. M. (Eds.). (2014). *Bullying in the workplace: Causes, symptoms, and remedies*. New York: Routledge Taylor & Francis Group.

McDonald, D. M. (2016). Examining scholarly identity through auto-fiction: A court jester's tale. *Tamara, 14*(1), 1–20.

McDonald, D. M. (in press). If I only had a brain: Scholarly identity at oddz in the world of academia. In B. Pohl & C. White (Eds.), *Social education: Narratives from the trenches*. Charlotte, NC: Information Age Publishing.

McDonald, D. M., Craig, C., Markello, C., & Kahn, M. (2016). Our academic sandbox: Scholarly identities shaped through play, tantrums, building castles, and rebuffing backyard bullies. *Qualitative Report, 21*(7), 1145–1163.

Milner, H. R. (2008). Disrupting deficit notions of difference: Counter-narratives of teachers and community in urban education. *Teaching and Teacher Education, 24*(6), 1573–1598. doi:10.1016/j.tate.2008.02.011

Nielsen, M. B., & Einarsen, S. V. (2018). What we know, what we do not know, and what we should and could have known about workplace bullying: An overview of the literature and agenda for future research. *Aggression and Violent Behavior, 42*, 71–83. doi:10.1016/j.avb.2018.06.007

Olson, M., & Craig, C. (2009). 'Small' stories and meganarratives: Accountability in balance. *Teachers College Record, 111*, 547–572.

Sargent, A. G., & Scholssberg, N. K. (1988). Managing adult transition. *Training and Development Journal*, 58–60.

Sole, D., & Wilson, D. G. (2003). Storytelling in organizations: The power and traps of using stories to share knowledge in organizations (LILA Briefing Paper). Harvard University.

Sue, C. A. (2015). Hegemony and silence: Confronting state-sponsored silences in the field. *Journal of Contemporary Ethnography, 44*(1), 113–140. doi:10.1177/0891241614540211

Tennant, M. (2005). Transforming selves. *Journal of Transformative Education, 3*(2), 102–115. doi:10.1177/1541344604273421

Warwick, R. (2016). Doubt, uncertainty and vulnerability in leadership: Using fiction to enable reflection and voice. *Tamara, 14*(4), 127–137.

Chapter 10
In the Midst of the Maelstrom:
Struggling Through the Revulsions of Academic Mobbing While Maintaining One's Ethical Compass

Caroline M. Crawford
University of Houston – Clear Lake, USA

ABSTRACT

Academic mobbing's impact upon the target and the target's professional world can throw one's world off kilter to the point that the target has difficulty maintaining a semblance of psychological and cognitive balance. This story is one target's approach towards maintaining a semblance of balance within the midst of the horrors of academic mobbing and bullying attacks. This target's ethical compass and balance are maintained through the support and guidance of outstanding colleagues, yet in more personal moments the target's sense of psychological equilibrium and emotional stability are drawn from the lifetime accumulation of quotations, lyrics, and poems that articulate one's ethical compass and steadfast psychological center.

DOI: 10.4018/978-1-5225-9485-7.ch010

INTRODUCTION

I found myself sitting in the pews of a memorial service for a faculty colleague whom I also called friend. The day was a perfect blue sky with fluffy clouds, a soothing breeze and just warm enough to bring a contented smile to the face of everyone enjoying such a lovely day in the city. I thought of the perfection of the day as I walked into her memorial service, knowing of her struggles with cancer and her grace through her battles as well as acceptance of the inevitable. The day was a perfect reflection of my friend and colleague. One song came to mind, by Nina Simone, with the specific lyric from her *Feeling Good* song:

Dragonfly out in the sun, you know what I mean, don't you know?
Butterflies all havin' fun, you know what I mean
Sleep in peace when day is done, that's what I mean
And this old world is a new world
And a bold world, for me (Simone, 1965, para. 5)

This second verse so perfectly described her grace as she walked through life, her acceptance, her strength, and so much of which I found deeply special in her soulfulness. This perfectly illustrated her legacy to me, and my memories of her.

On the drive home, I began thinking about other quotations from which I pull strength and why these quotes are so impactful to me throughout my own life's journey. Perhaps these quotations and poems reflect my own ethical compass, my own sense of integrity and depth of desire to actively respond to other's inaction in the face of injustices. The quotations always come to me during difficult times, soothing in a way that is sometimes indescribable. Perhaps, I reflect, this is why quotations of others have become so important throughout the maelstrom of academic mobbing that I've been journeying through for so many years now.

I then began thinking about the academic world in which I professionally live. The academic mobbing issues began almost as soon as I started with the institution, beginning with nasty suggestions about my personal life and rumors about which faculty colleagues were engaging in romantic trysts. There was no truth to any of it, but that didn't seem to matter; many of the same rumors continue to spread, even after a twenty year association with the institution. I was intrigued by the gossip, as the underlying suggestion was that I wasn't a capable academic and needed other ways to accomplish my professional achievements. I was naïve, to imagined that the academic mobbing would remain encapsulated and only associated with laughable gossip about my private life.

In the Midst of the Maelstrom

As the bullies slowly developed a level of comfort within the organization, having tested and learned that there would be no corrective action by administration nor by faculty colleagues viewing the attacks on what would become a continuous basis, the academic mobbing became more pronounced and directly impacting my work associated with teaching, research and service. It became so pronounced that my college dean actually wrote a contemptuously disdainful letter and placed it in my personnel file without issue or oversight, much less a date stamp that was expected of all files placed into the personnel files as procedurally mandated. This letter listed several non-documented and non-supported falsehoods with the urging to formally mandate that I attend anger management courses, and with the stated ultimate goal being to begin developing a documentation trail that would result in removal of tenure and firing from the institution. I was shocked and traumatized, that these types of falsehoods and misrepresentations of professional and personal character could be haphazardly and effortlessly inserted into formal documentation files without administrative alarm and rectification. There should be no documentation to support any of the claims in the letter, as none of the claims had ever occurred. Yet when I attempted to follow policy and formally request that the newly hired head of human resources revisit and remove the document from my personnel file, this request was rejected. My professional reputation and my personal reputation were under attack within the university, without anywhere to go for fair and impartial help. I felt revulsion by the actions of the bullies, but also revulsion by the inaction of the silent majority who watched as my professional reputation was unfairly torn apart, the gas lighting that I was constantly attempting to overcome in the work space, and the personal impact upon my cognitive and physical wellness, also including the vicarious impact upon people in my personal life.

Through the lens of quotations that are personally meaningful, while also supportive and reflective of my ethical compass, I shall journey through aspects of my academic mobbing journey. This is a difficult journey, as the maelstrom has long-term impact on both the physical and cognitive aspects of my being, but accepting a positive view of the journey as more deeply embedding and analyzing my own belief systems around what I view as *right* and *wrong* is an ethical compass and moral code exercise worthy of exploration.

BACKGROUND

Ethical leadership and healthy organizations are touted as vitally important within today's adult world of business. It is de rigueur for discussions around one's intelligence quotient (IQ), describing one's cognitive abilities, but overtaking discussions around one's IQ is a growing interest is the concept of emotional quotient (EQ), or one's self-awareness and ability to control one's emotions. I've found this to be a humorously oxymoronic, as equally impactful within today's society are discussions around organizational sickness, toxic work environments and, favored within the scholarly hallways of academia, is the reality of academic mobbing. Unless one has been involved in academia for quite a while or unhappily lands within an environment that tolerates or even supports academic mobbing, one might not realize what is occurring, either surreptitiously or directly. To better understand a holistic view of academic mobbing, Khoo describes it quite succinctly:

Academic mobbing is a non-violent, sophisticated, 'ganging up' behaviour adopted by academicians to "wear and tear" a colleague down emotionally through unjustified accusation, humiliation, general harassment and emotional abuse. These are directed at the target under a veil of lies and justifications so that they are "hidden" to others and difficult to prove. Bullies use mobbing activities to hide their own weaknesses and incompetence. Targets selected are often intelligent, innovative high achievers, with good integrity and principles. Mobbing activities appear trivial and innocuous on its own but the frequency and pattern of their occurrence over long period of time indicates an aggressive manipulation to "eliminate" the target. (Khoo, 2010, p. 61)

It's a curious world in academia, as the public face of it decries what is many times occurring behind the scenes. It's an interesting aspect of a toxic culture within an organizational structure that turns away from dealing with mistreatment amongst faculty, staff and administrative leadership. Yet this does not happen speedily. This is a slowly developing process wherein actions are not addressed and corrected, slowly growing into a cultural norm, and as new personnel are hired and enculturated into the normalcy of the toxic culture and less-than-ethical standards lower the expectations around acceptable integrity. As described by Seguin (2016):

The process begins when a small group of instigators decides to cast someone out on the pretext that he or she is threatening their interests. This concept covers a variety of cases; perhaps the target is not behaving the way they would like, does not share their view of the organization, earns more than they do or challenges questionable practices. Mobbers use negative communication as their powerful weapon of elimination. (para. 5)

In the Midst of the Maelstrom

It is unfortunate, but I have slowly begun to realize that I have been a target of outrageous and torturous academic mobbing behaviors, almost since arriving at the institution. I recognized that I worked in an unusual organization, with questionable integrity when viewed through my own moral compass, deeply repulsed and revolted by the actions of some people.

It has been a strangely curious reality to face, as my view of academia may be a bit different than many colleagues. Meaning, I believe in a work-life balance, maintaining a personal life distinctly separate and apart from my professional world. I have not found this to be true of many colleagues, who allow the professional career to overtake the personal life's necessary needs towards cognitive and physical necessities to relax, recoup and live a life separate and apart from the expectations of job responsibilities. Yes, I immensely enjoy my career and yes I enjoy the creativity and service aspect of not only adding to the knowledge base but also *passing it forward* as prior higher education faculty have done for me. But this is not my full life's ambition. Meaning, my perception is that of being of service for the greater good of humanity; not merely within the academic realm, but also in my personal life impact. Therein do I find a work-life balance.

Yet as I began trying to make sense of the nonsensical, my interest in academic mobbing grew. I saw myself in the descriptions of the targets, I realized the aggressive and passive mobbing activities were not merely other's psychological issues and inherent incompetence and ineptitude, but instead actively engaged attacks with an ultimate desire to ruin my professional reputation and career, not only ensuring my exit from the institution but also exit from academia as a profession. Albeit, this does not suggest my initial evaluations were flawed understandings. As described by Seguin (2016):

Workplace mobbing is a concerted process to get rid of an employee, who is better referred to as a "target" than a "victim" to emphasize the strategic nature of the process. The dynamic is reminiscent of Stalin's Moscow Trials: the targets are first convicted and evidence is later fabricated to justify the conviction. As sociologist of science Brian Martin put it, everything they say, are, write and do will be systematically used against them. (para. 3)

Further described by Khoo (2010):

Davenport et al. describes "mobbing" as a form of organizational pathology in which co-workers essentially "ganged up" and engaged in an ongoing rituals of humiliation, exclusion, unjustified accusations, emotional abuse and general harassment in their malicious attempt to force a targeted worker out of the workplace. It usually begins with one person who decides that he or she is threatened by a colleague and thus begins a desperate campaign that spreads through the workplace like a disease, infecting person after person with the desire to eliminate a target. (p. 62)

Davenport, Schwartz and Elliot (1999) as well as Halibur (2005) supported Khoo's (2010) explanation of academic mobbing, highlighting the insecurity and perceived threat to a person's position in the academic structure merely due to the psychological misappropriation and misplacement of one's own insecurity and possibly correct reflection of oneself as lacking, when compared to another colleague's hard work, ability and professional focus.

This is the institutional world in which my daily career was housed. Yet I was slow to recognize this academic mobbing as a concerted effort by the bullies. I was busily doing my job and living my personal life, without paying attention to the seeming growing issues wherein I was targeted. "Bullies use deception, amoral behaviour and abuse of power. A serial bully has a completely different mindset, often one that will never change except to improve their skills of manipulation, deception and evasion of accountability" (Khoo, 2012, para. 27). I began to realize that I needed help to deal with this academic bullying that was occurring from faculty colleagues through the topmost administrative leadership within the institution. I needed the support of ethical and honorable others throughout the institution, whom I'd recognized as holding integrity in high esteem and recognizing fairness and justice as inherent to all. I was not going to change the behaviors of the bullies, I was not going to successfully extinguish their seemingly rabid focus. Instead, the best that I could hope would be to connect with colleagues who were highly regarded through their inherent quality, ethical and displayed a strong moral compass. These generous and integral colleagues have brought forward solace and support, in adversarial situations that seemed ridiculous at the outset and cruelly focused upon the most significant opportunities for public impact. As well, I've found comfort and a sense of support through words of wisdom that come to me as quotations, poems and other forms of guidance. I share these words of wisdom, while framing the impact upon my attempt towards a graceful journey through life's hardships.

MORAL COMPASS THROUGH ANOTHER'S WORDS

It's a strange dichotomy that occurs in the midst of academic mobbing, that the target's cognitive abilities may diminish. The long-term stress responses over a long period of time impacts a target's brain's capacity, specifically the amygdala's capacity, due to damage from prolonged or intermittent yet continuous stressful situations. The amygdala, the part of the brain that impacts one's natural tendencies towards fight, flight, face or freeze responses, then lessens or shuts down other brain responses that will take away from the survival instinct. I found this to be true in my academic mobbing experiences, as the long-term impact of prolonged stress at my work site impacted my cognitive abilities.

I was finding it difficult to be professionally creative and analytic in my efforts, not only associated with my contractual obligations of instruction, research and publication, and even service; however, perhaps the most difficult cognitive tasks that I found difficult to comprehend and achieve were actually responses to the academic mobbing attacks. I was so shocked, so taken aback, by the ridiculousness of the claims, actions and untruths claimed by the bullies, that I had no idea how to respond. I was at a loss and literally could not analyze nor cognitively deal with the mobbing experiences. Conceptually, I was frozen. After so many years focused upon creating a viable reputation of integrity, honor and a moral academic, the bullies were attempting to tear apart the very core of my reputation and myself through "…rumours, complaints (often anonymous), conniving looks, mocking, gossip, misrepresenting facts, insinuations, hearsay, defamation, lies, secret meetings to discuss 'the case,' disparaging comments, police-like surveillance of the target's work and private life to gather 'evidence' that justifies the aggression, and so on" (Seguin, 2016, para. 6), but also "… includes unjustified accusations, manipulating or withholding information, sending menacing or hateful messages, calling purportedly friendly or disciplinary meetings, psychologically destabilizing the targets by incessantly accusing them of making mistakes, intimidation, tampering with their workstation, offering to 'help' with so-called adaptation problems, and public humiliation" (Seguin, 2016, para. 7). How could I possibly overcome these horrors while retaining a semblance of myself? I turned to the words of others, through quotations, poems, and even aspects of stories that rung true to the academic mobbing situation in which I found myself and towards reflecting a reminder of my own moral compass. This strategy reflects the positive post-it note concept that many people use as motivation and positivity (Brown & Wyatt, 2010; Garner, 2005; Glaveanu & Gillespie, 2014; Maurantonio, 2015; Ritter & Mostert, 2017; Weisenberg, 1997). How would I maintain my own integrity and moral compass, refusing to allow the bullies to succeed? I would focus upon positivity, gratitude for all the blessings in my life, and reminders of my moral compass that would see me through the academic mobbing journey. I share several of the quotations through this chapter, but I share more than mere quotes. I am sharing quotations but also reflective insights on those quotes.

Carroll's Land of Wonder and Madness

Lewis Carroll must have been thinking about the scholarly hallways of academia when he wrote this brilliant description, "There is a place like no place on earth. A land full of wonder, mystery, and danger. Some say, to survive it, you need to be as mad as a hatter" (Carroll, 1897, p. 100). Since my initial foray into doctoral studies and a graduate assistantship that saw me through five years of study, I have been curious of the academic goings-on and the reasons behind the quirkiness of the scholars. My doctoral experience was a joyous introduction to the world of academia and I looked forward to joining the tenure-track ranks of academics attempting to carve out their space amongst the creative and brilliant minds of yesterday, today and tomorrow.

Yet quirkiness shifted into a sense of cultural and organizational madness when I became a tenure-track part of the academic landscape, attempting to better understand the reasons behind why and how things happened in my newly adopted university. I began realizing that the Red Queen from Carroll's creative mind was not merely one person but an army of persons whom I began to call bullies and tyrants, due to the desire to rule by fear and cruelty:

As the Red Queen says to the Knave, "It is far better to be feared than loved." Her power is only used to increase fear—it is absurd, nonsensical, and arbitrary. Reason has no pull when cruelty rules the land, leaving madness as the means of resistance. (Callen, 2012, p. 122)

The madness of the environment became a cultural norm, baiting and shifting without reason. Lone bullies and tyrants slowly recognized strength in numbers, that grew into an academic mobbing situation in which I've languished for years.

As described by Callen, "Madness is very much nonsense, or perhaps it is un-nonsense—in any case, Alice in Wonderland is not a story of Alice's finding her way back home as it is of her becoming a 'self' through being with madness" (2012, p. 120). This comprehension around better understanding myself, my own professional abilities and personal cognitive and emotional strengths, amongst and within the academic mobbing brutality and malice is a worthy message. This has been an odyssey-laden account of a scholarly journey through the absurdity of academic mobbing, inclusive of a personalized professional sense of cognitive vulnerability that may appear on first glance to be a sense of madness, while in actuality my continued focus upon my own scholarly profession suggests a public and private resistance to the phenomenon. However, what is the outcome? What reformation occurs throughout this process?

When madness is the resistance that "revalues all values, to change one's life so as to change society as a whole" (Hardt, 2010, p. 158), is acting on liberating possibilities simply a therapeutic performance creating a line of flight where the Other no longer has to fly along the periphery nor live in the borderlands? Is society reformed . . . or are individual subjects reformed? (Callen, 2012, p. 124)

I have begun realizing my own revised sense of self, more so than if I hadn't been targeted and journeyed through this most difficult university site's torturous cruelty, and developed into a stronger sense of purpose and person. I have felt like a metamorphosis has been occurring throughout this academic mobbing journey. Although torturous and cruelly difficult, the transformation of my self from a naively trusting and immature view of the world as every person being worthy of value in my life, into a completely different view of the world in which my inherent values and moral compass remain the same, but the trusting belief in other's goodness and integrity-laden expectations has been forever dulled.

A Dr. Seuss Sentiment That's Not

Dr. Seuss was an amazing author, who brought forward adult themes through the joys of children books. Yet a quote that is normally designated as offered by Dr. Seuss and has been so beloved by many cannot be traced to Dr. Seuss; indeed, he never actually uttered it as a quotation: "Why fit in when you were born to stand out?" (Luechauer & Baum, 2015). The style of Dr. Seuss, the beauty of the simplicity of truth within such a *Seuss-ian* outlook, without actual articulation of this quotation. It's okay, this is still an outstanding quotation from someone, and reaches into the depth of a person's soul. Within a sick organization, a toxic environment, so many people are treated as understanding *their place* and as I was told by more than one well-meaning person, I needed to *stay in my lane* and descend into one of many silent sheep who were expected to go along with whatever the power-position bullies wanted to accomplish. Basically, I was told to *take it* by my colleagues. Yet as I watched other colleagues, both tenured and non-tenured be treated unfairly and unethically, I could not sit by and just watch what occurred. My own moral compass, my own sense of right and wrong, would not allow me to allow others to be professionally and personally demeaned. I would not, I could not, fit in to this style of professional behavior. If this is what it meant to fit in to a group of people, then I wanted nothing to do with it. Oppression of the creative mind, oppression of the creative heart and soul, were untenable. I had to *stand out* merely so that I could end my day knowing that I attempted to do the right thing by myself and by others. So the quotation that was not actually offered by Dr. Seuss, "why fit in when you were born to stand out?", reflects my disinterest in the mediocrity in which some colleagues are willing to survive. I want to thrive, and I cannot do my best job while watching others be bullied and careers ruined by insecure and jealous coworkers. This quotation is a reminder of my life's focus upon service and upon my needs to courageously support creativity, innovation and the quirkiness of an academic's personality that allows for not only long-term hard work but also the ability to think about things differently than what others have historically accomplished.

Niemoller's Quotation

Since my years in middle school, about twelve years old, the poem by Pastor Martin Niemoller has encapsulated my belief around standing up for what is right in this world. The students in my middle school were mandated to attend a guest speaker's presentation and, although much of the presentation is long forgotten, what I still have in my possession is a sticker with Niemoller's poem:

First they came for the socialists, and I did not speak out—
Because I was not a socialist.
Then they came for the trade unionists, and I did not speak out—
Because I was not a trade unionist.
Then they came for the Jews, and I did not speak out—
Because I was not a Jew.
Then they came for me—and there was no one left to speak for me. (Coohill,
2019, para. 3)

Niemoller was a German Lutheran pastor who initially supported Hitler and the National Socialists, living in Germany and wanting Germany to return to its esteemed position in Europe. Yet slowly, Niemoller began speaking out in opposition to Hitler. As occurred during the Nazi regime, people who spoke out against Hitler were arrested and sent to a concentration camp. After surviving Dachau and liberated from the concentration camp, he returned to show his wife where he was imprisoned and what struck him was that Dachau was active from 1933-1945; he was imprisoned in 1937, but one might suggest that his poem developed from his own moral compass, as describing Niemoller's thoughts:

"Where were you from 1933 until 1937?" — a very powerful message to get from his own conscience, and this is where he obviously began to develop his idea of being responsible for rationalizing his own inaction in the face of an advancing menace. Effectively, he was asking himself how he could morally justify standing by while other groups were taken. (Coohill, 2019, para. 12)

This was important to my own moral compass, long before I may have understood the nuances of World War II and Niemoller's experience that aligned with so many others who did not survive Dachau. I could not live a life of honor and morality, if I were afraid that someday I would have the question asked of me "Where were you? Why didn't you stand up for people without a voice, people who needed help?"

What I understood from a very young age, is that a person must do the right thing. It's every person's responsibility to speak up and speak out when one views or experiences an injustice. This poem has been impactful upon my own moral compass, as it's continuously reminded me to speak up on behalf of the victim. Yet when I became the target of academic mobbing, I couldn't conceive of myself as taking on the label of a *victim*. I don't choose to view myself as a victim; instead, I viewed myself as being treated unfairly and dealing with gas lighting by co-workers and administrative leadership. It wasn't until learning about academic mobbing that I found a sense of comfort in the label of *target*.

What I have found interesting throughout this academic mobbing experience, is that so many of the people whom I've actively and publicly supported during difficult periods within the institution and gone out of my way to help advance their careers through support and guidance, quickly disappeared when I became the target of academic mobbing bullies. This has been a curious side note to the targeting experience, and has highlighted the quality of colleagues who are happily willing to take advantage of my hard work during times of prosperity but quickly disappear into the silent spectators during difficult times. Yet along with the silent spectators, I have learned of the strength of collegial bonds amongst those of high quality, integrity and honor. I have been deeply touched and surprised by the number of colleagues who have come to my assistance, supporting me throughout this academic mobbing journey. I can revise the last line of Niemoller's poem from "Then they came for me – and there was no one left to speak for me" (Coohill, 2019, para. 12) to a recognition that my own reputation as an honorable and ethical colleague who did her best to protect and represent faculty during difficult times within the university's history that, when they came for me, the honorable and ethical amongst my colleagues joined together as a representation of quality academics who would *speak for me* when my own voice eluded me and I needed support.

As a side note, General Patton's army were the first into many of the concentration camps, liberating the prisoners. My great uncle Clark Worra was color blind, as it runs in my family, so he was on the front line of Patton's army and therefore was one of the first soldiers into the camps. As my mother's family were partially German and Lutheran, they would always write to Uncle Clark to keep a lookout for Pastor Niemoller. Uncle Clark was the soldier who found Pastor Niemoller on the day of Dachau's liberation. I found it especially intriguing that this poem spoke so deeply to me about doing the right thing in life, only to find out that my own beloved Uncle Clark was a part of this history.

Garver's Restrain One's Feelings

Will L. Garver published a book by the name *Brother of the Third Degree* (Garver, 1894) with many quotations that are impactful to my own sense of life understanding. One quotation that especially calls to me is "'Control yourself,' he said, 'the wise restrain their feelings'" (Garver, 1894, p. 69). Since first reading this line of the book, it's always made me stop and think about my own fiery disposition and calls out as a reminder to restrain my own emotional responses so as to protect my psychological and physical self from extreme emotions of frustration, anger, fright, and other equally impactful emotional responses.

I've called upon this quotation several times over the years that I've dealt with academic mobbing situations, stopping myself from responding with statements that I might later regret as being too forthright or offering responses that would reward the bullies' efforts. I can openly admit that my controlled response is not perfect, but I attempt towards restraining my feelings within public venues. As the years of bullying continue, I find that this journey has strengthened my ability to contain my emotional responses more so than earlier versions of myself; however, I do find that every thought and every emotion does continue to be viewable in my facial expression. This focus upon restraining my emotional responses has significantly supported and aided my moral compass, towards sustaining non-reactionary responses to difficult situations; instead of emotional responses, I step back in grace and take in both the situation and feelings that arise, prior to a formulated analysis of the situation.

This also offers me time to articulate the situation to trusted colleagues, who in turn may offer alternate considerations and a worthy assortment of responses to the situation. Recognizing that natural human responses within precarious situations are fight, flight, face or freeze, I have restrained my natural fight response, refuse the flight option, and instead am caught in the freeze response due to the traumatic nature of academic mobbing, before progressing towards facing the latest issue. Through the support of outstanding colleagues, I am able to face the bullying through a more structured and well developed documentation of argument.

Simone's Song Lyrics

I learned of Nina Simone's talents back in 1993 while watching the movie *Point of No Return* (2019), as I was just beginning my doctoral studies. I was lost in the music, the deep and earthy voice and the song's words. Nina Simone's web site described her as:

She was one of the most extraordinary artists of the twentieth century, an icon of American music. She was the consummate musical storyteller, a griot as she would come to learn, who used her remarkable talent to create a legacy of liberation, empowerment, passion, and love through a magnificent body of works. She earned the moniker 'High Priestess of Soul' for she could weave a spell so seductive and hypnotic that the listener lost track of time and space as they became absorbed in the moment. She was who the world would come to know as Nina Simone. (The Estate of Nina Simone, 2018, para. 1)

But I was lost in the lyrics of the song *Feeling Good*, especially the refrain:

It's a new dawn
It's a new day
It's a new life for me, yeah
It's a new dawn
It's a new day
It's a new life for me, ooh
And I'm feeling good (Simone, 1965, para. 2)

I've found that this refrain seems to align with my life's journey, always looking towards tomorrow, looking towards new beginnings and new opportunities. Hearing Simone sing this poetry, the message throughout the song, spoke quite deeply to me. Meaning, each new day is an opportunity for a new life, it's an excitingly positive way to view one's life that I thoroughly embraced as my own.

This refrain has been important throughout my academic life, especially as the academic mobbing situation ramped up and became unbearable at times. This refrain was a reminder that each new day was a new opportunity, that it's my own life and my own journey, and a strong reminder towards maintaining my self and my own sense of positivity throughout the bullying experiences that were focused upon destroying my reputation and feeling my own sense of self and sense of well-being torn apart. Simply, Simone's song, with a specific focus upon this refrain from her song *Feeling Good*, offered a continuous positivity and a reminder that each new day is worthy of esteem and potentials towards positivity.

Dove's Wisdom

I learned of Dr. Pearlie C. Dove from a professional colleague who became a dear confidant and trusted friend. Dr. Dove, an esteemed academic, offered a statement of principles that is so integral to a mirror of my identity that I have it attached to my university office door as the first thing that anyone sees as they enter to converse with me, whether this be faculty, student, staff or guest, as well as have it posted on my desk as a reminder to whomever I find in my office as well as when I have difficult professional or personal decisions in front of me:

I made my decisions based on DECENCY rather than EXPEDIENCY,
I strived for EXCELLENCE rather than MEDIOCRITY,
I believe ACTIONS should mirror WORDS, and
I prefer SUBSTANCE to SUPERFICIALITY. (Moffett & Dove, 2015, p. 190)

Concepts of decency, excellence, actions and a depth of substance are guiding descriptions that I have focused upon as decision-making tools throughout my professional and personal life. These are descriptions upon which I hope that the majority of others consider when describing my reputation and my personal self. My moral compass reverberates with the truth of these guiding expectations, and when this colleague shared his newly published work about Dr. Dove's life with me, I was impressed to the point that I began researching Dr. Dove and this is where I initially discovered the beautiful statement of responsibility, quality and integrity.

The wisdom of Dr. Dove's statement was offered during her retirement years, explained in a description of her amazing career's experiences:

As she basks in her retirement years, she devotes more quality time to her family and friends, patronizing the arts, and promoting historical preservation. In a biographical sketch for the 1941 Clark College Golden Anniversary Yearbook, she cited some principles, with God's grace, that continue to guide her journey. (Moffett, Frizzell & Brown, 2015, p. 20)

After a lifelong journey of quality and experience, these principles developed into a statement that reflected the quality of this outstanding woman who made such an impact upon the lives of others. As a reflection of my own moral compass I found that Dr. Dove's words felt as if they were my own, merely more powerfully articulated. Throughout my own academic mobbing experiences, I thought so many times that it would be easier to *fall in line*, *stay in my own lane* and allow the will of bullying others to negatively impact so many high quality professional careers. During these times I fell back upon Dr. Dove's principles, recognizing that my own moral compass, my own reputation would be impacted by making decisions that were not grounded in decency, excellence, actions and substance that reflected my own choices towards quality and integrity in life.

Einstein's A Life Worth Living

Einstein offered a quotation that I've come to realize reflects my life's journey. Being of service is how I have viewed my life, not only as a past and present understanding, but also looking into my future hopes, dreams and expectations. As quoted from Albert Einstein, by William Hermanns in a 1983 publication, although the original conversation occurred in 1948, "I believe in one thing – that only a life lived for others is a life worth living" (Hermanns, 1983, p. 102). This book by Hermanns is such an interesting read, as further into the text-based description of the discussion is offered a continuing of the conversation between Hermanns, a Protestant minister and Einstein, when Hermanns shares:

Einstein clasped his hands and leaned forward. "If you mean that your conscience tells you what to do, then I agree." After a short pause, "But conscience, of course, can be manipulated. Many of the Germans who chanted 'Heil Hitler' were eager churchgoers. I agree with you, intellect never has saved the world. If we want to improve the world we cannot do it with scientific knowledge but with ideals. … We must begin with the heart of man – with his conscience – and the values of conscience can only be manifested by selfless service to mankind. (Hermanns, 1983, p. 103)

Indeed, this is an intriguing discussion around conscience, intellect and ideals, leading towards an understanding of a life lived in service towards the support and betterment of humankind and the larger world in which we live.

From a depth of understanding around understandings of a life's mission, of a life's focused journey, being of service to others is a recognition that I've carried since my youth. It was initially ingrained in me from within my very traditional family structure, as a female was raised to serve the family, but later into my years as a high school teacher working my way through my master's degree. I began to realize that the larger understanding of service was a personal calling that was meaningful to me and my life's overarching purpose, leading me to focus a life's journey within academia as a reflection of service to offer quality education and experience to my students, to my institutional colleagues, as well as to the larger profession, if even in some small way.

This understanding around being of service to others was impacted by the academic mobbing experiences that have focused bullying behaviors upon me and my efforts. As I focused my job responsibilities and efforts towards being of service to others, the bullying that I've experienced has been especially egregious as it's struck deep into the heart of who I am, what I view as my life's purpose of service to others, and my well-meaning efforts to support the positivity and forward-leaning efforts of others to be treated well and fairly through ethical conscience, intellect, and ideals.

Thucydides's Understanding of Happiness, Freedom and Courage

A favorite internet-based quotation is from Thucydides, a fifth century BC historian of the Peloponnesian War is quoted as stating, "The secret to happiness is freedom, and the secret to freedom is courage." However, translations reflect something a bit different related to happiness' alignment with freedom and an alignment with courage:

Make them your examples, and, esteeming courage to be freedom and freedom to be happiness, do not weigh too nicely the perils of war. (Jowett)

This is one of those sentences where Thucydides becomes very terse, and leaves the reader to fill in the gaps: literally, "having judged happiness freedom, freedom courage". The sense is clear: happiness depends on freedom, and freedom depends on courage. It's a popular line on the internet, in many different forms, such as "The secret of happiness is freedom, and the secret of freedom is courage" (not clear where the 'secret' comes from, unless it's the influence of self-help books promising to reveal the secrets of a happy life). (Thucydides Project, 2019, para. 15-16)

The mention of Jowett as a reference in the quotation reflects a translation from 1881 by Benjamin Jowett, towards supporting our understanding of a fifth century BC statement.

Although the sentiment is not reflective of a true quotation, the impact is similarly focused upon one's happiness being dependent upon freedom, and subsequently one's freedom being dependent upon one's courage. I have found this to be a true statement throughout my life's journey, as only through the courage to follow my own journeying path successfully led me to a sense of my own freedom in life, beyond the bounds of having a master who would control my life choices or *allowing* me to make my own life choices. This has not been an easy path to choose nor to follow, but having the courage to stand apart from other's expectations and having the freedom to make my own life choices allowed me to fall but it has also allowed me to learn and to exceed far beyond the bounds of any dream that I could have dreamt. This gives me happiness and contentment with my own understanding of who I am as one person amongst so many, to have made my own way in the world, to have followed my own ethical compass and developed an honorable reputation that I hope has allowed me the ability to positively impact others.

Yet I suggest that this quotation also has a darker side, that people who envy one's sense of courage to choose between right and wrong, who envy those who have created a life that embraces freedom to follow their own life's path, and the clarity of one's happiness and contentment with life choices, no matter the outcome of choices made. I have learned that it is deeply troubling to some people, especially within the hallowed hallways of the ivory tower, that the ability of an academic colleague to have the courage to take the uncomfortable paths in research, teaching and service, may be threatening. That the courageous colleague whose teaching, research and service outcomes may be reflective of a creativity and an innovative nature that is respected by others in the academy may be envied by others. This jealousy, this envy, tears at the heart of the lesser man who cannot conceive of choosing a courageous path, to see where it may lead. This lesser man's understanding of freedom is only through one's own silo'd grabs towards power and control, diminishing another person's freedoms. The result being the detriment to happiness, contentment, and the ability for each academic colleague to create their own journey while adding to the larger knowledge base of the profession. This is wherein I view academic mobbing's birth and arising as the maelstrom that overtakes the strength and quality of an organization's strength, weakening the foundation upon which an organization is built and recreating the organization into a toxic work space, the sickness becoming more deeply embedded within the organizational structure until rooted out by those of courage, of freedom, of integrity and of honorable intent.

Jemison's View of Limitations

Dr. Mae Carol Jemison is quoted as stating, "Never be limited by other people's limited imaginations" (AZ Quotes, n.d., para. 5), with the full quotation offered as:

Never be limited by other people's limited imaginations. If you adopt their attitudes, then the possibility won't exist because you'll have already shut it out... You can hear other people's wisdom, but you've got to re-evaluate the world for yourself. (AZ Quotes, n.d., para. 7)

Although this quotation has always resonated with me, I did not know until many years later that Jemison was the first African American female astronaut in the United States of America, on board the Space Shuttle Endeavour. Recognizing her courage, her achievements, makes this quotation even more impactful to me, as I imagine that she struggled to achieve her accomplishments in the face of significant odds. Much as many people struggle to overcome in daily lives.

I have found this quotation to impact my own professional journey, as so much of the work that I strive towards accomplishing, so many of the academic colleagues and students with whom I have the honor to work, somehow have a feeling of constraint around not only what they can accomplish, but also what I can accomplish. I sometimes share the story that I have two groups of people with whom I work. When I share an idea with one group of people, I am informed that it's a stupid idea or that it can't be done; yet, when I share the same idea with another group of people, I become excited because this group of colleagues recreates, redefines and further develops my initial ideas into something new and stronger. Meaning, some people have such limited imaginations about what can be accomplished, and perhaps these people are happily embracing the status quo; however, some people see ideas as opportunities and pulling together these creatively imaginative people into teams can accomplish something even greater as a sum of all parts. Yet from these successes and the ability to create new and innovative ideas from what most people view as the status quo is something special in each person, and I value each person who comes into my life who possesses these strengths.

From an academic mobbing standpoint, people who choose to look beyond the status quo can be very uncomfortable for others who have invested significant time and effort not only upon maintaining the status quo, but have based their striving towards power and control upon developing environments that embrace the status quo. When creative others who have the ability to see beyond others perceptions of the world and of viewed possibilities are introduced into a status quo-laden environment, the discomfort that arises is so apparent that it can be physically and cognitively felt by others. The uncomfortableness, the fear associated with new possibilities and new ways of looking at traditionally accepted understandings can become jealousies, fears and somehow shift from envy into attacks. The rise of academic mobbing is realized. Seguin (2016) describes this situation well:

The process begins when a small group of instigators decides to cast someone out on the pretext that he or she is threatening their interests. This concept covers a variety of cases; perhaps the target is not behaving the way they would like, does not share their view of the organization, earns more than they do or challenges questionable practices. Mobbers use negative communication as their powerful weapon of elimination. (para. 5)

Reflecting this understanding, I was in a state of disbelief recently, after contemplating the level of incompetence associated with one of the bullies in my midst, and the attempts to not only misguide my work expectations but also the malice and unprofessionalism associated with this person's interactions with me. I asked a colleague, "Seriously, what does this person have against me?! What's so distasteful about just doing her job & offering each person a fair evaluation?!" (personal communication, 30 May 2019). The response received was, "She is severely insecure and you threaten her very core" (Confidant A, personal communication, 30 May 2019). As a response, I offered, "It makes her look worse, to constantly **** up. I don't threaten anybody … show up, do my job, & go away" (personal communication, 30 May 2019), reflecting my attempts to lessen the academic mobbing engagement with bullies within the organization. The understanding around Jemison's quotation supports my attempts towards following my own professional path, my own ethical compass. Even though others embedded within the academic mobbing behaviors choose their bullying behaviors, I continuously attempt to focus upon positively impacting the environment in which my professional efforts occur while not focusing too much detrimental attention upon those who attempt to maintain the status quo and reflect inadequate or restrictive imaginations.

de Grellet's Passing Through Life

The Etienne de Grellet quotation emphasizes one's journey through life and how one has the opportunity to positively impact others, "I shall pass this way but once; any good that I can do or any kindness I can show to any human being; let me do it now. Let me not defer nor neglect it, for I shall not pass this way again" (Goodreads,Inc., 2019, para. 1). This is a natural belief system that I attempt to follow, since I was in elementary school and received the full poem by de Grellet and framed the poem as reflecting who I wanted to be as a developing personality. The positivity of the quotation, the focus upon grace and kindness as one walked through life's journey, even at a young age reflected my ethical compass and understanding around how one should live and touch other's lives. Throughout the different adventures and experiences as my life has unfolded, de Grellet's words have encompassed my efforts. Being a decent person, passing forward kindness and support to others as we pass through each other's lives, all touched upon my understanding of life's meaning. The longer that I am in this world, the more that I realize the impact of a momentary connection with another, a kind word or even a gentle smile, can make upon another person's life journey. I suggest that de Grellett's quotation reflects my depth of belief in a life of service towards others, aligning with my desire to positively impact others through my own academic journey, whether this be a positive impact upon my students, colleagues, the profession or the larger knowledge base. Yet with this expectation towards grace and kindness, I find that there are many people on life's journey who imagine these personal attempts towards leading a life that reflects my own ethical compass and life understanding, perceive that my efforts are reflective of a person who is easily attacked and professionally hurt.

SOLUTIONS AND RECOMMENDATIONS

Recognizing academic mobbing as a reality within higher education can be a difficult recognition for many who have not yet found themselves in the midst of the maelstrom, many other colleagues throughout the higher education milieu have found themselves in the middle of academic mobbing situations, no matter whether the academic mobbing bullies themselves, the silent majority who passively watch as the academic mobbing occurs, the colleagues who actively engage in supporting and protest this bullying treatment of the targets, or even as the target her/himself. The depth of revulsive actions by the bullies is meant to ensure the desired outcome of expulsion of the target from the institution and the profession if the bullies' efforts are fully successful. Yet, consideration towards how targets can maintain, survive and hopefully reframe their professional lives to thrive within academic mobbing situations is a difficult thing to achieve. This manuscript reflects how one target has attempted to maintain her own ethical compass amidst a tragically strategic academic mobbing environment within a toxic organizational environment. This target's efforts towards maintaining her own ethical compass, integrity and sense of personal honor have been supported by her own personalized strengths as drawn from quotations, song lyrics, poems and other forms of reminders as pertains to her personal view of self, of life's journey and of her own sense of integrity and honor when dealing with the frustrations and horrors associated with academic mobbing experiences, attempting towards living a life journey of grace, kindness and service to others. Of intrigue is an article by Stillman (2018) that suggests a reason why more kindhearted and helpful people may be negatively viewed in the workplace environment:

But if you've ever been the office sweetheart, you know that what people claim to want and how they actually behave can be completely at odds. While everyone praises kindness and cooperation, exceptionally nice people often find their good deeds met with nastiness, ridicule, exploitation, and backstabbing. Why is that?

You could conclude (not entirely without foundation) that humans are sometimes nasty, hypocritical creatures, but according to a recent Canadian study the reason our stated ideals and our real-life actions fail to match up is more complicated than that. Niceness, the research found, can actually come across as threatening. (para. 3-4)

As further described by an article that delves further into the Canadian study, Pat Barclay of the University of Guelph and an undergraduate student named Aleta Pleasant found the following intriguing outcomes of the study:

It found that cooperative behaviour attracted punishment most often in groups whose members compete with each other. This was even the case when punishing or derogating the do-gooder lessened benefits for the entire group, including the punisher.

However, without competition, cooperation increased, the study said.

Being suspicious, jealous or hostile toward those who seem better or nicer or holier than us appears to run deep in the psychological makeup of humans, Barclay said. (American Association for the Advancement of Science, 2018, para. 7-9)

The natural inclination is towards *fighting fire with fire*, but in actually what does this accomplish? Rescinding one's own sense of right and wrong, one's own ethical compass, does nothing but further impact the target's sense of revulsion; however, the frustration, anger, angst and revulsion then turns inward, as the target departs from one's own ethical compass and takes on the lower qualities and traits of the bullies. The reality of the professional world in which we all live is a humanist understanding, wherein different people are living different perceptions of life. Some people look towards the greater good, highlighted by ethics, honor, kindness and service towards other; yet there are others who live in a jealous and hostile world in which lesser qualities of "nastiness, ridicule, exploitation, and backstabbing" (Stillman, 2018, para. 3) reflects their own internal status quo.

FUTURE RESEARCH DIRECTIONS

A developing understanding around the impact of academic mobbing upon not only the academic institution as an organizational entity, including the faculty and staff who are involved in academic mobbing behaviors, but a future research direction towards studying the impact of academic mobbing upon the students is an important next step in the progression of academic mobbing research. Another future research direction of intrigue is the organizational power shifts that occur due to the academic mobbing embedding within the university, looking at program-level, department-level and college-level academic mobbing impacts, while also looking at the upper administrative leadership impact that more fully impacts the organization and articulates a skewed understanding of an organization's mission, vision and values that may offer a more long-term structural concern.

CONCLUSION

Considering the terror achieved by bullies during academic mobbing experiences, it is difficult for a target to maintain a semblance of psychological and emotional balance, as well as cognitive engagement in the processes of the every day work environment expectations but especially through a need to document and explain the bullying maelstrom of misguided trauma and attacks to others who find the depth of revulsion associated with such unfounded and nonsensical, outrageously chilling attacks beyond the realm of possibility. As suggested by Seguin (2016), the bullies begin with whispers, intimations and gossipy rumors described as different forms of negative communications, yet:

The other side of negative communication is directed at the target and includes unjustified accusations, manipulating or withholding information, sending menacing or hateful messages, calling purportedly friendly or disciplinary meetings, psychologically destabilizing the targets by incessantly accusing them of making mistakes, intimidation, tampering with their workstation, offering to "help" with so-called adaptation problems, and public humiliation. (para. 7)

This academic mobbing becomes a form of gas lighting the target. The persons not involved in the bullying behaviors find these types of bullying behaviors difficult to understand, as academics are so busy achieving teaching, research and service recognition that the conception colleagues are focusing so much time, effort and strategic planning towards attacking a colleague at first appears ridiculous and revulsive. It takes time for others within the organization to begin recognizing the bullying is actually occurring, as the preponderance of evidence needs to arise for scholars to begin making the connections between initial concerns and the revulsive maelstrom that is academic mobbing. Throughout the initial months or years that the academic mobbing ramps up against the target, how does the target retain their own sense of balance? How does the target retain their own ethical compass and grounding, so as to not join the bullies in their unethical, cruel and horrific efforts? This author suggests maintaining one's ethical compass throughout the academic mobbing experiences through the positivity and grounding of meaningful quotations, poems, lyrics and other forms of reminders that emphasize the foundation of meaning upon which a person lives a life of meaning.

REFERENCES

American Association for the Advancement of Science (AAAS). (2018, July 20). People love to hate on do-gooders, especially at work. *EurekAlert!* Retrieved from https://eurekalert.org/pub_releases/2018-07/uog-plt072018.php

Brown, T., & Wyatt, J. (2010). Design thinking for social innovation. *Development Outreach*, *12*(1), 29–43. doi:10.1596/1020-797X_12_1_29

Callen, J. C. (2012). Impossible things: An investigation of madness as resistance in Tim Burton's *Alice in Wonderland*. *Administrative Theory & Praxis*, *34*(1), 120–124. doi:10.2753/ATP1084-1806340108

Carroll, L. (1897). *Alice's Adventures in Wonderland*. London: Macmillan.

Coohill, J. (2019). Martin Niemoller, "First They Came…" – quote or no quote? *Professor Buzzkill*. Retrieved from http://professorbuzzkill.com/niemoller-first-they-came/

Davenport, N. Z., Schwartz, R. D., & Elliot, G. P. (1999). *Emotional Abuse in the American Workplace*. Collins, IA: Civil Society Publishing.

Garner, R. (2005). Post-It® note persuasion: A sticky influence. *Journal of Consumer Psychology*, *15*(3), 230–237. doi:10.120715327663jcp1503_8

Garver, W. L. (1894). *Brother of the Third Degree*. Retrieved from https://www.sacred-texts.com/sro/botd/botd06.htm

Glaveanu, V. P., & Gillespie, A. (2014). Creativity out of difference: Theorising the semiotic, social and temporal origin of creative acts. In *Rethinking Creativity* (pp. 25–39). Routledge. doi:10.4324/9781315866949

Goodreads, Inc. (2019). Etienne de Grellet. *Goodreads*. Retrieved from https://www.goodreads.com/quotes/7502834-i-shall-pass-this-way-but-once-any-good-that

Halbur, K. (2005). Bullying in the academic workplace. *Academic Leader, 2*(11), 3-7.

Hardt, M. (2010). Militant life. *New Left Review, 64*, 151–160.

Hermanns, W. (1983). Einstein and the Poet. In *Search of the Cosmic Man*. Wellesley, MA: Branden Publishing Company.

Khoo, S. B. (2010). Academic mobbing: Hidden health hazard at workplace. *Malaysian Family Physician, 5*(2), 61-67. Retrieved from https://www.ncbi.nlm.nih.gov/pmc/articles/PMC4170397/

Luechauer, D., & Baum, N. (2015). Oh, the places you may go-just follow Dr. Seuss. *The Journal of Medical Practice Management: MPM, 30*(5), 341–344. PMID:26062332

Maurantonio, N. (2015). Material rhetoric, public memory, and the post-it note. *The Southern Communication Journal, 80*(2), 83–101. doi:10.1080/1041794X.2015.1011344

Moffett, N. L., & Dove, C. A. (Eds.). (2015). *Pearls of Wisdom from a woman of Color, Courage and Commitment: Pearlie Craft Dove*. Bloomington, IN: Xlibris.

Moffett, N. L., Frizzell, M. M., & Brown, D. C. (2015). Exemplar of pearls of wisdom for the academy. In M. Y. Zhou (Ed.), *Supporting ulticulturalism and Gender Diversity in University Settings* (pp. 1–22). Hershey, PA: Information Science Reference (an imprint of IGI Global). doi:10.4018/978-1-4666-8321-1.ch001

Point of No Return. (2019). In *IMDb.com Inc. online*. Retrieved from https://www.imdb.com/title/tt0107843/

Quotes, A. Z. (n.d.). *Mae Jemison Quotes*. Retrieved from https://www.azquotes.com/author/19683-Mae_Jemison

Ritter, S. M., & Mostert, N. (2017). Enhancement of creative thinking skills using a cognitive-based creativity training. *Journal of Cognitive Enhancement, 1*(3), 243–253. doi:10.100741465-016-0002-3

Seguin, E. (2016, September 19). Academic mobbing, or how to become campus tormentors. *University Affairs*. Retrieved from https://www.universityaffairs.ca/opinion/in-my-opinion/academic-mobbing-become-campus-tormentors/

Simone, N. (1965). *Feeling Good Lyrics*. Santa Monica, CA: UMG Recordings, Inc. Retrieved from https://genius.com/Nina-simone-feeling-good-lyrics

Stillman, J. (2018). Why being nice at work can backfire badly, according to psychology. *Inc*. Retrieved from https://www.inc.com/bill-murphy-jr/amazon-google-just-got-some-very-distressing-news.html

The Estate of Nina Simone. (2018). *Bio*. Retrieved from http://www.ninasimone.com/bio/

Thucydides Project. (2019). *11.43: Text and Translation*. University of Bristol, Department of Classics and Ancient History. Retrieved from http://www.bristol.ac.uk/classics/research/thucydides/ttt/text/

Weisenberg, R. C. (1997). Appropriate technology for the classroom--Using" Post-It Notes" as an active learning tool. *Journal of College Science Teaching*, 26(5), 339.

ADDITIONAL READING

Lutgen-Sandvik, P. (2013). *Adult Bullying—A Nasty Piece of Work: Translating a Decade of Research on Non-Sexual Harassment, Psychological Terror, Mobbing, and Emotional Abuse on the Job*. St. Louis, MO: ORCM Academic Press.

Pheko, M. M. (2018a). Autoethnography and cognitive adaptation: Two powerful buffers against the negative consequences of workplace bullying and academic mobbing. *International Journal of Qualitative Studies on Health and Well-being*, *13*(1), 1459134. doi:10.1080/17482631.2018.1459134 PMID:29667923

Pheko, M. M. (2018b). Rumors and gossip as tools of social undermining and social dominance in workplace bullying and mobbing practices: A closer look at perceived perpetrator motives. *Journal of Human Behavior in the Social Environment*, 1–17.

Towler, J. (2011). *Chaos and Academic Mobbing – The True Story of The Renison Affair*. Self-Published.

Westhues, K. (2005). *The Pope Versus the Professor: Benedict XVI and the Legitimation of Mobbing*. Edwin Mellen Press.

Westhues, K. (Ed.). (2006). *The Remedy and Prevention of Mobbing in Higher Education: Two Case Studies*. Lewiston, NY: The Edwin Mellen Press.

Wylie, P. (2018). My Campus Administration, Faculty Association and Me: Academic Mobbing and Sweetheart Unionism. *Workplace: A Journal for Academic Labor*, (31).

Yaman, E. (2010, Winter). Perception of faculty members exposed to mobbing about the organizational culture and climate. *Educational Sciences: Theory and Practice*, *10*(1), 567–578. Retrieved from https://files.eric.ed.gov/fulltext/EJ882735.pdf

KEY TERMS AND DEFINITIONS

Academic Mobbing: A style of individual harassment and attack upon a specific person, normally occurring by a group of people labeled as bullies, upon one specific person within the workplace referred to as a victim.

Bully: This label is given to each person who is actively engaged in attacking the target of academic mobbing.

Bullying Attack: This term is a label associated with each instance of a larger academic mobbing experience, strategically engaged in by bullies and focused upon a specific target.

Emotional Stability: This term focuses upon the need of the target to remain grounded and balanced, suggesting attempts towards retaining a calm disposition and recognition that the gas lighting events occurring are not a true reflection of the target nor of the target's reputation, during bulling attacks during academic mobbing experiences.

Ethical Compass: This is a term that refers to a person's sense of personal knowledge and assurance, perhaps described as one's core understanding and belief in oneself, in the midst of confusingly frustrated and bizarre or inexplicable events.

Maelstrom: Is defined within this discussion as a confusing and tumultuous situation that does not make sense from an inside viewpoint nor an external audience experience.

Psychological Center: The ability of a person to maintain a focused understanding of one's own behavior and one's own personality, continuously assessing the external occurrences against one's own knowledge of self.

Psychological Equilibrium: The ability of a person to maintain a balanced understanding related to external and internal dichotomies that may impact thought, behavior and attitude.

Silent Majority: This term refers to the persons who watch as academic mobbing occurs, yet who choose to remain quiet while the bullying and revulsive attacks occur, but who are not one of the bullies nor the target but who are equally culpable due to the choices made to not correct bullying behaviors based upon the fear of becoming a target oneself.

Target: This person is the focus of the bullying behaviors throughout the academic mobbing experiences.

Compilation of References

A Toxic Culture. (2016). *Internal Auditor*, 21-23. Retrieved from https://www.iia.nl /SiteFiles/IA/ia201612-dl.pdf

Adams, G. B. (2011). The problem of administrative evil in a culture of technical rationality. *Public Integrity, 13*, 275-285. doi:10.2753PIN1099-9922130307

Adams, G. B., & Balfour, D. L. (2009). *Unmasking administrative evil* (3rd ed.). Armonk, NY: M. E. Sharpe.

Aesop's Fables. (2011). *Online collection*. Retrieved from http://www.aesopfables.com /aesop4.html

Aldag, R. J., & Joseph, B. (2000). *Leadership and vision: 25 keys to motivation*. New York, NY: Lebhar-Friedman Books.

American Association for the Advancement of Science (AAAS). (2018, July 20). People love to hate on do-gooders, especially at work. *EurekAlert!* Retrieved from https://eurekalert.org/pub_releases/2018-07/uog-plt072018.php

American Association of University Professors. (2015a). *Ensuring academic freedom in politically controversial academic personnel decisions*. In AAUP policy documents and reports (pp. 32–36). Baltimore, MD: Johns Hopkins Press.

American Association of University Professors. (2015b). *On collegiality as a criterion for faculty evaluation: 2016 revision*. In AAUP policy documents and reports (pp. 227–228). Baltimore, MD: Johns Hopkins Press.

American Association of University Professors. (2015c). *On the relationship of faculty governance to academic freedom*. In AAUP policy documents and reports (pp. 123–125). Baltimore, MD: Johns Hopkins Press.

Andersson, L., & Pearson, C. (1999). Tit for tat? The spiraling effect of incivility in the workplace. *Academy of Management Review, 24*(3), 452–471. doi:10.5465/amr.1999.2202131

Appelbaum, S. H., & Girard, D. R. (2007). Toxins in the workplace: Affect on organizations and employees. *Corporate Governance, 7*(1), 17–28. doi:10.1108/14720700710727087

Arendt, H. (1963). *Eichmann in Jerusalem: A report on the banality of evil*. New York, NY: Viking Press.

Arendt, H. (1978). *The Jew as pariah - Jewish identity and politics in the modern age*. New York, NY: Grove Press.

Armstrong, J. (2012). Faculty animosity: A contextual view. *Journal of Thought, 47*(2), 85–104. doi:10.2307/jthought.47.2.85

Balthazard, P. A., Cooke, R. A., & Potter, R. E. (2006). Dysfunctional culture, dysfunctional organization: Capturing the behavioral norms that form organizational culture and drive performance. *Journal of Managerial Psychology, 21*(8), 709–732. doi:10.1108/02683940610713253

Bandura, A. (1973). *Aggression: A social learning analysis*. Englewood Cliffs, NJ: Prentice Hall.

Bandura, A. (1990). Mechanisms of moral disengagement. In W. Reich (Ed.), *Origins of terrorism: Psychologies, ideologies, theologies, states of mind* (pp. 161–191). Cambridge, UK: Cambridge University Press.

Banks, M. (1965). *How to live with yourself*. Sorrento, FL: Murmill Associates.

Barber, C. M., & Hamas, S. H. (2009). The media harassment of public figures from the ethical perspective of Madrid journalists. *Latin Magazine of Social Communication, 64*, 880–893. doi:10.4185/RLCS-64-2009-868-880-893

Barbuto, J., & Wheeler, D. (2007, October). Becoming a servant leader: Do you have what it takes? *NetGuide, 2000*. Retrieved November 1, 2014, from http://www.ianrpubs.unl.edu/epublic/live/g1481/build/g1481.pdf

Barone, T. (2007). A return to the gold standard? Questioning the future of narrative construction as educational research. *Qualitative Inquiry, 13*(4), 354–379. doi:10.1177/1077800406297667

Baron, R. (1996). Interpersonal relations in organizations. In K. Murphy (Ed.), *Individual differences* (pp. 334–370). San Francisco, CA: Jossey Bass.

Barrett-Pugh, L. G. B., & Krestelica, D. (2018). Bullying in higher education: Culture change requires more than policy. *Perspectives: Policy and Practice in Higher Education*. doi:10.1080/13603108.2018.1502211

Baumeister, R. F., & Dewall, C. M. (2005). The inner dimension of social exclusion: Intelligent thought and self-regulation among rejected persons. In K. D. Williams, J. P. Forgas, & W. von Hippel (Eds.), *The social outcast: Ostracism, social exclusion, rejection, and bullying* (pp. 53–73). New York, NY: Psychology Press.

Beckmann, C. A., Cannella, B. L., & Wantland, D. (2013). Faculty perception of bullying in schools of nursing. *Journal of Professional Nursing, 29*(5), 287–294. doi:10.1016/j.profnurs.2012.05.012 PMID:24075262

Compilation of References

Behr, R. (2010, September 21). Almost everything you know is wrong: Review of Being wrong: Adventures in the margin of error. *The Observer*.

Bergloff, L. M. (2014). *Correlation between self-reporting of exposure to workplace bullying behaviors and self-reporting of symptoms of anxiety and depression* (Doctoral dissertation). Available from ProQuest Dissertations and Theses database. (UMI No. 3708845)

Berraies, S., Chaher, M., & Ben Yahia, K. (2014). Employee empowerment and its importance for trust, innovation, and organizational performance. *Business Management and Strategy, 5*(2). Retrieved from https://pdfs.semanticscholar.org/3942/e29369ff7e50dc18c5fe0e26c1c1d43e46d6.pdf

Blau, G., & Andersson, L. (2005). Testing a measure of instigated workplace incivility. *Journal of Occupational and Organizational Psychology, 78*(4), 595–614. doi:10.1348/096317905X26822

Boddy, C. R. (2017). Psychopathic leadership: A case study of a corporate psychopath CEO. *Journal of Business Ethics, 145*(1), 141–156. doi:10.100710551-015-2908-6

Boje, D. (2008). *Storytelling organizations*. London: Sage Publications.

Bolman, L. G., & Deal, T. E. (2003). *Reframing organizations: Artistry, choice, and leadership* (3rd ed.). San Francisco, CA: Jossey Bass.

Bolman, L. G., & Deal, T. E. (2009). Battles and beliefs: Rethinking the roles of today's leaders. *Leadership in Action, 29*(5), 14–18. doi:10.1002/lia.1306

Borgatta, E. F., Bales, R. F., & Couch, A. S. (1954). Some findings relevant to the great man theory of leadership. *American Sociological Review, 19*(6), 755–759. doi:10.2307/2087923

Bourne, P. A. (2016). Leadership as a service: A new model for higher education in a new century. *Review of Public Administration and Management, 4*(3), 196. doi:-7844.1000196 doi:10.4172/2315

Bowman, J. S., & Wittmer, D. L. (2000). The unfashionable Drucker: Ethical and quality chic. *Journal of Management History, 6*(1), 13–29. doi:10.1108/13552520010316592

Branch, S., Ramsay, S., & Barker, M. (2013). Workplace bullying, mobbing and general harassment: A review. *International Journal of Management Reviews, 15*(3), 280–299. doi:10.1111/j.1468-2370.2012.00339.x

Braun, S., Aydin, N., Frey, D., & Peus, C. (2016). Leader narcissism predicts malicious envy and supervisor-targeted counterproductive work behavior: Evidence from field and experimental research. *Journal of Business Ethics*. http://dx.doi.org. ezproxylocal.library.nova.edu/10.1007/s10551-016-3224-5

Brodsky, C. M. (1976). *The harassed worker*. Toronto, Canada: Lexington Books.

Brown, A. D., & Humphreys, M. (2006). Organizational identity and place: A discursive exploration of hegemony and resistance. *Journal of Management Studies, 43*(2), 231–257. doi:10.1111/j.1467-6486.2006.00589.x

Brown, F., & Moshavi, D. (2002). Herding academic cats: Faculty reactions to transformational and contingent reward leadership by department chairs. *The Journal of Leadership Studies, 8*(3), 79–93. doi:10.1177/107179190200800307

Brown, T., & Wyatt, J. (2010). Design thinking for social innovation. *Development Outreach, 12*(1), 29–43. doi:10.1596/1020-797X_12_1_29

Burke, T. (2012). *Report of the Special Investigative Counsel Regarding the Actions of The Pennsylvania State University Related to the Child Sexual Abuse Committed by Gerald A. Sanduksy.* Retrieved from https://www.scribd.com/document/99901850/Freeh-Report-of-the-Actions-of-Penn-State-University?ad_group=33330X911648Xa7c6ee68af263f4e6d6fe721c2d688f3&campaign=SkimbitLtd&keyword=660149026&medium=affiliate&source=hp_affiliate

Caine, V., Murphy, M. S., Estefan, A., Clandinin, D. J., Steeves, P., & Huber, J. (2017). Exploring the purposes of fictionalization in narrative inquiry. *Qualitative Inquiry, 23*(3), 215–221. doi:10.1177/1077800416643997

Callen, J. C. (2012). Impossible things: An investigation of madness as resistance in Tim Burton's *Alice in Wonderland. Administrative Theory & Praxis, 34*(1), 120–124. doi:10.2753/ATP1084-1806340108

Campbell, W. K., Hoffman, B. J., Campbell, S. M., & Marchisio, G. (2011). Narcissism in organizational contexts. *Human Resource Management Review, 21,* 268–284. Retrieved from www.wkeithcampbell.com/wp-content/uploads/2013/08/CampbellHRMR2011.pdf

Caponecchia, C., & Wyatt, A. (2012). *Preventing workplace bullying: An evidence-based guide for managers and employees.* London, UK: Routledge Taylor & Francis Group.

Carroll, L. (1897). *Alice's Adventures in Wonderland.* London: Macmillan.

Catley, B., Blackwood, K., Forsyth, D., Tappin, D., & Bentley, T. (2017). Workplace bullying complaints: Lessons for "good HR practice.". *Personnel Review, 46*(1), 100–114. doi:10.1108/PR-04-2015-0107

Cawthon, D. L. (1996). Leadership: The great man theory revisited. *Business Horizons,* 1–4.

Centers for Disease Control and Prevention. (2012). *Principles of Epidemiology in Public Health Practice.* Retrieved from https://www.cdc.gov/ophss/csels/dsepd/ss1978/SS1978.pdf

Chakraborty, S. (2017). Using narratives in creativity research: Handling the subjective nature of creative process. *Qualitative Report, 22*(11), 2959–2973.

Chaleff, I. (2003). *The courageous follower: Standing up to and for our leaders.* San Francisco, CA: Berrett-Koehler.

Chamberlain, L. J., & Hodson, R. (2010). Toxic work environments: What helps and what hurts. *Sociological Perspectives, 53*(4), 455-477. doi:10.1525op.2010.53.4.455

Chave, S. (1958). Henry Whitehead and cholera in Broad Street. *Medical History*, *2*(2), 92–108. doi:10.1017/S0025727300023504 PMID:13526540

Cherry, K. (2018). *Understanding social exchange theory in psychology: How it influences relationships*. Retrieved from https://www.verywellmind.com/what-is-social-exchange-theory-2795882

Chin, J. L., & Trimble, J. E. (2015). *Diversity and leadership*. Los Angeles, CA: Sage.

Chua, S. M. Y., & Murray, D. W. (2015). How toxic leaders are perceived: Gender and information-processing. *Leadership and Organization Development Journal*, *36*(3), 292–307. doi:10.1108/LODJ-06-2013-0076

Çividilağ, A., & Sargin, N. (2013). Academics' Mobbing and Job Satisfaction Levels. *Online Journal of Counseling & Education, 2*(2).

Clair, R. P. (1998). *Organizing silence: A world of possibilities*. Albany, NY: State University of New York Press.

Clandinin, D. J., & Connelly, F. M. (1995). *Teachers' professional knowledge landscapes*. New York: Teachers College Press.

Clandinin, D. J., & Rosiek, J. (2007). Mapping a landscape of narrative inquiry: Borderland spaces and tensions. In D. J. Clandinin (Ed.), *Handbook of narrative inquiry: Mapping a methodology* (pp. 35–75). Thousand Oaks, CA: SAGE. doi:10.4135/9781452226552.n2

Clarke, A., & Erickson, G. (2003). Teacher inquiry: A defining feature of professional practice. In A. Clarke & G. Erickson (Eds.), *Teacher inquiry: Living the research in everyday practice* (pp. 1–6). London, UK: Routledge Palmer. doi:10.4324/9780203417669

Coohill, J. (2019). Martin Niemoller, "First They Came…" – quote or no quote? *Professor Buzzkill*. Retrieved from http://professorbuzzkill.com/niemoller-first-they-came/

Corsi-Bunker, A. (n.d.). *Guide to the education system in the United States*. Retrieved from https://isss.umn.edu/publications/USEducation/2.pdf

Cortés, M. T. (2012). *Metodología de la investigación*. Trillas.

Cortina, L. M., Magley, V. J., Williams, J. H., & Langhout, R. D. (2001). Incivility in the workplace: Incidence and impact. *Journal of Occupational Health Psychology*, *6*(1), 64–80. doi:10.1037/1076-8998.6.1.64 PMID:11199258

Costello, M. (2016). *After election day, the Trump effect: The impact of the 2016 presidential election on our nation's schools*. Montgomery, AL: Southern Poverty Law Center.

Covey, S. M. R. (2010). How can workplace learning and performance professionals instill trust in an organization's leaders? *T+D, 64*(10), 10-11.

Covey, S. R. (1989). *The 7 habits of highly effective people*. New York, NY: Simon and Schuster.

Cox Media Group. (2018). *A timeline of how the Atlanta school cheating scandal unfolded.* Retrieved from https://www.ajc.com/news/timeline-how-the-atlanta-school-cheating-scandal-unfolded/jn4vTk7GZUQoQRJTVR7UHK/

Cox, T. D. (2015). Adult education philosophy: The case of self-directed learning strategies in graduate teaching. *Journal of Learning in Higher Education, 11*(1), 17–22.

Cran, B. (2018, March 2). The academic mob and its fatal toll. *Quillette.*

Creswell, J. W. (2013). *Qualitative inquiry and research design: Choosing among five approaches* (3rd ed.). Thousand Oaks, CA: Sage Publications.

Creswell, J. W. (2014). *Research design: Qualitative, quantitative, and mixed methods approaches.* Thousand Oaks, CA: Sage Publications.

Crippen, C. (2010). Serve, teach, and lead: It's all about relationships. *A Journal of Scholarly Teaching, 5,* 27-36. Retrieved from https://eric.ed.gov/?id=EJ902861

Çubukcu, Z., Girmen, P., & Donmez, A. (2015). The investigation of mobbing events taking place at higher education institutions in Turkey considering the reflections on media. *Practice and Theory in Systems of Education, 10*(3), 245–256. doi:10.1515/ptse-2015-0022

Daft, R. L. (1991). *Management* (7th ed.). Chicago, IL: The Dryden Press.

Damasio, A. (2005). *En busca de Spinoza. Neurobiología de la emoción y los sentimientos.* Barcelona: Crítica.

Darling, N. (2007). Ecological systems theory: The person in the center of the circles. *Research in Human Development, 4*(3), 203–217. doi:10.1080/15427600701663023

Davenport, N. (2013). *Hannah Arendt: Battling the banality of evil.* Retrieved from https://www.spiked-online.com/2013/10/07/hannah-arendt-battling-the-banality-of-evil/

Davenport, N. Z., Schwartz, R. D., & Elliot, G. P. (1999). *Emotional Abuse in the American Workplace.* Collins, IA: Civil Society Publishing.

Davenport, N., Schwartz, R. D., & Elliott, G. P. (2005). *Mobbing: Emotional abuse in the American Workplace.* Ames, IA: Civil Society.

Davenport, N., Schwarz, R. D., & Elliot, G. P. (2003). *Mobbing and Emotional Abuse in the American Workplace.* Civil Society Publishers.

De la Garza, E. (2011). *Trabajo no clásico, organización y acción colectiva, Tomo I.* Universidad Autónoma Metropolitana, Unidad Iztapalapa.

Dean, D. (2014). Servant leadership for higher education: Principles and practices. *Review of Higher Education, 37*(2), 274–277. doi:10.1353/rhe.2014.0010

Compilation of References

Debenedictis, G. (2017). *UConn professor was 'bullied' out of a job in CSE department*. Retrieved from http://dailycampus.com/stories/2017/12/7/uconn-professor-was-bullied-out-of-job-in-cse-department

Deming, W. E. (1986). *Out of the crisis*. Cambridge, MA: Massachusetts Institute of Technology, Center for Advanced Engineering Study.

Denison, D. R., Hart, S. L., & Kahn, J. A. (1996). From chimneys to cross-functional teams: Developing and validating a diagnostic model. *Academy of Management Journal*, *39*(4), 1005–1023.

Denzin, N. K. (1978). *Sociological methods*. New York, NY: McGraw-Hill.

Dewey, J. (1989). *Freedom and culture*. Amherst, NY: Prometheus. (Original work published 1939)

Dictionary.com. (2018). *Sweetheart contract*. Retrieved from https://www.dictionary.com/browse/sweetheart-contract

Dobbs, J. M. (2014). *The relationship between perceived toxic leadership styles, leader effectiveness, and organizational cynicism*. Available from ProQuest Dissertations and Theses database. (UMI No. 3575052)

Dobson, J. (2001). *Discussion on the effects of bullying*. Retrieved December 12, 2018, from http://www.family.org

Donovan, M., Drasgow, F., & Munson, L. (1998). The Perceptions of Fair Interpersonal Treatment Scale: Development and validation of a measure of interpersonal treatment in the workplace. *The Journal of Applied Psychology*, *83*(5), 683–692. doi:10.1037/0021-9010.83.5.683 PMID:9806012

Doty, J., & Fenlason, J. (2013). Narcissism and toxic leaders. *Military Review*, 55–60.

Drucker, P. (1998). *Managing and leadership*. Retrieved November 1, 2014 from http://web.mit.edu/mbarker/www/ideas/drucker.html

Duffy, M. (2009). Preventing workplace mobbing and bullying with effective organizational consultation, policies, and legislation. *Consulting Psychology Journal: Practice and Research*, *61*(3), 242–262. doi:10.1037/a0016578

Duffy, M., & Sperry, L. (2007). Workplace mobbing: Individual and family health consequences. *The Family Journal (Alexandria, Va.)*, *15*(4), 398–404. doi:10.1177/1066480707305069

Duffy, M., & Sperry, L. (2014). *Overcoming mobbing: A recovery guide for workplace aggression and bullying*. Oxford, UK: Oxford University Press.

Dwyer, W. (1991). Humor, power, and change in organizations. *Human Relations*, *44*(1), 1–19. doi:10.1177/001872679104400101

Einarsen, S. (1999). The nature and causes of bullying at work. *International Journal of Manpower*, *20*(1/2), 16–27. doi:10.1108/01437729910268588

Einarsen, S., Hoel, H., & Notelaers, G. (2009). Measuring exposure to bullying and harassment at work: Validity, factor structure, and psychometric properties of the Negative Acts Questionnaire-Revised. *Work and Stress, 23*(1), 24–44. doi:10.1080/02678370902815673

Einarsen, S., Hoel, H., Zapf, D., & Cooper, C. L. (2011). The concept of bullying and harassment at work: The European tradition. In S. Einarsen, H. Hoel, D. Zapf, & C. L. Cooper (Eds.), *Bullying and harassment in the workplace: Developments in theory, research, and practice* (pp. 3–40). Boca Raton, FL: Taylor & Francis.

Emamzadeh, A. (2018, September 27). *Workplace bullying: Causes, effects, and prevention: A recent article discusses and reviews causes and effects of workplace bullying.* Retrieved from https://www.psychologytoday.com/us/blog/finding-new-home/201809/workplace-bullying-causes-effects-and-prevention

Epler, D. (2014). Identify your key goals and roles. *Strategic Finance, 96*(1), 13–15.

Eriksson, M., Ghazinour, M., & Hammarström, A. (2018). Different uses of Bronfenbrenner's ecological theory in public mental health research: What is their value for guiding public mental health policy and practice? *Social Theory & Health, 16*(4), 414–433. doi:10.105741285-018-0065-6

Facebook. (2018). *Mobbable.* Retrieved from https://www.facebook.com/Mobbable/

Faria, J. R., Mixon, F. G. Jr, & Salter, S. P. (2012). An economic model of workplace mobbing in academe. *Economics of Education Review, 31*(5), 720–726. doi:10.1016/j.econedurev.2012.04.004

Farley, S., & Sprigg, C. (2014, November 3). *Culture of cruelty: Why bullying thrives in higher education.* Retrieved from https://www.theguardian.com/higher-education-network/blog/2014/nov/03/why-bullying-thrives-higher-education

Farnsworth, K. A. (2007). *Leadership as service: A new model for higher education in a new century.* Westport, CT: Praeger.

Feather, N. (1989). Attitudes toward the high achiever: The fall of the tall poppy. *Australian Journal of Psychology, 41*(3), 239–267. doi:10.1080/00049538908260088

Field, T. (2002). *Tim Fields article on abuse.* Retrieved May 28, 2002, from http://www.shadesofsorrow.net/abuse/abusearticletimfields.htm

Flaherty, C. (2017). Worse than it seems. *Inside Higher Ed.* Retrieved from https://www.insidehighered.com/news/2017/07/18/study-finds-large-share-cases-involving-faculty-harassment-graduate-students-are

Fleming, P., & Spicer, A. (2003). Working at a cynical distance: Implications for subjectivity, power and resistance. *Organization, 10*(1), 157–179. doi:10.1177/1350508403010001376

Flum, H. (2015). Relationships and career development: An integrative approach. In P. J. Hartung, M. L. Savickas, & W. B. Walsh (Eds.), *APA handbook for career intervention* (pp. 145–158). doi:10.1037/14438-009

Flynn, G. (1999). Stop toxic managers before they stop you. *Workforce*, *78*, 40–45.

Fonseca, A. P. (2014). Pathogenic versus healthy biofilms: A metaphor for academic mobbing. *Workplace*, *24*, 52–55.

Furnham, A. (2010). *The Machiavellian leader. In the elephant in the boardroom*. London, UK: Palgrave Macmillan.

Gabriel, Y. (2000). *Storytelling in organizations: Facts, fictions, and fantasies*. Oxford, UK: Oxford University Press. doi:10.1093/acprof:oso/9780198290957.001.0001

Gans, H. (1972). The positive functions of poverty. *American Journal of Sociology*, *78*(2), 275–289. doi:10.1086/225324

Gardner Gilkes Benevides, S. (2012). *Mobbing: A not so new phenomenon* (Unpublished thesis). University of Phoenix, AZ.

Garner, R. (2005). Post-It® note persuasion: A sticky influence. *Journal of Consumer Psychology*, *15*(3), 230–237. doi:10.120715327663jcp1503_8

Garver, W. L. (1894). *Brother of the Third Degree*. Retrieved from https://www.sacred-texts.com/sro/botd/botd06.htm

Gilbert, P. (2006). Evolution and depression: Issues and implications. *Psychological Medicine*, *36*(3), 287–297. doi:10.1017/S0033291705006112 PMID:16236231

Ginsberg, B. (2011). *The Fall of the Faculty: The Rise of the All-Administrative University and Why It Matters*. New York: Oxford University Press.

Gkorezis, P., Petridou, E., & Krouklidou, T. (2015). The detrimental effect of Machiavellian leadership on employees' emotional exhaustion: Organizational cynicism as a mediator. *Europe's Journal of Psychology*, *11*(4), 619–631. doi:10.5964/ejop.v11i4.988 PMID:27247681

Glasø, L., Nielsen, M. B., & Einarsen, S. (2009). Interpersonal problems among targets and perpetrators of workplace bullying. *Journal of Applied Social Psychology*, *39*(6), 1316–1333. doi:10.1111/j.1559-1816.2009.00483.x

Glaveanu, V. P., & Gillespie, A. (2014). Creativity out of difference: Theorising the semiotic, social and temporal origin of creative acts. In *Rethinking Creativity* (pp. 25–39). Routledge. doi:10.4324/9781315866949

Glendinning, P. M. (2001). Workplace bullying: Curing the cancer of the American workplace. *Public Personnel Management*, *30*(3), 269–286. doi:10.1177/009102600103000301

Goffee, R., & Jones, G. (2003). *The character of a corporation – How your company's culture can make or break your business* (2nd ed.). New York, NY: Profile Books.

Gomori, M. (2017). *The Satir approach: Essence and essentials*. Retrieved from http://www.evolutionofpsychotherapy.com/download/handouts/Maria-Gomori-Essence-and-Essentials-Satir-handout.pdf

Goodreads, Inc. (2019). Etienne de Grellet. *Goodreads*. Retrieved from https://www.goodreads.com/quotes/7502834-i-shall-pass-this-way-but-once-any-good-that

Gorlewski, J., Gorlewski, D., & Porfilio, B. J. (2014). Beyond bullies and victims: Using case story, analysis and Freirean insight to address academic mobbing. *Workplace*, *24*, 9–18.

Gould, T. (2018, May 28). *Watch out for these 8 workplace bully personality types*. Retrieved from http://www.hrmorning.com/8-workplace-bully-personality-types/

Graeff, C. L. (1997). Evolution of situational leadership theory: A critical review. *The Leadership Quarterly*, *8*(2), 153–170. doi:10.1016/S1048-9843(97)90014-X

Gray, D. E. (2014). *Doing research in the real world*. Washington, DC: Sage Publications.

Greenleaf, R. K., & Spears, L. C. (2002). Servant leadership: A journey into the nature of legitimate power and greatness (25th anniversary ed.). New York, NY: Paulist Press.

Greenleaf, R. K. (1970). *The servant as leader*. Westfield, IN: Robert K. Greenleaf Publishing Center.

Greenleaf, R. K. (2009). *The institution as servant*. Westfield, IN: Robert K. Greenleaf Publishing Center.

Grijalva, E., & Newman, D. (2015). Narcissism and counterproductive work behavior: Meta-analysis and consideration of collectivist culture, big five personality, and narcissism's facet structure. *Applied Psychology*, *64*(1), 93–126. doi:10.1111/apps.12025

Guardian News and Media Limited. (2007). *The truth about lying and laughing*. Retrieved from https://www.theguardian.com/science/2007/apr/21/weekendmagazine

Gul, H. (2009). An important psychosocial risk in occupational health: Mobbing. *TAF Preventative Medicine Bulletin*, *8*(6), 515-520. Retrieved from https://www.ejmanager.com/mnstemps/1/khb_008_06-515.pdf?t=1561405895

Gunsalus, C. K. (2006). *The College Administrator's Survival Guide*. Cambridge, MA: Harvard University Press.

Hackman, M. Z., & Johnson, C. E. (2013). *Leadership: A communication perspective* (6th ed.). Long Grove, IL: Waveland Press.

Halbur, K. (2005). Bullying in the academic workplace. *Academic Leader*, *2*(11), 3-7.

Hardt, M. (2010). Militant life. *New Left Review*, *64*, 151–160.

Harper, J. (2013, March 28). *Surviving workplace mobbing: Identify the stages*. Retrieved on January 19, 2019 from https://www.psychologytoday.com/us/blog/beyond-bullying/201303/surviving-workplace-mobbing-identify-the-stages

Harper, J. (2013). *Mobbed! What to Do When They Really Are Out to Get You*. Tacoma: Backdoor Press.

Compilation of References

Harvey, M., Heames, J. T., Richey, R. G., & Leonard, N. (2006). Bullying: From the playground to the boardroom. *Journal of Leadership & Organizational Studies*, *12*(4), 1–11. doi:10.1177/107179190601200401

Hatch, M. J. (2013). *Organization theory: Modern, symbolic and postmodern perspectives* (3rd ed.). New York, NY: Oxford University Press.

Health & Safety Executive. (n.d.). *Healthy workplace, healthy workforce, better business delivery.* Retrieved on January 21, 2019 from http://www.hse.gov.uk/pubns/misc743.pdf

Healthy Workplace Bill. (n.d.). *Healthy Workplace Bill*. Retrieved from http://healthyworkplacebill.org/

Heim, P., Murphy, S. A., & Golant, S. K. (2003). *In the company of women: Indirect aggression among women: Why we hurt each other and how to stop*. New York, NY: Penguin Group.

Hendry, P. M. (2010). Narrative as inquiry. *The Journal of Educational Research*, *103*(2), 72–80. doi:10.1080/00220670903323354

Henry, M. (1706). *Exodus* (Vol. 1). Commentary on the Whole Bible. Retrieved from https://www.ccel.org/ccel/henry/mhc1.Ex.xxi.html

Hermanns, W. (1983). Einstein and the Poet. In *Search of the Cosmic Man*. Wellesley, MA: Branden Publishing Company.

Hirigoyen, M. F. (1999). *El acoso moral en la vida cotidiana*. Barcelona: Paidós Ibérica.

Hirigoyen, M. F. (2013). *El acoso moral en el trabajo. Distinguir lo verdadero de lo falso*. Barcelona: Paidós.

History of Leadership Studies and Evolution of Leadership Theories. (2012). Retrieved from hubpages.com: http://ecoggins.hubpages.com/hub/The-History-of-Leadership-Studies-and-Evolution-of-Leadership-Theories

Hodgins, M., & McNamara, P. M. (2017). Bullying and incivility in higher education workplaces: Micropolitics and the abuse of power. *Qualitative Research in Organizations and Management*, *12*(3), 190–206. doi:10.1108/QROM-03-2017-1508

Hoel, H., & Salin, D. (2003). Organisational antecedents of workplace bullying. In S. Einarsen, D. Zapf, & C. L. Cooper (Eds.), *Bullying and Emotional Abuse in the Workplace: International Perspectives in Research and Practice*. Taylor & Francis.

Honjo, K. (2004). Social epidemiology: Definition, history, and research examples. *Environmental Health and Preventive Medicine*, *9*(5), 193–199. doi:10.1007/BF02898100 PMID:21432303

Housker, J. E., & Saiz, S. G. (2006). *Warning: Mobbing is legal, work with caution*. Retrieved on January 21, 2019 from https://www.counseling.org/resources/library/vistas/vistas06_online-only/Housker.pdf

Humphreys, M., & Brown, A. D. (2002). Narratives of organizational identity and identification: A case study of hegemony and resistance. *Organization Studies*, *23*(3), 421–447. doi:10.1177/0170840602233005

Hur, E. H., Glassman, M., & Kim, Y. (2013). Finding autonomy in activity: Development and validation of a democratic classroom survey. *Educational Assessment, Evaluation and Accountability*, *25*(4), 303–320. doi:10.100711092-013-9173-y

Ibarra, E. (2001). *La universidad en México hoy: gubernamentalidad y modernización.* Universidad Nacional Autónoma de México, Universidad Autónoma Metropolitana, Unidad Iztapalapa, Unión de Universidades de América Latina y el Caribe.

Impressum. (2018). *Anti-mobbing: Help for scientists.* Retrieved on January 21, 2019, from http://www.antimobbing.eu/introduction/index.html

Institute of Health Equity. (2019). *About Professor Sir Michael Marmot.* Retrieved from http://www.instituteofhealthequity.org/about-us/about-professor-sir-michael-marmot

Izcara, S. (2014). *Manual de investigación cualitativa.* Fontamara.

Jamal, F., Bonell, C., Harden, A., & Lorenc, T. (2015). The social ecology of girls' bullying practices: Exploratory research in two London schools. *Sociology of Health & Illness*, *37*(5), 731–744. doi:10.1111/1467-9566.12231 PMID:25655642

Jensen, J., Patel, C., & Raver, J. (2014). Is it better to be average? High and low performance as predictors of employee victimization. *The Journal of Applied Psychology*, *99*(2), 296–309. doi:10.1037/a0034822 PMID:24219126

Johnson, P. (2014). Bullying in academia up close and personal: My story. *Workplace: A Journal for Academic Labor*, *24*, 33–41.

Johnson, C. E. (2009). *Meeting the ethical challenges of leadership: Casting light or shadow.* Thousand Oaks, CA: Sage.

Joyce, W. F., McGee, V. E., & Slocum, J. W. (1997). Designing lateral organizations: An analysis of the benefits, costs, and enablers of nonhierarchical organizational forms. *Decision Sciences*, *28*(1), 1–25. doi:10.1111/j.1540-5915.1997.tb01300.x

June, A. W. (2009, June 11). *Mobbing' can damage more than careers, professors are told at conference.* Retrieved from https://www.chronicle.com/article/Mobbing-Can-Damage-More-Than/47736

Kane, S. (2018, October 21). *Who is a workplace bully's target? Defend yourself against workplace bullies.* Retrieved from https://www.thebalancecareers.com/who-is-a-workplace-bully-s-target-2164323

Keashly, L., & Neuman, J. H. (2010). Faculty experiences with bullying in higher education: Causes, consequences, and management. *Administrative Theory & Praxis*, *32*(1), 48–70. doi:10.2753/ATP1084-1806320103

Compilation of References

Kein, J., & McDermott, J. C. (2007). *Consulting with academics: Mobbing, stress and workplaces of Violence.* Paper presented at the meeting of the American Psychological Association, San Francisco, CA.

Kellerman, B. (2008). *Followership: How followers are creating change and changing leaders.* Boston, MA: Harvard Business Press.

Khoo, S. B. (2010). Academic mobbing: Hidden health hazard at workplace. *Malaysian Family Physician, 5*(2), 61-67. Retrieved from https://www.ncbi.nlm.nih.gov/pmc/articles/PMC4170397/

Khoo, S. B. (2010). Academic mobbing: Hidden health hazard at workplace. *Malaysian Family Physician, 5*(2), 61-67. Retrieved from https://www.ncbi.nlm.nih.gov/pmc/articles/PMC4170397/

Khoo, S. (2010). Academic mobbing: Hidden health hazard at the workplace. *Malaysian Family Physician, 5*(2), 61–67. PMID:25606190

Khoo, S. B. (2010). Academic mobbing hidden health hazard at workplace. *Malaysian Family Physician, 5*(2), 61–67. PMID:25606190

Khoo, S. B. (2010). Academic mobbing: Hidden health hazard at workplace. *Malaysian Family Physician, 5*, 61–67. PMID:25606190

Khoo, S. B. (2010). Academic mobbing: Hidden health hazard in the workplace. *Malaysian Family Physician, 5*, 61–67. PMID:25606190

Knight, K. (2015). *Framing responsibility for bullying: An ethnographic content analysis* (Doctoral dissertation). Available from ProQuest Dissertations and Theses database. (UMI No. 1586807)

Kostev, K., Rex, J., Waehlert, L., Hog, D., & Heilmaier, C. (2014). Risk of psychiatric and neurological diseases in patients with workplace mobbing experience in Germany: A retrospective database analysis. *German Medical Science, 12*, 1–9. PMID:24872810

Lakoff, G., & Johnson, M. (1980). *Metaphors we live by.* Chicago: The University of Chicago Press.

Lawrence, R. D. (1986). *In Praise of Wolves.* New York: Henry Holt and Company.

Lee-Chai, A. Y., & Bargh, J. A. (2001). *The use and abuse of power: Multiple perspectives on the causes of corruption.* Philadelphia, PA: Taylor & Francis Group.

Levi, D. (2010). *Group dynamics for teams* (3rd ed.). Los Angeles, CA: Sage.

Lewis, S. E., & Oxford, J. (2005). Women's experiences of workplace bullying: Changes in social relationships. *Journal of Community & Applied Social Psychology, 15*(1), 29–47. doi:10.1002/casp.807

Leymann, H., & Gustavsson, A. (1984). Psykiskt våld i arbetslivet. Två explorative undersökningar [Psychological violence at work places: Two explorative studies]. Stockholm: Arbetarskyddsstyrelsen.

Leymann, H. (1993). *Mobbing: Psychoterror am arbeitsplatz und wie man sich dagegen wehren kann* [Mobbing: Psycho-terror in the workplace and how one can defend against it]. Hamburg, Germany: Rowolht.

Leymann, H. (1996). El contenido y desarrollo del mobbing en el trabajo. *European Journal of Work and Organizational Psychology, 5*(2), 165–184. doi:10.1080/13594329608414853

Lipinski, J., & Crothers, L. M. (Eds.). (2014). *Bullying in the workplace: Causes, symptoms, and remedies*. New York: Routledge Taylor & Francis Group.

Locke, E. A. (1982). The ideas of Frederick W. Taylor: An evaluation. *Academy of Management Review, 7*(1), 14–24. doi:10.5465/amr.1982.4285427

Lorenz, K. (1963). *Das sogenannte Böse zur Naturgeschichte der Aggression*. Verlag Dr. G Borotha-Schoeler.

Lorenz, K. (2016). *Sobre la agresión. El pretendido mal*. Siglo XXI Editores.

Luechauer, D., & Baum, N. (2015). Oh, the places you may go-just follow Dr. Seuss. *The Journal of Medical Practice Management: MPM, 30*(5), 341–344. PMID:26062332

Lutgen-Sandvik, P., & Tracy, S. J. (2011). Answering five key questions about workplace bullying: How communication scholarship provides thought leadership for transforming abuse at work. *Management Communication Quarterly, 26*(1), 3–47. doi:10.1177/0893318911414400

Luther, M., & Smith, R. (1999). *Martin Luther's Small Catechism (R. Smith, Trans.)*. Project Gutenberg. (Original work published 1529)

Maestripieri, D. (2007). *Macachiavellian Intelligence: How Rhesus Macaques and Humans Have Conquered the World*. Chicago: University of Chicago Press. doi:10.7208/chicago/9780226501215.001.0001

Manz, C. C., & Sims, H. P. (1987). Leading workers to lead themselves: The external leadership of self-managing work teams. *Administrative Science Quarterly, 32*(1), 106–128. doi:10.2307/2392745

Marmot, M., & Bell, R. (2010). Challenging health inequalities-implications for the workplace. *Occupational Medicine, 60*(3), 162–164. doi:10.1093/occmed/kqq008 PMID:20423942

Marquardt, M. J. (2011). *Building the learning organization: Achieving strategic advantage through a commitment to learning* (3rd ed.). Boston, MA: Nicholas Brealey.

Marraccini, M. E. (2013). *College students' perceptions of professor bullying*. Open Access Master's Theses. Paper 9. Retrieved from https://digitalcommons.uri.edu/theses/9

Martin, J.L. & Beese, J.A. (2018). Disappearing feminists: Remaining critical voices from academe. *Forum on Public Policy Online, 1*(22). Abstract retrieved from Walden University Library Databases.

Compilation of References

Martin, B. (2012). Suppression of Dissent: What It Is and What to Do About It. *Social Medicine (Social Medicine Publication Group)*, *6*(4), 246–248. Retrieved from http://www.socialmedicine.info/index.php/socialmedicine/article/view/582/1241

Martin, B., & Pena Saint Martin, F. (2014). *Public mobbing: A phenomenon and its features*. University of Wollongong. Retrieved from http://www.bmartin.cc/pubs/14Gonzalez.html

Martin, B., & Peña, F. (2011). *Mobbing* y anulación de la disidencia / descontento: Tras las huellas de sus interrelaciones. *Medicine and Society*, *4*(4), 284–296. Retrieved from http://www.medicinasocial.info/index.php/medicinasocial/article/view/633

Martínez, M. (2006). *Ciencia y arte en la metodología cualitativa*. Trillas.

Martínez, P. C. (2006). El método de estudio de caso. Estrategia metodológica de la investigación científica. *Pensamiento y Gestión*, *20*, 165–193.

Martin, R., & Hine, D. (2005). Development and validation of the Uncivil Workplace Behavior Questionnaire. *Journal of Occupational Health Psychology*, *10*(4), 477–490. doi:10.1037/1076-8998.10.4.477 PMID:16248694

Matteson, R. W. (2002). *A qualitative study of bullying behavior in federal law enforcement: An examination of former officers perceptions regarding the problem* (Doctoral dissertation). Available from ProQuest Dissertations and Theses database. (UMI No. 3072568)

Maurantonio, N. (2015). Material rhetoric, public memory, and the post-it note. *The Southern Communication Journal*, *80*(2), 83–101. doi:10.1080/1041794X.2015.1011344

May, F. (2010). *Thesis project in management science: The power of a lollipop, from theory to action*. Retrieved from Thesis.fr: http://www.theses.fr/s90114

McDonald, D. M. (2016). Examining scholarly identity through auto-fiction: A court jester's tale. *Tamara*, *14*(1), 1–20.

McDonald, D. M. (in press). If I only had a brain: Scholarly identity at oddz in the world of academia. In B. Pohl & C. White (Eds.), *Social education: Narratives from the trenches*. Charlotte, NC: Information Age Publishing.

McDonald, D. M., Craig, C., Markello, C., & Kahn, M. (2016). Our academic sandbox: Scholarly identities shaped through play, tantrums, building castles, and rebuffing backyard bullies. *Qualitative Report*, *21*(7), 1145–1163.

McDonald, T. W., Stockton, J. D., & Landrum, R. E. (2018). Civility and Academic Freedom: Who defines the former (and how) may imperil rights to the latter. *The College Quarterly*, *21*, 1.

McDonald, T. W., Stockton, J. D., & Landrum, R. E. (2018). Civility and academic freedom: Who defines the former (and how) may imperil rights to the latter. *The College Quarterly*, *21*. Retrieved from http://collegequarterly.ca/2018-vol21-num01-winter/civility-and-academic-freedom-who-defines-the-former-and-how-may-imperil-rights-to-the-latter.html

McIlveen, P. (2008). Autoethnography as a method for reflexive research and practice in vocational psychology. *Australian Journal of Career Development, 17*(2), 13–20. doi:10.1177/103841620801700204

McKay, R., Arnold, D. H., Fratzl, J., & Thomas, R. (2008). Workplace bully-ing in academia: A Canadian study. *Employee Responsibilities and Rights Journal, 20*(2), 77–100. doi:10.100710672-008-9073-3

McKoy, Y. D. (2013). The queen bee syndrome: A violent super bee. *Journal of Nursing Care Quality, 2*(3), 200–200. doi:10.4172/2167-1168.S1.004

McWray, K. (Producer). (1974). Little House on the Prairie [Television series]. Hollywood, CA: National Broadcasting Company.

Mehta, M. (2012). Situational leadership and personal effectiveness: Managers in Indian development organizations. *Foundation for Organizational Research & Education, 30*(1), 23–34.

Meiyun, F. U., Huawei, M. A., & Guoan, Y. U. E. (2014). Bystanders in workplace bullying: Roles, behaviors, and influence mechanism. *Advances in Psychological Science, 22*(6), 987–994. doi:10.3724/SP.J.1042.2014.00987

Metzger, A. M., Petit, A., & Sieber, S. (2015). Mentoring as a way to change a culture of academic bullying and mobbing in the humanities. *Higher Education for the Future, 2*(2), 139–150. doi:10.1177/2347631115584119

Meurs, J., Fox, S., Kessler, S., & Spector, P. (2013). It's all about me: The role of narcissism in exacerbating the relationship between stressors and counterproductive work behaviour. *Work and Stress, 27*(4), 368–382. doi:10.1080/02678373.2013.849776

Meyer, C., & Schwager, A. (2007). Understanding customer experience. *Harvard Business Review, 85*(2), 116. Retrieved from http://zurichhpdelivered.com/internet/zna/SiteCollectionDocuments/en/media/FINAL%20HBR%20Understanding%20Customer%20Experience.pdf PMID:17345685

Millage, A. (2016). When toxic culture hits home. *Internal Auditor, 73*(3), 7.

Millon, T., Grossman, S., Millon, C., Meagher, S., & Ramnath, R. (2004). *Personality disorders in modern life* (2nd ed.). Hoboken, NJ: John Wiley & Sons.

Milner, H. R. (2008). Disrupting deficit notions of difference: Counter-narratives of teachers and community in urban education. *Teaching and Teacher Education, 24*(6), 1573–1598. doi:10.1016/j.tate.2008.02.011

Moffett, N. L., & Dove, C. A. (Eds.). (2015). *Pearls of Wisdom from a woman of Color, Courage and Commitment: Pearlie Craft Dove*. Bloomington, IN: Xlibris.

Moffett, N. L., Frizzell, M. M., & Brown, D. C. (2015). Exemplar of pearls of wisdom for the academy. In M. Y. Zhou (Ed.), *Supporting ulticulturalism and Gender Diversity in University Settings* (pp. 1–22). Hershey, PA: Information Science Reference (an imprint of IGI Global). doi:10.4018/978-1-4666-8321-1.ch001

Compilation of References

Morreall, J. (2012). Philosophy of humor. *The Stanford Encyclopedia of Philosophy*. Retrieved from https://plato.stanford.edu/entries/humor/

Morrison, K. (2006). *Marx, Durkheim, Weber: Formations of modern social thought* (2nd ed.). London: SAGE.

Mulvey, P. W., & Padilla, A. (2010). The environment of destructive leadership. In B. Schyns & T. Hansbrough (Eds.), *When leadership goes wrong: Destructive leadership, mistakes, and ethical failures* (pp. 49–72). Charlotte, NC: Information Age Publishing.

Murphy, S. (2016). *The optimistic workplace: Creating an environment that employees everyone*. New York, NY: American Management Association.

Nahavandi, A. (2015). *The Art and Science of Leadership* (7th ed.). Upper Saddle River, NJ: Pearson Education.

Namie & Namie. (2000). *The Bulloy at Work: What You Can Do to Stop the Hurt and Reclaim Your Dignity on the Job*. Naperville, IL: Sourcebooks, Inc.

Namie, G. (2017). *Workplace Bullying Institute U.S. Workplace Bullying Survey: September 2007 report*. Retrieved from http://workplacebullying.org/multi/pdf/WBIsurvey2007.pdf

Namie, G., & Namie, R. (2001). *Workplace bullying*. Retrieved November 15, 2018, from http://www.bullybusters.org

Namie, G., & Namie, R. (2003). *The bully at work: What you can do to stop the hurt and reclaim your dignity on the job*. Naperville, IL: Sourcebooks.

Namie, G., & Namie, R. (2011). *The bully-free workplace: Stop jerks, weasels and snakes from killing your organization*. Hoboken, NJ: John Wiley and Sons, Inc.

Nielsen, M., & Einarsen, S. (2018). What we know, what we do not know, and what we should and could have known about workplace bullying: An overview of the literature and agenda for future research. *Aggression and Violent Behavior*, *42*, 71–83. doi:10.1016/j.avb.2018.06.007

Niemann, Y. (2016). The social ecology of tokenism in higher education. *Peace Review*, *28*(4), 451–458. doi:10.1080/10402659.2016.1237098

Noll, K., & Carter, J. (1998). *Taking the bully by the horns*. Greensboro, NC: Unicorn Press.

Norton, M. S. (2005). *Executive leadership for effective administration*. Boston, MA: Pearson.

O'Boyle, E., Forsyth, D., Banks, G., & McDaniel, M. (2012). A meta-analysis of the dark triad and work behavior: A social exchange perspective. *The Journal of Applied Psychology*, *97*(3), 557–579. doi:10.1037/a0025679 PMID:22023075

O'Reilly, C. III, Doerr, B., Caldwell, D., & Chatman, J. (2013). Narcissistic CEOs and executive compensation. *The Leadership Quarterly*, *25*(2), 218–231. doi:10.1016/j.leaqua.2013.08.002

Olson, M., & Craig, C. (2009). 'Small' stories and meganarratives: Accountability in balance. *Teachers College Record, 111*, 547–572.

OMS Organización Mundial de la Salud (2002). *Informe mundial sobre la violencia y la salud: resumen*. Ginebra: Organización Mundial de la Salud.

Osborne, D. (2009). Pathways into bullying. *Proceedings of the 4th Asia Pacific Conference on Educational Integrity*. Retrieved on September 14, 2018, from http://ro.uow.edu.au/apcei/09/papers/18/

Osborne, S., & Hammond, M. S. (2017). Effective employee engagement in the workplace. *International of Journal of Applied Management in Technology, 16*(1), 50–67. doi:10.5590/IJAMT.2017.16.104

Owen, D. (2017). *The new media's role in politics*. Retrieved from https://www.bbvaopenmind.com/en/articles/the-new-media-s-role-in-politics/

Owens, B. (2016). *Liberalism or how to turn good men into whiners, weenies and wimps*. New York, NY: Post Hill Press.

Parker, K. A. (2014). The workplace bully: The ultimate silencer. *Journal of Organizational Culture, Communications, and Conflict, 18*, 169–185.

Patton, M. Q. (1999). Enhancing the quality and credibility of qualitative analysis. *HSR: Health Services Research, 34*(5), 1189–1208. PMID:10591279

Pelletier, K. L. (2012). Perceptions of and reactions to leader toxicity: Do leader-follower 184 relationships and identification with victim matter? *The Leadership Quarterly, 23*(3), 412–424. doi:10.1016/j.leaqua.2011.09.011

Peña, F., & Fernández, K. (2016). *Mobbing en la academia mexicana*. Mexico City: Ediciones y Gráficos Eón, Red PRODEP Salud Condiciones de Vida y Políticas Sociales & Escuela Nacional de Antropología e Historia.

Pérez, G. (2017). Los desafíos sociales de la democracia en México. *Estudios Políticos, 41*, 27-53. Retrieved on June 13, 2019, from http://www.scielo.org.mx/pdf/ep/n41/0185-1616-ep-41-00027.pdf

Perry, C. (2015). The dark traits of sociopathic leaders: Could they be a threat to universities? *Australian Universities Review, 57*(2), 17–25.

Petrina, A., Matheson, S., & Ross, E. W. (2015). Threat convergence: The new academic work, bullying, mobbing & freedom. *Workplace, 24*, 58–69.

Petrina, S. (2012). The new critiquette and old scholactivism: A petit critique of academic manners, managers, matters, and freedom. *Workplace, 20*, 17–63.

Compilation of References

Pettway, A., & Phillips, H. (2018). *The Teaching Tolerance social justice standards: A professional development facilitator guide*. Southern Poverty Law Center. Retrieved from https://www.tolerance.org/sites/default/files/2018-11/TT-Social-Justice-Standards-Facilitator-Guide-WEB_0.pdf

Pheko, M. M. (2018). Autoethnography and cognitive adaptation: Two powerful buffers against the negative consequences of workplace bullying and academic mobbing. *International Journal of Qualitative Studies on Health and Well-being*, *13*(1), 1–12. doi:10.1080/17482631.2018.1459134 PMID:29667923

Pheko, M. M. (2018b). Rumors and gossip as tools of social undermining and social dominance in workplace bullying and mobbing practice: A closer look at perceived perpetrator motives. *Journal of Human Behavior in the Social Environment*, *28*(4), 449–465. doi:10.1080/10911359.2017.1421111

Pilch, I., & Turska, E. (2015). Relationships between Machiavellianism, organizational culture, and workplace bullying: Emotional abuse from the target's and the perpetrator's perspective. *Journal of Business Ethics*, *128*(1), 83–93. doi:10.100710551-014-2081-3

Piñuel, I. (2001). *Mobbing. Cómo sobrevivir el acoso psicológico en el trabajo*. Santander: Editorial Sal Terrae.

Piotrowski, C., & King, C. (2016). The enigma of adult bullying in higher education: A research-based conceptual framework. *Education*, *136*, 299–306.

Point of No Return. (2019). In *IMDb.com Inc. online*. Retrieved from https://www.imdb.com/title/tt0107843/

Pollack, J. M. (2015). *Understanding how organizational leaders describe the process of workplace bullying and enable capable guardians or mediators to prevent it* (Doctoral dissertation). Available from ProQuest Dissertations and Theses database. (UMI No. 10827825)

Pompili, M., Lester, D., Innamorati, M., De Pisa, E., Iliceto, P., Puccinno, M., ... Girardi, P. (2008). Suicide risk and exposure to mobbing. *Work (Reading, Mass.)*, *31*, 237–243. PMID:18957741

Popp, J. (2017). Social intelligence and the explanation of workplace abuse. *Journal of Workplace Rights*, *77*(2), 1–7.

Porter, S. (2018). *How academic mobbing works*. Retrieved from https://stephenporter.org/how-academic-mobbing-works/

Porter, L. J., & Parker, A. J. (1993). Total quality management: The critical success factors. *Total Quality Management*, *4*(1), 13–22. doi:10.1080/09544129300000003

President and Fellows of Harvard College. (2017). *The John H. and Elisabeth A. Hobbs Professor of Cognition and Education Adjunct Professor of Psychology, Faculty of Arts and Sciences*. Retrieved from https://www.gse.harvard.edu/faculty/howard-gardner

Prevost, C., & Hunt, E. (2018). Bullying and mobbing in academe: A literature review. *European Scientific Journal*, *14*(8), 1–15. doi:10.19044/esj.2018.v14n8p1

Quotes, A. Z. (n.d.). *Mae Jemison Quotes*. Retrieved from https://www.azquotes.com/author/19683-Mae_Jemison

Reasoner, R. (2000). *The true meaning of self-esteem*. Retrieved October 31, 2018, from http://www.self-esteem-nase.org/whatisselfesteem.html

Redmond, M. V. (2015). Social exchange theory. *English Technical Reports and White Papers, 5*. Retrieved from https://lib.dr.iastate.edu/cgi/viewcontent.cgi?article=1003&context=engl_reports

Reknes, I., Einarsen, S., Knardahl, S., & Lau, B. (2014). The prospective relationship between role stressors and new cases of self-reported workplace bullying. *Scandinavian Journal of Psychology, 55*(1), 45–52. doi:10.1111jop.12092 PMID:25271332

Ritter, S. M., & Mostert, N. (2017). Enhancement of creative thinking skills using a cognitive-based creativity training. *Journal of Cognitive Enhancement, 1*(3), 243–253. doi:10.100741465-016-0002-3

Ritzer, G., & Smart, B. (2001). *Handbook of social theory*. Thousand Oaks, CA: Sage;

Rodak, M. (2018). *Richie Incognito named ambassador of anti-bullying nonprofit group*. Retrieved from http://www.espn.com/nfl/story/_/id/24090452/nfl-offensive-lineman-richie-incognito-named-ambassador-anti-bullying-organization -boo2bullying

Roscigno, V. J., Lopez, S. H., & Hodson, R. (2009). Supervisory bullying, status inequalities, and organizational context. *Social Forces, 87*(3), 1561–1581. doi:10.1353of.0.0178

Rosenbach, W. E., Taylor, R. L., & Youndt, M. A. (2012). *Contemporary issues in leadership*. Boulder, CO: Westview Press.

Ross, D. B. (2008). Historical lecture on power for advanced school policy. *Fischler College of Education: Faculty Articles*, 1-7. Retrieved from http://works.bepress .com/david-ross/29/

Ross, D. B. (2017). Eight fundamentals of power: Information for policy and leadership courses. *Fischler College of Education: Faculty Articles*, 256. Retrieved from http://works.bepress.com/david-ross/256/

Ross, D. B., Matteson, R., & Exposito, J. (2014). Servant leadership to toxic leadership: Power of influence over power of control. *Fischler College of Education: Faculty Presentations*, 1-37. Retrieved from http://nsuworks.nova.edu/fse_facpres/244

Rossbacher, L. A. (2013). From the chair of the women's network executive council. *Network News, 1*(3), 1–10.

Ross, D. B., Sasso, M. T., Matteson, C. E., & Matteson, R. W. (2019). *Narcissistic and sociopathic leadership and the world of higher education: A place for mentoring, not mobbing*. Hershey, PA: IGI Global.

Russom, A. (2009). *Teacher and administrator perceptions of bullying: Gender and occupational differences* (Unpublished doctoral dissertation). Nova Southeastern University, Davie, FL.

Ryan, R., & Deci, E. (2000). Self-Determination theory and the facilitation of intrinsic motivation, social development, and well-being. *The American Psychologist*, *55*(1), 68–79. doi:10.1037/0003-066X.55.1.68 PMID:11392867

Sahawneh, F. G., & Benuto, L. T. (2018). The relationship between instructor servant leadership behaviors and satisfaction with instructors in an online setting. *Online Learning*, *22*(1), 107–129. doi:10.24059/olj.v22i1.1066

Samier, E. (2008). The problem of passive evil in educational administration: Moral implications of doing nothing. *International Studies in Educational Administration*, *36*, 2–21.

Sapolsky, R. M. (2017). *Behave: The biology of humans at our best and worst*. New York, NY: Penguin.

Sargent, A. G., & Scholssberg, N. K. (1988). Managing adult transition. *Training and Development Journal*, 58–60.

Sasso, M. T. (2017). *How narcissists cannot hold an organization together: A mixed method approach to a fictitious puzzle factory* (Doctoral dissertation). Available from ProQuest Dissertations and Theses database. (UMI No. 10819904)

Sasso, M. T., & Ross, D. B. (2019in press). Academic entitlement and the K-20 system: The importance of implementing policies to better the education system. In J. O'Connor (Ed.), *Strategic Leadership in PK-12 Settings*. Hershey, PA: IGI Global.

Satir, V. (1988). *The new people making*. Mountain View, CA: Science & Behavior Books.

Schefter, A., & Walker, J. (2014, February 15). *Incognito, others tormented Martin*. Retrieved from http://www.espn.com/nfl/story/_/id/10455447/miami-dolphins-bullying-report-released-richie-incognito-others-responsible-harassment

Schiel, T. (2015). Grappling with collegiality and academic freedom. *Academe*, *101*(6).

Schmidt, A. A. (2014). *An examination of toxic leadership, job outcomes, and the impact of military deployment*. Available from ProQuest Dissertations and Theses database. (UMI No. 3627674)

Schultz, J. R. (2014). Creating a culture of empowerment fosters the flexibility to change. *Global Business and Organizational Excellence*, *34*(1), 41–50. doi:10.1002/joe.21583

Schulz, L. C. (2010). The Dutch Hunger Winter and the developmental origins of health and disease. *Proceedings of the National Academy of Sciences of the United States of America*, *107*(39), 16757–16758. doi:10.1073/pnas.1012911107 PMID:20855592

Scott, H. S. (2018). Extending the Duluth Model to workplace bullying: A modification and adaptation of the Workplace Power-Control Wheel. *Workplace Health & Safety*, *66*(9), 444–452. doi:10.1177/2165079917750934 PMID:29582701

Seago, J. (2016). Toxic culture. *Internal Auditor*, *73*(3), 29–33.

Segal, L. (2010). The injury of mobbing in the workplace. *Conflict Remedy*. Retrieved from https://conflictremedy.com/the-injury-of-mobbing-in-the-workplace/

Seguin, E. (2016) Academic mobbing, or how to become campus tormentors. *University Affairs*. Retrieved from https://www.universityaffairs.ca/opinion/in-my-opinion/academic-freedom-and-the-faith-based-university/

Seguin, E. (2016). Academic mobbing or how to become campus tormentors. *University Affairs*. Retrieved on January 17, 2019 from https://www.universityaffairs.ca/opinion/in-my-opinion/academic-mobbing-become-campus-tormentors/

Seguin, E. (2016, September 19). Academic mobbing, or how to become campus tormentors. *University Affairs*. Retrieved from https://www.universityaffairs.ca/opinion/in-my-opinion/academic-mobbing-become-campus-tormentors/

Seguin, E. (2016). Academic Mobbing, or how to become campus tormentors. *University Affairs*.

Sennett, R. (2003). *Respect in a world of inequality*. New York: Norton.

Sepler, F. (2015). Workplace bullying: What it is and what to do about it. *Journal of Collective Bargaining in the Academy, 0*. Retrieved from http://thekeep.eiu.edu/jcba/vol0/iss10/42

Shaw, S. J. (2017). *Teachers' perceptions of the manifestation of horizontal workplace bullying in the K-12 setting* (Doctoral dissertation). Available from ProQuest Dissertations and Theses database. (UMI No. 10666730)

Simone, N. (1965). *Feeling Good Lyrics*. Santa Monica, CA: UMG Recordings, Inc. Retrieved from https://genius.com/Nina-simone-feeling-good-lyrics

Simon, L. S., Hurst, C., Kelley, K., & Judge, T. A. (2015). Understanding cycles of abuse: A multi-motive approach. *The Journal of Applied Psychology*, *100*(6), 1–10. doi:10.1037/apl0000031 PMID:26011719

Singh, S., & Kumar, R. (2013). Why do dysfunctional norms continue to exist in the workplace? *Journal of Organization and Human Beahviour*, *2*(2), 11–19.

Skousen, T. (2016, April 12). *Responsibility vs. Accountability*. Retrieved from https://www.partnersinleadership.com/insights-publications/responsibility-vs-accountability/

Smith, K., & Smith, M. (1966). *Cybernetic principles of learning and educational design*. Holt, Rinehart, Winston.

Sole, D., & Wilson, D. G. (2003). Storytelling in organizations: The power and traps of using stories to share knowledge in organizations (LILA Briefing Paper). Harvard University.

Stanley, D. J., Meyer, J. P., & Topolnytsky, L. (2005). Employee cynicism and resistance to organizational change. *Journal of Business and Psychology*, *19*(4), 429–459. doi:10.100710869-005-4518-2

Compilation of References

Staub, S. (2015). Mobbing in academia: Case analysis. *International Journal of School and Cognitive Psychology*, *2*(2), 121. doi:10.4172/2469-9837.1000121

Stillman, J. (2018). Why being nice at work can backfire badly, according to psychology. *Inc*. Retrieved from https://www.inc.com/bill-murphy-jr/amazon-google-just-got-some-very-distressing-news.html

Stogdill, R. M. (1974). *Handbook of leadership: A survey of theory and research*. New York, NY: Free Press.

Stokols, D. (1996). Translating social ecological theory into guidelines for community health promotion. *American Journal of Health Promotion*, *10*(4), 282–298. doi:10.4278/0890-1171-10.4.282 PMID:10159709

Stopbullying.gov. (n.d.). *Misdirections in bullying prevention and intervention*. Retrieved from https://www.stopbullying.gov/sites/default/files/2017-10/misdirections-in-prevention.pdf

Sue, C. A. (2015). Hegemony and silence: Confronting state-sponsored silences in the field. *Journal of Contemporary Ethnography*, *44*(1), 113–140. doi:10.1177/0891241614540211

Swick, A. (2013). *Student exposes bullying professor*. Retrieved from https://www.leadershipinstitute.org/News/?NR=10102

Tanzharikova, A. Z. (2012). The role of higher education system in human capital formation. *World Applied Sciences Journal*, *18*, 135–139. doi:10.5829/idosi.wasj.2012.18.120022

Taspinar, B., Taspinar, F., Guclu, S., Nalbart, A., Calik, B. B., Uslu, A., & Innal, S. (2013). Investigation of the association between mobbing and musculoskeletal discomfort in academicians. *The Japanese Psychological Research*, *55*(4), 400–408. doi:10.1111/jpr.120130

Taylor, F. W. (1914). *The principles of scientific management*. New York, NY: Harper & Brothers.

Teaching Tolerance. (n.d.). *Bullying: Guidelines for teachers*. Retrieved from https://www.tolerance.org/professional-development/bullying-guidelines-for-teachers

Tello, C. (2019). Austeridad, gasto público y crecimiento económico con justicia social. *Economía UNAM*, *46*(16), 54–60. Retrieved from http://www.economia.unam.mx/assets/pdfs/econunam/46/07Tello.pdf

Tennant, M. (2005). Transforming selves. *Journal of Transformative Education*, *3*(2), 102–115. doi:10.1177/1541344604273421

The Estate of Nina Simone. (2018). *Bio*. Retrieved from http://www.ninasimone.com/bio/

The Joint Commission. (2017). *Sentinel event policy and procedures*. Retrieved from https://www.jointcommission.org/sentinel_event_policy_and_procedures/

Thomas, M. E. (2016). How to spot a sociopath. *Psychology Today*. Retrieved from https://www.psychologytoday.com/us/articles/201305/how-spot-sociopath

Thomas, A. (2009). Internal grievance imperatives for universities. *African Journal of Business Ethics*, *4*, 25–36.

Thom, R. (1977). What is catastrophe theory about? In H. Haken (Ed.), *Synergetics. Springer Series in Synergetics, 2* (pp. 26–32). Berlin: Springer;

Thucydides Project. (2019). *11.43: Text and Translation*. University of Bristol, Department of Classics and Ancient History. Retrieved from http://www.bristol.ac.uk/classics/research/thucydides/ttt/text/

Tigrel, E.U. & Kokalan, O. (2009). Academic mobbing in Turkey. *International Journal of Social Behavioral, Educational, Economic, Business and Industrial Engineering*, *3*(7), 1473-1481.

Too, L., & Harvey, M. (2012). Toxic workplaces: The negative interface between the physical and social environments. *Journal of Corporate Real Estate*, *14*(3), 171- 181. http://dx.doi.org.ezproxylocal.library.nova.edu/10.1108187/14630011211285834

Twale, D. J., & De Luca, B. M. (2008). *Faculty incivility: The rise of the academic bully culture and what to do about it*. San Francisco, CA: Jossey-Bass.

U.S. Department of Health and Human Services. (2017). *How does bullying affect health and well-being?* Retrieved from https://www.nichd.nih.gov/health/topics/bullying/conditioninfo/health

Universities Canada. (2011, October 25). *Research Statement on Academic Freedom*. Retrieved from https://www.univcan.ca/media-room/media-releases/statement-on-academic-freedom/

University of British Columbia. (2016, July 12). *Invitation to engage from Professor Santa Ono* [email]. Author.

University of British Columbia. (2018). *Shaping UBC's Next Century: Strategic Plan 2018-2028*. Vancouver, BC: Author.

Valderas, J. M., Starfield, B., Sibbald, B., Salisbury, C., & Roland, M. (2009). Defining comorbidity: Implications for understanding health and health services. *Annals of Family Medicine*, *7*(4), 357–363. doi:10.1370/afm.983 PMID:19597174

Valenzuela, J. (1991). *Crítica del modelo neoliberal: el FMI y el cambio estructural*. Universidad Nacional Autónoma de México.

Van Seters, D. A., & Field, R. H. (1990). The evolution of leadership theory. *Journal of Organizational Change Management*, *3*(3), 29–45. doi:10.1108/09534819010142139

Vega, G., & Comer, D. R. (2005). Sticks and stones may break your bones, but words can break your spirit: Bullying in the workplace. *Journal of Business Ethics*, *58*(1-3), 101–109. doi:10.100710551-005-1422-7

Verhoef, P. C., Lemon, K. N., Parasuraman, A., Roggeveen, A., Tsiros, M., & Schlesinger, L. A. (2009). Customer experience creation: Determinants, dynamics and management strategies. *Journal of Retailing*, *85*(1), 31–41. doi:10.1016/j.jretai.2008.11.001

Vieyra, P. (2015). ¿Un nuevo tipo de individualismo? Las peculiaridades del individualismo mexicano. *Sociologica, 30*(85), 65–100. Retrieved from http://www.scielo.org.mx/pdf/soc/v30n85/v30n85a3.pdf

Vuger, D. (2017). Incubation of evil: Evil as the problem of human thinking and praxis. *Synthesis Philosophica, 32*(1), 51–66. doi:10.21464p32104

Vveinhardt, J., & Štreimikienė, D. (2017). Demographic, social, and organizational characteristics on the levels of mobbing and single cases of harassment: The Multicomplex approach. *Economics and Management, 20*(3), 52–68.

Walsh, B., Magley, V., Reeves, D., Davies-Schrils, K., Marmet, M., & Gallus, J. (2012). Assessing workgroup norms for civility: The development of the Civility Norms Questionnaire-Brief. *Journal of Business and Psychology, 27*(4), 407–420. doi:10.100710869-011-9251-4

Warwick, R. (2016). Doubt, uncertainty and vulnerability in leadership: Using fiction to enable reflection and voice. *Tamara, 14*(4), 127–137.

Weisenberg, R. C. (1997). Appropriate technology for the classroom--Using" Post-It Notes" as an active learning tool. *Journal of College Science Teaching, 26*(5), 339.

Welz, C. (2018). Facing the problem of evil: Visual, verbal, and mental images of (in)humanity. *Scandinavian Jewish Studies, 29*, 62–78.

Westhues, K. (2004). *Workplace mobbing in academe: reports from twenty universities.* Lewiston, NY: Edwin Mellen Press.

Westhues, K. (2005). *Workplace mobbing in academe: Reports from twenty universities.* London, UK: Mellen Press.

Westhues, K. (2006). *The envy of excellence: Administrative mobbing of high-achieving professors.* Lewiston, NY: Edwin Mellon Press.

Westhues, K. (2006). The unkindly art of mobbing. *The Journal of Higher Education*, 18–19.

Westhues, K. (Ed.). (2006). *The Remedy and Prevention Mobbing in Higher Education.* Lewiston, NY: Edwin Mellen Press.

Winter, D. G. (1973). *The power motive.* New York, NY: The Free Press.

Wise, J. (2010, October 17). *How psychopaths choose their victims just as sociopaths are a special breed, so too are their victims.* Retrieved from https://www.psychologytoday.com/us/blog/extreme-fear/201010/how-psychopaths-choose-their-victims

Wold, B., & Mittelmark, M. (2018). Health-promotion research over three decades: The social-ecological model and challenges in implementation of interventions. *Scandinavian Journal of Public Health, 46*(20_suppl), 20–26. doi:10.1177/1403494817743893 PMID:29552963

Workplace Bullying Institute. (n.d.). *Why U.S. employers do so little.* Retrieved from https://www.workplacebullying.org/individuals/problem/employer-reaction/

World Health Organization. (2019). *Suicide data*. Retrieved from https://www.who.int /mental_health/prevention/suicide/suicideprevent/en/

Wu Tsai Neurosciences Institute. (2019). *Robert Sapolsky*. Retrieved from https://neuroscience.stanford.edu/people/robert-sapolsky

Wyatt, J., & Hare, C. (1997). *Work abuse*. Rochester, VT: Schenkman Books.

Wylie, P. (2017). Memorandum of misunderstanding? Public accountability and the University of British Columbia, Okanagan Campus, 2004-17. *BC Studies*, *195*, 65–96.

Wylie, P. (2018a). The all-administrative campus: University of British Columbia, Okanagan. *Workplace*, *31*, 10–21.

Wylie, P. (2018b). Exclusionary and extractive campus management: The University of British Columbia, Okanagan. *Workplace*, *31*, 22–30.

Wylie, P. (2018c). My campus administration, Faculty Association and me: Academic mobbing and sweetheart unionism. *Workplace*, *31*, 31–41.

Wylie, P. (in press). The University of British Columbia's International Student Initiative: Implications for provincial public higher education. *Critical Education*.

Yaman, E. (2010). Perception of Faculty members exposed to mobbing about the organizational culture and climate. *Educational Sciences: Theory and Practice, 10*(10), 567-578.

Yildirim, N. (2017). Virginia Satir's family education and therapy model. *International Journal of Social Science Studies*, *5*(72). doi:10.11114/ijsss.v5i12.2778

Yin, K., Xing, L., Li, C., & Guo, Y. (2017). Are empowered employees more productive? The contingency of how they evaluate their leader. *Frontiers in Psychology*, *8*, 1802. doi:10.3389/fpsyg.2017.01802 PMID:29163249

Young, K. Z. (2017, Spring). Workplace bullying in higher education: The misunderstood academicus. *Practical Anthropology*, *39*(2), 14–17. doi:10.17730/0888-4552.39.2.14

Zapf, D., & Gross, C. (2001). Conflict escalation and coping with workplace bullying: A replication and extension. *European Journal of Work and Organizational Psychology*, *10*(4), 497–522. doi:10.1080/13594320143000834

Zapf, D., Knorz, C., & Kulla, M. (1996). On the relationship between mobbing factors, and job content, social work environment, and health outcomes. *European Journal of Work and Organizational Psychology*, *5*(2), 215–237. doi:10.1080/13594329608414856

Zimbardo, P. (2007). *The Lucifer Effect: Understanding how good people turn evil*. New York, NY: Random House.

About the Contributors

Caroline M. Crawford, Ed.D., is an Associate Professor of Instructional Technology at the University of Houston-Clear Lake in Houston, Texas, United States of America. She earned her doctoral degree from the University of Houston in Houston, Texas, United States of America, in 1998, with specialization areas in Instructional Technology and Curriculum Theory, and began her tenure at the University of Houston-Clear Lake (UHCL) the same year. At this point in Dr. Crawford's professional career, her main areas of interest focus upon communities of learning and the appropriate and successful integration of technologies into the learning environment; the learning environment may be envisioned as face-to-face, blended and online (virtual or text-driven) environments, as well as microlearning deliverables.

* * *

Sandina Begic is an assistant research professor at the Center for Health Policy at Boise State University. She earned her Ph.D. in Psychology from Clark University in 2013. During graduate school she completed considerable fieldwork in her native Bosnia-Herzegovina, conducting research on the lasting effects of the ethnic conflict that culminated in the 1992-1995 civil war; some of this work involved the stigma attached to children born of wartime rape and some also focused on the shattering of the social fabric that once existed in the former Yugoslavia. Her current research largely involves evaluating the impacts of evidence-based home visiting services for mothers, infants, and young children in households with many risk factors.

Silvia Karla Fernández Marin holds a BA in Political Sciences and Public Administration; a MA in Social and Political Studies, and a PhD in Social Sciences. She is currently the chair of the Graduate Program in Physical Anthropology, National School of Anthropology and History, Mexico. CV in Spanish: https://www.enah.edu.mx/images/documentos/lgac/af/silvia_karla_fernandez_marin.pdf.

Janice Harper was an Assistant Professor of Anthropology at the University of Tennessee when she was subjected to mobbing after reporting sexual harassment. Her tenure was initially denied by her Department Head for her alleged "negativity," which was followed by a series of accusations ultimately leading to the claim that she was building a hydrogen bomb. She was subjected to four levels of investigation by law enforcement, including what the FBI-Joint Terrorism Task Force described as an "aggressive investigation" by Homeland Security. Although ultimately exonerated of all charges against her, and the university paid her a substantial settlement for their actions, her tenure was denied and her career destroyed. She has since written a number of articles on mobbing for Psychology Today and The Huffington Post, and is the author of Mobbed! What to Do When They Really Are Out to Get You.

R. Eric Landrum is a professor of psychology at Boise State University, receiving his PhD in cognitive psychology from Southern Illinois University-Carbondale. His research interests center on the educational conditions that best facilitate student success as well as the use of SoTL strategies to advance the efforts of scientist-educators. He has over 425 professional presentations at conferences and published 3 edited texts, 23 books/textbooks, 29 book chapters, and has published over 85 professional articles in scholarly, peer-reviewed journals. He has worked with over 300 undergraduate research assistants and taught over 18,000 students in 26 years at Boise State. During Summer 2008, he led an American Psychological Association (APA) working group at the National Conference for Undergraduate Education in Psychology studying the desired results of an undergraduate psychology education. During the October 2014 Educational Leadership Conference in Washington, DC, Eric was presented with a Presidential Citation from then APA President Nadine Kaslow for his outstanding contributions to the teaching of psychology. With the launch of a new APA journal in 2015—Scholarship of Teaching and Learning in Psychology—he serves as one of its inaugural co-editors. He is a member of the American Psychological Association, a fellow in APA's Division Two (Society for the Teaching of Psychology or STP), served as STP Secretary (2009-2011) and STP President (2014). He is also a member of the Association for Psychological Science and was named a fellow in 2018. During 2016-2017 Eric he served as President of the Rocky Mountain Psychological Association (RMPA) and Eric served as President of Psi Chi, the International Honor Society in Psychology during 2017-2018.

Cortney E. Matteson is an educator in the Public Schools in Orange County Florida, the tenth largest school district in the United States. She earned a B.A. in Studio Art from Bloomsburg University, a Master's Degree in Education from Kutztown University and her Master's Thesis topic was Creating Curriculum and Lesson Plans for K-5 Art Educational Programs that were Inclusive of Math, Science, Social Studies and Language into Public School Fine Art Classes. She holds teaching certifications in Pennsylvania, Virginia and Florida. She has extensive teaching experience and serves as Department Chair and Lead Teacher Mentor in public schools in Florida, Pennsylvania and Virginia. Recently, her continued professional accomplishments led to being selected and awarded Teacher of the Year.

Rande W. Matteson retired in 2006, as a Senior Supervisory Special Agent (Federal Agent) after a 32-year law enforcement career having served in responsible international and domestic leadership-management, field and special covert assignments. During his career, Matteson served in various special project assignments and as an Agency Commander at the 2001 Winter Olympics in Salt Lake City, UT. He is a faculty member at Nova Southeastern University serving as a doctoral dissertation mentor and teaches graduate course in leadership. Previously, he served as an Associate Professor (department Chair) in the Department of Criminal Justice Flagship Program. He developed and taught undergraduate and graduate classes in law, leadership, economic crime, budgeting, violent crime, terrorism, ethics, criminal investigation and fiscal management. In addition to his scholarly publication record, he has served as an editor and on research committees for scholarly publications. His scholarly interests include complex global social and societal justice issues tied to dysfunctional leadership.

Denise M. McDonald, Ed.D, is Professor of Curriculum and Instruction at the University of Houston-Clear Lake. She teaches undergraduate and graduate courses in classroom management, curriculum planning, instructional strategies, professional development, and critical inquiry. Her research methodology includes critical ethnography, narrative inquiry, and self-study.

Theodore W. McDonald is a professor in the Department of Psychological Science at Boise State University. He earned his Ph.D. in Psychology from the University of Wisconsin-Milwaukee in 1998. A community psychologist, he works with agencies and organizations serving some of Idaho's most vulnerable citizens, including at-risk mothers and infants, youth in detention, refugees, and rural residents. He has published a number of articles on his work with these populations, as well as the book Post-Traumatic Stress Disorder in Refugee Communities: The Importance of Culturally Sensitive Screening, Diagnosis, and Treatment. His research and professional interests have recently expanded to the corporatization of college and university campuses, and the mistreatment of faculty and staff within academic institutions.

About the Contributors

Rebecca "Becky" L. Pearson is an associate professor in Central Washington University's Health Sciences Department. Becky teaches a variety of public health courses as well as designing and teaching courses for CWU's Douglas Honors College. Additionally, she currently serves as the university's first Director of General Education, after contributing to a significant university wide process that resulted in a new General Education program. Her academic agenda emphasizes community, and individual, capacity for improved health and wellbeing, with a focus on personal and societal food-related decisions and environments, as well as rights- and values-based approaches to health.

Florencia Peña Saint Martin holds a BA in Physical Anthropology, a MA in Social Medicine and a PhD in Anthropology. She is a full-time professor, Graduate Program in Physical Anthropology, National School of Anthropology and History, Mexico. CV in Spanish: http://www.antropologiafisica.org/florencia.htm.

Naomi Jeffery Petersen is a full professor in the Department of Curriculum, Supervision, & Educational Leadership at Central Washington University. In addition to coordinating the department's undergraduate programs, she teaches and researches education topics related to assessment, belief systems, and professional development. Her academic agenda is infused with the intersection of environment, culture, and technology, including such diverse applications as watersheds, railroads and military history, visual literacy, and informal learning environments. She fosters collaborations across disciples, such as geography and public health. She cultivated the partnerships resulting in the launch of CWU's interdisciplinary Accessibility Studies Program which she now directs. She actively promotes accessibility awareness and acceptance.

Gina L. Peyton, an Associate Professor at Nova Southeastern University, teaches doctoral level courses in organizational and higher education leadership, as well as master level leadership courses. Dr. Peyton earned her Doctorate in Organizational Leadership, specialization in Higher Education Leadership, Master of Science in Reading and Bachelor of Science in Psychology degrees from Nova Southeastern University. With almost 25 years of higher education experience, Dr. Peyton has extensive knowledge in leadership theories and practice, ethical leadership, strategic leadership, leading and managing organizational change, education, academic writing and research. Dr. Peyton is a dissertation chair and serves on numerous leadership committees.

About the Contributors

David B. Ross, a Professor at Nova Southeastern University, teaches doctoral level courses in educational, organizational, and higher educational leadership. Learning from many perspectives and philosophies from mentors while attending Northern Illinois University, the University of Alabama, and Florida Atlantic University, has assisted him in guiding students in the learning process. Dr. Ross earned his Doctorate in Educational Leadership, Master of Justice Policy Management with a Professional Certificate in Public Administration at Florida Atlantic University, and his Bachelor of Science Degree in Computer Science at Northern Illinois University. Dr. Ross regularly speaks at conferences and provides consultation and training in the areas of leadership and management, policy issues, critical thinking, team building, professional development, academic writing, education, and behavior management. He has written articles and book chapters on leadership, power, narcissism, organizational stress, academic integrity, plagiarism and fraud, entitlement, mobbing/bullying, Gerontechnology, policy development, professional development, and areas of homeland security. Dr. Ross is a co-editor of a book titled Higher Education Challenges for Migrant and Refugee Students in a Global World. Dr. Ross is a dissertation chair and a reviewer for the university's Institutional Review Board. Dr. Ross was named Professor of the Year 2015-2016 for the Abraham S. Fischler College of Education. Dr. Ross is a retired Criminal Investigator/Agent with extensive-applied supervisory and field operations experience involving complex federal, state, local, and international crime; covert-clandestine operative and worked with informants; smuggling, profiling and drug interdiction; public order crime; asset forfeiture, money laundering, and conspiracy; wire and mail fraud; development of evidence for use in sworn affidavits, arrest and search and seizure warrants, pen registers; public and political corruption, technical operations including wire-oral intercepts, high technical human, stationary and aircraft/marine surveillance; intelligence-led programs, and RICO Act crimes.

Melissa T. Sasso is an Italian Canadian native who grew up in Montreal, Quebec. She then moved to Florida, at the age of 16. Dr. Sasso attained her Bachelor of Arts in Psychology at Florida International University where she graduated with Cum Laude. She received both her Master's of Science in Exceptional Student Education and Doctorate in Education with a concentration in Organizational leadership at Nova Southeastern University, where she graduated with a 4.0 GPA in both degrees. Dr. Sasso has several years experience working with exceptional students who suffer from disabilities from Pre-K to grade 5 and is still interested in remaining within the education field. She has written articles with her Dissertation chair, Dr. David B.

Ross, which can be found in NSUWorks and has her published dissertation entitled How Narcissists Cannot Hold an Organization Together: A Mixed Method Approach to a Fictitious Puzzle Factory located in ProQuest. Her dissertation received a Dr. Charles L. Faires distinction award. Her research interests include stress, and she is a passionate researcher in the fields of toxic workplace environments, and narcissistic leadership.

Janelle Christine Simmons earned her B.A. in psychology from Michigan State University, She went on to earn her M.A. in Forensic Psychology from John Jay College of Criminal Justice, an M.Div. from Torch Trinity Graduate School of Theology and and Ed.S. in Curriculum and Instruction and an Ed.D. in Educational Leadership from Liberty University. Dr. Simmons is actively looking for a post-doctorate fellowship or a full-time lecturer position to apply what she has learned thus far. Her research interests center around multicultural leadership, multicultural education, issues of spirituality, workplace mobbing as well as other "event phenomenons" such as the Las Vegas shooting. Currently, she is volunteering, consulting and working on establishing a music museum.

Peter Wylie is an Associate Professor of Economics at the University of British Columbia (UBC), Okanagan Campus and past Head of the Economics, History, Philosophy, Political Science and Sociology Unit of the Barber School of Arts and Sciences, UBC Okanagan. He holds a BSc. In Economics from The Queen's University of Belfast and an MA and PhD in Economics from Queen's University at Kingston, Canada. He has been a consultant to the Treasury Board of Canada, Investment Canada, the former Northern Ireland Economic Council, and the BC Council on Admissions and Transfer (BCCAT, among others, and was Chair of the BCCAT Economics Articulation Committee 2007-12. He was awarded the BCCAT Leadership Award in 2015 for his work on BC higher education transfer arrangements. His current areas of research interest include higher education policy in BC, and he takes a keen and active interest in academic affairs.

Index

A

academia 5, 59, 77-78, 104-105, 111-112, 114-116, 118, 123, 131, 212, 214-215, 229, 237, 244-245, 248, 255
academic freedom 47, 50, 189, 195-198, 200-202, 204, 206-207, 210
academic mobbing 1, 3-5, 7-13, 19-24, 28-30, 34, 37, 40-42, 44-50, 52-60, 62, 104, 187-191, 194-195, 198, 200, 202, 205-207, 210, 241-249, 251-254, 256-263, 266
adjunct 1, 12-13, 17-18, 28, 77, 87
adult education 159, 161
All-Administrative 188, 210
All-Administrative University 210
autoethnography 1, 11, 23

B

bully(ies) 1, 4-7, 20, 29-32, 34, 36-39, 41-42, 45, 48-50, 56-61, 70, 72-75, 77, 80-81, 85-86, 89-91, 93, 109-112, 115, 117, 123-125, 170, 176, 213, 216-217, 230, 233, 243-244, 246-249, 251-252, 259-263, 266
Bullying Attack 266

C

civility 107, 112, 114, 118, 122-125, 131, 224
Climate for Civility 114, 131
collusion 109, 187-188, 191, 204, 207, 210, 230, 235
Comorbidity 108, 131
complicity 187, 191, 207, 210, 233-234
counterproductive work behavior 72, 80, 82, 84-85

D

Dark Triad Leadership 78
defamatory 197, 203

E

Emotional Stability 241, 266
Epidemiological Triad 117, 131
epidemiology 104, 116-117, 121
ethical compass 241-243, 257, 259-261, 263, 266
ethics 31, 153, 166, 179, 189, 261

F

Faculty Association 187-188, 192, 210

G

governance 57, 61, 120, 188, 193-194, 196, 199-200, 203-207, 210, 235

H

harassment 3, 9, 28, 33, 36, 40, 45-46, 71, 86-87, 136-138, 141-142, 148-149, 152, 187, 190, 197, 203, 214, 220, 229, 244-245, 266
hegemony 214, 228, 237

higher education 12, 46, 59, 69-72, 76, 78, 80-81, 87, 89-91, 94, 113, 121-123, 131-134, 138-139, 154, 159-163, 166, 170-172, 174-179, 211-212, 245, 260

I

institutions of higher education 81, 90, 121, 134, 138-139, 154, 159
investigation 48, 53, 86-87, 112, 117, 125, 131, 195-196, 199-204, 207, 210, 222, 230, 235

L

leadership and management 159, 163, 165, 170
lyrics 241, 253, 260, 263

M

maelstrom 241-243, 257, 260, 262-263, 266
mental health 50, 78, 168
metaphor 116, 212-213
mobbability 104-105, 107-108, 112, 117, 121-122, 125, 131
mobbing 1-13, 18-24, 28-42, 44-50, 52-62, 69-76, 80-82, 84-94, 104-121, 123-125, 132, 138, 140-141, 148-149, 151-153, 155, 158, 160, 170, 175-176, 187-191, 194-195, 198, 200, 202, 205-207, 210, 212, 214-215, 234, 241-249, 251-254, 256-263, 266
morality 36, 39, 110, 176, 251

N

narcissistic 48, 69-70, 79-80, 86, 162, 168
narrative 1, 12, 19, 188, 212
neoliberalism 134, 141-143, 150, 154, 158
neoliberal policies 132-134, 150

P

passive evil 44-45, 47-48, 50-60, 62
phases of mobbing 1, 6, 119
poems 241-242, 246-247, 260, 263

policy violations 44-45, 54, 222, 229-231
Psychological Center 241, 266
Psychological Equilibrium 241, 266
psychopathic 36, 41, 79, 219
psychoterror 46
public universities 132-133, 138

Q

qualitative 1, 11, 23-24, 107, 158
Qualitative Methods of Research 158
Queen Bee Syndrome 71, 77-78
quotations 241-243, 246-247, 252, 260, 263

R

Respectful Environment 196, 207, 210
Respectful Environment Policies 210

S

satire 212-214
selective moral disengagement 45, 54-56, 59
Self-study 188
senate 187-188, 190, 192-202, 207, 210
Sentinel Event 117, 131
servant leadership 159-162, 166-167, 170-171, 173-179
sham dealing 132, 137-145, 147-148, 152-155, 158
silent majority 243, 260, 266
social ecology 106, 112-113, 122, 125, 131
Sociopathic Leadership 69, 80
storytelling 211-213
suppression 132, 136-141, 143, 145-153, 155, 158, 195, 198, 200
sweetheart unionism 188, 191, 202, 206

T

targets 6-10, 32, 34, 36-38, 42, 57, 59, 61, 87-88, 105, 107, 110, 112, 115-116, 189, 212, 214-215, 218-220, 222, 226, 229-230, 244-245, 247, 260, 262
tenured professor 28, 88, 107, 190
toxic culture 82-83, 87, 159-160, 177, 244

Index

toxic leadership 81-82, 90, 159, 168, 171
TSTL survey 69, 90

U

unethical administrators 44-45, 47-48, 57, 61

W

wellbeing 106, 146

workplace abuse 108-109, 111, 118, 121
workplace aggression 29, 33, 35
workplace bullying 11, 36, 45-46, 48-49, 55, 59-62, 77, 90, 93, 132, 136, 138, 141, 147-149, 153-155, 158, 170, 214

Z

Zero-Empathy 110, 131

Purchase Print, E-Book, or Print + E-Book

IGI Global's reference books can now be purchased from three unique pricing formats:
Print Only, E-Book Only, or Print + E-Book.
Shipping fees may apply.

www.igi-global.com

Recommended Reference Books

Handbook of Research on Assessment Practices and Pedagogical Models for Immigrant Students
ISBN: 978-1-5225-9348-5
© 2019; 454 pp.
List Price: $255

Preparing the Higher Education Space for Gen Z
ISBN: 978-1-5225-7763-8
© 2019; 253 pp.
List Price: $175

Prevention and Detection of Academic Misconduct in Higher Education
ISBN: 978-1-5225-7531-3
© 2019; 324 pp.
List Price: $185

Care and Culturally Responsive Pedagogy in Online Settings
ISBN: 978-1-5225-7802-4
© 2019; 423 pp.
List Price: $195

Handbook of Research on School Violence in American K-12 Education
ISBN: 978-1-5225-6246-7
© 2019; 610 pp.
List Price: $275

Critical Assessment and Strategies for Increased Student Retention
ISBN: 978-1-5225-2998-9
© 2018; 352 pp.
List Price: $195

Looking for free content, product updates, news, and special offers?
Join IGI Global's mailing list today and start enjoying exclusive perks sent only to IGI Global members.
Add your name to the list at **www.igi-global.com/newsletters**.

Publisher of Peer-Reviewed, Timely, and Innovative Academic Research

IGI Global
DISSEMINATOR OF KNOWLEDGE

www.igi-global.com | Sign up at www.igi-global.com/newsletters | facebook.com/igiglobal | twitter.com/igiglobal

Ensure Quality Research is Introduced to the Academic Community

Become an IGI Global Reviewer for Authored Book Projects

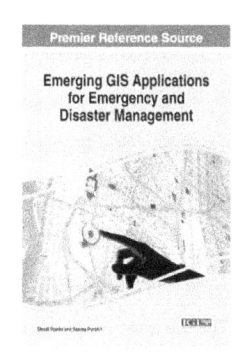

The overall success of an authored book project is dependent on quality and timely reviews.

In this competitive age of scholarly publishing, constructive and timely feedback significantly expedites the turnaround time of manuscripts from submission to acceptance, allowing the publication and discovery of forward-thinking research at a much more expeditious rate. Several IGI Global authored book projects are currently seeking highly-qualified experts in the field to fill vacancies on their respective editorial review boards:

Applications and Inquiries may be sent to:
development@igi-global.com

Applicants must have a doctorate (or an equivalent degree) as well as publishing and reviewing experience. Reviewers are asked to complete the open-ended evaluation questions with as much detail as possible in a timely, collegial, and constructive manner. All reviewers' tenures run for one-year terms on the editorial review boards and are expected to complete at least three reviews per term. Upon successful completion of this term, reviewers can be considered for an additional term.

If you have a colleague that may be interested in this opportunity, we encourage you to share this information with them.

IGI Global
DISSEMINATOR OF KNOWLEDGE
www.igi-global.com

IGI Global Proudly Partners with

eContent Pro International

Publication Services Provided by eContent Pro International:

Scientific & Scholarly Editing

English Language Copy Editing

Journal Recommendation

Typesetting & Publishing

Figure, Table, Chart & Equation Conversions

Translation

IGI Global Authors Save 25% on eContent Pro International's Services!

Scan the QR Code to Receive Your 25% Discount

The 25% discount is applied directly to your eContent Pro International shopping cart when placing an order through IGI Global's referral link. Use the QR code to access this referral link. eContent Pro International has the right to end or modify any promotion at any time.

Email: customerservice@econtentpro.com

econtentpro.com

InfoSci®-Books

Celebrating Over 30 Years of Scholarly Knowledge Creation & Dissemination

www.igi-global.com

InfoSci®-Books

A Database of Over 5,300+ Reference Books Containing Over 100,000+ Chapters Focusing on Emerging Research

GAIN ACCESS TO **THOUSANDS** OF REFERENCE BOOKS AT **A FRACTION** OF THEIR INDIVIDUAL LIST **PRICE**.

InfoSci®-Books Database

The **InfoSci®-Books** database is a collection of over 5,300+ IGI Global single and multi-volume reference books, handbooks of research, and encyclopedias, encompassing groundbreaking research from prominent experts worldwide that span over 350+ topics in 11 core subject areas including business, computer science, education, science and engineering, social sciences and more.

Open Access Fee Waiver (Offset Model) Initiative

For any library that invests in IGI Global's InfoSci-Journals and/or InfoSci-Books databases, IGI Global will match the library's investment with a fund of equal value to go toward **subsidizing the OA article processing charges (APCs) for their students, faculty, and staff** at that institution when their work is submitted and accepted under OA into an IGI Global journal.*

INFOSCI® PLATFORM FEATURES

- No DRM
- No Set-Up or Maintenance Fees
- A Guarantee of No More Than a 5% Annual Increase
- Full-Text HTML and PDF Viewing Options
- Downloadable MARC Records
- Unlimited Simultaneous Access
- COUNTER 5 Compliant Reports
- Formatted Citations With Ability to Export to RefWorks and EasyBib
- No Embargo of Content (Research is Available Months in Advance of the Print Release)

*The fund will be offered on an annual basis and expire at the end of the subscription period. The fund would renew as the subscription is renewed for each year thereafter. The open access fees will be waived after the student, faculty, or staff's paper has been vetted and accepted into an IGI Global journal and the fund can only be used toward publishing OA in an IGI Global journal. Libraries in developing countries will have the match on their investment doubled.

To Learn More or To Purchase This Database:
www.igi-global.com/infosci-books

eresources@igi-global.com • Toll Free: 1-866-342-6657 ext. 100 • Phone: 717-533-8845 x100

www.igi-global.com